SOME OTHER BLUES

SOME OTHER BLUES

NEW PERSPECTIVES ON AMIRI BARAKA

EDITED BY
JEAN-PHILIPPE MARCOUX

THE OHIO STATE UNIVERSITY PRESS
COLUMBUS

Library of Congress Cataloging-in-Publication Data

Names: Marcoux, Jean-Philippe, 1977– editor.

Title: Some other blues : new perspectives on Amiri Baraka / edited by Jean-Philippe Marcoux.

Description: Columbus : The Ohio State University Press, [2021] | Includes bibliographical references and index. | Summary: "Scholars and critics draw upon Amiri Baraka's oeuvre to reassess his political and literary legacy"—Provided by publisher.

Identifiers: LCCN 2020037850 | ISBN 9780814257845 (cloth) | ISBN 0814257844 (cloth) | ISBN 9780814281055 (ebook) | ISBN 0814281052 (ebook)

Subjects: LCSH: Baraka, Amiri, 1934–2014—Criticism and interpretation. | Baraka, Amiri, 1934–2014—Political and social views. | African Americans—Intellectual life—20th century. | African American authors—20th century. | Jazz in literature. | Black power—United States—History—20th century.

Classification: LCC PS3552.A583 Z884 2021 | DDC 813/.54—dc23

LC record available at https://lccn.loc.gov/2020037850

Cover design by Susan Zucker
Text design by Juliet Williams
Type set in Adobe Minion Pro

Dedicated to Amiri Baraka, Amina Baraka, and the entire Baraka family

CONTENTS

Side B   The Music (Ideations and Renegotiations)

PART II · IN THE TRADITION: REASSESSMENTS, RECOLLECTIONS, LEGACIES

FOREWORD

"We Seen It, Too"

FRED MOTEN

FAMOUSLY, and with the deepest lyrical rigor, Amiri Baraka described himself as loud in the changing of his ways. Loud, and musically profligate, and precise in the changing of his name, it was, in fact, LeRoi Jones who said this of Baraka, thereby rendering the description prophetic. And yet, as is proper for the one who wrote "The Changing Same"—the one who was so much more than one in the radical impropriety of his genius, which came from and was given back to the people who loved him and whom he loved, the people who have many names though one name is not just one among many—we must remember that Baraka was loud, also, in the continuity of his fundamental and absolute commitment to the general project he called "social development." That commitment was manifest in the constant gift economy that swirled around him, fugitively, centrifugally, like that striated common groove he laid down all over the place in the furious hospitality of his writing, and in the writerly grace of his hospitality.

The dual force of welcome and refusal, of welcome in common refusal of the brutal world, of welcome to unity and struggle in difference and love, was what greeted you at Amina and Amiri Baraka's home, their salon in New Ark, which they called "Kimako's Blues People" in memory of his sister. The walls there were supple with music and aroma, because something good was always cooking, turning a house into the heart and lungs of Amilcar Cabral's revolutionary friendship. Visitors, who'd come from some of everywhere, were welcome there, and made welcome to refuse, in common, in pursuit of something else in the way the music refuses and pursues. Baraka remains our host, in this regard, and we remain alive in him, and through his gifts, which bear the gifts of our tradition. His writing welcomes us again and again, silently or LOUD, to the changing of our ways in the sameness of our changing, which he shares. He lives in the ongoing frenzy of, and for, what we are and what we will be, which is the only possible register of what and how we bear in and out of being's precincts. This unbearable doubleness in the way of all that something else in the music's way, and in the music's ways, is that other thing (which is other than thingliness) in some other blues he called "something in the way of things," whose late solemnity we chant, en masse, as celebrants of a black mass for the black life of mo(u)rning. "I seen something," Baraka says. "I SEEN something / And you seen it, too."[1] And what he sees, so he could see the evil that chases and surrounds us, so that he could see it and name name name name name it, is *that* he seen it, and that *we* seen it, too. Our name is we seen it, too, and he never stops sounding that, transbluesently, so that that sounding is the lens we see through.

I heard him talk about all that just a few years ago, one night in Durham, North Carolina. He'd come to read for us. He read "Something in the Way of Things (In Town)" and the room was aflame because he was still on fire, still the same through all the changes, which he once again announced, whispering so loudly I can still hear, after I walked up to him to say, Man, you were burning! "Really?" he whispered. "Sometimes I wonder if I've done anything at all." I couldn't hear above the roar and boom in my head that came with the wonder that he could wonder such a thing, and that music is still with me though my wondering is cut by the ongoing realization that his humility and the depth of his commitment were the source and constancy and constant transformation of a gift and giving that can't be calculated. The depth of his question remains beyond him, as he remains, because it wasn't about him, which is why he was deep and beautiful, because it was about so much more than whether he had done anything at all. In having done all and everything, it was as if he were seeing through the work of seeing and naming, which is the poet's calling and the poet's fallenness. It is absolutely terrible and absolutely beautiful to see (through) all, as all, in giving all, in leaving all its names for all to say. He sees that in us and we see that through him. We share that with

---

1. Baraka recited this poem many times and recorded it with The Roots. It was released on their 2002 album *Phrenology*, MCA Records—112 996–2. Another excellent version, in which Baraka is accompanied by saxophonist Rob Brown, is available here: https://www.youtube.com/watch?v=bArO35pbn6Q.

him and here's the vicious miracle. Amiri Baraka's loss can never be repaired; his furious blessing can never be repaid; but he remains, the same and changing, to be found.

New York—June 10, 2020

ACKNOWLEDGMENTS

THE EDITOR would like to thank the following people:

First and foremost, my deepest gratitude goes to the contributors of the book. Thank you for trusting me with your work and for sharing your insights. You make this volume what it is. Also, thank you for your notes of encouragement and support. They meant a lot along the way.

Thank you to Ana Maria Jimenez-Moreno, the editor at the press. You have believed in this project from the very first day and have been a source of support and guidance ever since. Your name might not appear on the cover of the book, but you are on every page in spirit. Thank you for believing in my vision. Thank to everyone at The Ohio State University Press who worked on the book's production.

Thank you to Aldon Nielsen, William J. Harris, Ben Lee, Kathy Lou Schultz, and James Smethurst, who were the first ones to embark on this adventure, even when the project was still looking for its footing. Billy Joe, you provided the core riff.

Thank you to the many friends of this project: Evie Shockley, Keith D. Leonard, Annette Debo, Emily Lordi, Richard Flynn, Jerry Ward, Donna Akiba Sullivan Harper, Anna Everett, Shirley Moody Turner, Komozi Woodard, Margo Crawford, Meta Jones, and Askia Touré.

Thank you to Aldon Nielsen for his friendship and mentorship, and for the many conversations about the music; they inspired this project.

Thank you to my friends and family, as well as to my colleagues and students for the continuous support. Thank you to my wife Isabelle and my son Alexandre, for always believing in me even when I don't, and for the purity of your love.

Thank you to Amiri Baraka for doing the work. For *Unity Music*.

The editor and authors gratefully acknowledge the following entities for permission to reprint material included in this collection:

"Black Dada Nihilismus"; "Black Art"; "Wise 1"; "In the Tradition"; "AM/ TRAK"; "A Poem for Deep Thinkers"; "In Memory of Radio"; "Y's 18"; "'There Was Something I Wanted to Tell You.' Why"; "A Poem for Willie Best"; "A Poem Some People Will Need to Understand"; "The People Burning"; "Preface to a Twenty Volume Suicide Note"; "Poem for Half-White College Students." From *S.O.S POEMS 1961–2013*. Copyright © 2014 by the Estate of Amiri Baraka. Used by permission of Grove/ Atlantic, Inc. Any third-party use of this material, outside of this publication, is prohibited.

All other poems from Amiri Baraka: Permission by Chris Calhoun Agency, © Estate of Amiri Baraka.

Permission to quote from "An Education" by Lorenzo Thomas in chapter 7 of this collection has been granted by the literary executors for Lorenzo Thomas.

Chapter 10 in this collection was originally printed in *Brick City Vanguard: Amiri Baraka, Black Music, Black Modernity*. Copyright © 2020 by the University of Massachusetts Press.

Thanks to Aja Monet for permission to quote from "Is that all you got" from *My Mother was a Freedom Fighter* (2017). Courtesy of Haymarket Books.

INTRODUCTION

JEAN-PHILIPPE MARCOUX

T HIS IS a story of origins in two asymmetrical parts.

Amiri Baraka read with Amina and a jazz quartet in small club on the Bowery, in the Lower East Side of New York City. That night, Baraka concluded with "Somebody Blew Up America" performed in its entirely. The prologue to the poetry reading drew mostly from *Wise Whys Ys*. The jazz band followed the musical cues at the beginning of each section of *Wise*, Baraka's own riff on *Ask Your Mama*. Amina would come in once or twice to read her own poems, including her variation on "Strange Fruit." In between the sections, Baraka would lecture on jazz history, on his own experience as testifying witness to the developments in/of the music. He engaged with the music as an analogue to poetry, as well as to the history that gave birth to both music and poetry. In mapping out the geography of black cultural identity, Baraka laid claim to the conditions that demanded reparations in the form of rituals and performances of vernacular ancestry. Charting the parallel developments of black music and black history, the poet affirmed the need for unity and struggle, even though his bent back revealed the deep battle scars. He talked about the many phases of Coltrane, what each meant to young African Americans searching for forms of expressions of their experience. He talked about how sounds were vectors of political significance, means to probe cultural memory, to awaken a constantly refigured black consciousness. That night, Baraka, it seemed to the audience, had proceeded both to

1

reassess the meaning and import of his "sound," and to update his 1967 volume of jazz criticism and historiography, *Black Music*. Both texts interlink notions of identity and consciousness with vernacular culture, using the music as sounding on function of the poet.

In his 1959 "How You Sound," Baraka formulates his cultural identity as poet using language that conjures up jazz musicianship:

> The only "recognizable tradition" a poet needs to follow is himself . . . & with that, say, all those things out of tradition he can use, adapt. Work over, into something for himself. To broaden his voice with. (You have here to start and finish there . . . your own voice . . . how you sound). (16)[1]

While at that moment, Baraka's idea of tradition seems to be focusing on William Carlos Williams, the Beats, and Black Mountain poets—the "postmoderns" he is anthologized with in Donald Allen's seminal work—and while he is still not firmly ingrained in the tradition of black arts, as his early essay "A Dark Bag" shows, the language here echoes how jazz musicians develop their "sound." As Paul F. Berliner, in *Thinking in Jazz: The Infinite Art of Improvisation*, suggests, jazz musicians conceptualize and possess a jazz vocabulary, "store[s] of knowledge" (195) about the past musical traditions that they quote when improvising, when devising their sound. Their musical voice/sound is the result of their ability to converse with the tradition as they trade musical ideas with other musicians and, thus, assert their "broadened" sonic identity. Jazz improvisers, Berliner contends, become storytellers, archivists of the past, retelling "the tale" of the music's origins and changing meanings (201–205).[2] In that sense, every improviser is unique, for their relationship to tradition depends on their mastery of form and sensitivity to sonic evocations, which in turn informs their ability to quote, revise, and adapt. Their sound becomes their voice, their own telling of the tale of how improvised music is an affirmation of the individual within the collective.[3]

Baraka states a similar idea in "Expressive Language":

---

1. I refer here to the version republished in *The Leroi Jones/Amiri Baraka Reader,* edited by William J. Harris, 16–17.

2. Samuel A. Floyd Jr. believes that "black music [has been] expressive of cultural memory, and black music making [has been] the translation of the memory into sound and the sound into the memory." Floyd here echoes Sidney Bechet's concept of "remembering song" (9).

3. Lawrence Levine contends that in antiphonal rituals, the individual is placed "in continual dialogue with his community, allowing him . . . to preserve his voice as a distinct entity and to blend it with those of his fellows" (33).

An A flat played twice on the same saxophone by two different men does not have to sound the same. If these men have different ideas of what they want this note to do, the note will not sound the same. Culture is the form, the overall structure of organized thought (as well as emotion and spiritual pretension). (*Home* 170)[4]

Different musicians will have "different ideas" and, therefore, different approaches to sounding them. While they do borrow from the same cultural memory, they "translate"[5] and stylize according to their posture vis-à-vis what Scott Saul terms the "syncretic potential of an African-derived aesthetic" (93)—that is, the repertoire of traditions, the groundswell of experiential diasporic blackness that constitutes the basis of African American vernacular Baraka constantly turns to for inspiration and guidance, and which link he recognizes in *Blues People* (18). As he states later in the volume:

Music . . . is the result of thought. It is the result of thought perfected at its most empirical, i.e., as *attitude,* or *stance.* . . . The Negro's music changed as he changed, reflecting shifting attitudes or (and this is equally important) consistent attitudes within changed contexts. And it is *why* the music changed that seems most important to me. (152–153)

That he wanted to poeticize, literalize, and thematize the cultural history and experience of African Americans through vernacular poetics, through artistry as resistance, is made evident in Baraka's relentless questioning of the conditions under which black suffering resulted in new music. If, as James Smethurst writes, for Baraka "black music represented primarily a posture toward the world" (*Black Arts* 105), then it is unquestionable that Baraka hears in music one's sounding on the inevitable black revolution against a hostile world, a moment of creative sonic explosion correlating the ebullience of the revolutionary paradigm. In his *Autobiography,* he proclaims that "the fact of music was the [b]lack poet's basis for creation. And those of us in the BAM [Black Arts Movement] were drenched in black music and wanted our poetry to be black music. Not only that, we wanted our poetry to be armed with the spirit of the revolution" (237).[6] In many ways, the intersectionality between music, poetry, consciousness, and revolution is at the core of Baraka's oeuvre,

---

4. The essay was originally published in *Kulchur,* Winter 1963 edition. It is reproduced here from *Home: Social Essays.*

5. Here again, I wish to invoke Floyd's statement. See note 2.

6. Mary Ellison expands on this passage in "Jazz in the Poetry of Amiri Baraka and Roy Fisher."

marking each shift in identity with a corresponding, adaptive aesthetic and political "sound": a "broadened" Barakian voice.

Published at a time when he was a Black Arts architect and the most significant pursuer of Malcolm X's cultural objectives, Baraka sought, with *Black Music*, to show how the developments in the music correlated his growing dissatisfaction with the misrepresentation and misunderstanding of jazz by white critics, custodians of the co-optation of black sounds. Encoded in this posture is the deeply held belief that black identity and culture have, like jazz, suffered from a similar treatment at the hands of an oppressive society. The posture not only affirms, once again, Malcolm X's dictates that "Afro-American history and culture [are] indispensable weapons in the [b]lack quest for freedom" (Van Deburg 5), but also asserts the fundamentality of the music in narrativizing the black experience in ways the oppressor could never fathom—a tradition of vernacular resistance going back to plantation culture that Baraka will continue to invoke through his various political and ideological shifts.[7] That one constant belief that black music is black life ritualized is key to understanding how he perceived himself as a poet, as an activist, and a polemical aesthetician.[8]

Recollecting his writings on jazz from the early '60s to 1967, Baraka in *Black Music* often attacks white appreciation and unlearned rhetoric about a music experiencing important changes, the figurative blackening of swing's mismanagement of jazz. Baraka does this while historicizing the significance of New York jazz clubs in fostering an environment conducive to musical explorations and innovations. At the same time, Baraka navigates the vertical trajectories of black musical transformations, between uptown and downtown, between Harlem, the Village, and the Lower East Side.

It should not come as a surprise that *Black Music* opens with "Jazz and the White Critic" (11–20), in which Baraka takes issue with the ways critics have labeled bebop as "anti-jazz" and anti-music. As Baraka would later contend in "The Changing Same," failure to appreciate and understand the music was ultimately a failure to understand the conditions under which the music was created; the history of "black music" demanded redress, and the social consciousness that emerged from and was forged by the experiential predica-

---

7. On that tradition of vernacular resistance, I suggest the first chapter in Sterling Stuckey's *Slave Culture*, and Lawrence Levine's *Black Culture and Black Consciousness*.

8. For instance, in "Blues, Poetry, and the New Music," he affirms, "the new music is always rooted in historical certainty. . . . [I]t uses history, it is not paralyzed by it! . . . The new music reinforces the most valuable memories of a people but at the same time creates new forms, new modes of expression, to more precisely reflect contemporary experience!" (*The Music* 266–267).

ment that African Americans had to endure would define the terms of historiographic redress (*Black Music* 209–211). The corrective comes in "Minton's" (21–24), the second entry in *Black Music*. If the Lost Generation had Paris, then the generation of jazz innovators who found each other and assembled at Minton's had Harlem. It is there, Baraka recounts, on 118th Street in the Hotel Cecil, that they experimented with the new sounds, the new methodology that would be known as bebop (22). By looking at the history of the birthplace of bebop, Baraka celebrates the changes in the music's focus, from arranger to improviser, from performer to musician (22–23). That element of self-definition is what Baraka sees as a form of social protest, a nonconformist attitude to what a jazz musician should "sound" like. As bebop developed "antagonistically" (23) into new musical territories, Minton's role was to stage the musicians who were creating a new vocabulary.

But as Baraka concludes in "Minton's," the venue, like many before it, stopped being a part of the vanguard, settling instead for "replicas of what was highly experimental twenty-five years ago" (23). The new, new music, free jazz, could be heard on the Lower East Side, "in lofts, small bohemian-type clubs" (24), and cafés. The new sounds of free jazz, what Baraka calls "the newest expression of the black soul," would take some time to return "home" to Harlem (24).

The significance of downtown jazz clubs in the legitimation of the musician's craft is a central preoccupation of *Black Music*. In "Recent Monk" (26–33), Baraka outlines the impact of Monk's stay at the Five Spot in the Bowery—Monk also played the Old Bowery. Monk's innovative style, his supposedly "incomprehensible" sonic layerings, became a groundswell of musical depth that Coltrane would draw from as he developed his own stylization of jazz compositional structures (28–29). As Baraka states in "The Jazz Avant-Garde" (69–80), what musicians like Monk and Coltrane acquire through cross-fertilizing sessions and musical conversations is the ideation process that allows the musician to journey back to roots (69). For Baraka, downtown jazz innovators have roots as emotions. Blues, bebop, and free jazz are iterations of roots music (Benston 84).[9]

Umbra member Archie Shepp is another example of a roots musician who, for Baraka, extrapolates emotions into political consciousness.[10] As part of the Lower East Side scene, Shepp perceives "the jazz musician [as a] reporter, an aesthetic journalist of America," whose "purpose is to liberate [the nation] aesthetically and socially from its inhumanity" (*Black Music* 154). A privy witness

9. Kimberly Benston, in *Baraka: The Renegade and the Mask,* dedicates an entire chapter to Baraka's idea of roots music. See chapter 3, and especially pp. 84–88 on "roots" music.

10. In "New Tenor Archie Shepp Talking," from *Black Music* 145–155.

to the place jazz would occupy in the Black Arts project, Baraka understood the sublimation of black protest in the music—Clay recognizes this process of sublimation in the musical performances of Bessie Smith and Charlie Parker, roots artists, as he stares down "historical inevitability" in the New York subway (Dixon 76).

In his review of the Impulse LP *New Wave in Jazz,* Baraka celebrates the prowess of Albert Ayler, working in the tradition of Coltrane and Ornette Coleman, and whose music invoked "the black rhythm energy blues feeling" as "projected in the area of reflection" (*Black Music* 175). Named "New Black Music" by Baraka and recorded at the famous Village Gate located at the corner of Thompson and Bleeker, *New Wave* was actually a concert benefit for BARTS.[11] The concert illuminates New York City's vectorial fostering of black cultural identity projects: BARTS traveling downtown, dialoguing with a community of black spirits—black arts spirits. Downtown sounds needing to travel uptown, back home to Harlem. Sounds of blues emotions, born of oppression and hope, nurtured and sustained through extemporaneous ways to contest, means to redress a contested history. And Baraka navigates the scene with the poise of someone ready to explode, politically and aesthetically, contained mostly by the desire to translate in words the compositional explosion of the melodic lines.

This collection of moments testifies both to the "social consciousness" Baraka saw as inherent in jazz, and to the deep understanding of black music as "consciousness, the expression of where" African Americans "are" (*Black Music* 209, 210). The "changing same" might be a continuum of impulses transposed into musical ideas, but it is also an interpretative platform for experiential expressions of black selfhood that Baraka heard, most clearly and engagingly performed, on the various stages of jazz scenes. In essence, Baraka's entire oeuvre illuminates the evolution of his "sound." For how he sounds is who he is, in the moment of consciousness and identity.

Baraka is many sounds, many voices—the way he shifts positions and ideologies is part of a continuum of consciousness in constant permutation, a changing same. How Baraka sounds and how he "hears" sound are part of a similar a continuum: The developments in the music that he sees as part of the changing same of vernacular resistance parallel (and vice versa) his oft-changing postulations of self-definition as artist and activist. What instantiates the changing is his cultural identity in constant (re)formation and his desire for freedom, like the many phases of Coltrane, like some other blues provid-

---

11. From the 1965 essay "New Black Music: A Concert Benefits of the Black Arts Repertory Theatre/School Live," reproduced in *Black Music* 172–176.

ing foundation to new, innovative explorations of the improvisatory moment, waiting to be called upon and responded to.[12]

The jazz performance in the Lower East Side venue that night both invoked and evoked Baraka's transitions from bohemian avant-gardism to black nationalism that one can read in the pages of *Black Music*. In it, Baraka is showing us the new pathways, the shifts, the breaks. As a return to one of his first "homes" in the vanguard space of experimentation of the Lower East Side, the performance was embedded in a still-to-be-written and deeply felt compendium to Baraka's polytextual politics and poetics. In many ways, *Some Other Blues* attempts to unpack Baraka's career-spanning performance.

•

The year 2018 marked the fifteenth anniversary of the publication of the special number of *African American Review* on Amiri Baraka edited by Aldon Lynn Nielsen, William Joe Harris, and Kalamu ya Salaam.[13] Produced both in the context and the aftermath of the controversy stirred over Baraka's poem about 9/11, "Somebody Blew Up America," the number that Nielsen, Harris, and ya Salaam assembled sought to propose engaging ways of looking at Baraka's oeuvre, exploring up-to-then neglected work, and envisioning a new phase in Baraka criticism. The call for new critical approaches on Baraka's work had been made. In January of 2018, *Some Other Blues* thus began as a response.

The pathway to substantive responses had begun prior with important, trailblazing works. After *Black Chant* (1995), Aldon Nielsen's *Integral Music* (2004) continued its dedication to providing close readings of black postmodern poetry and innovative black poetics, with resounding analyses of Baraka's work. In 2005, James Smethurst published his field-changing *The Black Arts Movement* that historicized the many strands of black activism and artistry

---

12. As he writes in "The Changing Same" about Coltrane's approach to music, "Freedom [is] the change" (*Black Music* 197).

13. I would like to acknowledge the importance of the founding of the Amiri Baraka Society in 2015, spearheaded by Aldon Nielsen, Gregory Pierrot, and me. The goal was to organize panel discussions with scholars invested in Baraka studies, fellow critics willing to engage the work in new and innovative ways. The Society has been present on the critical scene, organizing panels and round tables every year at the American Literature Association annual conference, the Modern Language Association conference, and the College Language Association conference, among others. This presence of the Society on the critical stage has drawn sustained interest from contemporary scholars looking to engage the Black Arts Movement, African American avant-garde poetics, and performative poetics in groundbreaking ways. The efforts of the Society to bring awareness to Baraka's vast body of work culminate in the impressive number of scholars assembled for this collection.

that coalesced in the movement spearheaded by Baraka. In 2014, John H. Bracey, Black Arts alum Sonia Sanchez, and Smethurst published *SOS—Calling All Black People: A Black Arts Movement Reader,* which revived interest in the movement and provided access to poems, plays, essays, and statements previously difficult to obtain. One year later, Paul Vangelisti published an attempt at a collected edition of poems, *SOS: Poems 1961–2013.* More recently, fellow Black Arts artists Haki Madhubuti and Sanchez, along with Michael Simanga (who published the important *Amiri Baraka and the Congress of African People: History and Memory* in 2015) and Woodie King Jr., published, through Third World Press, *Brilliant Flame!: Poetry, Plays & Politics for the People.* The book is a superb collection of poems, eulogies, and interviews that honor and celebrate Baraka. It also contains short critical commentary (one to three pages) on Baraka by fellow poets and scholars. Despite the brevity of the criticism it includes, *Brilliant Flame!* would be the closest monograph to map out the way poets and scholars have perceived Baraka since Kimberly Benston's 1978 *Amiri Baraka: A Collection of Critical Essays.*

The last few years have also seen a resurgence in publications of Baraka's work with works by Meta Jones, Kathy Lou Schultz, Margo Crawford, Anthony Reed, David Grundy, and myself, attempting to shed light on new aspects of Baraka's poetics.[14] Smethurst's *Brick Songs: Amiri Baraka, Black Music, Black Modernity, and Black Vanguard* (University of Massachusetts Press, 2020) is the latest addition to the critical canon. And Aldon Nielsen is finishing a book-length study of Baraka's work with musicians. Still, it is undeniable that there is still work to do to respond fully to Harris, Nielsen, and ya Salaam's timely invitation to produce new critical material on Baraka's literary work. *Some Other Blues* intends both to answer the special number's call for active engagement with Baraka's poetics and to address the critical lacunae on his understudied work. Baraka needs to be studied as both artist and polemist, as both aesthetic and political revolutionary, as both public intellectual and philosopher, as both Leroi and Amiri. In that sense, Lloyd Brown, despite his sometimes harsh criticism of the work, was right: It is the "wholeness" (52) of Baraka's work, its many competing ideas and values, that makes him such a towering presence in African American literature and culture, and in the larger American canon. That "wholeness" intermixes aesthetic, political, spiritual, vernacular, philosophical, and historical preoccupations with the pro-

---

14. See Meta Jones's *The Muse Is Music*; Margo Crawford's *Black Post-Blackness* (chapters 2 and 5); Kathy Lou Schultz's *The Afro-Modernist Epic and Literary History* (chapters 5 and 6); Anthony Reed's forthcoming *Soundworks: Race, Sound, and Poetry in Production*; David Grundy's *A Black Arts Poetry Machine: Amiri Baraka and the Umbra Poets*; and the fourth chapter in my *Jazz Griots*.

found desire to represent African American communal beauty, resilience, and sensitivity as well as the means and rituals via which black people have upheld their humanity in the face of constant violence, aggression, and suppression.

Some Other Blues is not only the first attempt to present the results of two decades of innovative research on Baraka, but it is also the product of many ongoing conversations between the scholars gathered to honor, celebrate, and assess the work Baraka bequeathed to his readers. It certainly feels like the time is right to have new critical insights into Baraka's oeuvre, as he not only would have had a lot to say about the current political climate, but he would also be proud to see how he continues to influence generations of African American poets trying to negotiate mainstream society.

Some Other Blues is modeled after the call-response pattern of black vernacular music—it is, after all, the "mode of (musical) expression" (*Black Music* 181) that has remained central to Baraka's idea of black expressive traditions and to his translation of the black cultural memory into verse and text, what in "New Music/New Poetry" he calls "speech *musicked*" (*The Music* 243).[15] Structurally and thematically, each part and each chapter of this collection is antiphonally connected; for instance, the first essay of each "side" of *Some Other Blues* issues a call in the form of a shorter Harris essay, which is responded to by the ensuing chapters. Part II responds to the idea of legacy mapped out critically in Part I. And Fred Moten provides us with the core riff on Baraka's impact and centrality.

In Part 1 Side A, William J. Harris proposes a poetics of place—27 Cooper Square—that becomes a space Baraka uses to experiment with traditions, forms, and aesthetics at the same time as he fashions an identity that anticipates a deep immersion in black vernacular culture (in Side B). The first response comes from Aldon Nielsen, who studied under Baraka and shared a friendship with him. Nielsen tackles the significance of the Winter 1963 issue of *Kulchur* in fashioning the new direction of black poetics in the context of the early '60s. Kathy Lou Schultz engages Baraka's experimentalism and vanguard aesthetics, this time through *6 Persons*, a multivocalic experimental memoir that, she argues, constructs black subjectivity. Tyrone Williams riffs on the idea of tradition by drawing links and establishing thematic correspon-

---

15. See *The Music* 243–245. Fahamisha Brown terms this process "song/talk." Brown writes, "The language of African American music informs the language of African American poetry. . . . Song functions in African American vernacular culture as primary recorder, the means of documentation of life and experience. Making music, then, continuing the song/talk that records and passes on the story, documents the events, celebrates the heroes, exposes the evils, and exhorts the people to keep on keeping on is the mission of the poet as well. The contemporary African American poet sings to a community and from a vibrant oral tradition by making song/talk" (82).

dences between Countee Cullen, Baraka, and Natasha Trethewey. Emily Ruth Rutter focuses on Baraka's less-explored writings about sports, which become opportunities to address issues related to resistance, appropriation, and co-optation. In the last essay of the first part, Jeremy Matthew Glick provides a transition between Sides: He places Hegel's short essay entitled "Who Thinks Abstractly?" in conversation with tracks from the 1982 jazz album *New Music/ New Poetry*, especially "Strunza Med," which allows him to reconsider politics of revolution, nation building, and black internationalism.

In the opening remarks to Part I Side B, Harris highlights the significance of Baraka attending the Five Spot, where he experiences the power of black jazz musicians, especially Thelonious Monk and John Coltrane, creating a black avant-garde music. Harris argues that for Baraka, the club is "a black space, a new cultural space." In this second call, Harris lays the groundwork for assessing the means of absorption and the resultant work: vernacularized poetics and politics.

In the first response, John Lowney considers how Baraka's later long jazz poems, especially "In the Tradition," respond to Hughes's aesthetic legacy despite their vexed relationship—Lowney calls it "dissonance"—as radical jazz poets. In his contribution, Grégory Pierrot charts the history of how Baraka defended the "New Music" as a music critic and promoted free jazz artists in his tenure at the Black Arts Repertory Theatre in Harlem, and later in New-ark, performing and recording with free jazz musicians throughout his career. James Smethurst takes on a new topic: Baraka's work as writer of LP liner notes. Smethurst's objective is to trace not simply how Baraka's liner notes become a sort of literary sub-genre, but also how they transform to express his radicalized ideas about class, nation, and modernity, ideas that gestured toward a socialist future. In "Baraka's Speculative Revolutions," Ben Lee pro-poses an original premise: "Answers in Progress" is a fictional account—jazz and science fiction–inspired, as Lee contends—of a revolution that never materialized. The essay invokes Sun Ra and Afrofuturism as a way to inter-rogate notions of community and revolutionary potential. Michael J. New's contribution analyzes the relationship and cross-fertilizations between Baraka and Gil Scott-Heron. New focuses on the ways in which each writer concep-tualizes, theorizes, and synthesizes art and political engagement, thereby illu-minating how they satirized the world they lived in as a means of fostering community and of affirming their cultural politics. Aidan Levy's contribu-tion analyzes how the cultural politics of jazz reflects Amiri Baraka's evolving Marxism through an analysis of "Essay/'Poem' on Money (from *Why You Say-ing This: A Novel*)," an unpublished essay Levy found in the Baraka archive.

Levy studies how Baraka creates a coinage for the penny: the "Clifford," neologized as a homage to Clifford Brown. Finally, Anthony Reed's essay returns to Harris's premise: Reed theorizes what he calls Baraka's "vernacular avant-garde" praxes, most perceptive in his recording politics and performances. To do so, Reed uses Baraka's recording with the Spirit House Movers, especially the album *Black and Beautiful . . . Soul and Madness* as a primary example of vernacular avant-garde praxes and political assertiveness.

Part II of *Some Other Blues* unpacks a series of essays that read as testimonies, tributes, and reconsiderations of Baraka's meaning and legacy as poet-activist-philosopher. Lauri Scheyer provides a short assessment of Baraka's place in the canons of American and African American poetries. She refers to Baraka's 1960s work in order to show how Baraka had to negotiate his place among "new American poets." In his contribution, Howard Rambsy II engages the politics of anthologizing Baraka's work. Rambsy proposes a Baraka poetry database and data management tools that allow him to look at *how* Baraka is anthologized in order to assess both his literary legacy and the means via which it is archived.

Laura Vrana's essay is concerned with the notion of influence; she examines the aesthetic and ideological legacy of Baraka for young female poets such as Aja Monet and Jamila Woods, more specifically in terms of political art. Vrana explores Baraka as model for claiming and creating a contemporary black feminist poetics that differ from so-called academic poets. Taking the issue of gender in a new, innovative direction, Amy Abugo Ongiri employs the traumatic murders of Baraka's sister and daughter, as well as his relationship with his second wife Amina, as moments that signal a change in his view of black femininity and sexuality and black feminist politics. Part personal account of her meeting with Amina Baraka, part literary history of a seminal voice, Kim McMillon's essay focuses on Amina Baraka, on her artistry and her development as an activist. Often relegated to the wings because of her husband's commanding presence, Amina, McMillon suggests, is a foundational and preeminent figure in the black liberation movements, especially in Newark. Michael Simanga, a longtime friend of Baraka, prescriptively illuminates the legacy of Baraka's mentorship, teaching, and guidance on generations of African Americans. Kalamu ya Salaam takes us on a journey, historical and literary, into the heart of liberation struggles. A contemporary of Baraka and an active participant in the Black Arts South movement through the Free Southern Theatre initiative, ya Salaam identifies Baraka's key works that, to him, highlight what the black consciousness theorists and artists and black aestheticians were trying to achieve politically and artistically. In his "Blues/

Funk Outro," Tony Bolden echoes Simanga and ya Salaam, and proposes a funk aesthetic to reengage Baraka's role as poet and prescient voice of black struggles and unity.

The scholars who have agreed to collaborate on this collection are some of the most active and well-regarded critics in the field of African American poetry, critics whose outputs have been sustained and theoretically sophisticated. They have produced monographs, anthologies, and critical essays that remain, to this day, among the most oft-cited works in African American poetry. Together, these scholars cover twenty years of active engagement with Amiri Baraka; they represent two generations of scholars participating in an ongoing dialogue about the status of Baraka's work in the American literary and cultural canons. And they all listen to Coltrane and the blues.

PART I

PERSPECTIVES ON RECORD

Side A

Home (A Cultural Space of Experiment)

1
=

Amiri Baraka
Among the Bohemians

27 Cooper Square

WILLIAM J. HARRIS

N 1957, after being discharged "undesirably" from the United States Air Force, Amiri Baraka, then known as LeRoi Jones, arrived in New York's Lower East Side. In this two-part essay, I explore two Lower East Side, New York, bohemian locations that were central to Baraka's development: 27 Cooper Square, the home he shared with Hettie Jones, his first wife, and the Five Spot, a nearby jazz club where the new black avant-garde jazz was burgeoning. In the course of this essay we will enter these buildings, these spaces, these two environments and discover their respective importance. Both locations of the Five Spot are gone. 27 Cooper Square not only still exists, but Hettie Jones still lives there, and we will hear from her shortly. Baraka moved out not long after the assassination of Malcolm X on February 21, 1965, heading uptown to Harlem in March of that year. The building is presently surrounded by the Standard Hotel; in fact, the lobby of the Standard is the first floor of 27 Cooper Square. Hettie has made a deal with management; she told them: "I just want to stay here till I croak" ("High-Rise Eats Tenement"), and they accepted her terms.

Both Amiri Baraka and Hettie Jones explore places, locations, and spaces; in essence, they tell their biographies through places—both reveal their lives through places they have lived. Baraka ticks off his changing consciousness (self) by relating it to specific spaces. Both have written important autobiographies, *How I Became Hettie Jones* (1990) and *The Autobiography of LeRoi Jones*

/ *Amiri Baraka* (1997), in which they detail their experiences from specific spaces and locations. For example, Hettie Jones titles most of her chapters after places where she has lived, areas where their apartments were located, starting with Morton Street and ending with Cooper Square. In this study, places are small worlds that are cultural, ideological, and artistic spaces, filled with persuasive and influential people and situations. These distinct bohemian localities represent contrasting mental and psychological spaces through which we trace changing conceptions of self. In short, they are transformative sites.

Therefore, in the first section I explore the house, the people who live there, their domestic space, and their activities. In the second section I explore the Five Spot in two moments and places. Beginning in 1957, Baraka attended the Five Spot often, and in this mixed club he experienced the black avant-garde genius of the music, articulated through particular musicians, most notably Thelonious Monk and John Coltrane. What is important about this world, unlike the world of the house, is that black original and highly accomplished jazz musicians are the artists in sight and in control; they are creating and defining an art that grows out of black culture.

We thus have two communities, the primarily white bohemian community of the house and the black avant-garde community that Baraka finds at the mixed jazz club.

THE HOUSE SPACE

My essay was inspired by the commemorative plaque on the right side of the door at 27 Cooper Square. Their daughter, Kellie Jones, who lived there as a child also and is an art historian, said at a reading promoting her latest book, *South of Pico: African American Artists in Los Angeles in the 1960s and 1970s* (2017): "I write about artists in groups because I grew up among artists in groups." In an email to me, Hettie wrote of the plaque:

> I thought it important to remind that the "East Village" only came into being because my generation of artists had in the late 50s sought a low-rent area and the Lower East Side was convenient to Greenwich Village, the traditional bohemian "home" for us. (December 9, 2017)

For her, space comes about because of economics; the community settles there because of cheap rents, an old bohemian story. The plaque is different from many because it celebrates several people and their talents instead of one individual and his or her genius. Who lived there? The top floor was occupied by the writers Amiri and Hettie; they edited the influential little magazine *Yugen* and the avant-garde press Totem—we will return those publications in a moment. Archie Shepp, the great free jazz saxophonist, and his family lived on the second floor, and so that adds music to the space. Finally, the painter and MacArthur recipient Elizabeth Murray, influenced by abstract expressionism and cubism, and her first husband, sculptor Don Sunseri, lived in another apartment. What their individual arts had in common was a desire to fashion avant-gardism in their particular field. In that space, we have artists in various disciplines living under one roof, and they influence each other both because they have similar goals and because of their proximity.

The house is the Lower East Side in miniature. Frank O'Hara's poem "Why I Am Not a Painter," written in 1956, demonstrates the lifestyle and acts as a sort of manifesto. O'Hara's poem is a witty narrative about a poet, O'Hara, learning techniques from a painter, Mike Goldberg; more importantly, the poem is about the creative process that unites them as contemporary radical artists. Still, the poem is also about more than this unity. Let us look at the story in more details. O'Hara "drop[s] in" (*Collected Poems* 261–262, line 5) on Goldberg in his studio, where he is creating a new painting. O'Hara notices it has sardines in it. Goldberg says, "Yes, it needed something there" (9). Then, on another day, he visits and realizes the sardines are gone, and Goldberg explains, "It was too much" (16). On O'Hara's part, when he writes a poem about the color orange, he never mentions the word in the poem. It is important that the painter influenced the poet and shared a creative process. At the same time, it is equally important that one influenced the other, because they lived in the same artistic community and shared the same avant-garde goals. They are friends, and what unites them is their collective desire to make avant-garde art, to make it "new" and contemporary, whether it is a painting or a poem. The poet Anne Waldman, echoing O'Hara, said of the period and place: "During the '60s and '70s collaborations were made possible by a particular bohemian lifestyle. You dropped in on painters at work, they dropped in on you" (211). In short, 27 Cooper Square was a house comprised of artists collaborating, interconnecting, artists in groups, and artists as couples; these are artists practicing different arts, exchanging ideas, feelings, and techniques. They were close! And, this is the world Kellie Jones grew up in. This is the house she grew up in. The world she talks about in her book evokes her mother's words:

> Because we published our magazines and books, LeRoi and I had been at the
> New York center of the writers/artists of the "Beat Generation" as well as the

downtown contingent of the New York School of poets. We were the party place, in other words. We moved to the top floor of 27 Cooper Square in January 1962, and whenever either one of the two lofts downstairs was vacant, we managed to get our friends in (preferably those with kids who needed space.) This is how Archie Shepp and family arrived, as did Elizabeth Murray and family after the Shepps. The parties continued, especially since this place is quite private, so we could use all available floors, and the kids could play in the halls. (Hettie Jones, email to William J. Harris, December 9, 2017)

That the place, as the center of bohemian New York, was also a party center makes sense because Hettie realizes the importance of parties as places to meet people, swap ideas, and expand horizons. In other words, parties are serious business and need to be studied as part of literary history.

In reality, we are involved in an expanded literary history, history beyond the individual genius, which is usually male and white. This is a story of a community relating to each other. This is a history that mixes the domestic, the social, the cultural, and the artistic. Talking about space/place allows us to see these complex worlds interrelate. Moreover, this history adds voices and perspectives, including female voices.

THE FAMILY

It is important to know that 27 Cooper Square is a domestic place, a family place, as well as an artistic one. In a 1963 photo, we can see Roi with Lisa on his shoulders, and Kellie, the future art historian, on Hettie's lap. Hettie in her email refers to the children who grew up with the atmosphere of this "happy energy in place." She says:

> The children/now adults who grew up here absorbed this, I think, and have gone on to express it in various ways. Accra Shepp is the younger son of Archie and well-known as a photographer, teaching at ICP [International Center of Photography], and of course there is the wonderful Kellie as well as my younger daughter Lisa Jones, also a writer (Bulletproof Diva), who used to have a column in the Village Voice and has written Spike Lee's books about the making of his movies.

The space was permeated with values that impacted not only adults but the children also.

Of the place, Amiri says: "The Cooper Square apartment had an ambience, a sense of place, as Charles Olson would have called it, that was unlike either West 20th Street or East 14 Street. Perhaps, for one thing, it was my own deepening sense of myself that was at large within those rooms" (*Autobiography* 255). However, this self is divided. As he observes: "I began to feel, even though I was definitely still a member of the downtown set, somewhat alienated from my old buddies. . . . I peeped some distance had sprung up between us" (255–256).

A PLACE OF WORK

It was also the place of work, the place of both the important avant-garde press Totem and the avant-garde magazine *Yugen,* edited by Amiri and Hettie. Totem published Baraka's *Preface to a Twenty Volume Suicide Note,* Ed Dorn's *Hands Up,* Jack Kerouac's *The Golden Scriptures of Golden Eternity,* and Gary Snyder's *Myth & Texts.* Amiri wrote *Dutchman* and *Blues People* there, while Hettie wrote *How I Became Hettie Jones* in the same space. Let us look at *Yugen* for a moment, numbers 1 and 5, as well as at the people published there. In number 1, Philip Whalen, Judson Crews, Diane Di Prima, and Allen Ginsberg—future stars of avant-garde poetry—appear alongside four young black poets, Tom Postell, Allen Polite, Bobb Hamilton, and Baraka. Interesting to note how black poets disappear from the magazine after the second issue, except Baraka. We will return to that story in a moment. In the fifth number, more New American poet stars are featured. The great poet A. R. Ammons said to me that what was incredible about *Yugen* was that each issue was a gem. By that time, though, Hettie is demoted to an assistant editor. What does that mean?

COOPER SQUARE: THE IN-BETWEEN SPACE

The plaque next to the door of 27 Cooper Square reads:

> In the 1960s, this 1845 former rooming house became a laboratory for artistic, literary and political currents. Writers LeRoi Jones (later Amiri Baraka) and Hettie Jones, their *Yugen* Magazine and Totem Press, musician Archie Shepp and painter Elizabeth Murray all had homes here. The vacant building was transformed into a vital hub of cultural life, attracting leading figures including those from the Beat and the world of jazz.

The literary critic Claudia Pisano says of Cooper Square:

> In the early '60s, Cooper Square would have been considered something of
> an in-between space, not quite here or there. Abutting the Lower East Side,
> the East Village, the Bowery, and the section of Bleecker Street heading into
> Greenwich Village, rents would have been low and space abundant. . . . For
> radical, experimental artists, staying downtown but out of the already com-
> modified Greenwich Village, the East Village and Lower East Side were key
> in "artists' resistance to being co-opted by the kinds of mainstream activity
> [of] the late 1950s West Village scene (Kane 2)." (85)

For his part, Amiri Baraka writes:

> In one sense our showing up on Cooper Square was right in tune with the
> whole movement of people east, away from the West Village with its high
> rents and older bohemians. Cooper Square was sort of the borderline; when
> you crossed it, you were really on the Lower East Side, no shit. (*Autobiog-
> raphy* 258)

However, this in-between place is still primarily a white space.[1]

BLACKNESS IN THE HOUSE

Baraka started wondering what this white avant-garde world had done to him.
Baraka was feeling seduced by the white avant-garde world, like the young
black hero, Clay, who was also intellectually enticed by the white temptress
and murderer, Lula, on the subway in *Dutchman.* Let us not forget about the
issue I raised earlier about the absence of black poets by the third issue of
Yugen. Finally, Baraka reflects on his position in the white avant-garde world:

> But there is only one black writer, LeRoi Jones. . . . Ernie, Ed, Steve, Tim,
> Bobb Hamilton, Allen Polite, Tom Postell are not there. But I was not with
> them socially either. . . . I was "open" to all schools within the circle of white
> poets of all faiths and flags. But what had happened to the blacks? What
> had happened to me? How is it that there's only the one colored guy? . . . So
> obviously my social focus had gotten much whiter. White wife, co-editor.

---

1. See Kane 79–90.

The weekend hollering and drinking trysts were hooked to the same social focus. (*Autobiography* 231)

But blackness crept into Cooper Square. Of course, it was already there in terms of Archie Shepp, a black free jazz musician. Baraka said, "We had some bigger, wilder parties at Cooper Square, in Archie's loft, with some of the hippest music of the time" (*Autobiography* 262). So, black music happened in the white avant-garde house. Marion Brown, a member of Shepp's circle, wrote a free jazz composition, "27 Cooper Square" (1966), that alludes to the times he practiced there with Archie Shepp, and perhaps partied there too (Weiss 145). Brown recalls: "We used to practice at 27 Cooper Square, and he [Baraka] lived in that building on the top floor. Archie Shepp lived on the second floor. So he knew what we were doing all along, because he was upstairs listening" (146). As he becomes more disillusioned with the white world, Baraka started using 27 Cooper Square to meet with black intellectuals:

> There was clearly something forming, something about to come about to come into being. . . . I had said outright that the black and white thing was over, but I did not think I could act. For one thing, the little girls, now, were walking around and there was certainly both a deep love and a pressing responsibility there. (*Autobiography* 289)

Hettie Jones observes: "Increasingly the racial balance in our house shifted, as a black avant-garde . . . became part of the new East Village, just coming into that name" (*How* 172). Baraka stops hanging out at the Cedar Bar, a white space where white artists and poets gathered and dominated, and starts going to jazz clubs, coffeehouses, and lofts, mixed spaces culturally dominated by blacks.

The System of Dante's Hell was published in 1965, but it was written in the late '50s, early '60s (Reilly *Conversations* 100; *System* 153), the years of Baraka's growing struggles with the white avant-garde. This book reflects his struggles. In that novel, he tries to break away from the white avant-garde aesthetic. He tells D. H. Melhem: "The things that I try in the Dante I really wasn't even aware of, in a sense, I was just trying to stop writing like other people. And it's interesting that years later I read where Aime Cesaire did the same thing to get away from French Symbolist" (Melhem, *Heroism*, 228). In his essay "Aime Cesaire," from *Daggers and Javelins*, Baraka says: "These young [Negritude] poets were looking for a mode of expression, a method of saying what was uniquely theirs to say, and at the same time denouncing all sterile imitations of the colonial masters" (193). Baraka adds, "Blacks wanted to use surrealism a different way. For Cesaire, it represented a destruction of French literary tradition, which he felt stifled by" (194). As Baraka contends, "Cesaire . . . defines Negritude in 1959 as 'the awareness of being black, the simple acknowledgment of a fact'" (197). In that sense, jazz is Baraka's Negritude, a way to become himself.

2

=

Kulchur Wars

ALDON LYNN NIELSEN

WHILE THE EDITORS of the journal *Kulchur* always aimed for time-
liness and surprise, the Winter 1963 issue was more than usually
unusual; it had much breaking news for a nation breaking apart
to contend with. The issue was dedicated to the memory of W. E. B. Du Bois,
though readers did not learn that till they reached page 31 and the conclusion of the issue's special section, titled "Rights: Some Personal Reactions."
That special section was devoted to reflections in the wake of the preced-
ing summer's March on Washington. Du Bois had died in Accra the night
before the march, and in those days, when the World Wide Web was woven
of paper, rumor, and telegraph lines, most of those assembled on the grounds
of the Lincoln Memorial learned of the passing of Du Bois when Roy Wilkins
announced the news from the platform. In the wake of the march, the editors
of *Kulchur* had elicited commentaries on race and rights from eight American writers, three black and five white. Readers only learned the questions
that had been mailed to the respondents in the last of the contributions, the
one submitted by Denise Levertov, who couched her answers in the form of
a letter to LeRoi Jones, in those days listed on the masthead as the journal's
music editor. Levertov writes that she "does not feel capable of answering the
public question except in a private context" (29), hence the epistolary form of
her writing, an "open letter." But that in turn is rendered somewhat strange
by the fact that her salutation, "Dear Leroi," uses the pre–Howard University

orthography of Jones's name, with a small "r," even as the journal's heading on her piece, "Letter to LeRoi Jones," follows the example of all of his published work to that date by using the capital "R." And in a fashion unusual in correspondence, Levertov's letter, posted from Maine on September 1, follows a Q&A format. Hers is the only one of the responses that mentions the existence of a questionnaire, though joel oppenheimer's essay has headlined segments hinting at the questions. But when that issue of *Kulchur* appeared, though Levertov was listed on the rear cover among all the contributors to issue 12, in order to learn that she was a part of the forum on rights a reader would have to lift a last-minute tipped-in note on the Kennedy assassination to see that she was there among the respondents on rights; the Kennedy Assassination had literally obscured readers' vision of Levertov on civil rights.

And that was not the only tipped-in anomaly in the Winter 1963 issue. Between pages 86 and 87, there was an additional page, printed on a different paper from the rest and glued along its left side to page 87 beneath it. The added sheet bore a poem by LeRoi Jones titled "Exaugural Address," a poem which was never to appear in any of his subsequent books. The poem is dated November 26, 1963, just four days after the assassination, and in *Kulchur* it interrupts a review of Allen Ginsberg's *Reality Sandwiches*. That review was written by Baraka, and so the placement is readily understood on that basis, but there is another reason this poem is placed in the middle of this review; its subtitle, which we shall come to in a bit, revises and responds to a comment Baraka had made in his review.

Kulchur, its name borrowed from Pound, was primarily a journal of commentary, though it printed, as in that instance, an occasional poem, and published a drama issue edited by Baraka, which included his play *The Toilet*. (Notably, Baraka rejected Douglas Turner Ward's *Day of Absence* on the grounds that it was derivative of Ray Bradbury's "Way in the Middle of the Air.") The journal had been founded by Marc Schliefer. In Baraka's description, Schliefer "had come out of the university of Pennsylvania as an arch conservative, then was transformed by the various Village forces and became more radical than most of" Baraka's other colleagues (*Autobiography* 253). Lita Hornick, who lived on Park Avenue, not in the Village, bought the magazine from Schliefer as a means of continuing her burgeoning interests in the Beat arts scene, and eventually took over as chief editor. Baraka was originally listed as music editor of *Kulchur*, but later became contributing editor. Other staff members included Frank O'Hara, Joseph LeSeur, A. B. Spellman, Bill Berkson, Gilbert Sorrentino, and Charles Olson. Baraka saw the publication as being "still another vehicle for expression of our broad common aesthetic" that "allowed us to resume our attack on the academy . . . at an even higher level than *Zazen* provided," using the pseudonym for the journal *Yugen* that he edited with his then wife, Hettie Cohen (*Autobiography* 254). The scope of *Kulchur* is evident from an ad for back issues in number 19, highlighting "otherwise unavailable work by" Ginsberg, Creeley, Zukofsky, Koch, Rothenberg, Warhol, Guest, Beck, Dorn, Goodman, Kelly, Merwin, Kael, Corman, Blackburn, Oppen, Feldman, and many others. A sense of *Kulchur*'s international reach and combative sensibility can be found in number 15's "COMMENTS? FROM ABROAD" (104–105), in the form of a "Manifesto on Hungrealistic Poetry" that had come in from a group of young Bengali poets in Kolkata, India. The manifesto argues: "Poetry is not the caging of belches within form. It should convey the brutal sound of the breaking values and startling tremors of the rebellious soul" (104).

Though Schliefer was no longer on the editorial board by the time of issue number 12, his legacy is visible in the presence of Robert Williams among the contributors to the symposium on rights. Baraka had traveled with Williams during the trip to Cuba that led to his essay "Cuba Libre," first published in 1960 in *Evergreen Review*. Schliefer conducted a three-hour interview with Williams in Havana, which was later broadcast over WBAI, and was the editor of Williams's 1962 book, *Negroes with Guns*.

Kulchur's "Rights" symposium gets off to an odd beginning with Baraka's own contribution. He had already been registering dissidence with the strategies of the Southern civil rights movement. As he puts it in the *Autobiography*, he "was now taking potshots at the nonviolence movement" (266) in essays like "Tokenism: 300 Years for Five Cents," which appeared in *Kulchur*. So while the tenor of Baraka's symposium contribution isn't especially surprising, its subject matter is. The editorial note that introduces the section says: "The contributors to 'Rights' were asked to supply us with a variety of personal reactions to the civil rights crisis. Their comments are as varied as they are personal" (2). Perhaps none is so variant and personal as Baraka's, which is the review "Brief Reflections on Two Hot Shots," his dual takedown of Peter Abrahams and James Baldwin. From the distance of more than a half century, and in the wake of the international success of the Baldwin film *I Am Not Your Negro* (not to mention Baraka's later positive comments about Baldwin on film and in print), the heat of Baraka's rejection may come as a shock. "Abrahams and Baldwin want the hopeless filth of enforced ignorance to be stopped only because they are sometimes confused with the sufferers" (3), writes the young Baraka. "Men like Baldwin and Abrahams want to live free from such 'ugly' things as 'the racial struggle' because (they imply) they simply cannot stand what it does to men" (4). This last is itself a seemingly strange concoction, but we see in Baraka's view the problem with these writers, or at least a problem, is

their reduction of the struggle to questions of misunderstanding and sensitivity, and while this judgment is undoubtedly unfair to Baldwin and Abrahams,
Baraka's complaint must seem kindred to contemporary critical race studies
judgments about the problematic approaches of diversity management. Baraka
claims that "if Abrahams and Baldwin were turned white . . . there would be
no more noise from them" (5). This is clearly just the sort of potshot at mainstream civil rights discourse Baraka recollects in his *Autobiography*. He is still
two years away from writing "A Poem for Black Hearts" and decamping from
the Village, but, as can be seen from the essays gathered in the volume *Home,*
he was already well on his way to the more violently radical rhetoric that was
to mark the rest of the decade. He closes his consideration of the South African and the American novelists by imploring, "Somebody turn them! And
then perhaps the rest of us can get down to the work at hand. Cutting throats!"
(5) We do not as yet have the sorts of reception studies that would tell us what
contemporaneous readers made of this entry. *Kulchur's* audience had to have
been taken aback at seeing the first personal response to the "civil rights crisis"
recorded in the journal appear in the form of a brutal review of two prominent novelists, but even an audience weaned on the theater of the absurd, let
alone the theater of cruelty, must have been caught off balance when an essay
responding to the March on Washington took such a desperately violent turn
at its end. Add to this the fact that readers of *Kulchur* number 12 came to
Baraka's essay turning directly to it from that tipped-in editorial expression of
grief and indignation at the violence of the Kennedy assassination.

The remaining contributions to the special section all engage more directly
with the express subject of the personal responses, and in those responses we
can read the increasing tensions and ideological shifts arising in the short
months between the March on Washington and the Kennedy assassination.
Looking back, Baraka has acknowledged his own participation in the general
sense of progressive movement that so many Americans had felt with the pronouncements of the New Frontier heard in the Kennedy inauguration address.
"Kennedy for many of us," he writes, "even unconsciously represented something positive" (*Autobiography* 272). He even takes note of the naming of one
of the period's most interesting new jazz groups, The J. F. K. Quintet. Yet, by
summer of 1963, the Kennedy administration's ofttimes slow and sometimes
even grudging responses to growing demands for basic constitutional rights
for black Americans was edging African American writers progressively farther away from the King model of passive resistance.

A. B. Spellman's essay, directly following Baraka's review, shows in its very
title that black artists were growing restive with liberal ameliorationist stagings.
The essay is titled after Manet's painting "Luncheon on the Grass." What did

August's march prove to the liberal press, in Spellman's view? Only that "such a crowd could be assembled, 225,000 people who threatened nobody" (5). In Spellman's view, the march placed more emphasis "on non-violence than on civil-disobedience" (6), and thus was compromised from the outset. The violent note at the end of Baraka's essay was sign enough, if any were needed, that America was already past being transformed peacefully by demonstrations of brotherhood. The impression left by the gathered ministerial representatives at the march was that "racial discrimination is practiced only by other people" (10), a sentiment still hovering dangerously around white reception of much African American writing. And it is Spellman who acknowledges the passing of Du Bois, condemning the march speakers for speaking apologetically of the ninety-three-year-old Du Bois's "Marxist path" (11). Virtually predicting what was shortly to come in the movement for black rights, Spellman complains that "our leaders think in terms of persuasion rather than power" (13). Less than three years later, the field staff of the Student Non-Violent Coordinating Committee (SNCC) would reassert the slogan of Black Power, unalterably moving the politics of liberation toward new strategies.

Of course, an early proponent of Black Power was Robert F. Williams, whose book *Negroes with Guns* had been published the year before the march. Williams was a strong advocate of armed self-defense, and had even gotten a charter from the National Rifle Association (NRA; how greatly things have changed since) for a local chapter that he named the Black Armed Guard. Williams's rhetoric follows a familiar pattern. He says his "criticism is not of nonviolence and love, but of the fact that these so-called moralists are endeavoring to peddle their Ghandian wares to the wrong market" (15), and while it is true that King, Lewis, and others certainly favored the Klan abandoning strategies of racist violence, it was equally true that few prominent American political figures were then making it their business to preach active measures for ending racism to their white constituents. Williams is writing his response from exile, but his distance from his home country is not the self-exile of Baldwin, though the two share a common sense of what may be coming. "The flames of racial unrest sweep the USA like an all consuming firestorm," Williams says of the fire next time, "and only bold, decisive and honest action will stave off complete desolation of the land" (19).

Baraka and the editorial staff of *Kulchur* organized the symposium with the three black contributors appearing first, followed by five white writers, most of whom were the representatives of different branches of the New American Writing with connections to Baraka. It is clear from the responses that the contributors had all been asked their opinion of Elijah Muhammed's Nation of Islam, and Gilbert Sorrentino devotes his pages specifically to "A

Note on the Muslims." Sorrentino begins by confessing complete ignorance of the inner workings of the Black Muslims. That, however, was no impediment to his delivering himself of opinions on their efficacy. Oddly, he holds that a weakness of this black separatist movement is that "they have ignored the larger, and more politically efficacious body of disaffiliates and renegades which exists among the white populace" (19), a judgment that only comes to make a modicum of sense when we arrive at Sorrentino's stated belief that the only potential for a real breakthrough rests with the creation of a third party. Elijah Muhammed's Muslim organization, it must be recalled, disavowed most modes of practical political activity. Indeed, this was one of the sources of growing friction between Malcolm and Minister Muhammed. So, Sorrentino's expressed hope that the Muslim organization might "move from their currently hermetic position to one of general political activity" (21) might be best read as evidence of his professed ignorance of the workings of the organization about which he is writing.

Then, too, there is a rhetorical feature in Sorrentino's note that points up a divide between the writers in this symposium. One of his assertions begins with the words, "As many Negroes have noted . . ." (19). No doubt many Negroes might have noted just what he says they had, and yet in the absence of any citation, any reference to any actual Negroes, what we are left with is once again a white writer positing what black people more generally are thinking. I think joel oppenheimer is trying to gently attack such white thinking with the title of his own piece, "Some of My Best Peers." Before oppenheimer, though, comes a short offering from Ed Dorn, not even two full pages. Given how close Dorn and Baraka were, and how Dorn's political instincts were one of the bases for that closeness, his contribution here seems little more than a shrug of the poet's shoulders. In the end, Dorn's is the quietest position. "Race is an exotic recognition, mostly visual," he observes, and "always a momentary interest" (23). Race was about to prove itself a far from momentary interest to Baraka, and already had a perilously long life span in the nation. Dorn claims a peculiar poet's ethic, by which he claims it a point of honor and responsibility that he not number among his friends a cop, the president, a gangster, or anyone who thinks "Negroes should stay in their place" (23). Baraka would hardly be the only one to argue that responsibility extends farther than simply not befriending racists. oppenheimer, in sharp contrast, though he opens with one of those self-deprecating claims to be unable to add anything of interest to the subject that marks and mars so much white writing on race, concludes that the only position he can take is indeed that of Robert Williams. History has shown him that "americans are terrified of the thought of free men fighting to make their own space" (24). As if to prove that assertion, the next contribution in the gathering is from transplanted Southerner Donald Windham. Speaking of Georgia in the thirties, Windham writes: "I was unaware . . . of any such thing as prejudice against Negroes" (28). Windham follows that bit of dishonesty with one of the hoariest of Southern defenses against interventions to protect rights: "As long as the change comes from the outside, not from an increased examination by individuals of their feelings and acts . . . new targets will be found" (29). No doubt there will always be new targets, but someone who cannot even summon sufficient self-awareness to acknowledge that racial prejudice existed in the South in the thirties seems a poor choice to advise the rest of us. And in such moments of the *Kulchur* symposium, we can see delineated the obtuseness and white resistance that would lead Baraka and others to sever many ties to the communities of writers in which they had come of age.

Denise Levertov's open letter to Baraka, which closes out the set, rests somewhere between the quietism of Dorn and the revanchist ramblings of Windham. Those familiar with her subsequent politicalization might be taken aback by her observation that becoming politically active would "rob" time from her roles as wife, mother, poet, and friend. It also rests uncomfortably with her closing assertion that one cannot look at civil rights and the peace movement separately. We might note that few did—witness King's commitments to the peace movement—but as with Dorn, Levertov's letter leaves us somehow adhering to a movement without taking much if any time to do anything about it.

Tellingly, the editors close out the symposium with that dedication to the memory of the recently deceased Du Bois. Significantly, that dedication makes clear that it is the entire issue, not just the symposium, that is so dedicated. They close the dedication with that ringing rhetorical question Du Bois posited six decades earlier, "How does it feel to be a problem?" (31). One wonders how many white readers of *Kulchur* saw that question as directed at them.

The tipped-in interruptions of *Kulchur* number 12 manifest the multiplying fissures and ruptures that mark the '60s. If the Kennedy assassination was a death knell for the '50s in American culture, tolling the transformation of the New Frontier into a newer apocalypse, *Kulchur* both reflected and anticipated the many cleavages that were shifting the cultural terrain from 1963 to 1968: black from white, civil disobedience from revolution, New American writings from themselves. The pasting in of assassination news and verse was a last-minute reopening of all ideological questions as America and the world ripped themselves apart.

Kulchur was not the only literary/cultural formation torn by this moment. In the autobiographical fiction *6 Persons*, Baraka, using his pseudonym for the Umbra writers group, writes:

> At Eclipse they argued whether a poem accusing Kennedy of being an Imperialist Dog shd be printed a few weeks after his ice-ing. In fact the group broke up behind that. & the mad souls who sd print the muhfuh, they drew closer together & w/others like them. (365)

There were, of course, many factors feeding into the dissolution of the Umbra group, but there is no doubting the ferocity of debate around this question of post-assassination publishing. The piece at issue was Ray Durem's "A Decoration for the President." Durem's work, written in the years prior to Kennedy's assassination, was in the form of an open letter, inscribing an analogy between the death of a child in an American-sponsored bombing raid on Cuba and the murder of Emmett Till. The conceit of this composition is that the letter is accompanied by a "decoration," a human hand—the ring-bearing hand of the fourteen-year-old Emilio, killed when a bomb struck the outskirts of Havana. (We have to wonder if Durem was also counting on readers to recall something about the murder of Emmett Till just eight years before. Till's body had been unrecognizable when discovered, identified only by the ring he was wearing, bearing the initials "L. T." It was his late father's ring, passed to young Emmett by his mother, Mamie, just before his trip to the South. And there's this, too, probably known to as well-read a poet as Ray Durem: Louis Till, as we learn in Pound's *Cantos*, had shared a prison camp with the poet prior to being executed.) Sentences like the one closing the work's second paragraph give a sense of why some among the Umbra group hesitated to publish Durem's work so soon after Kennedy's death. It reads: "You may melt the gold and add it to your millions, or you may want to give it to little Caroline." Durem's "Decoration" was in the end not published by Umbra, eventually appearing in Durem's collection in the Paul Breman Heritage series book *Take No Prisoners* in 1971.

The disputes among the Umbra poets that year closely tracked with the disputes coming into view in the *Kulchur* symposium and within Baraka himself. Baraka writes of this moment in both the *Autobiography* and in *6 Persons*. In the novel, he writes that the Kennedy election had brought a widespread sense of "increase," but "the world had changed a great deal by the time he was iced" (343):

Even tho Camelot rose, ditto the inner contradictions, the different directions and destinations implicit in the origins of our gang. . . . The American
morality vs the need for a higher morality if they were supposed to be representing something of value. (344)

It is precisely such cleaving of values that is visible in *Kulchur*'s symposium on
rights, in *Umbra*'s internal fracturing, and in Baraka's own sense of himself in
the world. In the *Autobiography* he remembers his friend, painter Bob Thompson, weeping openly in the street at the news of Kennedy's death in Dallas:

Though I was disturbed, curious, about the assassination, I hadn't realized it
until I saw Bob sitting now on the curb, weeping uncontrollably. . . . I wrote
a poem which had to be tipped into the winter issue of *Kulchur*. . . . I was
trying to move to a revolutionary position, but I was still ready to weep for
Jacqueline Bouvier Kennedy. (273)

Baraka's poem, never subsequently collected, presents itself in the form of
an "Exaugural Address," an address whose rhetoric runs directly counter to
the generation-shifting discourse of Kennedy in 1961.[1] Baraka's poem begins:
"All hopes of the sweet millennium / vanished into the insanity of television."
It is interesting to think of this work in conjunction with Lorenzo Thomas's
inauguration poem, which also presents itself in stark counterpoint to the
mood of the ceremony on January 20, 1961. Thomas's poem inserts itself into
the rhetoric of the poem recited by Robert Frost on that occasion, offering a
satiric argument against Frost's too-easy possessive investment in whiteness.
Baraka's poem is a rhetoric of thwarted expectation, the death of what now
is seen as a false hope. He depicts "the submarine of state" now "submerged
again, to survive / and sustain itself in the holy blue moisture of darkness." At
poem's close, he has seen the Kennedy mythos as a counterfeit raising of our
wished-for democratic vistas:

And this will be the payback for our desires.
For history, like the ringing coin

that will not bend
when we bite it.

---

1. In *Kulchur* no. 12. The poem was inserted between pages 86 and 87.

The poem bears a dateline, just four days after the assassination. Though presented as an address, with all the implications of public delivery attendant upon that title, the poem is dedicated to the president's widow. That said, when Baraka remarks that his efforts to become truly revolutionary had not prevented his sympathies for the aggrieved Jackie—and I think we can take that sympathy as a trope for his feelings for the nation—Baraka's sympathies were not going to find expression in greeting card tones. The dedication reads, "for Jacqueline Bouvier Kennedy, who has had to eat too much shit."

If I might be forgiven for noting that this poem is sandwiched between the pages of Baraka's review of *Reality Sandwiches,* Allen Ginsberg's then latest book, it is also the case that this poem, tipped-in as it is, operates rhetorically within the arguments of that review. The Baraka poem comes between a passage from Ginsberg's "The Green Automobile" and a quotation from "My Alba." But the subject of Jacqueline Kennedy had already been raised in Baraka's review prior to the assassination and the writing of "Exaugural Address." Concluding his commentary on Ginsberg's "sandwiches," and pursuing the class-based arguments that had always been at the heart of his writing, even this long before his move to Marxism, Baraka asks: "Who has not eaten shit? I'm afraid there are too many people who have not. Has Jacqueline Kennedy eaten shit? I hope not, because if she has, then eating shit can no longer be the measure. Dig?" (87). So, reading the late addition of the poem within our reading of the Ginsberg review, we see that Baraka is answering his own rhetorical question with a new piece of rhetoric, just weeks after the first writing, a sign of just how fast things were moving in 1963. If Jacqueline Kennedy has had to eat too much shit, then, at least in this regard, she is just like the rest of us, and that can no longer be the measure. To put it in terms Baraka himself was to use, if America would do this to its own, what would it not do to those it refuses to recognize as its own? Baraka's address is not just an exaugural marking the exit of Kennedy, and Camelot with him (though it is important to recall that the myth of Kennedy's Camelot, like Baraka's poem, came *after* the assassination); it is an exaugural for an American idea.

That idea was at the heart of the contradictions exposed in the personal responses to *Kulchur*'s queries about rights, and its exauguration was impelled by the violence of 1963, culminating in the violence of 1968. The fires predicted in 1963 by Robert Williams and James Baldwin were upon us. Some hoped to extinguish the flames. Some looked on in rapt wonder. Baraka sought to turn up the heat.

3
=

"Other Autobiographies"

Racial and Spiritual Consciousness and the
Prism of Identity in Amiri Baraka's 6 Persons

KATHY LOU SCHULTZ

N *FIGURES IN BLACK,* Henry Louis Gates Jr. describes literary theory as a "prism" one uses "to refract different spectral patterns of language use in a text" (xvii). Taking this a step further by borrowing the principle of "total internal reflection" from physics, this essay shows how Amiri Baraka's use of multiple narrators in *6 Persons* allows him to see multiple subject positions simultaneously, as light inside a prism hitting one of the surfaces at a sufficiently steep angle allows a total internal reflection in which all of the different wavelengths that compose light are reflected simultaneously.[1] Rather than holding himself up to a mirror, Baraka reflects on his life as if through a prism, in order to understand the multiple "wavelengths" of his experiences. Employing as narrators the various subject positions or "you"s that Baraka occupied throughout his life, *6 Persons* charts his struggle to achieve a true consciousness, both racial and spiritual. The narrator of the chapter called "He" articulates the depths of this struggle: "But a black man, where does he go? How does he come to consciousness in this bloodstained nightmare?" (283). He must find the "whole story," or "holiness," of existence through the prisms of "I"—multiplied as a homophonic "eye" or seer/seeker of light. To

---

1. See, for example, Sal Khan, "Total Internal Reflection" [Video], *Khan Academy,* https://www.khanacademy.org/science/physics/geometric-optics/reflection-refraction/v/total-internal-reflection.

find the light that will illuminate consciousness, the prismatic "I" must learn to see though what Baraka calls the "whiteout" obscuring his true identity.

Baraka's multidimensional narrative stratagem is not mere "technique," nor representative of a "shattered" modern identity. Rather, in his search for the "holiness" of his prismatic identity, Baraka demonstrates how, as theorist LaCapra explains, "identity is probably best understood as a problematic constellation or more or less changing configuration of subject positions. And subject positions themselves are not necessarily fixed or complacent (even when they become fixations)" (5). While Baraka's many highly pronounced name, political, and aesthetic changes (or "fixations") may prompt in readers a desire for a linear narrative explaining how he evolved from "LeRoy" to "Amiri," 6 Persons recharts temporal relations suggesting, at times, the simultaneity, backward motion, or palimpsestic overlay of memories. Baraka follows the multiple narrators through the process that will enable him to create not just an "I" or "we," but a "We & All" with which to fight against what he calls the "whiteout," the physical, emotional, intellectual, spiritual, and financial consequences of living under white supremacy. Like the white "correction" fluid that obliterates the former presence of the black typewritten words beneath it, the whiteout annihilates the black man, his story, his consciousness, his identity, and his own understanding of who he is. "The whiteout worked when it did. It crippled you brother. It drove you down crazy paths before you got back home. But the world is there to be used, to be created in, to love and live in, to triumph in. If you wd but collect yrself, yr memory and will" (Baraka, 6 Persons 271). Indeed, in this experimental memoir, Baraka retains belief in the power of creativity—despite the nightmare in which the narrators find themselves—to perform, linguistically and formally, the process of "collecting" a "self."

Collecting a self in this way demonstrates an active development of identity. However, historian John E. Toews, analyzing LaCapra's theories of identity formation, notes that there are both active and passive sides to identity. Toews's description provides one way of understanding the form of 6 Persons, in which Baraka sets multiple subject positions in motion within their sociohistorical contexts; he writes: "There is clearly a passive side to identity—subject positions are historically given—but the process of making an identity out of them is an experimental and ultimately ethical activity" (685). Baraka's ethical positioning, including both political and spiritual dimensions, enables him to find wholeness/holiness as he struggles against the whiteout. Thus, Toews explains, for LaCapra (and, this essay argues, for Baraka as well), identity is not "an essence," but "an active (and endless) process of choice, selection, and integration among the 'subject positions' that are given as discursive possibilities within the various networks of cultural meaning" (685). Succinctly, "we experience subject positions passively as possibilities imposed on us by the various discursive worlds we inhabit—but we actively configure (and reconfigure) those positions in the processes of identity production, and we experience ourselves as actors in these processes" (685). Baraka's prismatic selves actively configure an identity that generates the possibilities of freedom, but also experience discursive *im*possibilities, rendered most obviously through structural racism's shutting off of opportunities for black men, but also through other mechanisms, such as family and class cultural codes that set particular expectations for the black middle class.

Utilizing the active method of identity formation, *6 Persons* engages memory and language to trace the "verbal process ongoing" that makes up multiple forms and perspectives of "I." Baraka's sense of the multiplicity of prismatic identity is evident in the chapter titles of *6 Persons*—"I"; "You"; "He"; "They (Them Theirs Theyres &c)"; "You, Yall, Ya"; "We"; and "We & All"—all of which reflect aspects of Baraka's persona, sometimes called "L," "LJ," "Bro," "AB," or various proper names. Even "Leroi" and "Leroi Jones" make appearances beside the other "you"s. As Aldon Lynn Nielsen remarks, "The six persons of the book's title are the shifting grammatical and historic points of view from which Baraka constructs the ever-shifting narrative of his book and himself" (*Integral* 103). Or, as the narrator in the last chapter of *6 Persons*, "We & All," describes: "Endless series of selves resolve, and at each pt of progress, we are whoever we must be to develop + reunderstand reality" (449). Re-understanding reality finally creates wholeness (holiness) to bring the narrator back home to himself and back home physically to Newark, modeling the epic hero's journey. The book moves from "the streets of Newark to Howard University, the U.S. Air Force, Greenwich Village, Harlem, and back to Newark" (Lacey 230), but Baraka explores the impossibility of a straightforward narrative if one remains true to the forms of life experience: "But if I wanted to make a strict chronicle of I. And not be rent and twisted by the weighted flashes booming in, the cackles and silences. The simple shut doors and screams inside my head. It wd be difficult. To make such a straightforward document of my life" (234). Put another way, *6 Persons* strives to fulfill the dictate of Baraka's infamous essay, "The Revolutionary Theatre," to "show up the insides of these humans, look into black skulls" to reveal the innermost thoughts of the black subjects in his work, to conduct his own "total internal reflection" (Jones, "Revolutionary").

Written in 1973–74, *6 Persons* is in some sense Baraka's "original" memoir, having been completed five years before what we know as his "autobiography": *The Autobiography of LeRoi Jones* by Amiri Baraka. *The Autobiography* was written in 1979 (five years after *6 Persons*) during the time when Baraka was incarcerated for "48 consecutive weekends in a Harlem halfway house for assault and resisting arrest" (Baraka, *Reader* 340). First published in 1984 by Freundlich Books, the *Autobiography* was reissued by Lawrence Hill Books in 1997 with a statement remarking that the first edition by Freundlich suffered from substantial cuts by the publisher. "This new Lawrence Hill Books Edition," a note states, "has reinstated all the excised material under the careful direction of the author. What you will read here is in effect the first complete edition of *The Autobiography of LeRoi Jones*" (ix). This was the only autobiography of Baraka's in print because the manuscript of *6 Persons*, Nielsen explains, sat "unpublished, in a cardboard box in the basement of Howard University's Founder's Library until the year 2000" (*Integral* 100). Nielsen explains that *6 Persons* was written in response to Putnam editor-in-chief William Targ's solicitation (following the public acclaim of Baraka's play *Dutchman*) for a "popular novel" with "strong plotting" that would be a "successor to *The Godfather*" (99–100). What Baraka produced instead—a manuscript never published by Putnam—is the multivoiced, decidedly not "strongly plotted" experimental memoir *6 Persons*. While the first chapter of *6 Persons* ("I") originally appeared in *Selected Plays and Prose of Amiri Baraka/LeRoi Jones* published by Morrow in 1979, the text was not published in its entirety until the release of *The Fiction of LeRoi Jones/Amiri Baraka* by Lawrence Hill Books of Chicago in 2000.

In "A Longish Poem About a Dude: An Introduction to *6 Persons*," Henry C. Lacey, who edited the complete manuscript for publication, recounts the difficulties the long-forgotten manuscript presented for eventual publication: "The long-ignored manuscript of *6 Persons* presented a number of problems. It consisted of 229 pages of primitive photocopy with frequently indistinguishable punctuation; missing words; occasionally indecipherable handwritten additions, corrections, and abbreviations; and orthographic inconsistencies. Moreover, there was, on occasion, evidence of missing text" (229). In exchanges with Baraka, Lacey achieved "agreement on the standardization of those aforementioned problematic areas as well as the general revising and critiquing of the overall manuscript" (229), resulting in the publication of *6 Persons*. Along with *6 Persons*, the 2000 fiction collection includes *The System of Dante's Hell* (1965), *Tales* (1967), and four previously uncollected short stories: "Suppose Sorrow Was a Time Machine" (1958), "Round Trip" (1959), "the man who sold pictures of god" (1960), and "God and Machine" (1973). The works are arranged chronologically, making *6 Persons* the last text in the book. Rather than fulfilling a mainstream audience's desire for an ethnic novel, revealing "certain racial authenticity or flavor" (Nielsen, *Integral* 100) that Targ sought, 6 Persons explores states of consciousness using a variety of language registers to more closely chart the movement of the mind and qualities of perception.

Baraka's experiments with narrative, temporal relations, and points of view, including the multiple narrators that are all parts of "I"—"Yes, it was me. All these parts to the same I" (240)—allow some of the personas to be present at the same time. This, in turn, allows for a prismatic representation of multiple selves that, taken together, can give us a sense of the whole self. This simultaneity is signaled in the first chapter when we find out that some of the other persons who will be introduced later in the book are more in touch with reality (not blinded by the whiteout), and thus have a stronger, more cohesive identity: "Yet the others (I will talk about those eyes as I's as others, as theys, after . . .) many times have a thing, a bigger more positive (active in touch with reality) self. An I" (240). Being in touch with reality requires seeing through the haze of the whiteout and decolonizing the mind.

Presenting the narrative personas simultaneously allows them to collide and sometimes interact with one another. For example, the third chapter, "He," begins by noting: "The dude talking wasn't the dude I was talking about, but then who'm I?" and that "He and Me, me and I, first came in touch with each other in New York state just before winter," referring to the period of time in which Jones joined the Air Force (273). The prismatic view allows "Me" to be present at the same time as "He" who is arriving for basic training after having left (been kicked out of) college. As "I" (me) narrates this section, talking about the "dude" (who is also "He"), we can conclude that these two personas—"I" and "He"—are part of the same larger self that the narrative is investigating. Furthermore, these questions of selfhood remain in play because "I" still doubts his own identity at this early point in the memoir: "Who'm I?"

Exploring his own origin story, Baraka notes at the beginning of 6 Persons, "Who can speak of their birth? Years later someone can testify as to its alleged meaning, heaping on years of subsequent rhythms, edging it toward whatever ideal has come to please them" (233). What we retain of our births is the stories that are passed on to us; furthermore, the hopes and expectations that precede our entrances into the world begin our life stories before we possess language capabilities ourselves. Baraka stresses that each young black man's "be-ing" has spiritual significance: "We are all projections of some one, some great being, some be-ing, a verbal process ongoing even today the window presses its sunny-rainy presence, young bloods laugh fight hug day to them. On-going. Be-ing. So I, is a process, a be-ing" (233). Because "I" is a "process," Baraka's experimental memoir follows the patterns of the multiple, prismatic projections of light—of holiness—rather than outlining predetermined conclusions. Discussing his earlier autobiographical writings, along with those of his first wife, Hettie Jones, and their daughter, Lisa Jones, Deborah Thompson identifies "a larger issue in these autobiographical writings: the belief that identity is not a matter of 'being,' but of 'becoming.' Identity is always in process. . . . From the 1950s to the 1980s, LeRoi and Hettie continually speak of their selfhoods in the language of 'becoming'" (85), which is evident in both of Baraka's "autobiographies." However, this is enacted formally in *6 Persons* in ways that it is not in the more conventional narrative of *The Autobiography of LeRoi Jones*.

In *6 Persons*, the narrators must inhabit the process of becoming in order to gain consciousness of the self and its relationship to something larger than the individual, here called "some great being." This concept is similar to what is called the "World Spirit" in "The Revolutionary Theatre." First published in 1965, the essay explains: "This should be a theatre of World Spirit. Where the spirit can be shown to be the most competent force in the world. Force. Spirit. Feeling" (Jones, "Revolutionary"). The essay insists that "people must be taught to trust true scientists (knowers, diggers, oddballs) and that the holiness of life is the constant possibility of widening the consciousness" ("Revolutionary"). The "true scientists" ("knowers, diggers, oddballs") are jazz musicians, writers, and artists who can tap into the spirit or holiness through acts of creation. Thus, the imagination is tied directly to the process of developing racial and spiritual consciousness; indeed, imagination is what in "The Revolutionary Theatre" Baraka calls a "practical vector from the soul."

The focus on the spirit is presented in *6 Persons* through the metaphor of light. Observing the writing process, "he" (the "dude" in chapter 3) summons the light that brings himself into being: "The dude telling the story, he crossed his legs, long limber, unfolded out the chair, and stood. He raised his hand, and spun slowly around . . . and the room, though dark and empty, seemed to light up at least there at the center where he was" (273), thus bringing us back to the metaphor of the prism. His physical description is rendered in poetic, rhythmic fashion, employing slant rhyme, assonance, and alliteration: "It was the brother, the brother, the dude in green glove leather, and high brown suede boots. He had on one big ring, and a big bush" (273). The ring channels the light that will allow the "dude" to come to voice: "The slender strain of light beat upon the ring, and he whirled in and out of the beam, until his terrible voice seemed to scream" (273). The voice produces a "bad song" (which here could mean good) "talking to the whole thing that listens" (the World Spirit), which allows him to tell his tale, "a longish poem, about a dude," (273), which is as apt a description of the genre of this book as any you will find.

In *6 Persons*, Baraka actively creates genre slippage, which contributed not only to the difficulty of getting the work published, but also to the challenge of keeping it in print and eliciting scholarly attention. What genre is *6 Persons*? In addition to a "longish poem about a dude," some possible labels include *Bildungsroman*, novel, and autobiography, all of which must be considered provisional. Of the few critics who have published on this work, James Liner calls *6 Persons* a "novelistic experiment in collectivity" (249). While Nielsen primarily frames the book as a novel in his essay "Six Plus One Persons: 'a longish poem about a dude,'" he also refers to it as a poem/novel, life narrative, and fictive memoir, revealing that the book resists categorization. Greg Tate asserts: "The degree to which *Dante's Hell, Tales* and *6 Persons* read as a warped strain of autobiographical literature is the degree to which they yield the most pleasure" (x). However, Baraka once stated that "while his work is admittedly autobiographical," the books included in the 2000 fiction collection "are not an extended memoir" (Reid). Yet, reading across Baraka's work—poems, essays, plays, "fiction," and what is called *The Autobiography of LeRoi Jones* by Amiri Baraka—one does find the same events retold and reinterpreted, as well as repetition of the same images, even in the same language.

I am calling *6 Persons* Baraka's "other autobiography" in large degree because several of the same events are recalled in both *6 Persons* and *The Autobiography*, though interpreted differently. For example, in the *Autobiography*, Baraka recounts discovering a bookstore in Chicago called the Green Door while he was on leave from the Air Force where he served from 1954–57 (an experience he labels the "Error Farce"). The books the young LeRoi Jones selects on that first visit to the Green Door are *Portrait of the Artist as a Young Man* by James Joyce and *Portrait of the Artist as a Young Dog* by Dylan Thomas, and he returns in a couple weeks to purchase Joyce's *Ulysses*. Of his encounter with Irish and Welsh modernism, Baraka writes: "All kinds of new connections yammered in my head. My heart beat faster my skin tingled. I could understand now a little better what was happening. I needed to learn. I wanted to study. But I wanted to learn and study stuff I wanted to learn and study. Serious, uncommon weird stuff! At that moment my life was changed" (*Reader* 344). The "serious, uncommon weird stuff" of modernism that allows a young man then calling himself LeRoi Jones to make "all kinds of new connections" also influences him to explore alternate methods of storytelling.

In contrast, in the earlier *6 Persons*, the narrator's encounter with European and Euro-American modernist authors in a bookstore—called the Red Door—is understood as part of the damning experience of the whiteout. Ezra

Pound, in particular, is a target of criticism as the narrator of "They (Them Theirs Theyres &c)" works to rediscover what all the reading he undertook while in the Air Force means to his development of a real consciousness. His critique of Pound is also a self-critique: "The fact that Pound was a fascist made him the true object of niggers' worship. The fact that he sd outright he hated them made him the object of fond regard" (322). Here, digging "esoteric" modernism is tainted by the self-hate he finds inherent in "worshipping" an author noted for his own hatred of black people. Yet, the reinterpretation of his relationship to modernism that is offered in the later *Autobiography* echoes back to Baraka's 1963 introduction to *The Moderns*. Here, he notes in an observation on the "New American Poetry" (a movement in which Jones played a central role) that "the concerns that made the poetry seem so new were merely that the writers who were identified with this recent poetic renaissance were continuing the tradition of twentieth-century modernism that had been initiated in the early part of this century" (Introduction, *The Moderns* x). Finding a continuum between early twentieth-century modernism and the "New American Poetry," he anticipates later scholarship in the "new" modernist studies that sees American modernism, particularly African American modernism, developing in an arc from the New Negro Renaissance to the experimental poetry of Langston Hughes at mid-century.

This new modernism also expresses itself through varieties of colloquial speech, what Mikhail M. Bakhtin defines as "social heteroglossia," "a blending of world views through language that creates complex unity" (Wills). Throughout *6 Persons,* Baraka displays acute attention to spoken language, what might be called black vernacular(s), as well as other language registers. In "From the Prehistory of Novelistic Discourse," Bakhtin writes: "The novel senses itself on the border between the completed, dominant literary language and the extraliterary languages that know heteroglossia" (67). If we update Bakhtin's argument to see how it may apply to twentieth-century African American texts, it is clear that rather than fighting for what Bakhtin calls the "renovation of an antiquated literary language," Baraka fights for the oral multiplicities of African American speech that exist "outside the centralizing and unifying influence of the artistic and ideological norm established by the dominant literary language" (Bakhtin 67) as various dialects collide, moving in and out, showing the daily experience of listening, be-ing in language.

An example is worth quoting at length to illustrate Baraka's acute attention to sound:

> And then to funky Rutgers, checkin' out Princeton dropouts (who now say you're the cia—). German professor down on Rector street sd, "You vant to

learn cherman, eh?" And he cd dig it, you know. "You vant to learn cherman, eh?" Ol' bad-head dude. He probly was, in the movies, like a German
professor, or mad doctor. Doktor Mengele, perhaps. Perhaps. Mishaps. No
haps, bro. Remember, you used to say that? "What's happening captain?"
"No haps, my man. Ain't nothin' shakin' but the bacon, and that don't matter cause that's in the platter." "Duh vord fur vater iss vasser." (*6 Persons* 254)

In this selection, the reader "is confronted with several heterogeneous stylistic unities, often located on different linguistic levels and subject to different stylistic controls" that are "multiform in style and variform in speech and
voice" (Bakhtin 261). For example, Baraka transcribes the sounds of the German teacher's speaking voice, "You vant to learn cherman, eh?," contrasting
his pronunciation of the English word "water" as "vater" with the German,
pronounced "vasser." Baraka is then able to switch from the German-inflected
English to what was hip black vernacular to give readers the texture of the
sound of a remembered conversation. The focus on sound is primary, over-
riding conventional spelling.

Baraka's experiments with colloquial speech enable him to construct an
alternate space outside of the ideological norms of whiteness. His encounters
with whiteness at college ("Colored School," i.e., Howard University) are also
encounters with assimilation and death. "Cracker are you alive anywhere, no.
You ain' alive. Yr dust ain' alive, it cnt fertilize a nut" (245). The suffocation and
sterility of this whiteness is reflected in the university's curriculum:

> And they kept Frazier under wraps. You heard of him in wraps. And Locke
> in wraps, tho he rapped a sweeter line for yella niggers. Chancellor Wms,
> they kept him under wraps. And absolute insanity wd strut across the land-
> scape with a Harvard bookbag, teaching classics, and being cultural attaché
> to the Vatican. We said he's a heavy dude, meaning this Snowden, but that
> name should have been a giveaway, snowed-in, froze to death by whiteness.
> (263)

E. Franklin Frazier's *Black Bourgeoisie* and Alain Locke's *New Negro* are kept
"under wraps," while Sterling Brown, an important mentor for Baraka, is
forced by "the school bourgeois dictatorship" to teach his jazz course in the
dormitory; "it was not really music after all" (262). The historical value of jazz,
an aesthetic touchstone for Baraka (particularly the hard bop of Coltrane) is
obscured by the whiteout at the assimilationist "Colored School."

Moving beyond the whiteout requires that one first understand how the
institution of white supremacy is constructed and maintained. "Trying to

explain how all this goes down, how the whiteout is made, how it seems like something else how its form is functional to freak us" (285), the narrator begs his black brothers and sisters to see "through the broken and jagged window of eyes" (284). The homophone "I"/"eye" is an important device used throughout the memoir. In the first chapter, the narrator recalls that he was a "bigeyed boy" teased for being "Popeye," which might have meant he was "omnivisioned spectacularly endowed in the seein' dept., or just funny looking" (240). "Hey I's! This man can definitely SEE!" the other boys signify, causing the narrator to conclude ironically that "I was, on a very low level, a seer," giving an early indication that the narrator will eventually see through the whiteout and construct a space outside of it (240). Yet, despite his ability to "see," "the world came down in fragments and splinters. In flashes and rhythmic thuds, rather than whole and initialed, considered like history, real and usable" (240). Therefore, in order to understand the whole story (and thus himself), the narrator must re-see these fractured memories together. Fundamentally, "we need a whole story to see whole, to be really and truly holy. Meaning in tune with every thing. All the reality, its multiple addresses, and parallel appearances" (240) reflected through the prism.

Fundamentally, he must first confront the narrators tainted by the false consciousness of Negro petit bourgeois striving, of a black middle class who sought to assimilate their children through education into the proper professions. At "Colored School," he is "there to be drawn warmly into the middle class" (261). As the narrator of "He" notes, the only variable in the "fixed and static" system in which L finds himself is the choice of occupation. "Be a postman, doctor, boxer (not really), teacher, cowboy, somethin,' the only variable, but all the rest was answered by what you saw . . . but did not understand" (284). This is how he is expected to fulfill his function in the whiteout, resulting in the obliteration of true consciousness and death of the self. Note that Baraka's criticism of the black bourgeoise is always and first a criticism of himself, even as he tries to find a path beyond it. "And the petty bourgeois nigger in you, LJ, clung to the edge and cried and stormed and fabricated another life outside the ritual of worship for master" (261). Trying to fashion this other life, he plans to move to New York after having been kicked out of another institution—the Air Force—that could ensure his place within the black middle class.

In chapter 6, "They (Them Theirs Theyres &c)," young L returns to Newark, having been spat out of the two endeavors that could enable access to the "middle class Negro fantasy" (305): college and the military. The latter is of great concern to his family as well as L himself:

Hadn't nobody in that family *never* been kicked out of the army before. Who cd visualize that? Not them. Not him. Not you, jim, if you'd been in Colored School, planning for success—vaguely but definitely. Niggers been slung around, drug around, tricked, sold into slavery, killed and cursed. But hadn't NEVER nobody we know been kicked outta no service before. (303)

The narrator continues: "And to top it off what if they knew that he had did it (L had) to hisself, cause, like, he just wanted to split? . . . What ain't he gonna get kicked out of cd've been the rim of question circling his parents' minds" (304). At this point, "L" decides to move to Greenwich Village and become an artist.

As he forms his ideas about moving to New York and imagines the person he might become there, the plan is too ludicrous to share with his family: "'Yeah. I'll go back to school in New York.' He was gonna say, 'I want to be a writer,' except he thought it was too corny to come in somebody who knew you's house and say something like that" (302) and "his mother wanted something heroic to come out of his mouth, not no vague dizzy garbage about no writin'" (303). Yet, New York represents the possibility of throwing off the static, putting him back in motion and continuing the process of becoming: "And suddenly L was in The Big Apple, an anonymous exotic wanderin' in and out of purposively strange places. A huge I again, like a rolling me, set loose to tell the story of the world any kind of way" (304). New York itself, it seems, will draw together the edges of what he must become, though he has little practical knowledge of what that might actually entail. "But now they sat in the apartment trying to decide to be painters or writers . . . How do they be an artist? (painter or writer?) Just shadup and be it" (306). He writes on yellow pads of paper with his feet in the oven to keep them warm in a "cold water flat on the east side, truly run down, gipsies and shit running around with the door open in the middle of winter" (304), considering the possibilities of freedom in his new surroundings: "Cut loose, cast adrift, let out the slam to grow again. The air swept him up. The air. Coffeeful air. The air smelled like the hundreds of coffee shops. And they prepared all this for him? No, he was anonymous again, but this time he liked it more" (304). Young L emerges in an American Western, "gunfighter style, he roamed in another place, a weird place, a different place. Yeh, it was fantasy, now that they sat around him on all sides" (305). Yet the buoyancy of this fantasy is at the same time pierced through by "Europa the bull. The white bull, the father of racism and capitalism, Amen" (307). In this place he calls "Oz," where, and as whom, has he arrived?

"Leaving implies arriving somewhere else. L crossed the water into the east side, of stinking hallways, and, unlike any place he'd been, whites" (304). While he certainly has had encounters with white people throughout his life, he now shares intimate interior spaces with whites in a way entirely new to him. He contemplates the question, "How did white folks get in there?," declaring, "If they cd trace the way the other folks got to where zen white boys cd wash their sox in they crib!" (308). In addition, "they got hooked up w/ these mousie Jewish babes & then one day all they knew was lil' Jewish babes, or Italian babes—very few Americans" (327), bringing to mind, of course, Hettie Cohen and Diane di Prima, but also raising a question of how, in spite of the continual othering of Jews in the text, these Jewish and Italian women remain somehow, in his mind, outside of the churning machine of Americanness. Yet, the interracial bohemian nexus is essential to the artistic identity that Jones claims. For a "*Bohemian* at the time meant a lot to these niggers. It meant deep and away from the dead grey factory hell of their youth. Away from the quiet agony, the wine bandit screaming, the motionless consciousness from the street that is now named after some bad nigger, hopefully" (328). These themes—the necessity, then failure of the Greenwich Village integrated artistic community—are central to other works by Baraka. As James Smethurst argues, "It is interracialism as a defining characteristic of downtown bohemia that Baraka engages negatively in his play *Dutchman*. Without this fundamental bohemian interracialism, it is not possible for bohemia to fail black artists in Baraka's play" (*Black Arts* 44). Interracial bohemia not only fails the young writer, whites also control and proscribe the young black artist's range of opportunities.

Thus, while whites now occupy blacks' interior domestic spaces in a way heretofore unimaginable (washing their dirty socks at your house!), whites also inhabit black culture to the extent of being able to own and control it. For example, through an early job sorting records, "they met all the whites that controlled critical thought about black music" (311). This is central to Baraka's development as a writer, for these same people are the gatekeepers determining L's possible "career" as a music critic. Recounting this experience, the text breaks into verse.

In the basement w/ the records
Studying the history of niggers + niggers + white folks +
America
Imitating rich conservative liberal white boys
Writing a short story on yellow legal pad
A "critic" becoming (311)

Of the white man who allows L to begin writing music reviews, he states, "The job is to harness the nigger energy. From slave trade to multinational corp, the job's intent is similar" because "this order has to . . . catch new energy and harness it up to feed itself" (313). Black music is exploited as fuel to keep the white capitalist system running. Thus, the young black artist, new to New York, had "an identity, a 'uniqueness' it was necessary to destroy so as better to control" (308). The birth of this new person, LeRoi Jones the writer, is still threated by death and destruction, from inside and out.

Photographs of the young Jones during his time in Greenwich Village show him sometimes smiling broadly or sweetly: Jones holding his baby daughter Kellie (1959); Jones and Frank O'Hara leaning into one another, likely following a reading at the Living Theatre (1959); Jones and Diane di Prima at the Cedar Tavern (1960). Yet, "All he's change, cross the ancient river, and become they," Baraka writes, "a warm abstract, all creation dumps its garbage on. Two theys conflict, this time in the streets of NYC, The Big Apple" (307). The "two theys" refracted through Baraka's prism exist at the same time in memory and in the text as the memoir charts our protagonists' move from the Village to Harlem after the murder of Malcolm X. This period shows the Black Arts impetus to use art to fight against the "enemies" while at the same time revealing the challenges of properly identifying who they might be. "Yet the struggle inside us, but a reflection of the world's struggle. Let us locate ourselves properly in that world & fight against the enemies. & who are these?" (449). There is no resting point; rather, there are "points of progress" along the way, and reality must be constantly reevaluated and re-understood using the multiple perspectives of the prism, revealing how such "looking back" may actually appear in the mind.

After his move to Harlem, the narrator of "You, Yall, Ya" repeatedly interrogates his (bro's) motivations and actions. "You'd arrived bro. . . . But to do what? Whattya mean? To do what? Askin'!" (381). As Nielsen notes, "Baraka doesn't let himself off this hook, and he wonders aloud about the direction of poetics in these times" of black cultural and political nationalism (*Six Plus 13*). Furthermore, as Tate explains, "the interior battles described in [Baraka's] fictional prose are acutely resonant of the times they were written in, where every value white America held as sacrosanct was being challenged and overturned, if not pillaged and burned" (Tate xi). Eventually, "You, Yall, Ya" learn from Malcolm X that "it was all corrupt & finally, dig it, that it wasn't even about color" (380). Thus, we see that "the years during which Baraka composed *Six Persons* bridge the period of his movement from Cultural Nationalism to Marxism" (Nielsen, *Six Plus* 3) as the ravages of white supremacy are analyzed within the larger rubric of capitalist imperialism.

Finally the narrator at the end of 6 *Persons* states, "Our agony + alienation can be pointed at & its source destroyed," a remarkable clarity that the narrators have struggled for (462). In fact, the book concludes with "We & All" at a family gathering, including seven children, reading *Afrikan Red Family* together (462).

> Our roads to get to here, where we are Black + Green + Red. Where we are revolutionary nationalists struggling to see Afrika liberated. PanAfrikanists fighting for an end to world oppression. Socialists pushing for a new beginning for all people. It is a long warm slow embrace today. Amidst the children's noise. They are looking for the ultimate weapon. Organization. The only one the people have. Victory to all peoples, we are singing to each other, just before lunch. Victory to all peoples. (462)

The multiple identities revealed through Baraka's prismatic form lend their knowledge to create wholeness, revealing holiness through a vision of socialist, "PanAfrikanist" freedom. Using political organization as the "ultimate weapon," victory for "We & All" can be foreseen at last.

4

=

Baraka, Cullen, Trethewey

Incidents

TYRONE WILLIAMS

AMIRI BARAKA'S "Incident" appears in the third and last section, "Black
Art: 1965–1966," of his first collected book of poems, *Black Magic:
Poetry 1961–1967.* As critic Lynn Nwuneli reminds us, this poem,
like all of Baraka's writing, can only be understood within the manifold of its
various contexts, including its location within the book.[1] That is, the poems
that precede it ("Black Art") and that follow it ("For a lady i know") literally
and figuratively frame "Incident." The former's infamous clarion call for a new
aesthetic, the latter's no less controversial call for a different kind of personal,
perhaps post-marriage, relationship, situate "Incident" as an example of what
the new, however understood (new aesthetics, new culture, new politics, new
sociality, etc.), must overcome. Because *Black Magic* delineates the concerns of
a pre-Marxist Baraka, the "new," for the most part, demands less an *ex nihilo*
originality than a return to, or recovery of, what slavery and racism, on the
one hand, and Christianity and capitalism, on the other, have driven from collective consciousness into individual subconsciousnesses.[2] Thus "Black Art"

---

1. Lynn Nwuneli, "Variety of Styles and Complexity of Vision in Baraka's *Black Magic
Poetry.*"

2. In *Introduction to Black Studies,* Maulana Karenga makes it clear that black art, like
black economics, politics, and culture, must transform black consciousness ("Black people must
rebuild themselves by rebuilding their culture" [209]). But while black is always Pan-African
for Karenga, Pan-Africanism is apparently insufficient for Larry Neal. Departing from the neo-

(*Black Magic* 116–117) and "For a lady i know" (119) offer, respectively, aesthetic and affective solutions to the problem of insulated individuation depicted in "Incident" (118).

Leaping over some of those other important contexts—the significance of the fact that 1965 is the year of the assassination of Malcolm X, and LeRoi Jones's decision to divorce his first wife, Hettie Jones, and move out of the East Village to Harlem, where he founds the Black Arts Repertory Theater (BART), often cited as the official (if not actual) beginning of the Black Arts Movement—we might also note that Baraka's "Incident" alludes to, is contextualized by, Countee Cullen's earlier, more famous, "Incident," first published in 1925 (15).[3] At the same time, Baraka's "Incident" precedes, and perhaps foreshadows, Natasha Trethewey's poem of the same title (Trethewey 41).[4] However, while Cullen's and Trethewey's "incidents" concern menacing acts of, respectively, verbal and pyromaniacal racist threats, Baraka's poem concerns physical, lethal intraracial violence.[5] At the same time, Baraka's deployment of the first-person plural pronoun throughout "Incident" resonates with Natasha Trethewey's use of the same pronoun in her poem. For both poets, "we" only signifies unconnected individuals grouped together by circumstance: a neighborhood (Baraka) or blood (Trethewey).[6] Since forty years lie between Baraka's and Trethewey's criticism of what we may understand as the false col-

---

Marxism of Etheridge Knight (e.g., "And the Black artist, in creating his own aesthetic, must be accountable for it only to the Black People. Further, he must hasten his own dissolution as an individual (in the Western sense)—painful, though, the process may be, having been breast-fed the poison of 'individual experience'" [Neal "Black Arts Movement," 64]), Neal offers this corrective: "First, we assume that there is already in existence the basis for such an aesthetic. Essentially, it consists of an African-American cultural tradition. But this aesthetic is finally, by implication, broader than that tradition. It encompasses most of the usable elements of Third World culture" (64).

3. The Jones/Baraka–Cullen connection is reinforced by the fact that the former's "For a lady i know" is a rewriting and, perhaps, rebuttal of Cullen's sardonic "For A Lady I Know." In truth, Cullen's four-line attack on the black bourgeoisie ("She even thinks that up in heaven / Her class lies late and snores // While poor black cherubs rise at seven // To do celestial chores") anticipates much of Baraka's own polemics.

4. While Cullen's poem is an aphoristic lyric that dramatizes a young black boy's presumably first encounter with racism—he's called a nigger by a white man—Trethewey's "Incident" recounts a family story about a KKK cross-burning outside their house.

5. Although the race of each "he" in "Incident" is never identified, the nonreactions of the "we" that narrate the poem suggest black-on-black crime. Nevertheless, insofar as the affectless narration is in large part the focus of my analysis, one can argue that Baraka is making an even stronger argument: Even in the face of white-on-black or black-on-white crime, the community's nonchalant attitude remains its indictment.

6. Baraka's and Trethewey's poems refer to incidents that occurred in the early 1960s, though Trethewey's "Incident" is, like Cullen's, a poem more about memory, personal (Cullen) and family (Trethewey), than the actual event.

lective subconsciousness of a decadent "we," or a collection of unconnected, politically and culturally retrograde consciousnesses, one might wonder if the singular "I" of Cullen's poem represents the kind of personal trauma that, writ large, aborted the possibility of an unalienated "we," a "we" that would no longer have required qualifying scare quotes—in short, a "we" that might have embodied a "true" collective consciousness fully recovered from the collective trauma of the Atlantic slave trade. On the other hand, Cullen's "I" may merely suggest that an individual black consciousness grapples with the far-reaching implications of racism by simply never forgetting, that the long night of this wrestling with historical trauma only "ends" in the ripple effects of callous intraracial in-fighting and opportunistic indifference.[7] Thus, we might read Cullen's and Trethewey's depictions of psychological trauma at, respectively, the individual and collective levels as classic, if such a word can be used in this context, examples of Afro-American pessimism.

If Baraka's and Trethewey's poems are connected by the first-person plural pronoun, Cullen's and Trethewey's poems are connected by geography; each "incident" takes place in the South. Unlike the setting of Trethewey's poem in her home state of Mississippi,[8] part of the so-called Deep South, Baltimore, the site of Cullen's poem, is one of those border towns, situated culturally, if not geographically, "between" the North and the South.[9] But if Cullen's and Trethewey's poems together erase the distinction between the South and the Deep South, between Maryland and Mississippi, between verbal assault ("he poked out / His tongue, and called me, "Nigger"; lines 7–8) and nonverbal assault ("When they were done, the men left quietly"; line 14), Baraka's poem, probably set in Harlem or Newark, conflates not only North and South as sites

7. It is important to remember that Cullen was born in the Caribbean and that "Incident" is dedicated to the Caribbean-born Eric D. Walrond, his roommate and, according to Cullen, lover. Along with Baraka's notorious homophobia, the African American / African Caribbean divide, emblematized in the Caribbean activist Marcus Garvey and the thoroughly American (at least in the 1920s) W. E. B. Du Bois, also explains why a concept like a collective unconscious is difficult to apply, coherently and consistently, to the members of the African diaspora.

8. Here is Trethewey on the contexts that informed "Incident": "The incident itself—the cross-burning—happened the week after the church across the street from my grandmother's house in Mississippi had been holding a voter registration drive to get disenfranchised African Americans registered to vote. And my mother and father and I were all living together in the same house at the time. The church didn't have its own driveway, so my grandmother used to let the church park their church bus in her driveway. So that's where they [KKK members] burned the cross, and we never knew then if the cross burning was about the voter registration drive or if it was about us, the interracial family in the house" (Sebree).

9. As Patrick Ottenhoff demonstrates in his brief overview of the "southernness" of Washington, DC, the border between the North and South depends on psychological and cultural perspectives as much as it does the geographical debates. See his "Where Does the South Begin?"

where black people live under the threat of assault from ordinary white boys ("And he was no whit bigger"; Cullen 6) and extraordinary men ("white as angels in their gowns"; Trethewey 10) but also implies that white male interracial violence dovetails with black male intraracial violence precisely at the nexus of gender.[10] Although Baraka can only think of this "problem" in heteronormative terms, affirmed by, for example, "Black Art" and "For a lady I know," he appears to recognize, by the apposition of "he" and "we" throughout "Incident," the problem of what it means to be a "man" at the beginning of widespread political, social, and cultural unrest and upheaval across the United States and, more generally, the so-called Third World. As we know all too well, Baraka's heterosexism will contaminate his writing throughout his career even as it remains marked by his unceasing interrogation of masculinity.[11] For a poet like Baraka, one must, or perhaps one prefers to, confront this problem first through the modality of language and, more narrowly, through the function of the proper name.[12]

Thus, it is important to recall that the mid-'60s "Incident" was written by LeRoi Jones, not Amiri Baraka. As the above reference to some of the events of 1965 suggests, *Black Magic* in general, and the section (and poem) "Black Art" in particular, mark a crucial transitional phase in Baraka's ethical, political, cultural, and aesthetic values and decisions. However mythical the narrative, the story recounted in interviews, articles, and books and thus sealed into historical memory is that Baraka, having been upbraided by leftist writers and artists during his 1960 trip to Cuba with members of the Harlem Writers Club, returns to the United States determined to abandon his East Village bohemian lifestyle and Beat aesthetics. These drastic changes include divorcing his white and worse, Jewish, wife and abandoning his mixed-race daughters.[13] In 1967 the poet was still LeRoi Jones; he would not adopt Imamu Amiri Baraka until

---

10. All three poems depict males as the instigators of verbal, nonverbal, and physical violence.

11. See Marlon B. Ross's brilliant analysis of Baraka's use of camp and the dozens to fend off challenges to his own conception of black manhood in "Camping the Dirty Dozens: The Queer Resources of Black Nationalist Invective."

12. The history of renaming oneself in African American history is too long land complex to be summarized here. Suffice it to say that the influence of Maulana (ne Ron) Karenga, his US organization and his adaptation of the Swahili concept of *kawaida* had a profound influence on Baraka during and "after" his cultural nationalist period.

13. As other critics have before, David L. Smith argues that Baraka's bohemian (that is, Beat) aesthetic marks all his writing from black nationalism to his Third World Leninist-Maoist phases. Smith also argues that Baraka's notorious antisemitism, while a motif threading throughout his writings, was also, in *Black Magic*, a calculated ploy to curry favor, so to speak, with the hostility and resentment toward Jewish storeowners in black communities. On the relative stability of *white* vis-à-vis an array of changing names for African Americans, see

1968, a year after the publication of *Black Magic*. Thus, *Black Magic* is a record of LeRoi Jones's struggles to overcome his middle-class background and orientation, his isolation from the experiences of "common" black people, and his self-confessed apolitical aestheticism. In these poems, he is sometimes LeRoi Jones and sometimes the man he will later name Amiri Baraka. In short, he is sometimes one kind of man and sometimes another kind of man. Hence, despite the exhortations, bombast, and calculated anti-aesthetic "ugliness" of specific poems, ambivalence characterizes *Black Magic* as a whole. And nowhere is this more apparent than in "Incident."

"Incident" is written as though it were the sketch for a short story that Edgar Allan Poe would have endorsed: short, dense, and psychologically disturbing. At the same time, it reads like a treatment for a film noir script: Ambivalence is its central stance, an *homme fatale* its lead character. Moreover, the description of the killing reads, in part, like a police blotter. Baraka achieves all these effects by drawing from his memories of radio dramas and films from the '40s, '50s, and early '60s, reducing his characters to pronouns (*he, him, we*), and deploying repetition and redundancies of key words and phrases. The flattening of language, characterization, and description results in a mesmerizing monotone.

Composed of five free verse tercets and three single lines (two single lines separate the first three tercet stanzas from the next two tercet stanzas and a final single line), the poem opens with five of its nine iterations of "he" and four of its five iterations of "shot" in the first stanza alone. Likewise, the phrase "came back" appears twice in the opening stanza and once thereafter, in stanza four, the same stanza that contains the last two iterations of "he" and the last iteration of "shot." The effect is twofold: We readers know *what* has happened, but we don't know, and as it happens, never find out, *why* it happened. The last clause of the poem affirms "our" ignorance: "We know nothing." Between that closing laconic admission and the equally terse opening—"He came back"— the poem crawls forward, backs up over itself, adding details, some of which ("the speeding bullet tore his face / and blood sprayed fine over the killer and the grey light"; 5–6) seem merely gratuitous. Other details function like camera shots from different angles. In the first stanza, "he fell, stumbling, past the / shadow wood, down, shot, dying, dead, to full halt" (2–3) (I will return to that last clause). The very next stanza begins, "At the bottom, bleeding, shot dead" (4). Details zoom in—the killer "shot only once into his victim's / stare, and left him quickly when the blood ran out" (13–14). Speculations zoom out—"We know // the killer was skillful, quick, and silent, and that the victim/ probably knew him" (13–15).[14] But all the other cinematic, journalistic, and law enforcement tenets—who, where, when, why—are either absent or useless. Who was involved? All we are told is that one "he" was the "killer" (second and fourth stanzas) and the other "he" was the "victim" (stanzas three and four). When did this happen? The only "timeline" is the past tense of a verb, "He came back," repeated twice in the first line and a half. Whence our killer? All we know is that "he came back, from somewhere."

In the first stanza, we have all the essential details of this incident. Some "he" becomes a murder victim when he is "shot" and dies "to full halt." The discourse of this clause that closes the first stanza derives from linguistics; more specifically, it is the kind of language an early learning, or non-native, speaker of English might use.[15] Another, perhaps more probable, possibility is that "full halt" derives from the discourse of telegrams, as though the details of this murder are being wired to a newspaper by a cigar-chomping beat reporter. Since, however, this clause is spoken by "we," the collective narrator of this poem, it implies a distance between "us" and the killer and victim. "We" remain aloof (no pathos regarding the killing appears in the poem), objective professionals, like a journalist, a police detective (and photographer), or a community so used to violence that another shrug of the shoulder is all "we" can manage.

However, as the brutal harshness of that last clause—"we know nothing"—indicates, Jones cannot quite maintain the poker-face demeanor of the professional or a community inured to murder. LeRoi Jones, poet and judge, makes an appearance at the end of "Incident." "Our" know-nothing immunity to outrage, fear, disgust, and so on is part and parcel of our willingness to accept the dehumanization of men (stripped of their proper names, reduced to pronouns, etc.), good and bad, victims and killers. Jones includes himself in this condemnation because his "Incident" shares one feature with Cullen's "Incident": an objective description of a horrific event. Whereas Cullen's objectivity is achieved by the chronological distance between his narrator's youthfulness ("Now I was eight and very small"; 5) when the incident occurs and his

14. Compulsive repetition is one of the symptoms of trauma, and one can certainly argue that the poem delineates the collective trauma of a black community. Trethewey deploys the palindrome to achieve the same effect, at the family level, in her "Incident."

15. I once taught an English as a second language (ESL) class, and when students would read English sentences out loud, many would say "full halt" or "full stop" instead of "period." However, a reader of this essay suggests the term may be a naval one. As a note, "full stop" is also more commonly British English for "period."

late teen/early twenties "adulthood," the poem as scar over a psychological trauma ("Of all the things that happened there / That's all that I remember"; 11–12), Jones achieves objectivity by impersonating the impersonal discourse of outsiders and insiders, not only professionals (law enforcement, journalism, etc.) but also ordinary citizens, the quotidian "we." Jones's "Incident" is less a traumatic experience seared into an individual brain than an autopsy of a community having succumbed to multiple organ—linguistic, aesthetic, cultural, social—failure. At the same time, we might read "Incident" as simply a summary of the murder of LeRoi Jones by Amiri Baraka as recorded by no-longer-Jones-not-yet-Baraka, recorded—that is, by another "we." The person Jones will soon become, Baraka, is indicated in those famous opening lines of the book's most infamous poem, "Black Art" (*Black Magic* 116): "Poems are bullshit unless they are / teeth or trees or lemons piled / on a step" (1–3). This accusing finger—"Poems are bullshit"—is pointed at LeRoi Jones. Amiri Baraka's poems must become "teeth or trees or lemons piled / on a step," must take on the materiality of physical objects, must be poems that *be,* not (merely) *mean.* However, both Jones's and Cullen's "incidents" sacrifice *being* to meaning, sacrifice males (a boy, a man) to other males (a white man, a black man with a gun), and no one—not Cullen's "I," not Jones's "we"—appears upset, angry, or frightened. Except for—and this is not insignificant—the inside outsider, the poet, whatever his name, who literally gets the last words: "We know nothing" (18).

Just as Jones must destroy himself in order to become Baraka, so too each member of the community's "we" must transform him- or herself into new black men and women. As he puts it in "For a lady i know," the poem that immediately follows "Incident,"

> Talk the talk I need
> you, as you resurrect
> your consciousness above
> the street. (1–4)

The street is, of course, in its colloquial sense, precisely what "Incident" delineates, a poem that seems to serve as Exhibit A in Baraka's prosecution of a *lumpenproletariat,* looking forward to his endorsement of what will retrospectively be deemed an errant cultural nationalism as he consolidates his political and cultural positions into a syncretic, if not unique, Third World Leninism-Marxism. In brief, the "we," no less than the "I," of his pre-1965 poems are not identical to the "we" and "I" of his post-1965 poems, even if Baraka will condemn and exhort the "same" black communities, the "same" individuals within those communities. Truth to tell, there are many degrees and kinds of "we" and "I" throughout the oeuvre.

All this bears on the "we" that narrates Natasha Trethewey's 2007 "Incident," published almost forty years after Baraka's "Incident" and is, as noted above, more like Cullen's 1925 "Incident" despite the span of eighty-two years. Yet Trethewey's poem, like Baraka's, is also a condemnation of "we." Whereas Baraka thematizes his execration in the last line of his poem—"we know nothing"—Trethewey deploys the formal proceduralism of the palindrome to send her message home. In both poems, futility is formalized as redundancy and repetition; Baraka's flat monotone becomes Trethewey's mindless ritualism: "We tell the story every year" (20). Although framed as a predictable family saga, Trethewey's "Incident" might easily be expanded to embrace the black family in general, the way we tell the same story—the Middle Passage, slavery, segregation, and so on—every February during Black History Month. In moving from Trethewey's specific family to a general black family, we turn her family into a synecdoche and example of everything "we" are, of everything "wrong" and "right" with us. Like Baraka, we not only have our dates, attached to epochal names—Emancipation, Reconstruction, civil rights, and the like— we also have our different kinds, different degrees, of we. For example, to "resurrect" our "consciousness above the street" can entail middle-class over-achievement, neo-Africana cultural practices (Kwanzaa), and a radical politics far left of the cultural conservatism of those we once knew as race men and race women. Conversely, to "resurrect" our "consciousness above the street" can be positioned against establishing one's "street cred" via hip-hop-inflected colloquialisms, hooking up with the local gang and wearing the latest sartorial fashions. Black Americans, to say nothing of African Americans, Negroes, and colored people, occupy all these positions, and more.

Is "we" then, no less than "I," a convenient abstraction of grammar and syntax, a mode of wishful thinking, a first volley of bombast, prophecy on the one hand and mixed metaphors, infelicitous similes, on the other? Depends. After all, not every person who uses first-person pronouns in the singular or plural is a pontiff. And those who are, aren't always. "Incident" finds Baraka in an especial un-pontificating mood. It is a poem we can imagine him writing before the assassination of Malcolm X, before Cuba. And whether we claim that "Incident" slides seamlessly into its place in *Black Magic* or seems to stick out like the sore thumb of a man standing too long beside a road, looking too long for a ride, *how* we read and imagine this poem in relation to *Black Magic*, to all Baraka's books of poetry, depends on nothing less than who we are—or believe we are.

5

"Legitimate Black Heroes"

Amiri Baraka's Prescient Views
on the Politics of Sports

EMILY RUTH RUTTER

PORTS HAS long been an arena in which African Americans have made an outsized sociocultural impact. Yet on the fields, courts, and rings where athletes of African descent have achieved heroic feats, they have also experienced the simultaneity of racial hypervisibility and personal invisibility, making sports, not unlike the entertainment industry, one of the most paradoxical sites for black socioeconomic mobility and political empowerment. Ever the shrewd cultural commentator, Amiri Baraka delineated these complexities first in regard to boxing in his essay "The Dempsey-Liston Fight" (1964) and later in regard to baseball in *The Autobiography of LeRoi Jones* (1984), which rues the fracturing of black solidarity that occurred when the Negro Leagues folded as a consequence of Major League desegregation. For Baraka, a key danger for black athletes lies in the forsaking of communal struggles for individual gains, particularly as the sports industrial complex hinges on a divide-and-conquer strategy that thwarts collective black empowerment and potentially ensnares black athletes in an exploitative scheme in which they are doing the bidding of white capitalists.

As this essay also contends, Baraka's asseverations about the political stakes of both boxing and baseball forecasted current dialogues about what it means for black athletes, especially in the NFL and the NBA, to participate in a white-dominated sports industry. While not typically considered a sports writer, Baraka's cautious appraisal of athletics as a vehicle for black empowerment remains relevant as players and pundits alike consider what it means to be, as William Rhoden provocatively terms it, "40 million dollar slaves," a consequence of the fact that "integration ended up merely allowing black athletes to join a corrupt system" (260). Returning to Baraka's writings about sports thus provides further evidence of his uniquely discerning voice on the relationships between black cultural production, white exploitation, and political resistance.

A "MOCK CONTEST"

Written in 1963 and first published under the title "In the Ring" in a 1964 issue of *The Nation*, "The Dempsey-Liston Fight" was subsequently reprinted in Baraka's *Home: Social Essays* (1966), which tracks the writer's evolving sociopolitical consciousness from his transformational visit to Cuba in 1960 ("Cuba Libre") to his full-throated commitment to cultural nationalism in 1965 ("The Legacy of Malcolm X, and the Coming of the Black Nation"). Within those years, Baraka pondered the social meaning of boxing, prompted specifically by a December 1963 issue of *Esquire* magazine, featuring a close-up portrait of then-heavyweight champion Sonny Liston donning a Santa hat. This *Esquire* cover, designed by the advertising pathbreaker George Lois, disarms the formidable boxer on the one hand and signals that his image has been commodified on the other. Responding not only to this cover but also to "The Greatest Fights of the Century" (1963), an article within the magazine's pages that heroicizes the former white heavyweight champion Jack Dempsey, "The Dempsey-Liston Fight" is a critique of the ways in which the sporting world reproduces the racial stratifications that structure American society writ large.

In particular, Baraka exposes the psychic trap of believing that black representation in white-controlled sports will result in increased opportunities for the majority of people of African descent. Accordingly, the essay begins with a series of interrogatives that call on his readers to open their eyes to the endemic racism hidden in plain sight: "See? See him dream? See the white man dream?" ("Dempsey-Liston" 179). The essay then outlines the particular scripts that boxers Sonny Liston and Floyd Patterson have unwittingly been enacting in their attempts to use the boxing arena in order to escape the poverty into which both were born. Liston, as Baraka describes, has been cast as "the big black Negro in every white man's hallway, waiting to do him in, deal him under for all the hurts white men, through their arbitrary order, have been able to inflict on the world" (179), whereas Patterson is "the tardy black Horatio Alger, the glad hand of integration" ("Dempsey-Liston" 180). In sum, "they painted Liston Black. They painted Patterson White. And that was the simple conflict" ("Dempsey-Liston" 180). Key here is that "they" (white hegemonic power structures, including the press) have pitted Liston and Patterson against each other, portraying Patterson as the embodiment of the values of the white status quo and Liston as a menacing threat to them, and thereby thwarting the possibility that these pugilists might work in solidarity to address the collective concerns of black Americans.

In 1962, the year before Baraka published this essay, Liston bested Patterson to win boxing's heavyweight title, and, as Baraka suggests, few relished his victory. President John F. Kennedy even phoned Patterson before the fight to emphasize "that it would not be in 'the Negroes' best interest' if Liston won" (qtd. in Zirin 136). Presumably, Kennedy's fear was that Patterson's defeat would undermine the propaganda that piety and a steadfast belief in American meritocracy were prerequisites for being a champion. Despite his victory, therefore, "Liston, the unreformed, Liston, the vulgar, Liston, the violent" was a consistent target of ridicule ("Dempsey-Liston" 180). In the rematch between Liston and Patterson—an event Baraka describes as a "mock contest" (179)—the two boxers were once again engaged in a fight orchestrated to affirm the righteousness of Patterson's Christian piety and belief in bootstrap capitalism, while delegitimizing the "mad-bad big black bad guy" Liston ("Dempsey-Liston" 182).

Indeed, Baraka exposes the ways in which the media and the white American public were keen to exploit the symbolic values ascribed to the fighters:

> Pollsters wanted the colored man in the street's opinion. "Sir, who do you *hope* comes out on top in the fight?" A lot of Negroes said Patterson. (That old hope comes back on you, that somehow this *is* my country, and ought'n I be allowed to live in it, I mean, to make it. From the bottom to the top? Only the poorest black men have never fallen, at least temporarily, for the success story.) A lot of Negroes said Liston. ("Dempsey-Liston" 180)

As Baraka implies, this media interest in which boxer members of the black community supported was not ideologically innocent but instead rooted in a pervasive white anxiety about how black Americans were responding to their second-class citizenship. Namely, will they continue to countenance racial and socioeconomic hierarchies in the hope of ascending "from the bottom to the top"? Or, have they decided, like Liston, to capitalize on the space carved out for black men in boxing without capitulating to the politics of respectability? According to Baraka, black Americans were swayed by both options, but his essay adumbrates a third way in which the "white man['s] dream" is framing neither the question nor the answer. In other words, in anatomizing these divisive racial schemas within boxing, Baraka warns readers about media attempts to use athletes and other famous black figures as pawns in a divide-and-conquer strategy ultimately designed to blunt collective black empowerment.

Moreover, "The Greatest Fights of the Century" (1963), the *Esquire* article that Baraka's piece engages, imagines not the ascendancy of Liston and other black boxers but instead their demise in the form of a series of fantastical match-ups with retrofitted "great white hope"[1] Rocky Marciano, the heavyweight champion from 1952 to 1956, and Jack Dempsey, the heavyweight champion from 1919 to 1926. Interpolating this article with his own commentary, Baraka exposes the endemic racism underwriting these imagined contests:

> In the [*Esquire*] magazine, Liston beats Marciano, "the most brutal first round ever seen," and he also beats [Joe] Louis, "Louis flew back five feet, fell, and rolled on his face." And having set this up, Dempsey comes marching in like drunk Ward Bond whistling a cavalry tune, to straighten everything out. . . ." Liston turned and fell heavily to the floor, his right glove under his face. In the posture of sleep, like a gypsy in the desert, a *fellaheen*. "At six, he rolled over and, back now in his corner, Dempsey smiled." ("Dempsey-Liston" 182)

In this anachronistic fantasy, Liston is initially portrayed as a "brutal" fighter who dominates not only the white Marciano but also the second black heavyweight champion, the "Brown Bomber" Joe Louis, who held the title from 1937 to 1949. Penetrating the writer's hegemonic gaze, Baraka mocks the notion that Dempsey would then be the one to topple Liston, who (magically, it seems) is stripped of his "brutal" strength by the sixth round. According to Baraka, the ending to this fantastical fight—"Liston vs. Dempsey. . . . . . Dempsey, K. O., 1:44 of the ninth" ("Dempsey-Liston" 183)—is meant to quell the fears of the white American public by assuring them that white men such as Dempsey are still ultimately in control ("Dempsey smiled").

However, when Baraka pivots to Muhammad Ali (Cassius Clay) in the essay's postscript, "Dempsey-Liston Addenda," he glimpses the possibilities

---

1. The term "great white hope" was furnished for Jim Jeffries, who was persuaded to come out of retirement in 1910 to reclaim the title from Jack Johnson, who had defeated Tommy Burns in 1908 to become the first black heavyweight champion. The Johnson–Jeffries fight was designed to give proof to the ideology of white supremacy, but Johnson decisively defeated Jeffries.

for boxing in particular and sports in general to become a revolutionary arena. Although he remains cautious in his optimism—"he [Ali] is now just angry rather than intellectually (socio-politically) motivated" (184)—Baraka sees the potential for what he terms "a new and more complicated generation" of boxers ("Dempsey-Liston" 183). At the same time, Baraka notes the continued efforts of the white mainstream to resist any black efforts to use their public platforms to challenge sociopolitical injustices. Specifically, Baraka refers to the 1964 fight between Liston and Ali, which marked the beginning of the end of Liston's boxing career:

> The Liston-Clay fight seemed to be on the up and up to me. Liston was just way out of shape, expecting young X [Ali was then known as Muhammad X] to be just another weak-faced American. But Cassius can box, and Liston in shape might have trouble spearing the very quick X. But poor Sonny's in jail now, where most of the white world would have him. (Shades of Jack Johnson!). ("Dempsey-Liston" 184)

In 1964, Ali upset Liston to become heavyweight champion, and he made use of the media coverage to publicly announce his conversion to the Nation of Islam the following day (Zirin 137). As Baraka notes, boxing's upper echelons, as much as they were appalled with Ali's religious convictions, were not keen to see Liston on top again, either.

In his parenthetical aside about Jack Johnson, the first black heavyweight champion, Baraka also indicates a pattern of retribution in response to black athletes' defiance of white-supremacist codes. For example, Johnson consistently broke rules of de jure and de facto segregation, sleeping with and marrying white women, and flaunting his riches at a time when African Americans were being lynched for the smallest (even perceived) infraction against a white patriarchal order. Consequently, Johnson "faced harassment and persecution for most of his life. He was forced into exile in 1913 on the trumped-up charge of transporting a white woman across state lines for prostitution" (Zirin 44). In turn, Liston's arrest for drunk driving on December 25, 1964, a day when courts were closed, was not the result of a random police stop, but instead an example of the ways in which the sports industrial complex has long colluded with the criminal justice system to delimit black agency, even (and perhaps especially) within cultural spaces in which people of African descent have been the highest achievers. As "The Dempsey-Liston Fight" concludes, the sporting arena is an unstable site for black social mobility, for heightened visibility and acclaim also engenders increased white surveillance and often public punishment.

"LIKE A GARMENT OF FEELING"

Whereas Baraka's account of boxing is rendered through the incisive lens of a cultural critic, in *The Autobiography*'s chapter entitled "Young," Baraka's tone is wistful as he recalls the affection for black baseball inculcated by his father. "The specialist feelings," Baraka recalls, "was when my father took me down to Ruppert Stadium some Sundays to see the Newark Eagles, the black pro team. Very little was as heightened (in anticipation and reward) for me than that" (*Autobiography* 42). In the transom of nostalgic memory, Baraka offers a distinctly different portrait of sports than the one he outlines in "The Dempsey-Liston Fight." Here, watching the Newark Eagles play, the young Baraka (then LeRoi Jones) feels the swell of pride in a display of black excellence that implicitly resists white supremacy. As he describes it, these games had "a *politics* . . . that still makes me shudder" (*Autobiography* 42).

For Baraka, therefore, sports (in this case, baseball) can be a site of black empowerment, as long as the players remain connected to their communities and are not beholden to white capitalists. Instead of bemoaning the so-called gentlemen's agreement among owners that resulted in black exclusion from the Major Leagues,[2] Baraka champions the all-black professional baseball organization, the Negro Leagues, as a vital cultural institution: "The Newark Eagles would have your heart there on the field, from what they was doing. From how they looked. But these were professional ballplayers. Legitimate black heroes. And we were intimate with them in a way and they were extensions of all of us, there, in a way that the Yankees and Dodgers and whatnot could never be!" (*Autobiography* 42). As Baraka remembers them, Negro League games fostered a strong sense of black solidarity that eschewed the white hegemonic gaze. Indeed, Newark Eagles games teemed with a collective sense of liberation: "We were wilder and calmer there. Louder and happier, without hysteria. Just digging ourselves stretch out is what, and all that love and noise and color and excitement surrounded me like a garment of feeling" (*Autobiography* 43). In this effusive portrait, Baraka suggests that when blacks control their sporting life, the games become a place for children to gain the self-confidence and self-love so often denied in a white-dominated society.

Conversely, when players cede their collective power to white owners and fans, the sports enterprise becomes as exploitative as it was for Sonny Liston and Floyd Patterson. Under this rubric, the first black Major Leaguer, Jackie Robinson, is a "synthetic colored guy," a "skin-covered humanoid" (45), who

---

2. Roberta J. Newman and Joel Nathan Rosen explain, "Baseball's color line, drawn in 1883, led to the formation of a series of loosely organized leagues and independent teams generally referred to collectively though not entirely accurately as the Negro Leagues" (3).

ushered in an era in which black baseball fans could no longer bask in the "self-love" and "collective black aura" of Negro League games (46). For Baraka, Robinson bears responsibility for the demise of black baseball, for he was persuaded to become a cog in the white capitalist machine:

> And you be standin' there and all of a sudden you hear about—what?— Jeckie Rawbeanson. . . . I don't want to get political and talk bad about "integration." Like what a straight-out trick it was. To rip off what you had in the name of what you ain't never get. Is that what the cry was on those Afric' shores when the European capitalists and African feudal lords got together and palmed our future? "We're going to the big leagues!" (*Autobiography* 45)

Comparing the integration of the "national pastime" to the trans-Atlantic slave trade, Baraka refuses the prototypical notion of progress associated with Robinson's debut with the Brooklyn Dodgers on April 15, 1947, particularly as it signaled the demise of black autonomy within baseball. Further, not unlike the dichotomous Patterson (good) versus Liston (evil) script designed to distract from the exploitation that all black Americans endured, Baraka views the signing of Robinson as a ruse ("a straight-out trick") to detract from broader sociopolitical inequities and exigencies.

Baraka's dismissal of Robinson is also rooted in his commitment to the collectivism of Third-World Marxism, the political stance he adopted in 1974 and that stands in contrast to Robinson's investment in capitalist enterprise as a means of achieving social mobility.[3] As Robert Nowatzki further observes, "For Baraka, the racial pride produced by the Negro Leagues far surpassed Robinson's inclusion in major league baseball" (108). Baraka also never forgave Robinson for testifying against Paul Robeson, another premier athlete (football), actor, singer, and social activist, who was called before the House Un-American Activities Committee (HUAC) for his Communist sympathies.[4] In *The Autobiography*, Baraka writes, "So Jackie came down to D. C. town and

---

3. As Baraka notes in *The Autobiography of LeRoi Jones*, he and his wife, Amina, publicly declared their commitment to socialism on October 7, 1974 (445), having rejected black nationalism with the realization that "just black faces in high places could never bring the change we seek" (443). By contrast, in *I Never Had It Made*, Robinson notes that the "two keys to the advancement of blacks in America" were "the ballot and the buck" (183).

4. Robeson gained football fame first at Rutgers University and then professionally during the 1921 season before the NFL barred black players. His subsequent celebrity as an actor and a singer, coupled with his anticapitalist, antiracist activism, also made him a target of the House Un-American Activities Committee, but he never confirmed the committee's accusations. When called before HUAC for the second time in 1956, Robeson invoked the Fifth Amendment, and ended the interrogation by admonishing the committee: "You are the nonpatriots, and you are the un-Americans, and you ought to be ashamed of yourselves" (qtd. in Bryant xi).

they got his ass to put Paul Robeson down!! I remember that, out of the side of my head I checked that. I wondered. What did it mean? What was he saying? And was it supposed to represent me?" (46). The older Baraka, of course, knows that the answer to the final question is decidedly "no," but here he reflects on the destructive example that he believes Robinson set by conspiring with congressional conservatives to impugn Robeson's reputation. For Baraka, when athletes privilege their individual success over the collective, they sacrifice the opportunity to use the sports arena as a platform for black liberation.

Of course, Robinson's statement before the committee was more complicated than Baraka makes it out to be. In his own autobiography, *I Never Had It Made* (1972), Robinson recalls telling the members of HUAC in 1949, "I am a religious man. Therefore I cherish America where I am free to worship as I please, a privilege which some countries do not give" (86). Robinson then offers an important rejoinder: "But that doesn't mean that we're going to stop fighting race discrimination in this country until we get it licked. It means that we're going to fight it all the harder because our stake in the future is so big. We can win our fight without the Communists and we don't want their help" (86). While ostensibly testifying against Robeson, Robinson also used the opportunity to denounce the second-class citizenship that black Americans continued to experience. Recounting this testimony over two decades later, Robinson also bookends the memory with his evolved outlook: "In those days I had much more faith in the ultimate justice of the American white man than I have today. I would reject such an invitation today" (84). Further, "I have grown wiser and closer to painful truths about America's destructiveness. And I do have an increased respect for Paul Robeson who, over the span of that twenty years, sacrificed himself, his career, and the wealth and comfort he enjoyed because, I believe, he was sincerely trying to help his people" (86). Baraka, had he given Robinson a second look, might have recognized perhaps not a fellow traveler but certainly a man with whom he shared a similar aptitude for self-reflection and sociopolitical evolution. Nonetheless, what stands out most in Baraka's memories of the Negro Leagues is the belief that the sporting arena has a political potency that *can* be marshalled for collective black ends, but that such a pursuit requires both solidarity and a steadfast resolve to resist white exploitation.

THE LEGACY OF BARAKA'S INSIGHTS

While baseball and boxing are no longer the central stages in which these racialized sporting dramas are being played out, both *The Autobiography* and "The Dempsey-Liston Fight" lay out a case for the paradoxical aspects of sports for athletes of African descent that remains strikingly relevant. As Howard Bryant recently noted, "Until 2017, all four major professional sports leagues combined had one black owner" (184), even while the NFL is 70 percent black, and the NBA is 80 percent black (Bryant 185). As Baraka predicted in *The Autobiography*, "going to the big leagues!" (45) has meant enriching the material wealth of individual black players but more or less gutting the sociopolitical agency that the black community as a whole might have been able to leverage. This is what Rhoden referred to earlier as the experience of "40 million dollar slaves," black athletes who are awash in cash and make up the majority of NFL and NBA rosters but whose institutional power within those organizations remains anemic.

Moreover, as Baraka observes in "The Dempsey-Liston Fight," white America is keen to exploit the symbolic values ascribed to black athletes in order to advance antiblack political agendas. For example, many Americans have responded to the former San Francisco 49ers quarterback Colin Kaepernick and the NBA forward LeBron James in ways that hark back to the treatment of Muhammad Ali, Jack Johnson, and so many other black athletes who refused to adapt their beliefs and circumscribe their behavior to comport with white Americans' expectations. Beginning in 2016, Kaepernick's peaceful pregame protests, whereby he sat or took a knee rather than stand for the national anthem, were designed to draw attention to racial discrimination within the criminal justice system and, by extension, the nation at large. This symbolic gesture was taken up by athletes across the sports landscape, and is now commonly shorthanded as the Take-a-Knee movement. In 2017, President Donald Trump publicly denounced Kaepernick and his followers: "Wouldn't you love to see one of these NFL owners, when somebody disrespects our flag, to say, 'Get that son of a bitch off the field right now, out, he's fired!'" (qtd. in Remnick). Eventually, the NFL essentially heeded Trump's call, with Commissioner Roger Goodell announcing a new policy in May 2018: "A club will be fined by the League if its personnel are on the field and do not stand and show respect for the flag and the anthem" ("Roger Goodell's Statement"). However, by the start of the 2019 season, the NFL and the NFL Players Association had still not come to an agreement about the policy, so the precise outcome remains uncertain. What is clear is that Kaepernick, with "shades of Jack Johnson," as Baraka might say, has remained unsigned by an NFL team since the end of the 2016 season; in fact, he reached a multi-million-dollar settlement in February 2019 in a joint case with his teammate Eric Reid that accused the thirty-two NFL teams of colluding to exclude them from the sport (Belson).

While the NBA has been more supportive of its players' social justice activism,[5] LeBron James, arguably the most acclaimed player in the sport, has experienced the public degradation that, as Baraka suggested in mapping a genealogy that includes Jack Johnson, Sonny Liston, and Muhammad Ali, accompanies defiance of paternalistic expectations for black athletes. For example, in 2017, James's Los Angeles home was defiled with a racist slur. As James lamented, "No matter how much money you have, no matter how famous you are, no matter how many people admire you, being black in America is tough" (qtd. in McKirdy). These words could have easily been spoken by any of the athletes that Baraka cites. Moreover, James has been the recipient, like Kaepernick, of Trump's vitriolic tweets, which have included a replay of the divide-and-conquer strategy Baraka identified in the media coverage of the Liston–Patterson fights. In response to an interview with CNN's Don Lemon in which James criticized Trump, the President tweeted: "LeBron James was just interviewed by the dumbest man on television, Don Lemon. He made LeBron look smart, which isn't easy to do." He then followed these disparaging remarks with: "I like Mike," a reference to Michael Jordan, to whom James is often compared in debates about the greatest basketball player of all time (qtd. in Stelter and Chavez). In this foiling of James and Jordan, we can hear echoes of Baraka's description of the media's portrait of Liston as the "mad-bad big black bad guy" (182) and Patterson as the "glad hand of integration" (180), who makes white America feel secure in its own righteousness.

Arguably, James, Kaepernick, and other socially conscious players have maintained their resolve by marshalling their resources in the service of something other than a "dream" conjured by white men, and signifying instead what Baraka envisaged in "The Dempsey-Liston Fight" as "a new and more complicated generation" of athletes (183). In Kaepernick and the Take-a-Knee movement he catalyzed, we can see the potential for Baraka's argument for sports as a vehicle for communal solidarity and self-determination. To this end, the Colin Kaepernick Foundation's stated mission is "to fight oppression of all kinds globally, through education and social activism." Moreover, he has used his public platform and economic capital to advance collective interests, resisting the white exploitation disguised as meritocracy that Baraka identified in the boxing arena in the 1960s and in his retrospective account of the

---

5. As John Branch recently noted, "The NFL has been unable to extract itself from the sticky web of the anthem controversy. The NBA, meanwhile, has avoided any such entanglement. Its star players and coaches have confidently dived into the political debates without retribution and with the support of the league commissioner and many team owners, if not all of them."

dissolution of the Negro Leagues after the Major League teams began signing Robinson and other black players.

In several respects, James has also acted in accordance with the communal ethos outlined in Baraka's *Autobiography*. Rather than pursuing purely individualized goals or feeling beholden to the white power structures that control not only basketball but also the entire sports industry, James has seen "the white man dream" and has turned his attention to the advancement of underprivileged youth in particular. The LeBron James Family Foundation provides the funding for the I Promise School in the player's hometown of Akron, Ohio. Opening its doors in 2018, I Promise "specifically targets low-performing students, identifying a pool of at-risk children and then hosting a lottery to decide who gets in" (McShane). Also in 2018, James launched a three-part Showtime series entitled *Shut Up and Dribble,* the title of which is an overt rejoinder to the calls of right-wing pundit Laura Ingraham specifically and conservative NBA fans and commentators more generally who have expressed their disdain for players using the court to express their outrage at antiblack racism (Bieler).

As we survey the contemporary sports landscape, we might also consider the neglect of Baraka's warnings about the sports industrial complex's use of individual African Americans (à la Floyd Patterson and Jackie Robinson) as shields against calls for addressing structural inequities. In this regard, in August 2019, the hip-hop mogul Jay-Z and his company, Roc Nation, agreed to manage the NFL's social justice initiatives in exchange for creative control over the Super Bowl entertainment program and other high-profile events. In a press conference with Commissioner Roger Goodell, Jay-Z opined, "I think we've moved past kneeling and I think it is time to go into actionable items"— a statement that did not sit well with Kaepernick and other players who have risked their careers for reforms that have yet to be enacted (Schilken). Given his concerns about the divide-and-conquer playbook utilized by boxing and baseball executives, it's difficult to imagine Baraka being convinced by Jay-Z's reasoning that the Take-a-Knee movement has run its course, and that his seat at the NFL table as the putative spokesperson for the black community will ensure equitable change.[6] Moreover, one might interpret James's efforts as both enabling some lucky children's socioeconomic mobility and challenging conservative pundits, yet not fully leveraging his social and economic capital to confront the racially skewed balance of power within the NBA. Kaepernick's recent Nike advertisement—"Believe in something, even if it means

---

6. For distinct reactions to Jay-Z's partnership with the NFL, see Cameron's Wolfe's "Stills Criticizes Jay-Z: He's Never Been on a Knee."

sacrificing everything"—could likewise be seen as a commodification of the Take-a-Knee movement, even as this marketing campaign has ensured that the black liberation platform he is fighting for in his post-NFL career remains in the public consciousness.[7] However one interprets these varied developments, it is clear that the incisive commentary Baraka published decades ago remains relevant to vigorous debates about the sociopolitical possibilities for and the limitations of sports.

Indeed, revisiting "The Dempsey-Liston Fight" and *The Autobiography of LeRoi Jones,* we can appreciate Baraka's perspicacity and prescience about the attendant dangers of black investment in white-dominated industries on the one hand and the productive sociopolitical roles that black athletes can perform for their communities on the other. Baraka especially highlights the need for players to place value on collective gains over individual achievements. Moreover, he imagines the sporting arena as a *potentially* revolutionary space that can facilitate black pride and liberation from oppression. On both accounts, Baraka seems to be whispering in the ears of James, Kaepernick, and their allies, even as they may not always heed his instructions. In addition to literature, music, and political activism, let us therefore add sports, if we had not already, to the list of fields upon which Baraka made his indelible mark.

---

7. Kaepernick's 2018 Nike campaign, which won an Emmy for the company in 2019, has multifaceted sociopolitical implications: It kept the Take-a-Knee movement in the spotlight during the start of the 2018 NFL season, while the campaign also generated a windfall of profits (and acclaim) for Nike. As Kevin Draper and Julie Creswell put it, "For Nike, the relationship resulted in tens of millions of dollars of free advertising and heightened credibility with the young, diverse consumers who look up to the player. For Kaepernick, the contract was lucrative and the might of one of the world's most powerful companies helped his goal of raising awareness of police brutality and systemic racial inequality."

6

=

Hegel off the Tracks

JEREMY MATTHEW GLICK

Einfuhlung (for this time)
We the kinda cats like to turn Hegel / upside
down just to see the pennies fallout![1]
—Amiri Baraka

A SCENE FROM Abel Ferrara's Depression-era film *The Funeral*: Christopher Walken's character pursues revenge against the person he believes killed his trade-unionist brother, played by Vincent Gallo. The alleged guilty party (Benicio del Toro) protests: "You have no right coming after me like this with that stupid mistake and idea that it was I who killed that stupid left-wing brother of yours, the anarchist." Walken's character, on the verge of committing homicide, resolutely retorts, "No no, no,—Johnny was a Communist!" (*The Funeral*). Walken's character precisely names the negation of the negation, the continuous becoming, the *hunting* as the surpassing of our current economic mode of production and its coeval imperialisms and national oppressions. For Amiri Baraka, the refusal to name is a hallmark of ideological complicity. A declaration embedded in his poem "In Town" asserts: "I seen something and you seen something too. / You just cant / call its name" (*Somebody* 18, lines 104–106).

This essay came out of my talks at the Philosophy Department of York University, The Columbia University Faculty Literary Theory Seminar, The Academy of Fine Arts, Vienna, Austria, the Caribbean Philosophical Association's Summer School at the University of Memphis, and the Gauss Seminar on *Hegel and the Humanities* at Princeton University. It is dedicated to my Summer School co-conspirator and dear friend Professor Hortense Spillers.

1. *Yugen,* no. 7, Masthead, edited by LeRoi Jones and Hettie Cohen, Totem Press, 1961.

PENNIES, PREFACES, AND ANTI-PROPAEDEUTICS

The epigraph announcing my endeavor, from the masthead of Amiri Bara-ka's journal *Yugen*, riffs on the Marxian procedure of turning Hegel "upside down" in order to mobilize its rational kernel. Its force-understanding strips the dialectic bare of theological properties, bringing such heady procedure out into the streets. Baraka's is aphoristic critique as upside-down yoke and shake-down. This essay frames a Baraka recording with and against Georg Wilhelm Friedrich Hegel to think about class-based aptitudes for abstract thinking. For Hegel, *abstrakt* signifies one-sidedness, absent of content, the antithesis of *konkret*. Both the particular and universal constitute *abstrakt* if disarticulated from both thought (as totality) and the sensory repertoire as a whole. Yet, this is neither a clarifying excursus on what Hegel actually meant by abstraction, nor a comprehensive analysis of Baraka's variations on the Hegelian dialectic.[2] Elsewhere, I provide a critical overview of Baraka's literary and political development (a critique of pragmatist-longing approaches to Baraka's poetics (Glick, "All I Do"), and a protracted analysis of Baraka's and Hegel's main political and analytic category: self-determination (Glick, *Black Radical Tragic* 9–24). Here, I place Hegel's short essay "Who Thinks Abstractly?" (1807–1808) in conversation with the 1982 jazz album *New Music–New Poetry* featuring Baraka with David Murray on tenor saxophone and bass clarinet and Steve McCall on drums. Telegraphing this essay's moves, Baraka's "Strunza Med" alongside Hegel and a William Parker recording dialectically complicate to the point of exploding black radical and Hegelian problematics pertaining to firsts and lasts, genesis and *telos*, contingency and necessity, closures and openings.[3] I conclude with a brief meditation on *Bildung* by way of highlighting problems of literary history and periodization, relating Baraka to both Erich Auerbach's Dante and broader biblical scholarship. "Strunza Med" proffers an occasion to

---

2. For an early example of Hegelian reading of Baraka's work, see Jackson. For a contemporary account of becoming in Baraka (more Deleuzian than Hegelian) of Baraka's self-referential fiction, see Liner.

3. James A. Snead in his "Repetition as a Figure of Black Culture" grabs hold of and wrestles from Hegel his so-called disavowal of African historicity in the lecture transcripts assembled by students of his *The Philosophy of History*: "In the main portion of Africa, there can really be no history. There is a succession of accidents and surprises" (Gates, *Black Literature* 62). Snead mobilizes such "accidents and surprises" in his theory of black expressive culture that in its nonaccrual challenges the logic of capital accumulation. Frank Kirkland, addressing the same topic of disavowal, argues to not rely "too heavily on what Hegel has said or not said rather than on what his philosophy is warranted to say or not." For Kirkland, Hegel's theory of development is both material and dialectical and does not preclude Africans or any of the world's people in principle as historical. "Entering history," according to such an interpretation, means engaging in revolutionary struggle.

think about translation as dialectical tension between abstract and concrete and particular and universal, a prerequisite for thinking and building an anti-capitalist revolutionary black inter(nationalism). "Strunza Med" as an exercise in attentive listening and poetic detection generates concepts contributing to such radical ends.

The concept, for Hegel, is the main unit and building block apropos philosophical discourse. It is dynamic, slow to cohere, patient, continuously forming and deforming—"the exertion of the Concept" (*die Anstrengung des Begriffs*) (Preface 88). From plant bud to blossom, blossom to fruit—Hegel's 1807 *The Phenomenology of Spirit's Preface* (composed after the main text and labeled by Herbert Marcuse as "one of the greatest philosophical undertakings of all time" [97]) engages the botanic to rehearse how movement subsumes parts and wholes.[4] It is a partisan declaration waging war against the propae-deutic, the thesis statement, and the preface itself. Narrative, for Hegel, lacks conceptual dynamism (the noun form *Begriff* as concept correlated in motion, integral to the verb form *Begriffen* to comprehend). For Hegel, in order to achieve the desired "seriousness of the concept" (*der Ernst des Begriffs*) (Pref-ace 10), philosophical process needs to be shown, not told. Perhaps this is one explanation for the fact that besides Plato's *Parmenides,* Kant, and a few others, proper names are conspicuously absent from Hegel's preface. Their preponderance would short-circuit his desired procedure to abstract thought to the grand level of the concept-in-motion.

Raya Dunayevskaya's *Rosa Luxemburg, Women's Liberation, and Marx's Philosophy of Revolution* mobilizes Hegel's main category of thought—REA-SON—as a plea to "perceive the Black dimension as Reason in our age" (81). Such dimension is part of the same world it labors to radically overhaul—not black dimension *of* reason but *as* reason; not an alternative modernity, but modernity as such. Such is the marching orders that animate this essay. Let us begin.

Amiri Baraka's 1964 essay and aphoristic declaration "Hunting Is Not Those Heads on the Wall" (*Home* 173–178) is a precision-capture of his open-ended praxis-based dialectic, demanding a strong-armed fastening on, a tarrying that requires precision in naming categories and phenomena, simultaneously conceding how such categories and phenomena are always in

---

4. Here I mean to evoke the following passage: "The bud disappears as the blossom bursts forth, and one could say that the former is refuted by the latter. In the same way, the fruit declares the blossom to be a false existence of the plant, and the fruit supplants the blossom as the truth of the plant. These forms do not only differ, they also displace each other because they are incompatible. Their fluid nature, however, makes them at the same time, elements of an organic unity in which they not only do not conflict, but in which one is as necessary as the other; and it is only this equal necessity that constitutes the life of the whole" (Preface 6–8).

motion, split, and propelled forward by what they are not. "Hunting" is a valu-
ation of process over product, verb over noun, protracted rigor and difficulty
over disposable *ready-mades,* trumpeting creative energy of negation in the
stick of entanglement as a condition of possibility for generating the new. In
the same text, Baraka elliptically asserts: "And even to name something, is to
wait for it in the place you think it will pass" (175). Names (like concepts) do
all kinds of work, including clarification of political tendencies. This aspect of
naming—the anxiety encapsulated by a naming procedure that strives to halt
or slow down perpetual motion—is hilariously captured by Baraka's friend
and co-collaborator Toni Cade Bambara in her 1980 thought piece "Working
at It in Five Parts": "And like tedious self-styled 'revolutionaries' (neo-magic-
marxists a sage at Atlanta U's poli sci dept tags'm) who want to come in, drink
up my wine, and categorically prove that Imamu is Lenin" (Bambara 34). In
his eulogy for Paul de Man, Jacques Derrida recalls how de Man and his son
engaged in a discussion as naming procedure after a Chicago jazz concert.
Their dance of proliferating interpretive possibilities is signaled by Derrida
as the expertise of technicians "who know how to call things by their name"
("Paul De Man" 75). Consider both Hegel's and "Hunting"'s resonant meditations on God and the proper name:

> Apart from the self that is limited or represented by the senses, it is above all
> the name as name that designates the pure subject, the empty unit void of
> Concept. For this reason it may be expedient, e.g. to avoid the name "God"
> because this world is not immediately also a Concept but rather the proper
> name, the fixed repose of the underlying subject, while, e.g. being or the
> One, the particular, the subject, etc., also immediately suggest Concepts.
> (Hegel, Preface 100)
>
> The Supermaker, is what the Greeks identified as "Gods." But here the
> emphasis is still muddled, since it is what the God can do that is really
> important, not the fact that he is the God. I speak of the *verb process,* the
> doing, the coming into being, the at-the-time-of. Which is why we think
> there is particular value in live music, contemplating the artifact as it arrives,
> listening to it emerge. *There* it is. And *There.* (Baraka, *Home* 198)

This juxtaposition marks the fundamental difference and overlap between
Hegel and Baraka's dialectic: Hegel's culmination in understanding privileges
the Concept, whereas Baraka's privileging of use takes the form of lauding
the *verb-process.* For both radical thinkers, God, the Spirit, and the Absolute
are all ciphers for movement and comprehension-as-movement in general. It
is the *doing* that is paramount. (It is not surprising that Paul Tillich's assertions "God is being itself" and "God is the ground of being" [Tillich qtd in

Walter Kaufmann's commentary to Hegel, Preface 101] are formulations from
the mind of both a theologian and socialist!) Seeking refuge in Zurich Library
at the outbreak of World War I, V. I. Lenin in September 1914 undertook a
comprehensive study of Hegel's *Major Logic*. Such endeavors are captured in
volume 38 of Lenin's *Collected Works—The Philosophical Notebooks*. The rigor
and provisional experimentation contained within function as a useful hedge
against contemporary efforts to evoke in order to dismiss Lenin, more often
than not based on caricatures of key forms such as vanguard party. Lenin at
his provocative best: "Aphorism: One cannot understand Marx's *Capital* and
in particular its first chapter without having studied the *whole* of Hegel's *Logic*.
Thus, a half a half century after Marx, not one Marxist understood Marx!" A
critical dialectic resists teleology privileging *latter* forms as key to understanding *prior*. In the same vein, I propose the following variation: One cannot
understand Hegel's *Phenomenology of Spirit* and in particular its preface without having studied Baraka's "Hunting Is Not Those Heads on the Wall." Thus,
for 157 years, not one understood Hegel!

Consider four enunciations informing my essay:

Actuality and thought—more precisely the Idea—are usually opposed to
one another in a trivial way, and hence we often hear it said therefore that,
although there is certainly nothing to be said against the correctness and
truth of a certain thought, still nothing like it is to be found or can be actually be put into effect. Those who talk like this, however, only demonstrated
that they have not adequately interpreted the nature either of thought or
actuality. For, on the one hand, in all talk of this kind, thought is assumed to
be synonymous with subjective representation, planning, and intention, and
so on; and, on the other hand, actuality is assumed to be synonymous with
external sensible existence. (Hegel, *The Encylopaedia Logic* 214)

You know Gil, you shouldn't be afraid of what is actual. (Amiri Baraka on
Gil Noble's *Like It Is,* 2002)[5]

Either I am wrong
or "he" is wrong. All right
I am wrong: but give me someone
to talk to. (Baraka, *Black Magic Poetry* 23–24, lines 40–43)

Blackness is necessary, but it is not sufficient. (Cox qtd. in Joseph 28)

---

5. https://www.youtube.com/watch?v=YuPwtgklEWM.

"You shouldn't be afraid of what is actual": This is the line said by Amiri Baraka as he breaks down a trajectory of consciousness along modified Hegelian lines to television host Gil Noble, altering Hegel's forms of consciousness and becoming knowledge in *The Phenomenology*.[6] Hegel charts a movement from Sense-Certainty to Perception to Force-Understanding (Reason). Sense-Certainty is essential, yet scorned for its immediacy. Necessary, but not sufficient. This is by no means an effort to conflate sense-certainty with Blackness, despite efforts toward such an end across wide ideological divides (for example, consult both attacks and defenses of so-called identity politics). Perhaps W. E. B. Du Bois's 1903 *The Souls of Black Folk*'s dismissal of "car window sociologists" (105) can be understood here as rallying against the limits of sense-certainty. For Baraka the militant, the arc of perception/consciousness starts with *sense-perception,* then *reason-rationale,* and (like Brecht) culminates in *use.* Baraka gestures with his hand to Mr. Noble a kind of topographic modeling of the trajectory he plots: sense-perception, reason, use. The culminating test of use only ignites the circuit anew—Count Basie and his orchestra's *April in Paris*: "Let's try it one more, once!"

ABSTRACTING "STRUNZA MED"

What follows is a meditation on the philosophical import for Hegel and Baraka on being cursed out—"Strunza Med": an Italian profanity containing multiple conflicting translations. Baraka's task is to establish some consensus of definition. "Strunza Med" is two minutes and seven seconds and begins with Baraka's unaccompanied narration: "When I was in Newark I went to a school, a high-school that had a lot of Italian students in it. And a lot of words they used to say when they got angry, I would listen to. And I never found out the definitions. This is a poem about one of those words. It's called *Strunza Med*" (Baraka, Murray, and McCall, "Strunza Med," *New Music*). The music encroaches frantically onto the recitation and Baraka repeats the curse, coupling it with a query and an assertion that "the world is a poem," itemizing characteristics of this poem world. There is a toggling of focus here: the mystery of affective response of the anger of "the Italians I went to school with" and the world as a whole. The anger, striving for accurate translation, proffers an opportunity to think poetic form in relation to the abstraction that is the

---

6. For the entire interview in five parts: https://www.youtube.com/playlist?list=PLgUUv
Xaa9wKZWF2FkngmQSpFCWjTS4AoR.

world. Michael McKeon's *The Secret History of Domesticity* makes an exacting argument for the virtues of abstraction characteristic of Marxian method:

> Abstraction is not a dogmatic shutting down but an experimental opening up of discovery, a way of generating concrete particularity by tentatively constituting a whole susceptible to analysis into part. Abstraction entails not the occlusion but the explication of concretion, just as system may work not to exclude but to ensure the acknowledgment of, contradiction. (xxv)

Likewise, Philip Brian Harper's *Abstractionist Aesthetics: Artistic Form and Social Critique in African American Culture* theorizes abstractionism as "resolute awareness that even the most realistic representation is precisely a representation," exhibiting a "distance from the social reality" by necessity (2). "Strunza Med" stages *social distance* from some playfully irate Italian schoolmates that necessitates a translation query and *social proximity* enough to be invested in such a query's results.

In Baraka's performance, the mystery of translation, from the concrete particularity of the mass, the concrete particularity of vulgar incensed sociality ("words they used to say when they got angry that I would listen to"), and the discovery of meaning ("I never found out the definitions") constitute both a form (a poem) and a whole (a world) "susceptible to analysis into parts." Baraka's performance posits analogical equivalence between poem and world—"beautiful, interesting, ugly, tragic, sad, but happy." He tops off his exhortation with a command to study: "Look at it fool!" To go through the world with active partisan perception, encountering its difficulty as praxis, its complexity and oblique presentation warrant a patient look, an immersive initiation that scorns what Hegel in the context of his preface of *The Phenomenology of Spirit* would dismiss as the "ready-made."

"Who Thinks Abstractly?" is the title of a short article by Hegel most likely from his Jena period—1807 to 1808. Michael Inwood provides a helpful gloss, an etymological backstory explicating its keyword:

> In the sixteenth century, *abstrahieren* ("to abstract") was borrowed from the Latin *abstrahere*, literally "to draw away, remove (something from something else)." The past participle of *abstrahae*, *abstractus*, gave rise, in the eighteenth century, to abstract and das *Abstrakte* ("the abstract") to characterize the products of such abstraction (*Abstraktion*). Similarly, *konkret* and das *Konkrete* derive from the past participle, *concretus* ("grown together, condensed"), of the Latin *concrescere* ("to grow together, condense").

The abstract is usually regarded as a THOUGHT, CONCEPT OR UNI-VERSAL, which we abstract from the concrete, the perceptible reality. But Kant, in many of his writings, insisted that *abstrahieren* should be used intransitively, to say, that is, not that we abstract something (especially a concept), but that the concept itself, or we in using a concept, abstract from (i.e. disregard) something, especially the inessential, contingent features of the concrete. Hegel too often uses *abstrahieren* intransitively, to say e.g. that the WILL, or the I* abstracts (itself from its concrete desires, etc.).

Another feature of Hegel's usage is that, in line with the noncommittal etymology of *abtrakt* and *konkret,* a sensory item or a PARTICULAR, as well as a thought or a universal, may be abstract (viz. cut off from a thought or from other sensory items), and a universal may be concrete (viz. "grown together" with other universals or with the sensory concrete), as well as abstract. (But Hegel also tends to see any item, whether sensory or intellectual, that is cut off, or abstracted, from other things as (abstractly) universal. (29)

In the article, Hegel's market woman generalized an accusation questioning the integral quality of her wares and breaks her accuser down to her component parts. Here is Hegel's market woman's retort to the accusation of selling rotten eggs:

Old woman, your eggs are rotten! The maid says to the market woman. What? She replies, my eggs rotten? You may be rotten! You say that about my eggs? You? Did no lice eat your father on the highways? Didn't your mother run away with the French, and didn't your grandmother die in a public hospital? Let her get a whole shirt instead of that flimsy scarf; we know well where she got that scarf and her hats: if it were not for those officers, many wouldn't be decked out like that these days, and if their ladyships paid more attention to their households, many would be in jail right now. Let her mend the holes in her stockings!

In brief, she does not leave one whole thread on her. She thinks abstractly and subsumes the other woman—scarf, hat, shirt, etc., as well as her fingers and other parts of her, and her father and whole family, too—solely under the crime that she has found the eggs rotten. Everything about her is colored through and through by these rotten eggs, while those officers of which the market woman spoke—if, as one may seriously doubt, there is anything to that—may have got to see very different things. ("Who Thinks" 117–118)

. . .

The uneducated, not the educated. Good society does not think abstractly because it is too easy, because it is too lowly (not referring to the external status)—not from an empty affectation or nobility that would place itself above that of which it is not capable, but on account of the inward inferiority of the matter. (116)

Hegel stages yet another example of abstract thinking: Prior to the market woman's outburst, an observer labels a murderer en route to his execution as "handsome." Such a compliment is offensive to the populace since the positive attribute of handsomeness introduces a multiplicity of characteristics to the murderer, who, in accordance with a so-called mass-based procedure of abstract thinking, is just a murderer. Hegel qualifies: "This is abstract thinking: to see nothing in the murderer except the abstract fact that he is a murderer, and to annul all other human essence in him with this simple quality" (116–117). I do not read this as an attack on abstract thinking as mass logic. Rather, Hegel's object of critique is an abstracting procedure that forsakes the responsibility of the dialectic, one that refuses to undercut the blanketing logic of abstraction (the murderer is just a murderer) with other mediations, myriad of particularities. A dialectical procedure that starts with a space of abstraction and journeys to a multiplicity of concrete mediations in constant motion contains both abstract and concrete in its very developmental design.

James Baldwin stages a similar logical interrogation in his meditation on the Atlanta child murders in his last essay, *The Evidence of Things Not Seen*. There is ironic play at work here with Hegel attributing abstract thinking to the masses—a satiric swipe against understanding philosophical reflection as elite praxis. Hegel insists on not decoupling abstraction procedures from consideration of how particularities mediate. In the context of African diasporic expressive culture, political praxis, and scholarship, Hegel's association of abstraction with the masses pushes back against tendencies to see action/ the real as the province of Africans in armed rebellion (Haiti, for example) and abstraction as theorization the province of European philosophy (Hegel). "Actuality and Thought—more precisely the idea"—Let's split this Hegelian formulation from *The Encylopaedia Logic* and constitute two sides of a ledger in order to proliferate associations. Actuality: "External sensible experience," nature, immediacy, improvisation/spontaneity, action. Thought: "Subjective Representation," Planning, Intention, Knowledge, Study. Taking the time to listen to the cursing market woman and Baraka's agitated school pals troubles such a divide. In the spirit of and against Paul Gilroy's *Black Atlantic*'s rallying "against the closure of categories with which we conduct our political lives" (xi), we may discover that Hegel's categories were never that. As Baraka asserts on *New Music–New Poetry*'s tribute to Abbie Hoffman: "There is no such thing as a last revolutionary" (Baraka, Murray, and McCall, "Last Revolutionary," *New Music*). Fredric Jameson reminds us in his Bach/Glenn Gould fugue-inflected title, *The Hegel Variations: On the Phenomenology of Spirit* (2014), that the Hegelian dialectic is fundamentally one of openness; it refuses closure, and its *Aufheben*/sublation procedure proliferates generative repetition, particularity in dialectical interplay with universality, the combinatory and the disaggregate, perpetual fusion and separation.

"FREDDIE'S DEAD" AND BLACK RADICAL *BILDUNG*

The immediacy of sensory perception is never reality. Consider as reading strategy—Hegel's *Phenomenology* (for that matter, Baraka's *System of Dante's Hell*) as *Bildungsroman*, a mono-narration from the standpoint of consciousness in its development. "Sound and Image," or Baraka's dialectical excursus from "The Changing Same (R&B and the New Black Music)": "Music makes an image" (*Black Music* 185). The *Phenomenology* as *Bildung* (image), a novel of education, initiation, and image building traces the development of its central character as consciousness. It is a science of the development of consciousness, traveling through negative examples (stoicism, skepticism, the unhappy consciousness). Such development is broken down in subchapters as sense-certainty, perception, and understanding: all three repeatable and sublated. Each stage develops its own particular, universal, and concept, simultaneous changes and consistencies in the spheres. For Hegel, it is "the spirit that educates[or forms] itself" (Preface 20)—*der sich bildende Geist*. The *Phenomenology* is a novel of apprenticeship and maturity—*Wilhelm Meister's Apprenticeship, Manchild in the Promised Land, Portrait of an Artist as a Young Man, The Catcher in the Rye* (for white people). Baraka's *Dante* couples its "result together with its becoming" (Hegel, Preface 10). Its protagonist traverses actual geography and its movement's culmination of absolute knowing is historical, yet the historical brought back inward onto an expansive consciousness of self: "the absolute pain our people must have felt when they came onto this shore." *The System of Dante's Hell* actualizes in its movement expansiveness of consciousness as historical development gestured toward in "The Changing Same"; its emphasis on total environment and consciousness of the total: self, environment, and world. As Baraka writes, "If we can bring back on ourselves, the absolute pain our people must have felt when they came onto this shore, we are more ourselves again, and can begin to put history back in our menu, and forget the propaganda of devils that they are not devils (*System of Dante's Hell* 158–159).

Music critic Ben Ratliff's liner notes for the vinyl re-reissue of Miles Davis's 1967 album *Sorcerer* quotes tenor saxophone Wayne Shorter, who composed most of the album's music—a first for Miles, who normally would not relinquish artistic control. Shorter asserts: "The word 'finished' is artificial' and 'First' is artificial too" (Ratliff). Origin and Death, the problem of both Christopher Columbus and the *telos*. One of Baraka's later recording endeavors is on bassist William Parker's 2010 *I Plan to Stay a Believer: The Inside Songs of Curtis Mayfield*. "Inside" resonates with the Hegelian insistence on immanence, entering into the protocols of the object or thought or system you want to transform, entering into in order to exit through. In Baraka/Parker's journey and versioning inside Mayfield's "Freddie's Dead" from the 1972 *Superfly* soundtrack, Baraka croons "Freddie's Dead," pushing his vocal register past resignation, past the finality of Freddie's final destination. In the eleven minute and twenty-six second track, Baraka consistently queries the use-value of dying: "Death is the worst shit we know. And we don't even know what it's for" (Baraka and Parker, "Freddie's Dead," *I Plan to Stay a Believer*). Such an excursus on the Reaper recalls an anecdotal Hegelian backstory. In an essay entitled "Hegel's Fool" for the 1978 edition of the journal *Semiotexte* entitled "Nietzsche's Return," Georges Bataille scholar and translator Denis Holier notes that this

> period of extreme anguish preceded . . . [Hegel's] *Phenomenology of the Mind,* but several years later, one of his students who had perhaps understood him better than his peers wrote, after leaving the class-room in a state of oppression, that he had been overcome by the impression that Death itself had been speaking from the pulpit. (Holier 126–127)[7]

Absence—Being-towards-death as the ultimate source of object-less anxiety versus object-dependent fear—the fact that we can generate conceptual language surrounding our being toward death but can never match it with experiential knowledge. The gap between affirmatively knowing and not know(ing) "what it's for." Perhaps this simultaneous avowal of knowing and disavowal of utilitarian value is an argument for why interpretation matters: "A text is not a text unless it hides from the first comer, from the first glance, the law of its composition and the rules of its game. A text remains, moreover, forever

---

7. Curiously, Alexandre Kojève's lecture on *The Phenomenology of Spirit*'s discussion of death is absent in the English translation of his infamous *Introduction to the Reading of Hegel*. See Kojève, "The Idea of Death."

imperceptible. Its laws and rules are not, however, harbored in the inaccessibility of a secret; it is simply that they can never be booked, in the present, into anything that could rigorously be called a perception" (Derrida, *Dissemination* 63). Baraka's poetics and political legacy offer a trove of resources we can use to recalibrate our collective desires to less research and more thinking, less product and more process and project.

I will conclude by gesturing to problems of textual interpretation and periodization, the figure of things to come. Embedded in *The Leroi Jones/Amiri Baraka Reader* is a charming debate between author and editor around this problem. In the "Preface to the Reader," Baraka writes a friendly retort to editor William J. Harris's periodization scheme:

> The typology that lists my ideological changes and so forth as "Beat-Black Nationalist-Communist" has brevity going for it, and there's something to be said for that, but, like notations of Monk, it doesn't show the complexity of real life.
>
> "You mean that's not accurate?" Dick or Dixie Dugan wd counter.
>
> "Well, yes and no," I'd drawl, acknowledging any mental disclaimer needed to sound so Zennish.
>
> But the truth is that in going toward and way from same name, some identifiable "headline" of one's life, the steps are names too, but we ain't that precise yet. We go from step 1 to step 2 and the crushed breath away from the "given" remains unknown swallowed by its profile as what makes distance. But there is real life between 1 and 2. There is the life of the speed, the time it takes, the life there in, in the middle of, the revelation, like perception, rational, and use. To go from any where to any there. (xi)

In Erich Auerbach's *"Figura,"* the weary philologist comments on the work of Tertullian, the African Berber Christian author from Carthage in the Roman province of Africa:

> In his polemic *Adversus Marcionem* Tertullian speaks of Oshea, son of Nun, whom Moses (according to *Numbers* 13:16) names Jehoshua Joshua:
>
> For the first time he is called Jesus. . . . This, then, we first observe, was a figure of things to come. For inasmuch as Jesus Christ was to introduce a new people, that is to say us, who are born in the wilderness of this world, into the promised land flowing with milk and honey, that is to say, into the possession of eternal life, than which nothing is sweeter; and that, too, was not to come through Moses, that is to say, through the discipline of the Law, but through the grace of the gospel, our circumcision being performed by a

knife of stone, that is to say, by Christ's precepts—for Christ is a rock; therefore a great man, who was prepared as a type of this sacrament, was even consecrated in figure with the Lord's name, and was called Jesus. (28–29)

For Auerbach, "The naming of Joshua-Jesus is a phenomenal prophecy or prefiguration of the future Saviour; *figura* is something real and historical which announces something else that is also real and historical. The relation between the two events is revealed by an accord or similarity" (29). The naming designation *Old and New Testament* binds together two books of scripture in consecutive relation that only one of the two religions (the latter) claims. The so-called Old Testament anticipates the New Testament Messiah—"figures of things to come." Perhaps the campaign to replace the periodization BC (before Christ) with BCE (before the Common Era) in the spirit of religious neutrality would be better served dislodging the prefixes *Old* and *New* from their respective Testaments. Periodization vis-à-vis Christ does not imply theological belief, whereas the prefixes *Old* and *New* perform continuity only true for one religion.

The African intellectual Tertullian's procedure of balancing the abstract and concrete, historical actuality and prophetic becoming, constitutes a more sophisticated endeavor. Tertullian does not (to employ Baraka's lexicon) confuse heads for hunting. As Auerbach notes, "Tertullian expressly denied that the literal and historical validity of the Old Testament was diminished by figural interpretation. He was definitely hostile to spiritualism and refused to consider the Old Testament as mere allegory; according to him, it had real, literal meaning throughout, and even when there was figural prophecy, the figure had just as much historical reality as what it prophesized" (30), let alone accordingly marking one's historical periodization. This has resonance for the interpretive problem of thinking about Baraka's political ideology as a metric or framework for periodization of his work. It opens up the kind of space to think the complexity of the world by going through (and listening to) such a world. "Strunza Med" as a listening exercise and political primer demonstrates as much. Tertullian and Baraka: two black intellectuals separated by millennia, deeply sharing concern for the interpretive project of calibrating concrete with abstract, particular with universal, the clarity of the poised, always aiming hunter balancing concrete actuality with contingent potentiality. Tertullian performs Hegel's *Aufheben* (sublation) procedure *avant la lettre,* to simultaneously negate, preserve, and transcend, and Baraka works within a critical open-endedness even in his most partisan moments.

In my apartment living room there is a drawing by Baraka (entitled "PLAY ON!") of a round-spectacled black man in a homburg hat. It includes a caption variation on the indefinite labor of *the absolute*: "Suppose you wanted to know The Truth about Everything!" Amiri became a Marxist the year before I was born. How to resist reading those commitments into his early work? Or for that matter treating earlier work as missteps toward a future road to arrival, reducing their anti-systemic force? How to resist prefiguring such commitments—to read like you know where the story ends, hubristically presuming the story even has an end to know? I spent years of my life alongside close friends and comrades writing political programs (equipped with maximum and minimum political demands) for campaigns with Amiri in the context of our organizational formation—*Unity & Struggle*. Even Amiri's comforting counsel (after the violent death of my father) channeled the dialectic: "Focus your subjective pain to clarify an objective path for struggle." The aesthetic playfulness and openness to "the world" (as poem) captured in the procedures of "Strunza Med," the eagerness to "find out the definitions" does not supplement the political as second-order artistic division of political struggle. Rather, the poetic complements the programmatic as dialectical contingency, an unlocked door and patiently waiting brim-filled wine glass welcoming future *prophe-bilities*, interpretive-insurgent forces against closure, what Baraka theorizes on a recorded musical excursus with the Billy Harper Sextet as "the zig-zag of chance, the improv" (Billy Harper Sextet).

Amiri was fond of reminding us that the urgent brilliance of Baldwin's *The Evidence of Things Not Seen* could be distilled in ten words: "The present social and political apparatus cannot serve human need" (124). I miss him every day.

Side B

The Music (Ideations and Renegotiations)

7

=

The Five Spot Café

WILLIAM J. HARRIS

N A FITTINGLY washed-out photograph of the old Five Spot Café, located at 5 Cooper Square, just down the street from the apartment 27 Cooper Square, sitting next to a pizza joint, stands the famous venue; one can see that it is an unprepossessing building. Hettie Jones remarks, "The Five Spot . . . [in] daylight [is] rendered shockingly nondescript" (*How* 163). The building does not look like one of the pivotal places where the revolution in black avant-garde music is about to occur.

The Termini brothers, Joe and Iggy, opened the Five Spot on August 30, 1956 (Kelley, *Monk* 227); it was a small club capable of seating seventy-six people—that is, legally (230). Among the white visual artists who came regularly were Willem de Kooning, Franz Kline, Alfred Leslie, Larry Rivers, Grace Hartigan, and Mike Goldberg, and some white writers like Jack Kerouac, Gregory Corso, Allen Ginsberg, and Frank O'Hara showed up at times as well (227). Kelley writes that "during the Five Spot's formative stage, the scene was nearly all-white and mostly male" (227). Ted Joans and Amiri Baraka were among the first blacks to frequent the club (227). David Amram, a white musician, brought Cecil Taylor and other black musicians to the Five Spot. The revolution in black music began there with Cecil Taylor (228). But things did not start out well: After Cecil Taylor broke the club's ancient piano, Joe declared he did not want him ever to play there again. Feeling a kinship with the black iconoclastic musician, the abstract expressionists demanded that Taylor stay;

83

the painters found that Taylor was engaged in a radical art that was akin to theirs—that is, it "was abstract expressionism in sound" (228). Like Baraka, who was drawn to the white avant-garde because of their innovativeness, these artists were drawn to Taylor because of his sound, but as the story unfolds, we see that these practices do not always concur. Still, "it was in the winter of 1956 that Cecil Taylor, there only by the insistence of the [white] artists, turned the Five Spot into the city's leading venue for experimental jazz, [mostly black music]" (228).

They were many outstanding black innovative musicians playing at the Five Spot over the years, including Ornette Coleman, Eric Dolphy, Randy Weston, Jaki Byard, Sunny Murray, and Charles Mingus, but the magic came with one Thelonious Monk, advanced bebop pianist and his quartet. Monk had two long gigs there, "the first late spring in the summer of 1957, with that beautiful quartet consisting of John Coltrane, Wilbur Ware and Shadow Wilson" (Baraka, *Black Music* 28), and from June 1963 to February 1964 with a different group—Frankie Dunlop on drums, Butch Warren on bass, and Charlie Rouse on saxophone (31) at the new location at 2 St. Marks Place. Baraka was there almost every night. Night after night, he scrutinized not only Monk but also his entire quartets. As Kelley writes, "Baraka didn't just come to dig the music; he *studied* Monk" ("What" 103). What does he learn there? What transforms him as a poet there? For the answer, I first turned to Baraka's quintessential work on the new music, *Black Music* (1968), and in particular to his 1963 essay "Recent Monk."

Being there during the historic thirteen-week run, Baraka observed: "Anyone who witnessed the transformation that playing with Monk sent John Coltrane through (opening night he was struggling with all the tunes), must understand the deepness and musical completeness that can come to a performer under the Monk influence" (*Black Music* 29). For Baraka, Monk is the great teacher of the radical elements of advanced bop and the blues traditions: He embodies both the most advanced and the oldest aspects of the African American musical tradition. In short, Monk was the head teacher, in a way that evokes how Charles Olson, even though not usually on the scene, was at 27 Cooper Square. Monk and Olson articulated the values of their respective places. And over time, Monk is not only Coltrane's teacher but also Baraka's: He is the teacher of the tradition. By using him as his model, Baraka could be both radical and black, and as such, he could escape white hegemony. In Baraka's essay "High Priest of BeBop," from his masterful impressionistic jazz writings, *Digging: The Afro-American Soul of American Classical Music* (2009), he more fully affirms Monk's place in the jazz tradition than in the earlier essay. He observes,

Monk's deep traditionalism allowed him to go as far out as he wanted to, yet shape what he did with something familiar as our collective memory. Something like "Four in One" . . . goes off into the Monkesphere alright, but at the same time sounds like Jelly Roll or James P. Johnson. Like we say, "in the Tradition," demonstrating continuously that time and space were an illusion squares hemmed you in with. (233)

Moreover, hearing the new music in general at the Five Spot was an educational experience for many. The poet Ira Sadoff, who was at the Five Spot in the summer of 1961, recalled on Facebook, "Now that was an education, tuition $3.50 at the bar, saw Baraka there of course, mostly from a distance."

Similarly, Lorenzo Thomas's poem about the Five Spot and the new music is appropriately called "An Education." The poem begins: "Our academy was the 5 Spot's FIRE door" (*Collected Poems* 486, line 1). Iggy Termini, one of the brothers who owned the Five Spot, left the fire door open because it was hot in the club; he also did so to allow people who could not pay to hear the music. Izzy was generous in that way, which is not typical of many club owners— Baraka even liked him. Thomas was a young poet and could only afford to pay once a month, so he camped out at the fire door, which allowed him to get his education. So what was this education? In the poem, he mentions a number of fine musicians who played the new music there; he calls Sunny Murray, the great drummer, a

> Soft-spoken Socrates
> In frayed blue jeans the essence of the Blues
> No love, he says, no money
> His own music too strange
> Even for sessions in the afternoon. (3–7)

Thomas is saying the new music comes out of the blues but in a radical new form. The poem ends:

> But the music was never so sweet
> As those hot nights
> When we eavesdropped
> As genius told the spirits
> Just how we humans feel (26–30)

Thomas learns the blues tradition; in essence, he learns how it feels to be human. The blues teaches how it feels to be human in terms of a specific culture—that is, it is black before it is universal. The collective pronoun *we* appears twice in the poem. First, it describes the group too poor to enter the club (the young artists); the second time, it defines humanity as a whole. The new music is teaching black poets how to be part of the tradition in a radical new way. Interestingly, Thomas does not mention Monk. Perhaps Monk was never there when Thomas was—the education was what counted.

Baraka says: "Of all the bop greats, Monk's influence seems second only to that of Charlie Parker among the younger musicians" (*Black Music* 28). That is, Monk is the figure behind the academy, the master teacher. And Baraka is likewise a teacher of the new music. The black Beat poet Ted Joans also sat at the Five Spot every set during the time Ornette Coleman was there. Baraka taught him how to listen to Coleman. Joans said: "[Baraka] told me to listen to Ornette's sounds not the notes and don't try to find conventional chordal structures or traditional solo structures. This bit of advice and some more true digging turned me onto Ornette" (*Poet Painter* 21). But in Baraka's liner notes to *Thelonious Monk Quartet with John Coltrane at Carnegie Hall*, he says:

> Of even more curious delight is that one can see how Trane's residency with that great band influenced the teacher as well. Check Monk's expansive backup arpeggios on "Monk's Mood," matching Trane's multi-noted zoom. "Epistrophy" shows the exactness the well-honed match that playing together over an extended period can produce. (6)

Even though Monk is the teacher, he is also the student in this highly disciplined interchange.

Monk is the door to The Out and The Gone—to evoke Baraka's 2007 volume of tales. As stated earlier, for Baraka, Monk is the guru in the house of jazz, connecting the jazz musicians to the foundations of the music and suggesting ways to achieve those connections. In "High Priest of BeBop," Baraka declares, "But Monk seemed to take me all the way where I wanted to go. . . . Monk was weird past just funny. Monk was 'deep,' 'heavy.' And in my unwinding literary mind, that was the quality I seemed to seek" (*Digging* 225). In his writings, Baraka wanted to emulate Monk in his radical weirdness, in his black avant-gardism. The artist Theodore Harris, an artist friend of Baraka's said on Facebook, "To Amiri, to be 'out' was his way of saying Avant-Garde." Monk and the other boppers were crazy, but "what was wrong with crazy, if sane in the late '40s and early '50s meant Harry Truman and Dwight D. Eisenhower?" (*Digging* 224). "For Monk," Baraka continues, "the seed was the blues, not just as genre or form, but as the emotional essence of its origins as feeling, as the self-conscious interior of the objective experience. . . . Blues as the deepest reservoir of black emotion" (229). For the jazz poet, the blues reflects the essence of black culture. He concludes: "The point too is that Monk never let anybody ban his oom boom ba boom" (234). This final sentence leads us to "Wise 1," from Baraka's epic poem, *Wise, Why's, Y's* (1995), which ends thusly:

> they ban your
> oom ba boom
> you in deep deep
> trouble
>
> humph!
>
> probably take you several hundred years
> to get
> out. (7, lines 12–19)

In a book that covers the history of blacks in America, this poem reflects on the period of slavery. White enslavers try to ban the "Oom ba boom," the talking drum; they try to destroy black cultural expression. "Humph!" is a title of a Monk song, which suggests inventiveness, wit, and the vernacular. In this poem, Baraka is declaring that Monk's New World Africanness, his and the culture's expression, cannot be destroyed.

There exists a famous photo of the Five Spot by Burt Glinn.[1] It is 1957. On the right side there is a white jazz musician, David Amram, the person responsible for bringing Cecil Taylor to the club, in deep concentration, playing a French horn with his cheeks puffed out. In front of him is a room packed with attentive listeners, mostly men. The room is not equally divided between blacks and whites, but there are many blacks there and everybody seems relaxed. This is a place that Baraka could feel comfortable in, at least for a while.

The Five Spot was a different dwelling place from 27 Cooper Square. Different values dominated. White avant-garde genius dominated the house at Cooper Square, and even though it was a mixed club owned by two white brothers, black artistic genius dominated the Five Spot: Black genius set the standards, not white genius. At 27 Cooper Square, Baraka, perhaps unconsciously, took on white aesthetic standards and values. Baraka says in 1965, "Having read all of whitie's books, I wanted to be an authority on them. Having been taught that art was 'what white men did,' I almost became one, to

---

1. You can see it here: http://blues.gr/profiles/blogs/ribute-to-david-amram-one-of-the-greatest-composers-conductor?overrideMobileRedirect=1.

have a go at it" (*Home* 10). His new teachers, headed by Monk, allowed him to follow his tradition, let him write in his own language, and freed him from fashioning his words "in the alien language of another tribe" (*Tales* 90). The music, like James Brown's, lets him identify with "a place and image in America" (*Black Music* 185).

The poet-anthologist Arnold Adoff, who often attended the Five Spot and managed Charles Mingus for a while, said that the black musicians were validated, respected, and well paid at the club (Private Harris Journal, July 14, 2018). Baraka could learn radical black art there; he could be true to his tradition there. But the story is a bit more complicated. According to Allen Ginsberg, the New Jersey–based great modernist William Carlos Williams brought Baraka back to the sound of Newark. He says, "Williams's practice. It brought Jones back to Newark, in a sense. If any literary influence had tended in that direction, Williams's tended to bring Jones back home to his own speech and to his own soul and to his own body and to his own color and to his own town" (*Spontaneous* 269). Interestingly, in 1960 before Baraka's disillusionment with the New American Poetry, he articulated a similar position regarding Williams (Reilly 6). The music critic Frank Kofsky says that the new black music contains "the voice of the urban Negro ghetto" (134), and so does the new black poetry.

Like Hughes and Williams, Baraka finds authenticity in the working class. But in the same way that Monk helped him get there, Williams provided techniques that would be helpful in creating the new poetry. In spite of Baraka's feelings that the white avant-garde was taking him away from his people, it still provided innovative modes and ideas that allowed him to incorporate the new music into his poetry—that is, both the black and white avant-gardes got him "home."

Yet Ginsberg overstates the case: Williams is a gateway, not an end—the new music is the end or beginning. Monk and the new music provided a communal and cultural model for Baraka to use to write about his people and himself because it contains "the deepest reservoir of black emotion" (*Digging* 234). With and through the music, Baraka recovered his own soul and reconnected with the tradition. Moreover, Baraka needed a dwelling place nourished by black genius to fully become himself; he needed a space free from white hegemony; he needed a space where he could pick and choose among ideas; and he needed a space where he could embrace black vanguard art unencumbered, free from the dictates and controlling consciousness of the white avant-garde. Even though Williams helped him along the way, if he had not found the music, he would not have found himself, because the music is grounded in the black blues/jazz tradition, the tradition of the Blues People.

8
=

"Of Langston and Langston Manifestos"

Langston Hughes and the Revolutionary
Jazz Poetry of Amiri Baraka

JOHN LOWNEY

WHEN AMIRI BARAKA writes "of Langston and Langston Manifestos" in his 1982 long poem "In the Tradition," he suggests the importance of Hughes for his Third-World Marxist revolutionary jazz poetics. This celebration of Hughes is even more pronounced, and more specific, in the introduction to *Wise, Why's, Y's,* when Baraka cites the precedent of *Ask Your Mama: 12 Moods for Jazz* (along with Melvin Tolson's *Libretto for the Republic of Liberia,* William Carlos Williams's *Paterson,* and Charles Olson's *Maximus Poems*). Recent books by Meta DuEwa Jones, Kathy Lou Schultz, and Jean-Philippe Marcoux have made compelling arguments for reconsidering Hughes's impact on Baraka's poetry.[1] In arguing specifically for the influence of Hughes's long jazz poems, *Montage of a Dream Deferred* and *Ask Your Mama,* they have extended earlier historiographic studies of the New Black Poetry by critics such as Aldon Nielsen, James Smethurst, and Lorenzo Thomas.[2] This essay will consider how Baraka's later jazz poetry collected in

---

1. Jones discusses the importance of Hughes's jazz poetics, especially in his jazz sequences, for subsequent generations of African American jazz and spoken word poetry. Marcoux considers the specific continuity of *Ask Your Mama* with Baraka's later jazz poetry, while Schultz concentrates on the long poems of Tolson, Hughes, and Baraka (*Wise Why's Y's*).

2. See Nielsen, *Black Chant* and his chapter on Baraka in *Integral Music* (98–147); Smethurst, *The Black Arts Movement* and "Don't Say Goodbye"; and Thomas, especially his chapter on the Black Arts Movement (*Extraordinary Measures* 118–144).

The Music (1987), including "In the Tradition" (104–112), responds to Hughes's precedent. In doing so, however, I will emphasize the initial distance—and dissonance—between Baraka and Hughes as much as their shared purpose as radical jazz "griots," as Marcoux has written. I will begin by discussing their correspondence from the Hughes archives in the Beinecke Library, which demonstrates their ambivalence about each other in the early 1960s. I will then consider how Baraka's reassessment of Hughes's politics and poetics, after the 1973 publication of Hughes's *Good Morning Revolution: Uncollected Social Protest Writings,* informs his constructions of the black radical tradition in his later poetry. In asserting a tradition of black resistance that includes Hughes's jazz writing, "In the Tradition" accentuates how the construction of this tradition is as much an active process of recovery and reclamation as it is a belated act of affirmation. "In the Tradition" exemplifies what Houston A. Baker Jr. has defined as black "critical memory." Distinguishing critical memory from "nostalgic" accounts of the past, he writes that critical memory is the "very faculty of revolution . . . cumulative, collective maintenance of a record that draws into relationship significant instants of time past and the always uprooted homelessness of now" ("Critical Memory" 7).[3] Through his revisionary linking of Hughes's radical social criticism with his own Marxist writing in the 1970s and 1980s, Baraka furthermore insists on an ongoing black liberation struggle that expands the historical and geographical parameters most commonly identified with the civil rights movement in the US.

In one of the most thoughtful considerations of Baraka's reputation after his January 2014 death, Marlon Ross wrote in *Callaloo* that, like Hughes, Baraka was a "larger-than-life public persona," which made it seem like "the truth about him . . . is assumed to be settled, answerable." Also like Hughes, "the extraordinary literary success of his youth encouraged his readers and critics to assume a fixed decline in the later work" ("Baraka's Truth" 473). Most of the Baraka obituaries written in the mainstream mass media confirm Ross's claims, as he is repeatedly labeled as "controversial." The primary evidence of his "incendiary" role as a public figure, as a "poet and playwright of pulsating rage" and "political firebrand," as Margalit Fox wrote for the *New York Times,* was of course his leadership as a radical black nationalist in the 1960s and early 1970s. There is minimal attention in the mainstream obituaries to his

---

3. Baker articulates the concept of "critical memory" in the influential 1995 collection *The Black Public Sphere.* Writing specifically about the legacy of the Reverend Dr. Martin Luther King Jr., he differentiates the allegorical rhetoric of nostalgia, which is "a purposive construction of a past filled with golden virtues, golden men and sterling events," from the rhetoric of critical memory, which "judges severely, censures righteously, renders hard ethical evaluations of the past that it never defines as well-passed" ("Critical Memory" 7).

extraordinary impact on the New American and New Black Poetries, as an editor and writer prior to the Black Arts Movement. And the second half of his life as a writer barely exists in most accounts, except for the 2002 "controversy" of "Somebody Blew Up America," often represented anachronistically as further evidence of his black nationalist anger (and anti-Semitism). Ross's reflection on the public response to Baraka's life and death, including his own initial response, exemplifies the "critical memory" of those who answered such reductive portrayals of Baraka with more nuanced and appreciative considerations of his legacy. The numerous online commemorations that simultaneously critique the insufficiency and inaccuracy of the mainstream obituaries and reflect on the complexity of Baraka's life attest to his profound impact on activists, artists, scholars, and students. One of the most insightful commemorations, Jelani Cobb's "The Path Cleared by Amiri Baraka," actually occurred in the *New Yorker,* a magazine not often associated with Baraka's writing. Like Ross, Cobb relates Baraka to Hughes, primarily as writers who had "combed the black vernacular for literary value." Noting that Baraka's importance as a public figure exceeded familiar categories—he was "part trickster and part provocateur, a brilliant juggler of genres, ideas, and identities"—Cobb asserts that the title "In the Tradition" also describes the continuity of Baraka's commitment to black ancestral traditions. He concludes: "To cast Baraka as a superannuated sixties radical is to miss the point: he understood himself, rightly, as a single link in an ancestral chain that is older than slavery and unbroken by history's detours and convolutions."

Despite such acknowledgments of the comparable predicament of Baraka and Hughes as African American public figures, there has been limited scholarly consideration of Baraka's response to Hughes's writing. The reason for this is precisely the problem that Ross identifies: The Black Arts Baraka of the 1960s hardly resembles the Harlem Renaissance Hughes of the 1920s. And their later work has not received enough attention to transform these identifications of their literary personae. When considering Baraka, however, it is always important to ask: Which Baraka? And why? These questions also apply to Hughes: Which Hughes? And why? What makes Baraka's lifelong engagement with Hughes's writing so fascinating is his recognition that these questions are inevitably political and thus require renewed inquiry as social conditions change. More specifically, these questions are also questions of which Baraka or which Hughes is legible and which has been erased. The story of Baraka's reconsideration of Hughes is, then, a complicated story of the politics of cultural memory. It is also a peculiar story, as the trajectory of Baraka's career doesn't exactly conform to dominant narratives of late twentieth-century literary or cultural history.

Hughes admired Baraka's talent, but he was skeptical about his early association with the Beat movement. On the other hand, Baraka respected Hughes, but he was initially uncertain about his writing, which seemed more populist to him than modernist. One of their first exchanges concerned Hughes's dismissal of the Beats at the 1959 American Society for African Culture Black Writers' conference. "Who wants to be beat?" he asked. "Not Negroes" (qtd. in Rampersad 309). Yet he soon qualified this claim with praise for Baraka in his *Chicago Defender* column: "LEROI JONES represents color within the Beat generation very well because his poetry is good and the little magazine he publishes in the Village, 'Yungen,' is quite worth reading. With his beard he looks like Othello. Beat—but all reet!" (qtd. in Rampersad 311). Given this initial tension, it is not surprising that the early correspondence between Baraka and Hughes suggests a pattern of missed connections and missed opportunities.[4] Much of their correspondence consists of invitations to literary events followed by notes of regret for missing each other. Most of the correspondence concerns readings and publications, including Hughes's submissions to *Yugen* and *The Floating Bear* and his selections of Baraka's poetry for *New Negro Poets U.S.A.* And while the exchange is mostly cordial, the distance between the Lower East Side and Harlem seems vast. So many of Baraka's letters to Hughes conclude with a statement like "I've either got to write you a long letter . . . or come up to see you as soon as I can" (April 29, 1959). And Hughes's letters to Baraka repeatedly close with invitations "to come up and have a drink" (March 29, 1960). It is strange enough to read written correspondence between writers who were both living in Manhattan, but it is stranger to see how many times they almost meet but do not. According to Baraka, when they finally do meet, at the Village Vanguard in 1959, Hughes was unaware that Jones was Jones because the noise was too loud to hear his name when he introduced himself (Rampersad 310–11).

Their correspondence from the Beinecke Library begins with a Baraka postcard inviting Hughes to a reception and reading for the then new little magazine *Yugen* in 1958 (May 5, 1958). While he did not attend the reception, Hughes subsequently wrote to Baraka and inquired about submitting some poems to the journal he persistently (and revealingly) called "*Yungen*" (May 26, 1958). While none of his poems were published in *Yugen*, Hughes later submitted a sequence from *Ask Your Mama* to *The Floating Bear*, the successor to *Yugen* that Baraka co-edited with Diane di Prima. With the submission

---

4. The Hughes–Baraka correspondence is in the Langston Hughes Papers, in the James Weldon Johnson Collection of the Beinecke Rare Book and Manuscript Library at Yale University. All references to this correspondence will be cited by the date of the letter.

of this sequence, "Horn of Plenty," on April 27, 1961, Hughes wrote: "Perhaps the enclosed sequence from ASK YOUR MAMA might be of interest to THE FLOATING BEAR—since the dozens are still news to lots of people" (*Selected Letters* 371). While the dozens apparently were not news enough for Baraka to publish "Horn of Plenty," one wonders how publication of *Ask Your Mama* in the interracial avant-garde context of *The Floating Bear* might have affected its reception. *Ask Your Mama* was published later in 1961 by Knopf, and while Hughes's book-length jazz sequence received mixed reviews, its first section, "Cultural Exchange," was reprinted in Dudley Randall's important anthology, *The Black Poets*, in 1971. It was also excerpted in Hughes's posthumous remix of earlier poems with his 1960s poems, *The Panther and the Lash: Poems of Our Times* (1967). Given that the musical structure and vernacular discursive mix of *Ask Your Mama* were aesthetically closer to Baraka's poetry than any previous Hughes book, Baraka's apparent silence about its publication is notable, even as many other readers were perplexed about its jazz enactment of the dozens.

Much of the correspondence initiated by Hughes between 1960 and 1964 concerns Baraka's inclusion in the anthology *New Negro Poets U.S.A.*, which, like many anthologies, took forever to assemble and publish. Given the momentous changes in African American culture that took place with the civil rights movement in the early 1960s, the poetry in the delayed anthology seemed almost anachronistic.[5] Nonetheless, Hughes's role in expanding the audience for a younger generation of African American poets was significant. The correspondence between Hughes and Baraka during these years also became increasingly political and increasingly revealing about their generational differences. In a letter dated March 17, 1960, with the heading "The Irish Marched," Hughes wrote:

> I'm just back from reading poetries in Georgia, and about to take off on another Southern Lecture tour. Those college kids down there are TREMEN-DOUS! The day I was in Atlanta the cops came charging into the A. U. campus drug store with a police dog and ordered all *"loiterers"* out. Not a soul left, asked for a definition of the word, *loitering,* threatened to kick the police DOG in the teeth. So the cops, redfaced, left—but said they'd be back. Hadn't up to the weekend, when I departed.
>
> I told the Morehouse-Spelman literati to get YUNGEN and read somebody new—YOU, etc . . . ." (March 17, 1960)

---

5. See Rampersad 375 on the reception of *New Negro Poets U.S.A.*

While Hughes reached out to Baraka as a younger writer, Baraka appealed to Hughes's experience when he made his transformative trip to Cuba in 1960. He discussed his meeting with Nicolás Guillen, and wrote to Hughes: "If the travel ban is lifted (& I have hopes that Senor Kennedy may lift it) you really ought to visit Cuba & see for yrself all the beautiful things going on down there. As apolitical as I was . . . I was deeply moved" (February 4, 1961). The social questions raised in these two exemplary letters suggest how timely the African diasporic scope of *Ask Your Mama* was, as they also foreshadow the increasingly political and international turn of Baraka's writing.

Hughes supported Baraka at least through 1964: He wrote a letter to support Baraka's application for a Whitney Foundation Fellowship, and he recommended the publication of *Blues People* as a reader for William Morrow. He even defended Baraka when he was charged, as editor of *The Floating Bear*, with sending "obscene materials through the mails." The "obscene material" was an issue of *The Floating Bear* that included an excerpt of *The System of Dante's Hell*, which had been sent to a young poet who was incarcerated in New Jersey. Coincidentally, the October 30, 1961, Baraka letter requesting Hughes's testimony for his "all around good fellowship and small talents" and the "integrity and seriousness" of *The Floating Bear* concludes with yet another account of a missed opportunity to meet: "I got up to the book party (bought a book) and sat down and listened to the Calypso. I wanted to stay longer and get to talk to you but I had to shoot down to a poetry reading a friend of mine (Robt Creeley) was giving at the YMHA." The book party Baraka mentions was probably for *The Best of Simple* (Rampersad 342), as Hughes's response to Baraka's request invokes the street smarts of Simple in his criticism of Baraka's questionable judgment:

> What I'll never understand is <u>why</u> did you-all send that particular BEAR to a guy in jail? Prisons have all kinds of stipulations as what an inmate CANNOT receive, including literature on SEX, RACE, POLITICS, and stuff—and the wardens read <u>all</u> incoming mail. I've got lots of jailhouse fans—some can't even send candy unless it comes from the factory! As for literature (that ain't Simple) God forbid! (November 1, 1961)

Hughes's tone is unmistakably paternal in his admonishment of Baraka, even as his anger expresses his own experience of authoritarian censorship. At the same time, there is a hint of African American literary solidarity with Baraka in the doubleness of the parenthetical Simple reference. Hughes acknowledges the presumably subversive threat of "literature that ain't Simple," while also underscoring his own expression of social criticism through the character—and language—that is deceptively "Simple."

Despite Hughes's growing reservations about the "obscene" language of Baraka's writing, which he expressed most publicly in a *New York Post* column called "That Boy LeRoi" (1965), Hughes continued to support Baraka. Baraka likewise treated Hughes respectfully, especially when he moved to Harlem, proposing to include him in planning the Black Arts Repertory Theatre programming. He wrote in 1965: "We want you to help us with the Black Arts as much as you're able" (undated 1965). Hughes was neither able nor especially willing to help with the Black Arts. As Baraka was moving uptown, Hughes was traveling through Europe and Africa on behalf of the US State Department. He was also becoming weary of the increasingly violent rhetoric of the Black Power movement. In 1967, Hughes's final books would be published, *The Panther and the Lash* and *Black Magic: A Pictorial History of the Negro in American Entertainment*. Two years later, Baraka would also publish a book called *Black Magic*. His *Black Magic* would not only eclipse Hughes's standing as an African American poet, it would also become a definitive text of the Black Arts Movement.

It is tempting to characterize Baraka's literary relationship with Hughes as evidence of the younger poet's "anxiety of influence." As Smethurst has written, Hughes was an "artistic *and* a political confidant and parental-figure" for Baraka and other writers associated with the Black Arts ("'Don't Say'" 1231). There is limited evidence, however, of Hughes's influence on Baraka's early poetry. It is William Carlos Williams, not Hughes, whom Baraka credits for learning how to "write in my own language—how to write the way I *speak* rather than the way I *think* a poem ought to be written—to write just the way it comes to me, in my own speech, utilizing the rhythms of speech rather than any metrical concept" (Ossman 6). Strangely, Baraka learned to employ the black vernacular in his poetry from white avant-garde poets such as Williams and Pound rather than black vernacular poets such as Hughes. If, as William J. Harris argues, Baraka's poetry revises that of his white poetic "fathers" and, in doing so, "transforms white forms and ideas into black ones through a jazz process" (*Poetry and Poetics* 16), how does such a "jazz process" relate to the poetry of a black poetic "father" such as Hughes? The answer—or answers—to this question underscore how misleading assertions of "influence" can be without specific attention to the historical circumstances informing reception and revision. Baraka was neither a "Beat" nor a "Black Arts" avant-garde poet forever, and the Hughes who became most important for him later was invisible to him during the older poet's lifetime.

When asked about Hughes in a 1976 interview with Werner Sollors, Baraka described him as one of his "main inspirations" (Sollors 249). And when he was asked in 1982 who his "most useful poetic influence" was, he answered, "Langston Hughes" (Melhem, "Revolution" 209). This recognition of Hughes seems remarkable, given their aesthetic and political differences after the emergence of the Black Arts Movement. So what happened? To put it simply, Baraka became a Marxist. And *Hughes* became a Marxist. By the mid-1970s, Baraka had become committed to Third-World Marxism as a revolutionary writer and activist.

Coinciding with this transformation was the publication of Hughes's *Good Morning Revolution* (in 1973), which featured poetry and prose that was *not* included in the *Selected Poems* or *The Langston Hughes Reader*. This collection, as editor Faith Berry wrote, reminds us that Hughes "wrote some of the most revolutionary works by any American writer of his generation" (xix). But it also reminds us that Hughes's reputation as the "poet laureate of the Negro race" excluded his revolutionary writing, which supposedly "represented an aberration, an isolated phase of his early career" (xix). Berry asserts and documents that this presumed "passing phase" of Hughes's career "actually lasted as long as he lived" (xix). The story of Hughes's interrogation by Joseph McCarthy's Senate Permanent Sub-Committee on Investigations is now well known.[6] Hughes's career as a writer and speaker was at stake, and he experienced censorship of his books and hostility at public appearances despite his cooperation with the subcommittee.[7] One result of this censorship was the limited and distorted memory of his most overtly revolutionary writing. Baraka notes the personal cost of this censorship for his own development as a writer: "The problem that I see is that that is 30 years of actual struggle, personal struggle. Given a good socialist education, I would have had *that* to build on" (Sollors 252). According to Baraka, *Good Morning Revolution* was "absolutely contemporary, as strong as any work I have seen by an American poet and very carefully hidden by American literary marshals" (Sollors 249). Baraka might be the only reader who described *Good Morning Revolution* as "absolutely contemporary" in the mid-1970s, and this unlikely convergence of the Marxist Baraka with the Marxist Hughes is understandably underappreciated.

---

6. The most comprehensive account of Hughes's interrogation can be found in Chinitz, which includes transcripts of Hughes's executive session testimony and his public testimony.

7. As Berry writes, after the McCarthy hearings, "Hughes's name was on a list of 'un-American' authors whose books were banned from U.S.I.A. libraries throughout the world. His books were also banned from the schools and libraries of certain states that passed anti-Communist laws" (xxi).

Baraka's reflections on the disappearance of Hughes's Marxist writings remain relevant, however, for his own poetry as well as Hughes's. Baraka, like many radical writers of his generation, had considered Hughes as "some kind of liberal spokesman," who had compromised his principles before the McCarthy Committee to protect his livelihood as a writer. The unavailability of Hughes's "Un-American" writings accentuated what Baraka called the "problem of history . . . the question of not being able to benefit from history" (Sollors 249, 253). As I will suggest, this "problem of history" animates the recovery and reconstruction of the black radical past in Baraka's later poetry, most notably in historiographic long poems such as "In the Tradition." It is no coincidence, then, that "In the Tradition" resembles the Hughes poem that Baraka could have published, *Ask Your Mama*. In recalling *Ask Your Mama* through the formal and rhetorical patterns of his own long poem, Baraka restores the radical continuity of Hughes's poetry, from his overtly Marxist protest writings through his more covertly radical jazz sequences.

The volume of Baraka's writing that engages with Hughes's precedent most intensively is *The Music: Reflections on Jazz and Blues* (1987). *The Music* features a section of poetry by Amina Baraka (Baraka's wife), followed by a section of poetry by Amiri Baraka, then his *Primitive World: An Anti-Nuclear Jazz Musical*, and concludes with a sequence of essays, reviews, and liner notes on black music, mostly jazz. It also includes illustrations of jazz performance by Vincent D. Smith and photographs of musicians by Stephanie Myers. Among the poems included is "In the Tradition," which was originally published separately as a pamphlet in 1982. Baraka cites Hughes, along with W. E. B. Du Bois and Frederick Douglass, in defining the significance of "the music" in his introduction. He in fact begins the book with a Hughes quote that introduces the collective importance of "the music" for African American culture: "Langston Hughes said, 'I want to capture the form and content of Negro Music.' Profundity rides profundity and our access, he instructed, is our most naturally extended and essential lives" (13). Hughes's literary adaptation of jazz is the primary precedent for Baraka's poetry in *The Music*, but he is also a link to earlier ancestors: Du Bois, whose *The Souls of Black Folk* is "the classic of structural diversity on a focused theme" (13), and Douglass, whose *Narrative* "laid his feelings, perception, and rationale, which can still instruct us as deeply as any sound" (15). All of these figures emphasize the power of African American music to sustain, emotionally and socially, a commitment to black liberation as well as a cultural continuity with African cultural traditions.[8]

---

8. Baraka makes similar claims about Hughes's revolutionary role in African American literary history in an earlier essay, "The Revolutionary Tradition in Afro-American Literature," which was published in *Daggers and Javelins* (1984). He emphasizes how "The Negro

The presence of Hughes's poetics is noticeable throughout *The Music,* in the formal practice of Baraka's jazz poetry and in the essays about jazz history, in which Baraka insists on the blues basis of jazz expression:

> Jazz incorporates blues, not just as a specific form, but as a cultural insistence, a feeling-matrix, a tonal memory. Blues is the national consciousness of jazz—its truthfulness in a lie world, its insistence that it is itself, its identification as the life expression of a specific people, the African-American nation. So that at its strongest and most intense and indeed most advanced, jazz expresses the highest consciousness of that people itself, combining its own history, as folk form and expression, with its more highly developed industrial environment, North America. (263–264)

While Baraka's claims for the blues are more explicitly Marxist than Hughes's, and more explicitly Marxist than his earlier claims in *Blues People,* there is considerable continuity between his understanding of the blues as African American "tonal memory" and the cultural significance of the blues that Hughes asserts, even as early as "The Negro Artist and the Racial Mountain."[9] There is also considerable continuity between the avant-garde African American jazz that Baraka promotes in the early 1980s (e.g., Arthur Blythe, David Murray, and Henry Threadgill) and the earlier generation of Charles Mingus and Randy Weston that Hughes favored in the later 1950s and 1960s. The poetry that invokes Hughes in *The Music* recognizes his precedent as a jazz poet primarily through its formal devices, but there are also three significant poems in which Hughes appears by name: "The Rare Birds," "I Love Music,"

Artist and the Racial Mountain" extends Du Bois's "total rejection of American racial paternalism and cultural aggression." Hughes, along with McKay, exemplifies the revolutionary nationalist implications of Harlem Renaissance literature: "It is a literature of the new city dwellers having left their rural pasts. It is a literature of revolt, it is anti-imperialist, and fights the cultural aggression that imperialism visits upon its colonial and nationally oppressed conquests—first by reflecting and proclaiming the beauty and strengths of the oppressed people themselves" (*Daggers* 317). The Harlem Renaissance, then, and Hughes's contribution specifically, was modern, urban, and nationalist. Baraka's Marxist revaluation of the Harlem Renaissance also insists on its internationalism, its influence on African diasporic culture worldwide, and its engagement with "oppressed nations and colonial peoples," most notably Haiti, where Hughes and McKay were recognized as influences on the *indigisme* movement. Baraka also notes the importance of Hughes's involvement with the Communist Party USA, evident in *Good Morning Revolution,* even though he subsequently "copped out before the inquisitors of HUAC" ("Revolutionary" 318).

9. As Smethurst notes, Hughes was most important for Black Arts writers who "posited a continuum of African-American culture from Africa to the U. S. present, including folk, popular, and avant-garde elements" ("'Don't Say'" 1229). While "The Negro Artist and the Racial Mountain" suggests this continuum, *Ask Your Mama* and Hughes's later essays on jazz define this continuum more explicitly.

and "In the Tradition." All of these poems situate Hughes within a jazz context, and in doing so, they play an active role in revising and renewing his reputation.

Although Hughes appears only briefly in "The Rare Birds" (80), he is distinctively situated within an interracial modernist canon of literary, jazz, and visual artists. "The Rare Birds" is dedicated to second-generation New York School poet Ted Berrigan, reminding us of Baraka's earlier close relationship with Frank O'Hara and the New York School more generally. Like O'Hara's (and Berrigan's) poetry, "The Rare Birds" is notable for its abundance of proper names. "The Rare Birds" also has an elegiac tone of "listening to another time," not unlike O'Hara's "The Day Lady Died." The music that Baraka remembers, though, is the music of such "birds" as "Yard and / Bean, or Langston grinning at you" (lines 5–6). While this brief but affectionate image of Hughes is more suggestive than definitive, he is clearly identified with the jazz tradition of Charlie "Yardbird" Parker and Coleman "Bean" Hawkins. But the poem also constructs a modernist collection of "rare birds" from the visual arts, "Brancusian" (9) birds, birds that evoke "that guy Pablo" (12), and "Jake's / colored colorful Colorado colormore colorcolor" (9–10), the "birds and their grimaces" (11) from Jacob Lawrence's Great Migration series. "Rare Birds" also quotes William Carlos Williams on "the smallness of this American century" (15). And while it is Williams who bridges the New York School interest in the visual arts with Baraka's vernacular poetics, the poem concludes with a more oblique reference to an unnamed "very rare bird" (21) whose influence likewise exceeds the aesthetic categories and traditions that Baraka invokes, the composer/musician of "*Impressions,*" John Coltrane (*The Music* 80). The title track of this album was first recorded at Coltrane's legendary November 1961 performance at the Village Vanguard. "Impressions" exemplifies Coltrane's practice of adapting unlikely compositions, in this case a theme from Morton Gould's popular 1939 *American Symphonette,* into profoundly expressive and often expansive performances. Coltrane is the jazz model for Baraka's transformation of "white forms and ideas into black ones through a jazz process" (Harris, *Poetry and Poetics* 16). As the "very rare bird" who translates the blues as well as "white" popular music into a transformative art whose "message" crosses musical boundaries, Coltrane inspires the jazz poet who extends the language of earlier birds such as Hughes and Williams into an ongoing "tradition of the new."[10]

---

10. Like the jazz "tradition of the new" that Baraka celebrates in "Blues, Poetry, and the New Music" from *The Music,* "The Rare Birds" exemplifies how his poetry "reinforces the most valuable memories of a people but at the same time creates new forms, new modes of expression, to more precisely reflect contemporary experience" (*The Music* 267).

While "The Rare Birds" is an oblique Coltrane poem that locates Hughes within an interracial jazz modernism, "I Love Music" (47–48) emphasizes a correlation between Coltrane and Hughes more overtly. "I Love Music" primarily celebrates Coltrane, as an inspirational "force for real good" (line 1) whose "love supreme" (15) is no less moving than it was in his lifetime. It thus recalls the elegiac association of Coltrane with Malcolm X in earlier Black Arts poetry, including Baraka's "AM/TRAK" (*Reader* 267–272), which characterizes Coltrane as "the spirit of the 60's / He was Malcolm X in New Super Bop Fire" (271, lines 255–256). The late Coltrane of "I Love Music," however, evokes a socialist utopian vision, a vision that celebrates Hughes as a sustaining ancestral presence. In rhythmically complex lines that evoke the expressive range and virtuosity of Coltrane, Baraka introduces Hughes as the culminating figure of an international pantheon of revolutionary figures. "Because of trane," he writes:

can be
sean ocasey in Ireland
can be, lu hsun in china
can be,
    brecht wailing
        gorky   riffing
           langston hughes steaming
              can be
            trane. (40–51)

Situating Hughes in this all-star band of socialist modern writers is a tribute to his own prior example of blending jazz and poetry: "Because of trane," Baraka can imagine such a band, but also because of Hughes, Baraka can imagine that "because of trane," he can imagine such a band. These lines distinctively resemble the "Bird in Orbit" mood in *Ask Your Mama,* in which Charlie Parker acts as the guiding star for an international galaxy of black liberation figures, African as well as African American. Baraka's subsequent reference to "trane" as "bird's main man" (52) furthers this intertextual tribute to *Ask Your Mama:* As "trane" inventively extends the bebop of "bird," "I Love Music" signifies on the signifying of *Ask Your Mama,* "all of it meaning, essence revelation, everything together, wailing in unison / a terrible / wholeness" (59–61).

Ask Your Mama is a curious intertext for the poetry of *The Music,* given Baraka's apparent disinterest in Hughes's long poem when it was first published and its disappearance from public discussion soon afterward. While it attracted a number of mostly perplexed reviews, there was hardly any subsequent discussion of its innovative formal blend of poetry and jazz prior to *The Music*. As Arnold Rampersad has written, "No scholar, whether black or white, apparently was prepared to take the poem seriously. No one was challenged sufficiently by its allusions and references, or by its possible novelty as a fusion of jazz and literary language" (344). Its structure is deceptively simple, as it consists of a dozen movements based on the recurring theme of "The Hesitation Blues," each of which rhetorically enacts the vernacular form of "the dozens." Each movement is also written as a score for performance, with specific marginal musical instructions juxtaposed with the lines of poetry. The marginal notes and the voices, scenes, and sections of the poem invoke a remarkable mix of music from the African diaspora and of sites of contemporaneous and earlier struggles for black liberation, in Africa, Europe, the Caribbean, and Latin America as well as the US. There are even end notes, or "liner notes," although they complicate rather than explicate each movement. With its unprecedented form and encyclopedic allusiveness to the diasporic history of black music, *Ask Your Mama* posed challenges even to readers with the expertise of Baraka. Only readers with a comprehensive knowledge of African diasporic music *and* history were able to appreciate the rhetorical complexity of Hughes's long poem.[11]

The poem from *The Music* that most dramatically invokes *Ask Your Mama* is "In the Tradition." Lorenzo Thomas has noted that "In the Tradition" extends the rhetorical strategy of celebratory "list making and repetition" that occurs in African American historiographic poetry as early as Melvin Tolson's "Dark Symphony" (*Extraordinary* 159). "In the Tradition" has also been read as an avant-garde Third-World Marxist text that extends as it politically transforms the Pan-Africanist poetics of Black Arts cultural nationalism.[12] Only Marcoux, however, has argued specifically for the precedent of *Ask Your Mama* for "In the Tradition," as an "intravernacular" historiographic long poem that enacts jazz performance as a revolutionary process of reclaiming black history.[13] As

11. See the discussion of the reception of *Ask Your Mama* in Lowney 565–566 and 584–585 (note 5). A representative selection of reviews can be found in Dace 635–646. Most reviewers of *Ask Your Mama* in mainstream newspapers and magazines were confused by its jazz form and/or its multiple allusions. African American reviewers were more likely to appreciate the performative structure of *Ask Your Mama* as well as its references to African American (and African diasporic) history and popular culture.

12. Harris initiated discussion of the avant-garde implications of "In the Tradition" (*Poetry and Poetics* 112–117). Kim develops the most compelling and comprehensive analysis of the Marxist avant-garde poetics of "In the Tradition." Spahr extends this discussion in considering the revolutionary aesthetics of the poem (152–154).

13. In emphasizing how *Ask Your Mama* and "In the Tradition" exemplify the modern role of the African griot through their jazz testimony of African diasporic history and cultural lega-

I will suggest, "In the Tradition" also foregrounds the importance of revising and reinventing the jazz literary tradition, of tradition *making*, through its allusions to Hughes and to the formal and rhetorical strategies of *Ask Your Mama*.

While "In the Tradition" is dedicated to Arthur Blythe, its reclamation of his importance in jazz history is simultaneously a reclamation of *Ask Your Mama*—and "Langston" more generally—within a revolutionary black tradition of jazz poetry. The motif of Blythe's album title *In the Tradition* functions similarly to Hughes's "Hesitation Blues" in *Ask Your Mama*, and Baraka's poem similarly blends references to black music, literature, and activism to suggest a continuum of revolutionary forms of expression. Blythe's recording itself enacts a continuum of jazz history, with compositions by Fats Waller ("Jitterbug Waltz"), Duke Ellington ("In a Sentimental Mood" and "Caravan"), and John Coltrane ("Naima") as well as by Blythe himself. *In the Tradition* exemplifies the jazz that Baraka celebrates in *The Music*: "The new music reinforces the most valuable memories of a people but at the same time creates new forms, new modes of expression, to more precisely reflect contemporary experience" ("Blues," *The Music* 267). Citing David Murray, Henry Threadgill, the World Saxophone Quartet, the Art Ensemble of Chicago, Olu Dara, and Craig Harris as well as Blythe, Baraka argues for jazz that invokes the musical history of African America, especially through the "tonal memory" of the blues (263), while advancing the "tradition of the new" (267). This tradition, personified by Coltrane in the 1960s, is implicitly a tradition of resistance as well as improvisation. And like *Ask Your Mama*, Baraka's "In the Tradition" accentuates earlier as well as contemporaneous modes of resistance.

Baraka dedicates "In the Tradition" specifically to "Black Arthur Blythe" (*The Music* 105), accentuating the "blackness" of his sound as much as the politics of naming. Blythe was listed as "Black Arthur Blythe" or "Black Arthur" on several recordings in the 1970s, and his formative experience as a musician in Los Angeles certainly positioned him within the Black Arts Movement. Before moving to New York and establishing his recording career as a lead musician, Blythe played with the pianist and bandleader Horace Tapscott in the 1960s and early 1970s. He was one of the founding members of the Union of God's Musicians and Artists Ascension, the Watts collective that was committed to the support of black performing and visual artists as well as to arts education. Baraka honors Blythe's considerable experience as a musician and activist through recognizing him as "Black Arthur," but he also

---

cies, Marcoux addresses how jazz poetry is "intravernacular" in its enactment of jazz sounds, phrasing, and patterns of improvisation in addition to its references to songs and musicians (7).

celebrates Blythe as an exemplary musician who in the late 1970s and early 1980s blended the early history of jazz, and especially the blues, with free jazz improvisation.[14] Because Blythe's music was grounded in African American folk forms even as it was associated with the post–free jazz loft scene in New York, Baraka identifies him as a key figure in the "class struggle" of 1970s jazz. Blythe resisted both the transformation of jazz into European concert music and the corporate pressure of jazz to conform to "the suffocating arena of middle-class unseriousness" (Baraka, "Jazz Writing," *The Music* 260). As an avant-garde musician whose sound was distinctively African American, Blythe epitomized what Baraka defines as "black music":

> But black music is an actual genre, whose most impressive styles and works have not only been created by the African-American people, but more importantly carry an aesthetic that is generally identifiable. For instance, it *swings* (is syncopated), it is *hot* (intense, rhythmic) even if it is presidentially insouciant. It is blues or bluesy or makes reference to blues (as life tone and cultural matrix). . . . It is improvised, and even its most Ducal arrangements and compositions provide room or allow for improvisation. ("Class Struggle," *The Music* 319)

Baraka identifies the "black music" that Blythe exemplified with the African American working class, as a music that represents the history of African America as a distinctive culture. He acknowledges the hybridity of African American music, but he underscores that "its main reference is itself," namely the history of black music and the social history from which it has emerged (320).[15]

Baraka's Marxist formulation of a populist jazz avant-garde certainly has implications for his poetry and for the history of jazz poetry more generally. In his introduction to a 1981 recording of his poetry with David Murray and Steve McCall, "*New Music–New Poetry*," Baraka defines poetry as "speech *musicked*," and the primary example he cites of "black music running into

---

14. Jazz critic Bill Shoemaker explains Blythe's identification as "Black Arthur Blythe" or "Black Arthur" in 1970s post–free jazz albums with India Navigation and Adelphi, prior to his contract with Columbia Records. Shoemaker notes that "at the time, the name was unremarkable to the extent that musicians changing or amending their name were a somewhat common experience. The fact that such consciousness movement-inspired name changes now are so rare may very well be a part of the legacy of the neo-cons' grasp on the generation that came after Blythe."

15. See Kim 356–357 for an incisive explanation of Blythe's significance for black avant-garde jazz in the late 1970s, specifically as an exemplary figure of what Stanley Crouch characterized as "Freedom Swing."

high speech" is Langston Hughes (*The Music* 244). Indeed, his explanation of his own "*poetrymusic*" (245) recalls Hughes's aspirational claims for African American poetry in "The Negro Artist and the Racial Mountain":

> The poetry I want to write is oral by tradition, mass aimed as its fundamental functional motive. Black poetry, in its mainstream, is oracular, sermonic; it incorporates the screams and shouts and moans and wails of the people inside and outside of the churches; the whispers and thunder vibrato and staccato of the inside and the outside of the people themselves, and it wants to be as real as anything else and as accessible as a song—a song about a real world, full of good and evil. (Baraka, "New Music," *The Music* 244)

Successful jazz poetry, then, or speech "*musicked,*" is "a song about a real world," but it is also music whose "main reference is itself." These two temporal axes for understanding jazz poetry, the present "real world" and the comprehensive history of black culture, inform the interpretive challenges of "In the Tradition." On the one hand, the poem is precisely oriented to the struggles of the "real world" of African American culture in the late 1970s and early 1980s, while on the other hand, it freely invokes names, sites, and movements throughout the history of the African diaspora. The recurring figure of "Black Arthur" keeps the poem both "real" and "traditional." Hughes meanwhile plays a more implicit role in Baraka's rendering of the tradition: Even though Hughes is mentioned only twice, *Ask Your Mama* figures as a formal "reference," but a reference that is renewed for the later twentieth century.

The challenge of interpreting the "real world" of "In the Tradition" is immediately apparent in the epigraph that follows the dedication to "Black Arthur Blythe": "*Not a White Shadow / But Black People / Will be Victorious*" (epigraph, lines 1–3). It is not immediately clear whether the "White Shadow" is "real" or a figure referring to African American history more generally. It becomes clearer soon after that the "White Shadow" refers to a popular television series contemporaneous with "In the Tradition," a series that featured a white basketball coach at a mostly black and Latino Los Angeles high school. The black art of basketball, of "skyman darrell / or double dippin hip doctors deadly in flight" (34–35), of "Magic or Kareem" (36), is only slowly introduced in contrast with the paternalistic "White Shadow." It is introduced within a densely allusive framework of contested images of African American popular culture, beginning with

Blues walk weeps ragtime
Painting slavery

women laid around
working feverishly for slavemaster romeos. (4–7)

The not-so-real world of the "White Shadow" is thus initially inserted within a too-real history of slavery and exploitation. Like the beginning of *Ask Your Mama*, "IN THE QUARTER OF THE NEGROES / WHERE THE DOORS ARE DOORS OF PAPER" (477, lines 3–4), the question of what's "real" is also a question of history, social and economic history, but also a history of representation. What's real depends on the medium and the economic basis of the medium, folk or mass, the testimony of the "blues" (67) or the "three networks idiot chatter" (41). And what's real depends on the perspective of the reader, with his or her knowledge of African American history and familiarity with the jazz poetic "tradition" of resistance to white supremacy.

Within the continuum of black creativity and racist exploitation that begins "In the Tradition" emerges the figure who reconciles the present with black history, Arthur Blythe. The tradition Blythe recalls is initially the tradition of slave revolt, the tradition of Douglass and

of David Walker
Garnett
Turner
Tubman. (48–52)

This tradition is closely aligned with the musical tradition of

Kings, & Counts, & Dukes
of Satchelmouths & SunRa's
of Bessies & Billies & Sassys
& Mas. (55–58)

The elaboration of this tradition that immediately follows celebrates new forms of black creativity, in a catalogue of rebels, race leaders, and writers, and of musicians whose expressive styles are evoked most extravagantly. This catalogue culminates in a crescendo of music and movement, of Blythe and basketball:

bee-doo dee doop bee-doo dee dooo doop (Arthur
tradition
of shooters
& silver fast dribblers

of real fancy motherfuckers
fancy as birds flight, sunward/high
    highhigh
    sunward
    arcs/swoops/spirals
in the tradition. (92–101)

Here, as elsewhere in the poem, "birds flight" suggests multiple forms of ascent, from the soaring sound of Blythe's saxophone to the graceful movement of black athletes to the determined flight to freedom evoked by the names of black activists.

Hughes stands out in "the tradition" as the first writer whose writing is named, initiating a catalogue that blends writing and music, literary artists and performing artists:

of Langston & Langston Manifestos
Tell us again about the negro artist
& the racial mountain so we will not
be negro artists, McKay Banjoes and
Homes in Harlem, Blue Black Boys &
Little Richard Wrights, Tradition of
For My People Margaret Walker & David Walker & Jr Walker. (107–113)

Baraka acknowledges the lasting influence of "The Negro Artist and the Racial Mountain" for black vernacular poetics, and the catalogue that follows locates that influence within a Marxist tradition of black writers. In accentuating the historical signification of the word "Negro," he also recalls the "Black Arts" of the 1960s, the generational tension between "Negro artists" and "Black artists." This tension is less emphatic, however, than the affirmation of what this tradition is "Basied on, we Blue Black wards strugglin / against a Big White Fog" (115–116). "Africa people," Baraka writes, "our fingerprints are / everywhere / on you America, our fingerprints are everywhere" (116–117). Generational differences, like diasporic cultural differences, are eventually less important than the shared commitment to resistance and self-determination that the poem asserts:

in the tradition
    of revolution
    Renaissance
    Negritude
    Blackness

Negrismo
Indigisme. (251–257)

This black internationalist tradition of celebrating African descent, with its corresponding modes of musical expression, suggests the intercultural literary work of Hughes as well as the Black Arts anticolonial commitment to black liberation worldwide, to an international as well as national "tradition of us / the reality not us the narrow fantasy" (264–265).

As "In the Tradition" concludes, the "wide panafrican / world" (120–121) that Baraka celebrates is identified explicitly with both Hughes and Blythe:

in the tradition of gorgeous africa blackness
says to us fight, it's all right, you beautiful
 as night, the tradition
thank you langstron/arthur
says sing
says fight
in the tradition, always clarifying, always new and centuries old. (306–312)

Although *Ask Your Mama* is not named in the poem, Baraka invokes Hughes's precedent through the African diasporic scope and rhetorical virtuosity of "In the Tradition." He furthermore invokes this precedent through a decidedly Marxist historiography that honors a black international list of Afrocentric writers associated with Hughes: "Cesaire, Damas, Depestre, Romain, Guillen" (131). As the jazz figure of "Black Arthur Blythe" renews "how / we is and bees / when we remember" (272–273), Baraka likewise restores Hughes to "our memory as the projection / of what is evolving / in struggle" (274–276). In dramatically enacting the revolutionary black tradition of "langstron/arthur" (309), Baraka not only recovers the radical continuity of Hughes's writing, he also asserts a continuity between his own writing and Hughes's that seemed so unlikely for the editor of *Yugen*—or "*Yungen*"—only two decades before.

9

Amiri Baraka and the Dream of Unity Music

GRÉGORY PIERROT

THAT AMIRI BARAKA'S poetry evolved in tune with his politics hardly needs to be stated. In his study of the first two decades of Baraka's writing career, Werner Sollors characterized Baraka's oeuvre as a "quest for populist modernism," aspiring to "a romantic unity of life and art, which must be wrested from 'bourgeois' systems of classification and separation of realms" (2). Throughout the journey that led him from the globally apolitical rejection of mainstream of his Beat years to Marxist-Leninism by way of black cultural nationalism, Baraka's changing convictions shaped verses increasingly designed with performance in mind and politics at heart. As Meta DuEwa Jones argues, Baraka's "work engages in a process of revision modeled upon the improvisatory ethos of jazz" ("Politics" 246). Yet if jazz as African American improvised music breathed its soul into Baraka's poetry, his own forays into music, notably his recordings, were not all New Thing. From the doo-wop harmonies of *Black & Beautiful, Soul & Madness* (1967) to his soul- and funk-inflected 1972 album *It's Nation Time* and late 1970s performances with funk band The Advanced Workers, Baraka showed time and again his readiness to engage with a broad spectrum of black music. As Jones makes clear, "a formal audio and visual analysis of Baraka's poetry-in-performance can potentially enrich our appreciation of his poetics" ("Politics" 246). In the same spirit, this essay will explore those recordings where Baraka engaged with popular African American musical genres in order to achieve the elusive dream of producing the "Unity music" he foresaw in his 1965 essay "The Changing Same" from *Black Music* (180–211).

For Baraka, music is "part of the answer to the question How did you get to be you?" (*Autobiography* 65). It was crucial to his personal growth and inspired him as he began writing poetry in the late 1950s in New York City's Greenwich Village, and soon it became such a staple in his own readings that fellow Beat and jazz poet Ted Joans claimed jazz readings to be Baraka's idea (Joans, "Le griot" 22). Baraka came to know and enjoy a variety of musical genres, yet the one that always featured most prominently was "*The Music,* meaning African American improvised music. What we've called, in our deeper moments, Jazz" (*Autobiography* 65). Baraka famously did much to promote free jazz musicians and their sound; as William J. Harris writes, "free jazz allowed Baraka . . . to come into a fuller sense of self, allowed him . . . both a musical and racial continuity in the discontinuity of the multiplicity of black sound" ("How You Sound??" 323). In this way the music is also irreversibly intertwined with Baraka's rising political consciousness and broader cultural and political radicalization at the turn of the 1960s: "It was in the air, it was in the minds of the people . . . coming out of people's horns, laid out in their music . . . there was a newness and a defiance, a demand for freedom, politically and creatively, it was all connected" (*Autobiography* 261). When he made the political decision to move to Harlem in 1964, Baraka found natural allies in the musicians he saw as a revolutionary artistic avant-garde: Uptown, Baraka founded the Black Arts Repertory Theatre, with the goal to create "an art that would reach the people," and among the first artists to follow him in his endeavor were free jazz musicians Sun Ra and Albert Ayler (*Autobiography* 298). The Black Arts Repertory Theatre took these streets by storm, offering poetry readings, dance spectacles, painting, and always music. Around the same time, Baraka began putting his musical readings to vinyl: In 1965, he contributed to the New York Art Quartet's self-titled debut album, reciting his poem "BLACK DADA NIHILISMUS" to their music. Later, Baraka's "Black Art" featured on Sunny Murray's *Sonny's Time Now* (the first release on Baraka's Newark-based independent record label Jihad Productions in 1967), providing a striking example of Baraka's "dramatic approach to recitation" (Nielsen, *Black Chant,* 191).

"Black Art" (*SOS* 149–150) opens with the infamously pithy pronouncement: "Poems are bullshit unless they are / teeth or trees or lemons piled / on a step" (lines 1–3), only to call for "poems like fists . . . dagger poems . . . Black poems" (12–15) and "Assassin poems" (20). The recording demonstrates just what those might sound like, merging Baraka's vocal evocations of strafing airplanes firing machine guns with Albert Ayler's high-pitched saxophone bursts. Much happens in Baraka's delivery of the last lines of the poem:

> We want a black poem. And a
> Black World.
> Let the world be a Black Poem
> And Let All Black People Speak This Poem
> Silently
> or LOUD. (50–55)

Over a decade later, in liner notes for *New Music–New Poetry*, a live recording of Baraka backed by David Murray and Steve McCall, Baraka would write: "The poetry of the dying epoch (racism and monopoly capitalism, imperialism) exists mostly on paper. . . . Black poetry begins as music running into words." Consider this recording a rebirth, then, and take the printed version of "Black Art" with a grain of salt. On the page, the word "LOUD" is capitalized, appearing to suggest typographically the very loudness we deem it to express. Yet in his recorded performance, Baraka appears to deny it: His "LOUD" may be the quietest word he utters in the entire recording. Baraka turns it into an injunction to change perspective. For Fred Moten, "that which appears on the page is not the poem but a visual-spatial representation of the poem that would approximate or indicate its sound and meaning, form and content, and the particular sculpted manifestation of language as their interanimations" (*Break*, 97). Yet some dimensions of the poem's sound go beyond language and into its essence as music: In that moment on the record, loudness comes courtesy of Sunny Murray's short flurry on the snare drum. If, as Jean-Philippe Marcoux notes, "sonically, the rhythmic irregularity that capitalized words create confers to the line a declamatory tonality akin to free jazz drumming" (152), it is a tonality that echoes, possibly summons the recording's. *This* is not the poetry of the dying epoch—this poem, Baraka suggests, exists, is meant to exist, mostly beyond paper: There are more ways to speak than just by uttering words, and maybe poems that kill, kill as softly as this song.

Who or what are assassin poems meant to kill, exactly? They must "wrestle cops into alleys / and take their weapons leaving them dead / with tongues pulled out and sent to Ireland" ("Black Art," *SOS* 21–23). Taken tongue in cheek, as it were, what we have in these gory lines is a drastic thought experiment in "cast[ing] off the white self, the white voice, the white sound" (Harris, "How You Sound??" 315): How would, how might Americans sound without Irish or other white tongues? Paralleling this gruesome back-to-Europe movement, we have to imagine the quest at the heart of Baraka's oeuvre, the same search for black origins at work in "BLACK DADA NIHILISMUS": For Fred Moten, it only uncovered "the absence, the irrecoverability of an originary and constitutive event; the impossibility of a return to an African, the impossibility of an arrival at an American, home" (*Break* 94). "Black Art," of course, in spite of it all, hopes to transcend this foregone conclusion: It is a prayer; it describes what we want, not necessarily what can be. Ablackadabra: The hope is also that Black Art, like (black) magic, might allow Baraka to create as he speaks, not on the page, but in the moment of performance.[1]

There is black magic in live performance, then, but it comes in many forms whose worth and power are for Baraka directly proportional to their proximity to blackness, or its spirit as embodied by "the Blues impulse . . . containing a race," the constant in the "Changing Same" of black music and arguably, in Baraka's own career (*Black Music* 180). If the arc of Baraka's artistic career can be described as a "migration from . . . aesthetic individualism to nationalist and Marxist vulgarity" (Moten, *Break* 86), one must also consider how these two ends share the somewhat counterintuitively elitist approach expressed in the very notion of avant-garde—wherein knowledge, science, illumination, and so on are conveyed to the masses by a group of singularly enlightened artists. In the latter days of his Village life, Baraka was increasingly made to face the inherent contradictions of his life—married to Hettie, a white woman, a bona fide star in hip circles, audiences for his "emotional antiwhite tirades" (Sollors 174) were principally white people. Bohemian values mean to contradict bourgeois values of good taste and consensus; bohemian talk of revolution, borrowing as it routinely does political rhetoric, remains for the most part safely circumscribed to matters of aesthetics and morals. In Baraka's developing outlook in the mid-1960s, the modernist necessity of avant-garde experimentation crossed that of racial authenticity—the former on a spectrum from convention to revolution, the latter on a spectrum from racial authenticity/origin to dilution and assimilation into white culture.

Two crucial paradoxes appear: The music of the black musical avant-garde "differs (or seems to differ) from Rhythm and Blues, R&B oriented jazz, or what the cat on the block digs" because its formal innovations (even as they might channel "the blues impulse") are often proximate to, and compatible with, similarly heady innovations in "white Euro-American music" (*Black Music* 188). Baraka defines avant-garde musicians as self-conscious, spiritual, "more conscious of a total self (or *want* to be) than the R&B people who, for

---

1. The formula "abracadabra" is thought to derive from an Aramaic phrase meaning "I will create as I speak." See Conley 66.

the most part, are all-expression. Emotional expression" (188). The unadulter-ated, carnal expression typical of R&B—but also soul, funk, and other popu-lar, unabashedly dance-driven forms of black music—has for ages been an essential influence in the broader American (read: white-controlled) musical mainstream. On both axes, Baraka describes, in "Jazz and the White Critic," a cycle of action and reaction, revolution and dilution, revolt and consen-sus, one that asserts the centrality of the blues impulse (*Black Music* 19–20). Proponents of black music on the two spectrums have this in common, that they eschew mediocrity: Though the risk that they might appeal to the much-dreaded tastes—or lack thereof—of the middle class does exist, it is through their utter dedication to spirituality for one and emotion for the other that they cyclically find ways to reinvigorate the changing same.

Baraka struggled to reconcile the elitist and populist elements of his out-look. His "R&B people" evoke nothing as much as Langston Hughes's "low-down folk"—portrayed as an endless source of inspiration for artists, likely to "accept what beauty is their own without question" (Hughes, "Negro Artist" 92), but also as incapable as a group of the sophistication necessary for self-conscious art, sophistication that in turn always threatens to corrupt the sin-cerity of black art. As a thought experiment, Baraka could dream of a "*Unity Music*" that would be simultaneously "jazz and blues, religious and secular . . . New Thing and Rhythm and Blues . . . a social spiritualism" (*Black Music* 210). However, in the real world, nothing he saw could quite cover the entire ground. The black masses he encountered in Harlem still favored the popular genres Baraka himself tended to look down on in spite of an early musical education shaped by the sounds of doo-wop quartets such as the Ravens or the Orioles—groups apt to "translate our real funk" (*Autobiography* 79), but also liable to reach broad, and therefore suspicious, success beyond the Afri-can American community. The appropriation of black music by mainstream white American culture evoked visions of industrial exploitation: "R&B now, with the same help from white America in its exploitation of energy for profit, the same as if it was a gold mine, strings that music out along a similar weak-ening line" (*Black Music* 180). R&B hit factories might produce unique jewels, but for Baraka their specialty was mechanical reproduction and therefore a certain reduction of inspiration to formula, the dilution of soul and aura. And yet: "Those artists, too, were reflecting the rising tide of the people's strug-gles. Martha and the Vandellas' "Dancing in the Streets" was like our national anthem" (*Autobiography* 305). Now living away from the Village in the mid-1960s, Baraka heard and saw daily reminders that mainstream popularity also did mean connection to the people.

By the end of 1965, Baraka's Harlem experiment had ended in disaster, but he started over with the same principles in Newark, opening at the Spirit House a base for operations that would at one point include a bookstore, a monthly newspaper, a publishing company and record label, a traveling theater troupe, the Spirit House Movers, and a band, The Jihad Singers. Their album *Black & Beautiful, Soul & Madness,* recorded at the Spirit House, was the second release on Baraka's label. It proposed to integrate R&B and free jazz influences in a package apt to make visible the intrinsic ties between the two styles. In a letter written for the album's 2009 reissue, Baraka states: "We thought of ourselves as cultural workers, revolutionary artists pushing the program as some of our cultural nationalist comrades were wont to say" ("September 2009"). Baraka and the Jihad Singers went about it in striking fashion. The album's original liner notes state that their music is "new blues . . . expanded to be more deadly by being stretched out with the new music" (Weusi). On first hearing, this may not seem obvious: The album's "dangerously contemporary" R&B numbers are performed almost a cappella, providing a stark aural counterpoint to the lush slickness of Motown, even as they ostensibly channel that sound. Thus, on the opener, "Beautiful Black Women," Baraka reads his eponymous poem while the Jihad Singers sing the chorus to Smokey Robinson and the Miracles' "Ooh Baby Baby" in a doo-wop loop, supported by Bobby Lyle's discreet bass. In the Miracles' song, these pleading words underlay Robinson's teary, remorseful address to a former lover, wronged and subsequently lost. Robinson's speaker has no illusions, but he can't abandon hope either: He is the illustration of Baraka's argument that in R&B lyrics love is practical, concrete, felt or lacking, embodied. By contrast, love in the New Music is a spiritual call; it has no object, it is love "for the sake of Loving." Baraka postulates that "Spiritual Concern . . . would be corn or maudlin, would not serve, in most R&B, because to the performers it would mean a formal church thing. But this will change, too" (*Black Music* 201). In this spirit of change and with unity music at heart, "Beautiful Black Women" stretches and complements the Miracles' song with Baraka's paean to Black women.

It is not to everyone's tastes: Jerry G. Watts quips that "to call this poem trite would be to point out the obvious" (Watts 233). While there is undoubtedly much in "Beautiful Black Women" that smacks of what Watts dubs the "requisite poetry-of-praise to black womanhood" he deems typical of the Black Arts era, there just as certainly is much more to this song than clichés. In order to see this, Watts would have to think of "Beautiful Black Women" as more than the text printed in *Black Magic Poetry 1961–1967* (*Black Magic*

148–149), a third of which he conveniently avoids reading. Indeed, he leaves out what is arguably the poem's most striking passage: "Ruby Dee weeps at the window, raining, being lost in her / life, being what we all will be, sentimental bitter frustrated / deprived of her fullest light" (lines 5–7). But only in the performance of this passage as recorded on the album—which Watts does not even mention—can we hear Baraka's signifying on the Miracles. On the "baby, baby" whose loss Robinson self-pityingly laments, Baraka superimposes a snapshot of Ruby Dee, evoking elements of her celebrated stage and screen performances as Ruth Younger in Lorraine Hansberry's *A Raisin in the Sun*. What is Ruby Dee weeping about? When her voice "hangs against the same wet glass" (12) and permeates all, "the lost heat, and the gray cold / buildings of our entrapment" (13–14) might refer to the decaying relationship sung by Robinson, to the petty horrors of living black that form the backdrop to *A Raisin in the Sun,* or to how the two might compound each other. Baraka riffs on the same chords of love, betrayal, and remorse as Robinson, only to elevate the singer's concrete, lover's plea to a more spiritual cry for help and cross-gender solidarity. Live performance is key: Take it from Ntozake Shange, who declares that this rendition of "Beautiful Black Women" was the moment "when [she] could say: 'I want to do that'" (Shange, "First Loves"). Elsewhere, she compared the combination of Baraka's recitation and the Jihad Singers' harmonies to "an Ave Maria. It is just holy" (Shange, "Interview" 487). For all the alleged triteness of this poem, it appears that as an effort at unity music, it managed to work magic in at least one pair of ears.

Many more heard Baraka and his collaborators, and the Spirit House quickly became a hub of artistic and political activity. "Our explosions inside the Spirit House were in tune with the whole siege of tension that stalked the day-to-day streets of the slowly simmering town," Baraka says of a year of lead that would culminate in the July 1967 Newark rebellion, which occurred a few months after the recording of *Black & Beautiful, Soul & Madness* (*Autobiography* 367). During the rebellion, Baraka was arrested and brutally beaten by Newark police, who alleged illegal possession of firearms to justify their behavior.[2] When the second Black Power Conference took place in Newark mere days later, as scheduled, public scrutiny guaranteed that Baraka was among its most prominent participants. Tellingly, in his reminiscences of the event, Baraka speaks in musical terms: "In rebellions . . . the song is a police siren," he writes. Describing people setting stores on fire, he muses: "They were the most rhythmic, the fire people, they dug the fire cause it danced so tough." Accounting for his own actions during the rebellion, he explains that

2. For details of the case, see Woodard.

he "tried to follow the hot music's beat. . . . A scale no musician could plumb" (*Autobiography* 368). Baraka spells out in hindsight a central concern of his own forays into music: how to channel the radical energy he thought he could perceive in the people around him into music that might mobilize the same people. If "'Dancing in the Street' provided a core of legitimate social feeling though 'mainly metaphorical and allegorical for Black People,'" it fell short of being revolutionary music: It was all emotion, no mobilization. With his increased involvement in local and national politics, Baraka also enhanced his engagement with "socially oriented" R&B (*Black Music* 208).

At the turn of the 1970s, Baraka had become a constant political and cultural presence both on the local and national scenes. He subscribed to Ron Karenga's Afrocentrist value system, Kawaida, and in that time period changed his name from LeRoi Jones to Amiri Baraka. His militant activities in Newark were instrumental in the election of the city's first black mayor, Kenneth Gibson, in 1970. Baraka was also delivering lectures on campuses around the country, becoming a national figurehead of cultural and political black nationalism at the national level, notably in helping organize the inaugural Atlanta Congress of African People in 1970, a gathering of black political and cultural figures from a wide-ranging political spectrum (Watts 381–388). On this occasion, he closed his statement as representative of the Committee for Unified New Ark with a mesmerizing, bravura performance of "It's Nation Time!," a poem that would find its way on Baraka's next foray into populist music: the 1972 album *It's Nation Time!: African Visionary Music*, released on the Motown's subsidiary label Black Forum. Baraka read alone in Atlanta; the recorded performance comes near the end of the LP's B-side, whose nine tracks run into each other without notable interruption. As bass, drums, and percussions play softly in the dying moments of the previous track ("The Spirit of Creation"), Baraka's announcement of the poem's title is answered by a frantic drum roll. The poet eases into a typically breathless psalmody, then the rhythm section picks up again, meeting a flurry of onomatopoeia with snare drum and cymbal hits and signaling the entrance of honking saxophone and clanging piano, with chance of electric guitar, a female voice accompanying Baraka's exhortations for a few seconds as poet and musicians reach the poem's climax. In the words of Meta DuEwa Jones, "his reading style concurrently encourages and mimics musical interaction" ("Politics" 249). Jones highlights how the differences between print and recorded versions of this poem—and between the different recorded versions of his performance—point to the aesthetic sophistication of texts routinely derided for their alleged crass simplicity. Baraka's improvisations in such political contexts as the Congress of African Peoples and the recording of

It's Nation Time! mean to instantiate unity music in awareness, and in spite, of the seeming impossibility of maintaining the collective spontaneity of jazz and the organizational demands of mass, black nationalist politics.

Both elements are featured heavily on the album. The cover evokes ancient Africa, and so does the music: On the opening "Chant," an all-female choir sings in Swahili, accompanied by percussions as Baraka recites a black nationalist creed celebrating the black man, the creator, and the seven principles of Nguzo Saba and Kawaida, "tradition and reason." With his increased attachment to Kawaida, Baraka's outlook on music took more pragmatic accents. As Scot Brown tells, "when describing an aesthetic blueprint for a Black nationalist societal alternative" around 1968, "Baraka did not differentiate between jazz and soul, asking the audience to 'dig the idea of buildings that look like John Coltrane's solos or automobiles that look like James Brown's singing'" (139). Musically, the album mostly hovers between percussion-heavy, recitation moments and free jazz–like instrumental outbursts. In all the seeming seriousness of Baraka's spiritual pronouncements, spread as they do on two sides where each new recitation and music blends into the next, two poems/performances stand out for their gleeful, humorous engagement with Baraka's theories of revolutionary aesthetics and popular music.

"Come See About Me," the album's third track, begins with Baraka soberly reciting over subdued percussions and bass the eponymous poem published simultaneously in *Spirit Reach* (*Selected* 209–210):

> O Allah
> all deity, jinn, spirit creation
> on the earth, where we live, cut off from
> righteousness
> by devil
> in corporated
> come see about
> we
> us
> Black people your first creationssss. (lines 1–10)

As he asks for divine intervention, Baraka picks up the pace, his voice rising and accelerating, but about a minute in, as he interpellates Allah, the band breaks into a cover of The Supremes' "Come See About Me," switching from traditional drumming to R&B. At first this urgent, accelerated version of the Motown hit cuts into Baraka's chant like a joke. Baraka, black priest lost in his mystic thoughts, is rudely interrupted by pop music, and for a second he appears in turn surprised and indignant: "God. Hey God! God!" he cries, as if the music might have distracted the All-Hearing. The staging of the divide between the spiritual and practical extremes of black music posited in "The Changing Same" could not possibly be set in more convincing and hilarious terms: R&B's emotion beats spiritual introspection any time. Yet Baraka takes it in stride. If it comes as a surprise, the band's interruption did not exactly come unannounced: It was summoned by the song's title, and by the injunction in Baraka's prayer, "Come see about we," both already borrowed from the Supremes' 1964 hit and the language of popular music. The interruption itself, then, is God's sign. "We here cut off in this devil's land, we need something to be strong, God," Baraka recites, over lines from the original song pleading with a lost lover to "return to ease the fire that within me burns."[3]

For all that he adapts his message to the music—much as he did with "Beautiful Black Women"—Baraka also appears to unlock meaning that already sat under the surface of the original R&B hit he quotes. As the piece picks up, trumpets joining the drums, guitar, and vocals, Baraka's delivery merges into the infectious drive of the song: "Let us Allah please move from where we at. Into ourselves is where, dig it! The pleasure boat of sweet black memory is where. Anywhere the whole being is, anywhere the total vibration is."[4] Separated from this performance, Baraka's spiritual injunctions might easily be derided as "corn or maudlin." Arguably, they are indeed derided as such in the performance itself. Jessica E. Teague has analyzed thoroughly how the stereophonic dynamics of the recording themselves "allows the track to perform the task of bringing the secularized (and saccharine) R&B closer to its spiritual roots" (29). The attention Baraka puts to the recording as sonic object turns it into "a black sonic space . . . a *space* in which a new Black Nation could be born" (Teague 29). In this, the change from "Come See About Me" to "Come See About We" is especially important, for the movement it operates from the possible individual and individualistic consumption of sound to the implications of collective enjoyment of music. "The cool world is around you, dig yourself!":[5] What is staged here is gleeful transcendence, a demonstration that when the Supremes ring out, *they* are where the total vibration is, and that this total vibration is an acceptable path toward forms of racial and political self-consciousness where individual epiphany might lead to collective illumination.

This, however, is a difficult path, and "Who Will Survive America," the album's final effort at producing a straight R&B number, exposes in rather

---

3. In the poem, the corresponding lines are fragmented three breaks, 15–18.
4. In the poem, the corresponding lines would be 29–35.
5. In the poem, those are lines 46–47.

stark fashion the limits of Baraka's approach. To the question in the title initially asked by Baraka, a choir offers this answer: "Few Americans / Very Few
Negroes / No crackers at all," subsequently repeated throughout the song. This
darkly playful, black nationalist fire-and-brimstone sermon evokes the apocalyptic tones of "BLACK DADA NIHILISMUS." Yet where the poem imagined
violence against "the white girls . . . their fathers . . . the mothers" and his own
friends, only to curtail his summoning of the frightful spirit of black dada
nihilismus with a final prayer to be saved "against the murders we intend," this
song celebrates the inevitable downfall of America, listing some of those she
will take with her. In Baraka's reading of "BLACK DADA NIHILISMUS" with
the New York Art Quartet, in the words of Aldon Nielsen, tensions grew "out
of the dissonance between the apocalyptic words of the poem and the almost
overly calm fashion in which Baraka reads it" (*Black Chant* 191). Here the contrast is between apocalyptic verse and joyous, raucous funk. This is a song of
joy, in the end, a song of joy *of* the end: the end of white America and its min-
ions. It builds a sonic experience still different from that delivered previously
on the record, a dialogic development. The evolution from the opening of
the album is drastic: "Come See About Me" collided spiritual chant and R&B
to eventually merge them. Here the funk seems born out of Baraka's words;
he calls out the refrain once and the bass rolls in, and by the time he repeats
the sequence the choir, guitar, and drums have joined him. The Imamu has
adapted: Where previously he'd had to pick up the song in his own words from
the interrupting choir, he now leads them, uniting the reflection of his lyrics
to the emotion of the musical form.

That Baraka should conceive of a time after the end only makes sense:
He wants to project the millenarist possibilities of the *tabula rasa,* imagine
what might happen if the "black sonic space" of the song should spread to
the entire world as it is and set it on fire. "Who Will Survive America?" presents a cast of common villains whose actions are deemed counterrevolution-
ary and antiblack: addiction to tobacco and other substances; women and
men not wearing their hair natural; black communists, loathed by cultural
nationalists; churchgoing lady, "shrinking from blackness"; old people; Chris-
tians—all are bound to be eradicated, along with white people, in the "heat
and fire / of actual change." Tellingly, Baraka used much the same vocabulary
to describe the effects the 1967 Newark rebellion had on him: "For me, the
rebellion was a cleansing fire. . . . I felt transformed, literally shot into the eye
of the black hurricane of coming revolution. I had been through the fire and
not been consumed. Instead, I reasoned, what must be consumed is all of my
contradictions to revolution. My individualism and randomness, my Western,

white addictions, my Negro intellectualism" (*Autobiography* 375).[6] This, perhaps, reveals the limit of Baraka's effort in *It's Nation Time!*, when the striving
toward unity music appears to circle back onto Baraka himself, and he appears
not quite to join the ranks of the people so much as perpetually see himself
one step ahead of them: a band leader in the production of unity music, with
all the paradox such a position suggests as regards a populist politics, and the
sublimation offered in the moment of performance.

Baraka's dedication to live performance did not wane after he reneged on
cultural nationalism to embrace Marxist-Leninist-Maoist orthodoxy in the
mid-1970s. In fact, while his turn to Marxism marked a distinct downturn
in Baraka's political visibility, it also coincided with the constitution of The
Advanced Workers, Baraka's most accomplished funk project. A recording of
a performance of Baraka and the band at a 1977 festival in Germany recently
made public reveals the band as a tight, groove-driven act worthy of better-
known contemporaries such as Funkadelic. Early on, Baraka channels Lenin
to explain the band's name: "By advance workers we mean those who are
already organizing and educating the class. . . . We the advanced workers
from the ghettoes of America" (Baraka and The Advanced Workers). There
is some irony in hearing college-educated Baraka define himself as one of
"those people who despite their stultifying labor in the factories all over the
world have so much strength and willpower that they can study and study
and study." His words evoke the fetishization of working-class status typical
of 1970s European and American Maoists. Yet, here also, one can argue that
what contradictions are at work in Baraka's political stance are subsumed in
the moment of performance. It is unclear whether Baraka was ever satisfied
that he had managed to produce the "unity music" he dreamed of in the mid-
1960s, but it is fair to imagine he never stopped trying, and this recovered
recording gives us a fascinating glimpse into somewhat lesser known efforts.
On "Like This Is What I Meant," he delivers a new creed: "Poetry must sing,
laugh and fight . . . so that even in our verse . . . even in our dancing, even
in our song, in our pure pure pure love songs: Revolution!" (Baraka and The
Advanced Workers).

Admittedly, this new creed is eerily similar to Baraka's older creed; strip
the ideological specifics and it could easily apply to any previous period in
Baraka's political life. Thus Watts's assessment might as easily seem accurate
when he declares: "The problem with Baraka's political art is Baraka. When-

---

6. Noted artists issued a public statement in support of Baraka on the occasion of his trial,
and Ginsberg helped raise money for his defense fund. See Watts 299–301.

ever Baraka has imagined himself as politically engaged, it has always been as self-anointed leader of the masses" (463). Purposefully or not, this merciless note echoes Werner Sollors's argument that "Baraka's own development" as an artist can be characterized "as 'The Changing Same'" (8)—how black music through time and place is simultaneously ever changing and always "the exact replication of The Black Man In The West" (*Black Music* 180). Yet where Watts might say that the "Black Man in the West" is actually Baraka himself, Sollors's riff on Baraka's famous phrase highlights the fact that Watts leaves performance entirely out of his treatment of Baraka's Marxist years. Judging Baraka's works strictly as text on pages is quite simply missing the point. In the process, one is bound to dismiss the possibility that Baraka's fundamental and ever-frustrated quest was truly not to extol his personal worth but rather to try to build a different politics—personal and collective. It may be impossible to transcend the apparent individualism of the single voice, but we should gainsay Baraka as band leader, and ponder what may be gained in hearing Baraka the soloist, with his words and voice part of the ensemble that is the real message: the Music, and what it can teach us about acting together for a greater good.

10

"A Marching Song for Some Strange Uncharted Country"

*The Black Nation, Black Revolution,
and Amiri Baraka's Liner Notes*

JAMES SMETHURST

T IS HARD to think of another major US writer who was more committed to ephemeral or occasional writing than Amiri Baraka throughout his life. Baraka consciously attempted to change ideas about both the marginal and ephemeral, collecting and republishing in book form his liner notes, reviews, and occasional pieces, blurring the lines between different modes of cultural transmission and reception—though, interestingly, it is for the most part his liner notes for "free jazz" or "New Thing" recordings on the Impulse label that he includes in the 1968 *Black Music* rather than those for Prestige Records that began his career as a writer of such notes.

What is of interest here is the close connection of Baraka's ostensible hack work of writing liner notes and other music industry–printed marginalia with his more overtly serious music criticism, which in turn is not separated from his poetry, plays, fiction, and political and social writing. The concern is not simply how for Baraka his liner notes and other music marginalia become of a piece with his more obviously literary work. It is also how his liner notes evolve to express Baraka's sense of radical black nationhood (including the emergence of a black working class, a process that he describes at length in his 1963 *Blues People* and in his later Marxist writing, particularly his autobiography), internationalism, and black modernity in a way that calls for social (and socialist) transformation. This sense of a radical black national and international vanguard, though clearly more elaborated as time goes by and Baraka moves emphatically into a Marxist stance, is suggested in embryo form even in Baraka's earliest notes.

Of course, bohemia here and abroad has long had an association with mass culture and hack work, particularly before employment in academia became widely available to black and white radical writers. Baraka was no exception in this bohemian engagement with the new New Grub Street. One frequent source of hack writing opportunities after his move to New York's downtown bohemia in the late 1950s was to write more than twenty sets of LP album liner notes between 1959 and 1986, the latter date being shortly before the first year (1988) when sales of compact discs topped those of LPs on vinyl.[1] The largest numbers of these notes were written as part of a semi-regular job for Prestige Records, a major jazz and blues label that operated between 1949 and 1971 (Baraka, *Autobiography* 172).

Prestige was a pioneer in its approach in using the new microgroove sound technologies and the extended-play vinyl disc. Though Prestige lagged behind Blue Note a bit in its approach to the visual aspects of LPs, soon it, and other labels, began to explore the visual as well as the audio potential of the new format. As Darren Mueller points out:

> The adoption and standardization of long-playing technology made recording labels rethink their overall presentation in other ways as well. Cover art became increasingly sophisticated, detailed, and creative. Record jackets began to feature liner notes that educated consumers about the music and new technologies or detailed the label's own history. Even the record sleeves, once simply a blank piece of paper, became an alternative place for advertising. (Mueller)

The earliest liner notes appeared in the 1930s and 1940s and antedated the microgroove technology of the LP, accompanying multidisc reissues of older recorded jazz (Piazza 3–4). However, by the 1950s, liner notes became far more common and took on new roles. Prestige was among the first to develop the use of liner notes to both inform listeners (or potential listeners browsing in a record shop) as well as to provide those listeners (or potential listeners) with a critical stance through which to interpret and evaluate the music.

Beyond the background information about the particulars of the session and more generally about the artist and her or his music, the writers of liner notes in the 1950s projected a certain sort of hip style or attitude. Jazz liner

---

1. Recording Industry Association of America, http://www.riaa.com/market/releases/statover.htm.

notes writers were often among the leading younger jazz critics whose pieces appeared in *Metronome, Down Beat,* and the *Jazz Journal,* the *Record Changer,* and other journals of the jazz press. These writers included Ira Gitler, Martin Williams, Nat Hentoff, Larry Gushee, Daniel Morgenstern, Orrin Keepnews, and Baraka, the only black critic of the group. These writers were encouraged to display a personal voice in their liner notes. As Tom Piazza says,

> Of course, liner notes provide factual information and are in fact the main source of printed factual data for some artists. But the best liner notes, whether historical, musicological, narrative, or impressionistic, have always provided something beyond facts: they tell the listener, in many subtle ways, what it means to be a jazz fan. They embody styles of appreciating the music, a range of possible attitudes toward it. It is in this extra dimension that the liner notes as a form really distinguishes itself. (1–2)

One might say that those liner notes tell not only "what it means to be a jazz fan" but also why one might want to be a jazz fan. That is to say, they are tools for recruitment, a sort of cultural polemic, albeit with a certain commercial purpose as far as the record label is concerned.

Brent Edwards perceptively observes that one should not assume that "ancillary genres" of jazz writing (including liner notes, interviews, and other writing immediately dependent on the actual recorded music) are necessarily "subordinate afterthoughts, stray jottings that are inherently of secondary importance in relation to the music" since they "can emphatically frame the way a record is heard" (11–12). The stance of a "jazz fan," then, is, among other things, one of an educated, "hip" consumer whose sense of having knowledge about "the music" is in part the objective of music industry marketing. This uncomfortable amalgamation of the commercial and the antibourgeois, if not actually anti-capitalist, is the archetypal bohemian condition, of which Baraka is aware and negotiates even as he uses liner notes to sound, so to speak, a black radical tradition and a critique of US politics and culture. Similarly, despite the commonplace about Baraka that he passed through bohemia to come to Blackness, one also sees in his liner notes notions of both African American tradition and black internationalism from the very beginning.

Baraka's first Prestige liner notes, for Eddie "Lockjaw" Davis's 1959 album *Bacalao,* appeared only eight years after what might be thought of as the liner note revolution. For the most part, one might see these notes as in the generic mode of informing an audience (or potential audience) about the music and providing that audience a critical context for receiving the music. Yet Baraka's voice is immediately recognizable, with flourishes and concerns that would characterize his work throughout his career. He opens, "Eddie Lockjaw Davis has for a long time now enjoyed a weird kind of fame and prestige among musicians," going on to discuss how even though Davis's broader reputation was as a blues "honking" saxophonist, he also was comfortable in a wide range of jazz styles, including the "modern." Here the reader sees the deployment of one of Baraka's signature words in his early career, "weird." It is a word that Baraka used to convey a variety of things, but which is often a shorthand for the contradictions and depths of black modernity and a vanguard black sensibility as it comes into contact with a "mainstream" white sensibility. One also finds here an early expression of Baraka's notion of a blues continuum embodied in his description of Davis.

It is also telling that Baraka, a year before his life-changing trip to revolutionary Cuba in 1960, writes, "It sounds like a political rally in Cuba. . . . I keep expecting someone to yell, 'Down with Batista!'" (Liner notes, Davis *Bacalao*). Here he uses *Bacalao*'s engagement with Afro-Cuban music to sound a radical black internationalism through the connection of the blues, "modern jazz," Afro-Cuban music, and the Cuban Revolution that had triumphed at the beginning of 1959, even during the height of Baraka's downtown countercultural phase, before what has been often represented as his more conscious turn toward blackness in Black Power and Black Arts. He also declares Davis's version of a James Moody tune, "Dobbin' with Redd Foxx," to be like a "marching tune for some strange uncharted country," a wonderfully suggestive statement anticipating his future artistic and political trajectory.

In his second set of Prestige liner notes for the 1960 LP *South Side Soul*, by the John Wright Trio, Baraka comments on the take of the pianist Wright and his group, all younger black musicians, on the blues tradition of Chicago that Baraka links to Harlem (and, by extension, the other termini of the Great Migration). Again, what is seen is another early expression of the "changing same" that maintains a sense and sensibility of tradition even as it both articulates, helps produce, and chronicles the forging of a black industrial working class:

> I am certain that the very ugliness of the city was enough to frighten some people into turning around and going right back. But those people who did hang on, anywhere in the North, and came together in those huge "black capitals" of the world, invested their parts with something, some kind of strength, that enabled them and enabled their children to ward off unspeakable coldness, harshness, and unreality of the cities. The South Side is not Chicago, but it certainly is. Harlem is not New York, but it couldn't exist anywhere else in the world. And in almost the same fashion, the boogie

woogie pianists and iterant blues singers of the early South Side (as well as Harlem) left a soul music, a musical legacy that is constantly being reinterpreted by the young.

Baraka is not simply talking here about history as an accounting of events as they occurred in this past. Neither is he only providing an analysis of deep structures of historical development, the motion of history, and social relationships shaped by modes of material production, or even a "structure of feeling." Baraka is concerned with all of those things, but this writing is also about black music as a shaper, expression, and indicator of a black historical consciousness, particularly a black working-class historical consciousness, of a people's sense of where they are located in history and in contemporary society. As he would take up at some length in *Blues People,* Baraka sees the blues as fundamentally an expression of the world view and psychology of the Southern black rural poor and the urban working class, declaring, "Such a thing as a *middle-class blues singer* is almost unheard of. It is, it seems to me, even a contradiction of terms" (140). That is why Baraka, in the liner notes, constantly mentions such words as "attitude," "interpretation," "a black landscape of need," "the minds of the many poor blacks," "the Negro's *conscious* appearance on the scene," and so on. Really, he is speaking of a revolutionary national consciousness of a "nation within a nation" with the black working class in the lead, even in such an unabashedly commercial enterprise as album liner notes.

It may be, as Werner Sollors and other perceptive writers have noted, that a traditional antibourgeois, anti–middle class, and anti-"middlebrow" (14) bohemian aesthetic attitude was the source of Baraka's earliest cultural criticism. However, as John Gennari points out, this criticism was also often one that centers the working class (254). After all, there is no inherent reason why in vilifying the pretensions and gaucheries of the black middle class, Baraka would need to lionize the black working class, its expressive culture, its psychology, and its social attitudes as, basically, the most advanced, most revolutionary section of the US population.

Even Baraka's most perfunctory, least inspired liner notes, such as those on the 1963 *Sonny Is King* recording of "folk" blues singer and harmonica player Sonny Terry, reflect *Blues People*'s argument that the blues and the "blues impulse" is at the heart of any black music that legitimately and accurately reflects the African American people in the US:

And no matter what wild "bag" some young man might get into, as far as the "new" and the advanced in jazz, it really doesn't matter, if the blues feeling is lost. And Sonny and Brownie demonstrate consistently on these tunes what that feeling is. And that feeling, that "blueness," is the most consistently available emotional predilection in American Negro music, whether it comes from Sonny Terry or Sonny Rollins.

As Baraka's liner notes evolved, he moved even farther from the informational or even personalized contextualization toward a lyric style of liner notes that resembled his poetry and such essays-manifestos as "The Changing Same." An early example of this lyric style is on the posthumous 1962 release of a Billie Holiday LP, *Ladylove*, on the United Artists Jazz label. Most of the tracks on the album are drawn from a live recording of a 1954 concert in West Germany augmented by several studio tracks recorded earlier in New York and Los Angeles. Baraka opens with an invocation of an old debate about whether Billie Holiday was "really" a blues singer and what the authentic blues were/are formally and what they meant/mean. He also indirectly engages questions of which sort of music truly sounds the "blues impulse" or the "blues continuum": the "soul jazz" and various sorts of revivalist attempts to restage older forms of the music that Baraka sees as clichés or appropriation or the "free jazz" that he views as more organically in the blues spirit. In his notes, Baraka proposes the proto–Black Arts idea of music as history, and history in turn as myth, which is to say some shape or form that makes sense of black experience in a manner that is useful to the survival of black people as human beings and as a people or nation:

> The myth of blues is dragged from people. Though some others make categories no one understands. A man told me Billie Holiday wasn't singing the blues, and he knew. O. K., but what I ask myself is what had she seen to shape her singing so? (*Black Music* 25)

Another way of restating Baraka's opening sentence of the *Ladylove* liner notes through a slight but significant alteration would be "The myth of blues is dragged from *a* people." Baraka's commentary on the unnamed person, some self-described scholar who "knew" that Holiday was not a blues singer, reminds one of the title of a 1979 essay of James Baldwin in the *New York Times*, "If Black Isn't a Language, Then Tell Me, What Is?" In other words, OK, if Billie Holiday is not singing the blues, then what is she singing? Yes, frequently she sings in the thirty-two-bar mode and other forms of the pop song and even in what might be thought of as adapted art song of the cabaret style, as she did in "Strange Fruit," rather than the twelve-bar form that many associated with the blues—though she sang the twelve-bar blues, too (as she does on *Lady Love* in "Billie's Blues"). Baraka argues that her music, even her renditions of pop standards, is both a history of black oppression and black resistance as well as a myth that gives shape to black life—in short, the blues. Interestingly, given Baraka's association with black masculinism during the Black Arts era, especially during the period of the late 1960s, when he was most influenced by Maulana Karenga and Karenga's Kawaida philosophy, he suggests that Holiday's music renders "a black landscape of need, and perhaps, suffocated desire" through a black woman's voice, which is to say, a black woman's sensibility:

> And even in the laughter, something other than brightness, completed the sound. A voice that grew from a singer's instrument to a woman's. And from that (those last records critics say are weak) to a black landscape of need, and perhaps, suffocated desire. (*Black Music* 25)

Baraka here perhaps consciously echoes Langston Hughes's notion of "a dream deferred" (and perhaps riffs on the opening of Eliot's "The Wasteland," with its invocation of a modernist white landscape of need and suffocated desire). But there is an interesting juxtaposition of "need" and "desire," of the impulse for self-determination (of a black woman, of a people) and repression from a working class as well as national perspective that is raised here in Baraka's sense that the blues is by definition an expression of the black working class. That is to say that what marks Billie Holiday as a "blues singer" is not primarily structural, though, again, she did on occasion employ forms that virtually anyone familiar with the genre would recognize as the blues. It is, instead, the intersection of race (or nation), class, and gender—though more in the mode of Claudia Jones's "triple oppression," perhaps, than of "intersectionality" in the twenty-first century.

What the reader (and prospective listener) does not get in the liner notes to *Ladylove* is any of the usual information about personnel, recording dates, account of the actual performance, and so on. That is provided by an extremely bland account of the concert by jazz critic Leonard Feather, who introduced Holiday to the German audience at the actual performance, part of a Jazz Club U.S.A. tour in Europe, held under the auspices of the *Jazz Club U.S.A.* radio program that Feather hosted on the Voice of America radio in the 1950s. However, Baraka's commentary suggests another dimension to the music that does not celebrate liberal US democracy, but provides a sharp critique of it. He gives another sort of historical context, the poetically condensed emotional history, the psychological history. This history suggests that the real nature of the blues is far more than the notion of the blues as a feeling; perhaps more important, it is a historically constituted expression of an oppressed people in which form is important, but process, the motion of history as it were, more so. This aspect of the notes is heightened when Baraka includes them in *Black Music,* a consciously radical, black nationalist collection of his shorter music writing.

Probably the most cited and most republished of Baraka's liner notes is the set he wrote for the 1964 Impulse recording *John Coltrane Live at Birdland,* which opened with the most pointed and direct assaults on the US, its society, and its place in the world:

> ONE OF THE most baffling things about America is that despite its essentially vile profile, so much beauty continues to exist here. Perhaps it's as so many thinkers have said, that it is because of the vileness, or call it adversity, that such beauty does exist. (As balance?) (*Black Music* 63)

On the face of it, Baraka would seem to be violating the basic purpose of the liner notes form, which is to draw in potential listeners, both confirmed fans of Coltrane as well as possible fans, without alienating others, to a degree that he had not done before—even in the Holiday notes. Writers of jazz liner notes (and indeed the recording companies themselves) generally employed a sort of marketing strategy of hipness, the suggestion that only the discerning or most "advanced" hipster would appreciate the music in question. Here, Baraka does not begin with the sound that separates the sheep from the goats, but with a declaration about the vileness of the profile of the United States. There is no doubt that potential listeners to the album might be alienated by that declaration. However, if one accepts Tom Piazza's aforementioned claim that, among other things, liner notes "tell the listener, in many subtle ways, what it means to be a jazz fan," then Baraka is advancing an argument about what it means to be a "jazz fan" in 1964, which is to say, again, what jazz means. Of course, as we have seen, by 1964 Baraka had already clearly articulated both his sense of what the music means and records, as well as of the historical process of ethnogenesis and black class formation that the music encodes and helps produce in *Blues People,* his poetry, drama, fiction, and essays, and to some extent in his earlier liner notes.

But, in *John Coltrane Live at Birdland* he makes those claims in a clearer way than he had before in other liner notes. Not only did Baraka feel empowered to declare the US vile, but he also attacked the jazz industry in an even more direct and extended fashion, suggesting that the capitalist corruption of the jazz club was a metonym for the US as a whole:

Thinking along these lines, even the title of this album (A-50) can be rendered "symbolic" and more directly meaningful. *John Coltrane Live at Birdland*. To me Birdland is a place no man should wander into unarmed, especially not an artist, and that is what John Coltrane is. But, too, Birdland is only America in microcosm, and we know how high the mortality rate is for artists in this instant tomb. Yet, the title tells us that John Coltrane is there *live*. In this tiny America where the most delirious happiness can only be caused by the dollar, a man continues to make daring reference to some other kind of thought. Impossible? Listen to "I Want to Talk about You." (*Black Music* 63–64)

One of the notable things about this is not simply that Baraka wrote the notes in this way, but that he felt free to do so in such an open fashion, and that Impulse Records included those notes, unedited, on the album. In other words, something had changed by 1964 in the jazz audience, the musicians themselves, and the African American community that made such liner notes possible on a commercial album released by a label whose niche was the new jazz, with Coltrane as their star.

The usual demarcation of the beginning of the Black Arts Movement has often been the creation of the Black Arts Repertory Theatre and School (BARTS) in Harlem in 1965, after the murder of Malcolm X. This certainly is a plausible beginning, especially since any event marking the advent of a cultural movement (or any movement) is always an arbitrary marker. Even in terms of Baraka, one might cite a variety of possible beginnings for his rupture with bohemia and his entry into a new sort of black radicalism that was only embryonic before. Certainly, the liner notes for *John Coltrane Live at Birdland* could be seen as moving beyond a transition into something new, even if, as noted before, with a long foreground. What if the beginning of the Black Arts Movement was not the founding of BARTS in Harlem, but the liner notes to *John Coltrane Live at Birdland?* The historian John Bracey describes what he saw as the impact of John Coltrane on him and his generation of black activists, artists, intellectuals, and indeed a mass constituency for Black Arts and Black Power:

What Coltrane was doing in his music was indicating that we had to move beyond the whole system of western thought, cosmology and culture. We needed a new sound, a new aesthetic for new times. If you were not a witness to this process it is difficult to convey the emotional impact of the step by step stripping away of western conceptions of melody, harmony, rhythm, structure that had dominated definitions of music since the mid 19th century. Coltrane was a major subject of Black Arts poetry and figured in numerous discussions of cultural and political change. It was his increasing relevance in these disparate arenas that validated my feeling that his musical accomplishments were vital to the political journey from civil rights and integration, to the politics of liberation and black nationalism. (653)

Bracey here evokes the same generational spirit of Baraka in the liner notes of *John Coltrane at Birdland,* which suggest that Coltrane's mission was one of profound black destruction and reconstruction, demolishing old notions of aesthetic and critical sense and suggesting the lines of something new:

> Entering "The Jazz Corner Of The World," a temple erected in praise of what God (?), and then finally amidst that noise and glare to hear a man destroy all of it, completely, like Sodom, with just the first few notes from his horn, your "critical" sense can be erased completely, and that experience can place you somewhere a long way off from anything ugly. Still, what was of musical value that I heard that night does remain, and the emotions . . . some of them completely new . . . that I experience at each "objective" rehearing of this music are as valuable as anything else I know about. (*Black Music* 64–65)

Obviously, other critics, including Baraka, had already written at length about Coltrane, but this was one of the first expositions of Coltrane's music as both a sounding and a catalyst of the new black political and cultural radicalism that Larry Neal would eventually term the "Black Arts Movement" (BAM). While Coltrane sometimes differed from BAM writer-critics, such as Baraka, A. B. Spellman, Jimmy Stewart, Askia Touré, Sonia Sanchez, and others in their assessments of his work, they provided readings of his music that made it more accessible to a mass of potential listeners, especially black listeners, in a manner that took the music as seriously as Coltrane intended it. In other words, one might see them as writing revolutionary liner notes whether or not their work appeared on the back of an album cover.

Interestingly, after the lyric opening, Baraka does what liner notes often do, which is describe the tunes on the record and the performance of the band's personnel. Still, even in this description, Baraka returns to the notion of a revolutionary aesthetic politics of destruction as well as a translation of historical events. Such events include the bombing of the 16th Street Baptist Church and other violence against civil rights participants in Alabama from the Pettis Bridge, and the dogs and fire hoses of Birmingham, as well as mass violent response by working-class black Birmingham residents in 1963:

The whole is a frightening emotional portrait of some place, in these musicians' feelings. If that "real" Alabama was the catalyst, more power to it, and may it be this beautiful, even in its destruction. (*Black Music* 66–67)

If Baraka's notes for *John Coltrane Live at Birdland* can be read as an inaugural event or declaration of independence of the not yet named Black Arts Movement, then his notes for *The New Wave in Jazz* (1965), a recording of a benefit concert for BARTS, is a report from the early days of the movement. The concert included many of the leading new jazz figures and groups, such as the classic Coltrane quartet; reed player Albert Ayler in a group with drummer Sunny Murray; Newark-born and raised trombonist Grachan Moncur with drummer Bill Harris, bassist Cecil McBee, and vibraphonist Bobby Hutcherson; tenor saxophonist Archie Shepp in a band with alto saxophonist Marion Brown; and trumpet player Charles Tolliver with McBee, Hutcherson, alto player James Spaulding, and drummer Billy Higgins. (Two other major artists and their groups, Sun Ra and his Arkestra and singer Betty Carter and her group, appeared at the concert but are not included on the record, for some unnamed reason.)

Baraka declares that the album demonstrates that a movement is under way, and in fact, has been under way, but is now being documented in a more coherent and concrete manner:

> But the album is also heavy evidence that something is really happening. Now. Has been happening, though generally ignored and/or reviled by middle-brow critics (usually white) who have no understanding of the emotional context this music comes to life in.
>
> This is some of the music of contemporary black culture. The people who make this music are intellectuals or mystics or both. The black rhythm energy blues feeling (sensibility) is projected into the area of reflection. Intentionally. As expression . . . where each term is equally respondent. (*Black Music* 175)

When Baraka declares that the record contains "some of the music of contemporary black culture," he insists that it is a piece of a larger black communal identity as well as a theorization of what a new liberated black culture and society with roots in a blues tradition might be. This is especially visible when he insists that the musicians on the record (and those who played at the concert but were not included on the record) "are intellectuals or mystics or both." That is, the new revolutionary black music and the new black culture have both a spiritual dimension and a materialist aspect, thereby echoing Larry

Neal's more explicit critique of the European Marxist tradition. This tradition, he argues, is essentially correct in its economic analysis of capitalism and capitalist exploitation, but lacking in the spiritual dimension, which is an essential human sphere, especially for African-descended people ("Reply" 6).

Baraka, too, makes a similar argument as he puts forward the principles he sees underlying the new black music as the expression of the new black culture inspiring new art in all media and genres advanced by BARTS and the incipient Black Arts Movement. Again, one finds another version of the connection of history and myth (in the sense of a pattern or archetype based on a certain vision of history) in which history is encoded and recorded in art, if you have the informed ears to hear it, sharp eyes to see, and spirit to feel it. But for Baraka, that is also a history that points the way forward. There is a certain sense in which Baraka's notes here might seem to assume a neo-primitivist stance in which the "reflection" of which Baraka writes is instinctive. However, this version of overcoming the old Cartesian split of mind and body, reason and instinct, yokes feeling to intelligence, a black intelligence. This black intelligence emerges in the modern world of capitalism, in slavery, Jim Crow, industrial revolution, and colonialism. Still, it transcends that world through a vanguard consciousness rooted in Black history and black lives, one that is nation-conscious rather than individualistic:

> That is, the spirit, the World Explanation, available in Black Lives, Culture,
> Art, speaks of a world more beautiful than the white man knows.
> All that is to make clear what we are speaking of. And that
> the music you hear (?) is an invention of Black Lives. (*Black Music* 175–176)
>
> . . . You hear on this record poets of the Black Nation.
> New Black Music is this: Find the self, then kill it. (176)

The evolution of Baraka's liner notes is not only an important index of his own ideological and aesthetic changes but also an important marker and influence on the emergence of the Black Arts Movement and its sense of African Americans as a people with a revolutionary tradition and revolutionary future that would be determined by black people themselves. Jazz critic and writer Stanley Crouch claimed that it was Baraka's liner notes for *John Coltrane Live at Birdland* that opened the possibility of a "poetic jazz criticism" that caught the spirit of the music and was a creative form in and of itself, not merely a parasitic commercial genre.

Again, if, as Tom Piazza argues, one function of the liner notes that flowered with the release of jazz on 33 1/3 LP albums in the 1950s was to instruct the listener (or potential listener) on what it meant to be a jazz fan, Baraka's liner notes from the very beginning were about the ways black music encoded black history, black international connections, and, ultimately, black nationalism and internationalism in ways both mundane and spiritual. In that way, to be a true jazz fan was to be black, and to be black was to be able to look back and look ahead along a continuum in which the new black music was a key expression of the new black culture. This new black culture is truly "postmodern" in that it exceeds, and ultimately transcends, the technologies, or discourses if you will, of power used by Europe and North America to dominate the world.

11

Baraka's Speculative Revolutions

BENJAMIN LEE

I N AMIRI BARAKA'S short story "Answers in Progress" (*Fiction* 219–222), aliens arrive in Newark on the fifth day of the revolution. The narrator and his black nationalist comrades control the streets, the courthouse, and the television stations. They kill the white men who resist and gather other white residents on the city playgrounds. They work to secure the city, its infrastructure, its wealth, and its historical records. They patrol the various quadrants of Newark, submit reports to headquarters, question prisoners for the TV news, and put on plays to update black people on a rebellion that has kicked off in other cities as well. Not all are as stable as Newark: "Some brothers came in from the west, Chicago, they had a bad thing going out there. Fires were still high as the buildings" (*Fiction* 221).

The aliens have come for a different reason: "Art Blakey records was what they were looking for" (219). The space men support the revolution, which they describe as "evolution," but their focus is elsewhere. They "wanted to know what happened after Blakey. They'd watched but couldn't get close enough to dig exactly what was happening." Though the narrator and his comrades have a revolution to manage, they take time to teach the blue spacemen about free jazz, about Albert Ayler and Sun Ra. They make time for conversation and mutual understanding. The spacemen "wanted to take one of us to a spot and lay for a minute, to dig what they were in to. Their culture and shit" (219, 220).

Baraka, then still LeRoi Jones, first published "Answers in Progress" in 1967 as the last story in *Tales*. In both *Tales* and in *The Fiction of LeRoi Jones/ Amiri Baraka* (2000), he dates the story "March 1967" (*Tales* 132; *Fiction* 222), a few months before the actual Newark riots. The riots, or what Baraka in his *Autobiography* (1983) calls "the Newark rebellion" (263), took place in July of 1967, and they did not play out as the rebellion does in "Answers in Progress." Most of the violence went in the other direction, starting with the beating of the black cab driver by white police officers that sparked the riot and ending with deaths numbering somewhere in the low to mid-twenties, most of them among Newark's black citizens. "The official score was 21 blacks killed and 2 whites, a policeman and a fireman" (263), Baraka writes in his *Autobiography*. "But there were many more blacks killed, their bodies on roofs and in back alleys, spirited away and stuck in secret holes" (263). Whereas in "Answers in Progress" the narrator's black nationalist organization controls the city, in July 1967 the police, the National Guard, and New Jersey state troopers occupied Newark. Baraka's narrator in "Answers in Progress" dreams of heading home at the end of the fifth day of the revolution, to get high and eat a home-cooked meal. But in July of 1967, Baraka was "locked up the first night of the Newark rebellion" (263). He was dragged from his van by police, beaten severely, and charged with weapons possession, charges Baraka has always maintained were fabricated to justify his beating. He spent the remaining five days of the riots in the Essex County Prison (263).[1]

What, then, to make of "Answers in Progress," a short fictional account of a revolution that never took place, or that took place as predicted but differently? Baraka's title underscores the speculative, dialectical quality of his thinking: his constantly changing understandings of self and situation. "Answers in Progress" is another of the narrative, lyric, and/or rhetorical compositions he generates throughout his career as a way of trying to understand, personally and historically, where he stands while writing whatever he is writing at the time, and how he feels about his position. We might say it engages in what Jonathan Flatley calls "affective mapping" (4), or what Lauren Berlant describes as "the activity of being reflexive about a contemporary historicity as one lives it" (5). As Berlant and Flatley argue about other texts, and as Nathaniel Mackey argues quite explicitly about Baraka's poetry, this activity takes place at the levels of affect as well as intellect—of shifting moods and experiences felt as well as perceived—and gets transmitted formally as well as through content or explicit statement.

---

1. See also Woodard's account of the rebellion in the context of political organizing in Newark before and after July 1967, 69–90.

One encounters Baraka's emphasis on feeling everywhere in his oeuvre, in poems and fiction as well as in his criticism, where he famously links it to music. This emphasis, as Mackey argues, "is not so much a repudiation of thought as an effort to rethink, to as it were *un*think the perversions of thought endemic to an unjust social order" (42). Emotional responses to a particular text, cultural practice, or historical situation motivate us to explain why we object to or are fascinated by them. "Feeling," as Baraka puts it, "predicts intelligence" (*Black Music* 175; *Transbluesency* 132). The musicians who interest him most respond at the level of composition or technique to some primary and collectively experienced structure of feeling, what in *Black Music* he calls "social feeling" (208) or "the emotional context this music comes to life in" (175). For Baraka in the 1960s, the blues and bop are affective registers as much as technical or historical designations. John Coltrane represents "a scope of feeling" (173). "More than I have felt to say" (25), he writes unforgettably of Billie Holiday, "she says always" (72).

As Mackey's discussion of Baraka's work in the late 1960s and early 1970s helps us understand, Baraka's speculative, jazz and science fiction–inflected response to the urban uprisings he had been following in the news—the Watts riots in the summer of 1965, the Hough riots in Cleveland in the summer of 1966—gets filtered through the black nationalism he had been working to realize through the Black Arts Repertory Theatre in Harlem, the Spirit House in Newark, and the Black Convention Movement.[2] As such, "Answers in Progress" also tells us something about the representational politics of Black Arts texts, which are so often characterized as propaganda—manipulative and oversimplified—and yet reveal themselves upon closer examination as complex, expansive, internally contradictory or discrepant. In Baraka's story, brief, almost whimsical descriptions of alien culture overlap with fantasies of antiwhite revolution, and armed revolutionaries get characterized somewhat paradoxically by their commitment to the continuous and noninstrumental activities of aesthetic enjoyment and interpretation. The pace of revolutionary activity in the story—patrolling the streets, questioning prisoners, reporting to headquarters—seems at once urgent and strangely relaxed. The revolution, it turns out, requires a lot of sitting around, talking, exchanging ideas. It goes in search of new media, new temporalities, an expanded range of affective and political modalities.

---

2. On the Black Arts Movement in Harlem and Newark, see Baraka's *Autobiography*, 295–446, and Smethurst, *The Black Arts Movement*, 100–178. On the Modern Black Convention Movement, see Woodard, especially xiii–xv, 1–45. On Baraka's embrace of black nationalism and then Marxism, see his *Autobiography*, Mackey, and Baraka's "Preface to the Reader" and William Harris's introduction, chronology, and editorial notes to the selections in *The LeRoi Jones/Amiri Baraka Reader*, xi–xiv, xvii–xxxiii, and following.

One might say that "Answers in Progress" is about a revolution that needs to happen, since power needs to be redistributed, by force if necessary, whether or not those in power are willing to participate. But it is also about a revolution already happening in Baraka's thinking and writing from the 1960s, which struggle to articulate the thoughts and feelings of black communities like those in Newark or Harlem (which are not, of course, without their divisions and disagreements), and to connect them (as his spacemen help signify) to cultures and communities elsewhere. The play between here and there, now and then, inside and out in "Answers in Progress" thus anticipates what Fred Moten has described as "the temporal paradox of optimism" in black studies, in which "a necessarily futurial attitude" coexists with "assertion[s] of the necessity, rightness, and essential timelessness of the already existing" (*Stolen Life* 159–160). This is a discrepant complexity, as I will argue, that characterizes much of Baraka's writing of the Black Arts period, just as it characterizes his engagement, starting in the mid-1960s, with the poetry, music, and philosophy of Sun Ra.[3]

•

Where does the music go after Art Blakey's Jazz Messengers? It is no accident that Sun Ra emerges as the most convincing answer to the question the aliens come to Newark to have answered, even if, according to Baraka's speculative and affective mode as I have described it, this hardly answers the question for good. Baraka's story gives us other sounds to consider, from Albert Ayler's honking riffs to the new and improved Smokey Robinson, no longer crying over unrequited love but now "straight up fast and winging," offering Newark's citizens "the beauty of the whole" (*Fiction* 221). And yet, the narrator and his comrades devote time and energy to piping the music of the revolution into the streets, and there is little doubt he thinks he knows what the aliens need to hear to get the answers they're looking for. "I hope they play Sun-Ra for them blue cats," he remarks, "so they can dig where we at" (221). Later, as the narrator talks with the aliens' leader about music and painting, it is when a Sun Ra tape begins to play that "this blue dude really opened up. He dug the hell out of it. Perfect harmony these cats had too" (222).

---

3. My use of *discrepant,* here and elsewhere in the essay, is meant to underscore my debt to Mackey: not just his attentiveness to affect in Baraka, or his insistence on Baraka's movements across media and disciplinary boundaries, but his fundamentally dialectical reading—Baraka swinging constantly between thinking and feeling, idealism and material fact. This reading remains "discrepant" inasmuch as it allows the gaps, fissures, contradictions, and dissonances in Baraka's writings (or in Baraka's writings, for example, in relation to Sun Ra's poetry and music) to sound as loudly as their harmonies or points of agreement.

These scenes remind us how taken Baraka was in the late 1960s with Sun Ra's distinctive articulations of Afrofuturism and musical enlightenment, which Baraka interpreted as part of a larger movement in music and culture that included Black Arts, black nationalism, and free jazz, or what Baraka called "the new thing," "new music," or "the jazz avant-garde." John Szwed writes of Sun Ra's long involvement with Baraka, starting with their work together, in 1964, in support of the Black Arts Repertory Theatre and School (BARTS). Sun Ra's Arkestra was featured in both the concert Baraka organized to raise money to open BARTS and the parade he organized to announce its arrival in Harlem. In the months that followed, Ra "came up to the Black Arts office almost daily and held forth to whoever would listen" (210). The Arkestra was often featured when BARTS sent trucks out into Harlem loaded with performers (poets, dancers, actors, and musicians) intent on bringing new black culture to the people, a practice Baraka continued in Newark when he returned to his hometown in late 1965. The Arkestra dressed in fanciful Egyptian robes and headdresses; Sun Ra would play his new "sun organ," "which played colors as well as sounds" (210), a reflection of Ra's symbolist poetics and precursor, as Baraka liked to point out, to the swirling light shows of the psychedelic era. Baraka, Szwed notes, saw, "as no one else, the spiritual or visionary nature of Ra's music as inherently political" (210). "What Trane spoke of," Szwed quotes Baraka as asserting, "what Ra means, where Pharaoh would like to go, is clearly another world. In (w)hich we are literally (and further) 'free'" (210).

Sun Ra's spoken-word piece, "The Music Is Like a Mirror," reinforces Baraka's assertion while also giving us a chance to consider the problem it raises, namely that of translating Ra's own characteristic rhetoric and imagery into the "inherently political" claims Ra's most perceptive critics—Baraka and Szwed among them—discover there. How can we describe the freedom Baraka hears in Ra? How can it be at once literal and the expression of a further and presumably as-yet-unrealized form? Does it jibe with the freedoms Baraka imagines in "Answers in Progress"? Released by Norton Records in 2013 but recorded sometime soon after Ra moved to Philadelphia in the fall of 1968, "The Music Is Like a Mirror" captures Ra's remarkable capacity for meandering, seemingly extemporaneous aesthetico-philosophical speech, the kind that helped earn Ra a reputation in some circles as a crazy person or kook and yet whose sly consistency and intellectual force has long fascinated his admirers.[4]

---

4. Edwards indexes "the easy response to Ra, which wants to brand him a kook, a space freak, talking nonsense, *out*" (121). Szwed addresses long-standing dismissals of Sun Ra— "Genius or Charlatan?," "madman," "silly"—in opening and closing his book and quotes or paraphrases skeptical opinions throughout, noting, for example, that Baraka was "initially suspicious" of Ra and "saw him as a '"modernist' faddist" (xvii, 209, 387).

"This music is like a mirror," Ra begins. "You keep on listening to it and you can see something. You can see your alter self; you can see beyond tomorrow. You can discard the future." Ra's initial meditations on mathematics and nature, including on his own natural gifts as a musician, indicate that, as with Moten's observations on "the temporal paradox of optimism," the answers in progress are also already available, present in the patterns of nature, mathematics, and, by extension, the musical and articulated wisdoms Ra offers us in this and other recordings, poems, and live performances. Solutions to the social ills Ra invokes a bit later in his discourse—overcrowded cities or corrupt legal systems—are available to us as well if we can only manage to pay attention and to interpret the signs.

In the meantime, Ra observes, "the people are not doing so well." The unequal distribution of land and wealth has created so much "misery and suffering" that Earth has become "a real liability," "a cursed planet." "Leaders" and "rulers," Ra suspects, are already preparing to leave the planet behind, to save themselves before the environment is further corrupted or the people begin to object. If the people get wise, they will harness the power of the space age and travel to other planets as well, freeing themselves from the "sentence of death" they experience in "this jurisdiction." Outer space functions as a figure for socialism, or for the redistribution of wealth to all humans, regardless of "nation" (a word that also carries racial connotations in Ra's poems) or economic status. Its transformative potential inheres in the possibility of living under different laws and with an equal distribution of territory. "My idea is to give everyone some parts of the universe, so everybody [would] have some land, everybody would have some collateral, and everybody would share in the universe," Ra offers. "If every person had a share in the universe," he continues, "everyone would be wealthy"; "if everyone had some collateral, everyone would have credit."

One imagines this is what Sun Ra might have sounded like sitting and talking with Baraka and others in Harlem in 1965 or in the Spirit House in Newark in 1966 or 1967. In one oft-cited recollection of a party Baraka and his wife Amina hosted in Newark, Baraka remembers that Ra "held court" in their basement theater, conveying the impression of "the grand salons of advanced civilizations, where philosophers and intellectuals and artists could hold forth in open, pleasurable, serious discussion about the whole world and profound reality" (*Eulogies* 220). In another short story from *Tales*, "Now and Then," a barely fictionalized sketch of the jazz avant-garde scene in the era of black nationalism, conversations become fraught and combative, and one character is said to "lecture like Sun-Ra" when getting his points across (*Fiction* 216). It seems reasonable, based on such anecdotes, to take the discussions Sun Ra convened in Black Arts settings as models for the conversations between

revolutionaries and spacemen in "Answers in Progress," always the final destination of street patrols in the story and just as significant a collective activity.

Nor would there have been any question for Baraka that the visions of
outer space Sun Ra offers in "The Music Is Like a Mirror" are responses to
real suffering, in this case that of black Americans confined in designated
neighborhoods and subject to laws and police forces overwhelmingly hostile to their interests. Space travel in "The Music Is Like a Mirror" offers a
cosmic solution to racism and economic insecurity; it implies that a proper
understanding of nature and mathematics and of the long-standing curses
determining life on Earth prepares one for the peace and prosperity of outer
space. "Space," as Szwed puts it in a reading that overlaps with Baraka's, functions for Ra as "both a metaphor of exclusion and of reterritorialization," a
means of "claiming the 'outside' as one's own" and "of tying a revised and cor-
rected past to a claimed future" (140). The idea that one might discard a dam-
aged future and lay claim to a new one Baraka heard not as escapism or idle
fantasy but rather as a critique of present conditions and a call to transform
them: through open rebellion, as one saw in Newark in the summer of 1967
and again in the summer of 1968, but also through electoral politics, local and
national organizing, cultural activism and art.[5]

Not that Sun Ra would have agreed with such an interpretation. As critics
like Szwed, Brent Hayes Edwards, and Anthony Reed have all observed, Ra
dissented from Baraka's black nationalism, not to mention his readings of jazz
history. Ra took issue with bebop (it showcased great improvisers but lacked
great composers) and free jazz ("no sense of humor," not precise enough,
struggled to connect with audiences) and raised objections about many of
the progressive or revolutionary claims of the era, including those associated
with the 1967 riots in Newark and Detroit (Szwed 149–150, 235–236, 249).[6]
His "rejection of the label 'avant-garde,'" Reed argues, "and broader rejection of common narratives of music history and development . . . might also
be understood as a rejection of political vanguardism" (123). When Sun Ra,
Edwards notes, in an observation that applies quite brilliantly to "The Music
Is Like a Mirror," "refigures the so called black nationalist *land question*—or,
in another discourse, the Communist Party 'Black Belt' thesis that African
Americans formed an 'internally colonized' nation in the U.S. South—into

---

5. Woodard captures vividly the extent to which the racial politics and economic effects
of housing, policing, and educational policy were pressing concerns for Baraka in the months
leading up to and the years after the riots, as were political races in Newark and in other cities
across the US.

6. See Szwed's extended discussion of Sun Ra's "views on race and the role of black people
on Earth," including his relationship to black nationalism in the 1960s, 310–316.

the *space question,* we are not quite in recognizable nationalist strategy any-
more" (123).

All these observations, however, point not to irreconcilable differences
between Baraka and Sun Ra but rather to the necessity of translating one
complex and expansive mode of thinking and feeling into another. Provocative as a form of illuminated nonsense or space age esoterica—what Jonathan
Eburne calls "outsider theory"[7]—Sun Ra's conspiracy theories and interplan-
etary prophesies present themselves as hermeneutical exercises in need of further interpretation, magic equations in search of new variables. Baraka had
ample justification for interpreting them through and across his disagreements with Ra, since further interpretation was what Ra called for and delivered, in song after song, poem after poem, conversation after conversation.[8]
More to the point, as I want to argue in a final reading of "Answers in Progress," Baraka found common cause with Sun Ra as an artist whose rhetorical
provocations and formal, compositional strategies one might hear as a call for
ideological transformations profound enough to have political effects. What
if the racism structuring everyday life and subjectivity were razed or erased
as if by magic, or because the truth became apparent to all? What if everyone
suddenly agreed that wealth should be redistributed?[9] This is utopic thinking,
no doubt, though in Baraka's case always qualified by his tendency to swerve
away from speculation and return our attention to the "hard facts" of forcing
those in power to relinquish their privilege.[10] In Baraka's case as well as Sun
Ra's, one hastens to add, utopic speculation was combined with a tireless commitment to all those mundane, unromantic tasks involved in writing, publishing, rehearsing, booking and publicizing events, local organizing, political

---

7. See Eburne's introduction in *Outsider Theory.*

8. See Edwards on Ra's "poetics of recombination or *exegetical* poetics" (145–153).

9. For Reed, outer space in Sun Ra functions not as a metaphor for historically specific
inequalities but rather as a "catachresis" (a misuse, mixed metaphor, or intentional mistake)
meant "to remove or circumvent . . . ideology itself," the terms and frameworks within which
we understand our everyday lives and might imagine making political demands in the first
place (121). For Edwards, writing in a similar vein, Sun Ra's favored use of the word *impossible*
conveys "the recognition that the radically different . . . is inconceivable, and yet paradoxically
exactly that which must be conceived" (124). For Eburne, "what is 'alien' in [Ra's] method is
its promise rather than its premise: we know, or we think we know, that thought does not
really come from outer space," and yet we combine this method with others as a means of
destabilizing and "intervening in the domains of power" and of reified thought (361–364).

10. *Hard Facts* is the title of Baraka's 1972 collection, his first as a Marxist. In one poem
from that collection, "A Poem for Deep Thinkers," "skymen" come down "out of the clouds,"
much like the aliens in "Answers in Progress." Unlike the aliens, however, who understand and
support the revolution, the skymen of "A Poem for Deep Thinkers" are "blinded by sun, and
their own images of things." They need to be guided to "the battlefield" and forced to take sides
(*Transbluesency,* 165–167).

activism, paying salaries, running community arts centers, and/or managing a jazz orchestra for the better part of four decades.

Before returning to Baraka's short story, it is important to remember how literally his critics have tended to take his writings, most famously poems like "Black People" and "Somebody Blew Up America." These they have read neither as poetry nor as provocation—even less as speculative, dialectical, or self-critical—but rather as straightforward calls for violence or expressions of anti-Semitism.[11] Interpreting Baraka through Sun Ra hardly clears him of these charges or insulates him from critique on other grounds. Utopic thinking, Reed reminds us, has often devolved into authoritarianism (119). The successful rebellion in "Answers in Progress" only preemptively reverses the police state New Jersey's white governor imposed in July 1967; it imagines black militants gunning down and imprisoning the white leaders who would soon order black people off the streets under threat of gunfire or imprisonment. Baraka's story trades in homophobic insults and leaves black women at home to cook for the revolutionaries and to care for their children. Baraka scholarship can hardly overlook such missteps, which are part of the record, and which Baraka himself has acknowledged. It needs to theorize them carefully, however, and insist that these stumbles and stutters deepen or expand rather than reducing the complexity of a remarkably capacious set of texts. What new work might these writings, always somewhat troubled and troubling, still help make possible? What sorts of connections, disagreements, and thought experiments might they help us articulate?[12]

•

One such project, I have been arguing, is that of charting Baraka's shifting moods over time, the "affective maps" he produced, year by year and decade by decade, as a means of remaining interested and engaged—rather than sim-

---

11. See Harris and Nielsen's "Somebody Blew Off Baraka," which discusses the controversy around "Somebody Blew Up America" and describes Baraka as "a poet who . . . heard his own poetry read back to him by a sentencing judge as evidence that he [was] a dangerous man who should be put away" (186). This description refers to Baraka's sentencing for weapons possession in the wake of the Newark riots, during which, as Baraka puts it in his *Autobiography*, the judge "amazed me by prefacing my sentencing by reading a poem of mine, 'Black People,' with the lines that became ubiquitous: 'Up against the wall, motherfucker, this is a stickup!" (380). Baraka's sentence was later thrown out on appeal.

12. White's *Dear Angel of Death* represents one such thought experiment, that of revisiting many of the fundamental assumptions of Baraka's writings, including his emphasis on black music as freedom, an emphasis extended so brilliantly in the work of Mackey and Moten. "I'm asking whether the music we have, today," she writes, "not the music we used to have or the music we imagine, continues to offer up . . . something we might look to as a prophecy of being different in blackness" (137).

ply disaffected, angry, or depressed—and of understanding his own emotional responses to the world as collective, a potential source of connection or disagreement with others.[13] Like his most well-known poems from the period, "Answers in Progress" challenges black readers to dispense with white, European standards of value (including the Marxist perspective he would later adopt), and to assert their own values and assert the legitimacy of their own experiences. It imagines destroying one civilization in order to construct a new one, a form of symbolic violence meant, as Phillip Brian Harper argues, to be "*heard*" by white audiences, whose racial privilege it insists should be destroyed as well, and "*over*heard" by black audiences, whose own social divisions Baraka's rhetoric implies and even helps to produce ("Nationalism" 251). This was a moment, as Harper reminds us, when "*black* . . . represented an emergent identification among nationalist activists and intellectuals and not a generic nomenclature by which any person of African descent might be referenced" (251). Who, then, could respond to Baraka's story but "those whose political consciousness [was] sufficiently developed . . . to subscribe to the designation *black* in the first place," as opposed to "Negro" or "colored" (251), designations Baraka and other black nationalists rejected in the strongest possible terms? Baraka's short story commits to a vision of racial unity it knows is aspirational more than actual, and to a sense of imminent, ongoing transformation it describes in affective and musical terms. "We thought about the changing reference of our new world," Baraka's narrator muses as the story closes. "As it stood already in the old ruins. And we all felt like Bird. The old altosaxophonist . . . but the limits opened out into the pure lyric tone of powerful beings" (222). This is the structure of feeling invoked as well when the music of Sun Ra plays in the story, or when the narration is interrupted suddenly by a lyric poem. The transformation Charlie Parker, "the old altosaxophonist," suggested within the recognizable structures of the American popular song now expands beyond those limits, as a "pure lyric tone" or timeless, ever-expanding collectivity.

Midway through "Answers in Progress," its hip, vernacular prose comes abruptly to a halt. Baraka's first-person narration, its "I" shifting frequently to the "we" of the narrator and one or more fellow militants, gives way to a three-stanza poem. I quote the first two stanzas:

> Walk through life
> beautiful more than anything
> stand in the sunlight
> walk through life

---

13. See Flatley 1–10 and elsewhere.

love all the things
that make you strong, be lovers, be anything
for all the people of
earth.

You have brothers,
you love each other, change up
and look at the world
now, it's
ours, take it slow
we've got a long time, a long way
to go. (220, lines 1–15)

The violence of the story recedes as Baraka turns to poetry, as does its underlying black–white antagonism, and "all the people of / earth" take their place.
The first-person, play-by-play narration of the speech and movements of the
revolutionaries is replaced by the second-person, imperative mood so typical,
as Harper emphasizes, of Black Arts poetry as a field. If the "you" addressed in
Baraka's lyric is to flourish, he or she needs—or they need—to "walk," "stand,"
"love," "be" "change up," "look," and "take it slow." The "you" could be a woman
who loves her "brothers," a man who loves his, a collective "you"; the mascu-
line camaraderie of the story proper gets replaced or supplemented here by a
more fluid set of possibilities. The portrait of social division Harper discovers
in the second-person address of Black Arts poems, while perhaps implied here
as well, takes on an easier, more inviting cast. There are no compromised, inte-
grationist "negroes" or "Half white College Students" in Baraka's lyric (or, for
that matter, in the story proper), set there as foils for the fully realized "black
consciousness" of the speaker.[14] Which is not to say that Baraka's short story
isn't meant to shock and provoke, to challenge, and even to exclude readers who are not yet ready to contemplate revolution. And yet the mood and
temporality of that intervention have shifted: Folded into the confrontation is
the pleasure of sociability and sunlight, of language and music, of interpretation and reassurance and debate. Rhyming with the necessary push into the
future—"we've got a long time, a long way / to go"—is the call to extend and
enjoy the essential rightness and beauty of "the world / now." "Take it slow,"
Baraka's lyric speaker admonishes.

---

14. See Harper's discussion in "Nationalism and Social Division in Black Arts Poetry of the
1960s" of Baraka's "Poem for Half White College Students" and June Jordan's "Okay, Negroes,"
alongside other poems by Baraka, Sonia Sanchez, Nikki Giovanni, and Haki Madhubuti (Don
L. Lee).

Baraka's poetry, as Mackey has written, is characterized by a "fugitive . . . impulse" or "obliquity": an insistence on "sliding away from the proposed" (43). This is an impulse that leads him to "test" or "qualify" not just individual statements or poems but individual words, phrases, even syllables. As Baraka's feelings changed in response to historical events or events in his own life—his visit to Cuba in 1960, for instance, or the assassination of Malcolm X in 1965—he expressed those changes by qualifying or veering away from his own previous positions, or by capturing his own complicated feelings in the discrepant, sometimes contradictory movements of an individual poem or work of prose. Such is the case with "Answers in Progress," which juxtaposes poetry and prose and responds to Baraka's hopes and frustrations with racial politics in Newark in 1967 with images of symbolic violence against a white power structure but also with expressions of shared pleasure and sociability among black voices suddenly set free.

It is difficult, when reading Baraka's "Answers in Progress," or when reading accounts of the historical uprising that followed, not to think of more recent protests against police violence that then turned into occupations of black neighborhoods by local police departments now armed with tear gas as well as rifles and batons and supported, as in Newark in 1967, by the National Guard. One thinks Ferguson, of course, and of Minneapolis and Louisville, and of subsequent demands to divest from the police and invest instead in free educational access, community control, and a guaranteed livable income.[15] We might read Baraka's proleptic counterfactual tale as an early vision of what Joshua Clover has called "riot as modality," a hypothesis—the riot as a "struggle with the state" in the era of deindustrialization, with "the police now stand[ing] *in the place of* the economy" (124–125)—that emerges in part from Clover's analysis the riots of 1967 in Watts, Detroit, and Chicago as well as Newark. As for Baraka, rioting for Clover is literal but also speculative and poetic: It is the revolution one imagines and proclaims as a way of reinforcing one's ongoing resistance to what Sun Ra might have called "white rules and laws," or "the history of this enforced 'reality'" (*Immeasurable*, 265, 414). It is a mode of sociality that is analytical and resistant but also aesthetic and adhesive, leveraging the collective experience of beauty and interpretation— felt as well as thought, urgent but also unhurried, extended—to reinforce the solidarities of the street.

---

15. See, as a representative example, the platform the Movement for Black Lives issued in 2016, in the wake of protests in Ferguson, Cleveland, and elsewhere, and updated in 2020 in response to COVID-19 and the deaths of George Floyd and Breonna Taylor. https://m4bl.org/policy-platforms/.

12

Black and Blues

Amiri Baraka and Gil Scott-Heron's
Political Poetry

MICHAEL J. NEW

MIRI BARAKA describes his return to Newark and partnering with Amina as the completion of a "full circle" (*Autobiography* 240). He writes: "To have gone away so far, so many places, yet to be back with a black woman from the Central Ward. The irony was somehow mocking. I told her how many steps we'd wasted only to come back to our source, love in black life" (240). Leaving behind the Black Arts Repertory Theatre and going home to Newark was a further immersion in black communal space and political consciousness. In 1966, Amiri and Amina Baraka moved into their new home on Stirling Street, which they later called the "Spirit House." It was an important communal arts space, educational and spiritual center, and hub of social activism. Such an arrangement extended Baraka's work in Harlem and drew further inspiration from the Panthers' Black House in Oakland, where the couple spent a significant time in the spring of 1967.

At the Spirit House, there were deep connections between vanguard politics and performance art. The idea to combine experimental music, theater, and writing and to distribute it to the masses on long-play records exemplifies Baraka's populist vanguard aesthetic, his belief that revolutionary art would connect with people if it spoke to them in their own language.[1] In Newark,

---

1. Literary historian James Smethurst explains that innovators like Amiri Baraka, Larry Neal, Askia Touré, Sonia Sanchez, A. B. Spellman, James Stewart, and others were "initiators of the Black Arts movement in the East" who "synthesized and revised a cultural inheritance

the Barakas built a way of life drawn from Afrocentric nationalist ideologies, connected with the local black community, and served their needs while expanding consciousness through experimental art. His coupling with Amina allegorizes the poet's social and cultural return to his black self and, ultimately, political identification with the black nation. Newark represented a common tongue, shared history, familial connections, and political agency—home and homeland.

The backstory of the Spirit House in Newark is crucial for understanding the relationship between Gil Scott-Heron and Amiri Baraka. The site of their initial meeting was the center of Baraka's effort to organize and leverage black Newark's political power after the 1967 rebellion and during Kenneth Gibson's mayoral bid.[2] Just months after the Barakas' return from the West Coast, during the long hot summer of 1967, Newark police officers beat and arrested a black taxi driver named John Smith, triggering long-standing grievances against corruption and systemic racism in Newark's city government and police department. Over the following week, tensions spilled over into an uprising, resulting in dozens of deaths and hundreds of injuries. Thousands of law enforcement officers, including the National Guard, were called in to subdue the protesters—Baraka himself was assaulted by the police and jailed.[3] In the wake of the rebellion, electing Newark's first black mayor became a unifying, tangible prospect.[4] Coalition building and connections to what Baraka describes as the "more politically oriented middle class" helped lead Kenneth Gibson to his mayoral win in July 1970 (*Autobiography* 268). Baraka, too, threw the weight of his radical reputation behind Gibson's bid, even helping raise funds and his profile by bringing Isaac Hayes, James Brown, the Staple Singers, Stevie Wonder, and the Supremes to "[ride] around on the back of a truck all day, singing and pushing the program" (283). The campaign was not only a watershed for Newark but also a beacon beyond city limits: "Every

derived significantly from the Popular Front, using the 'new thing' jazz or 'free jazz' of the late 1950s and the 1960s as a model for a popular avant-garde" (Smethurst, *Black Arts* 59).

2. For an in-depth analysis of race and rebellion in Newark, see Kevin Mumford's *Newark: A History of Race, Rights, and Riots in America*. For a more condensed narrative of racial tensions that contributed to the 1967 uprising, see Tuttle 153–166.

3. This episode is detailed in his autobiography and glimpsed in his poem "AM/TRAK."

4. Historian Donna Murch traces a similar shift in the Black Panther Party's ideology in the early 1970s, especially with Bobby Seale's candidacy for mayor of Oakland in 1972: "African Americans' drive for electoral power had strong affective dimensions that tapped into their collective history of displacement and exclusion. The hope was that new black majorities could transform cities in their own image and thereby redeem the long history of disfranchisement and expropriation" (194). She cites "two important national developments" that "empowered the Panthers to take on municipal campaigns: the candidacy of Shirley Chisholm for president of the United States and the National Black Political Convention in Gary, Indiana" (195).

weekend busloads of students came in and walked the streets" (284). Among those who joined in the consciousness-raising efforts were Lincoln University students Gil Scott-Heron and Ron Welburn (Baraka and Baraka, *The Music* 237).[5]

I begin with the concept of "home" as a potent metaphor for black consciousness as a shared struggle, one demanding an experimental model of social organization rooted in black communal values. I argue that this "source"—"love in black life," as Baraka put it—is the foundation from which he and Gil Scott-Heron built their political perspectives and developed their poetic techniques. Home is foundational to that period, for Newark was also the launching pad for Baraka's experiments with recording his poetic and theatrical work in collaboration with experimental jazz musicians. The synthesis of art and activism, as well as the innovative blend of poetry and music, had a profound impact on the direction of Scott-Heron's work as the poet-musician was also experiencing the effects of a return.[6]

In the fall of 1969, Scott-Heron had recently returned to coursework after a disastrous start at Lincoln and then a yearlong sabbatical during which he secured a contract from the World Publishing Company for his first novel, *The Vulture,* and book of poems, *Small Talk at 125th and Lenox.* The same semester he returned to school, Scott-Heron began collaborating with songwriter Brian Jackson; they formed their first band, called Black and Blues, and they began building a repertoire of songs now considered classics. Scott-Heron was already becoming known as a musician and writer, but he soon took the spotlight in a new role as an activist and community organizer as well. Returning from a weekend trip to see the Last Poets in New York, he learned that the drummer in his recently formed band, who was asthmatic, had died largely due to inadequate health care facilities on campus. Relying on the authority and discipline of the Vietnam veterans at Lincoln, Scott-Heron led a student strike. He composed a list of seven nonnegotiable demands and called an impromptu all-campus meeting. Distributing the demands to the student

---

5. Marcus Baram suggests that it was the Gibson campaign that brought Scott-Heron and Brian Jackson to Newark to perform in 1969 and that Scott-Heron returned later to read his poetry at Baraka's invitation (55). Scott-Heron's memoir does not recount his introduction to Baraka, but he writes about similar trips during the time, including one to Fayette, Mississippi, where he "witness[ed] the election of Charles Evers, Medgar Evers's brother, who was . . . the first Black mayor elected in the south since Reconstruction" (*The Last Holiday* 133). He also recalls making monthly trips to New York with bandmates to visit Abiodun Oyewole and catch the Last Poets during their "East Wind thing" (134).

6. While the musical approach of Scott-Heron's early recordings may owe more to the Last Poets, I would argue that Baraka's literary voice is a stronger influence on Scott-Heron's writing and the direction of his future work.

body and administration, he recalls feeling that "everything boiled down to my ability as a writer" (*The Last Holiday* 139). Within weeks, the striking students secured a twenty-four-hour campus clinic, inspections of the campus's medical facilities by a trained professional, the dismissal of the current physician and the hiring of a new one, and the purchase of a dedicated ambulance managed by campus security.

From their earliest encounter, Baraka understood that Scott-Heron had committed himself to synthesizing art and political activism. He explains that "even as a college student," Scott-Heron's poetry "was part of the movement of the masses of black people to liberate ourselves to destroy the legacy of slavery and humiliation which has always been our lot in white racist monopoly capitalist America" (*The Music* 237). It was no exaggeration for Baraka to write of his initial encounter with Scott-Heron as that of a teacher and student. "Imamu," the title Baraka had then recently adopted, did mean "teacher" or "spiritual leader," after all. If Scott-Heron was the "New Black Poet" as the cover of his album, *Small Talk at 125th and Lenox*, proclaimed, then Baraka was an established artist and leader of a movement to which Scott-Heron felt he belonged. But it was not long before Scott-Heron had published three books, released two LPs, and found himself in a master's program teaching creative writing. "Despite having a second album on the way," Scott-Heron recalls, "as far as I was concerned I was still a student. And if I tried to picture myself doing something professionally, it was as a novelist, not a musician" (*The Last Holiday* 160). Baraka's impact on Scott-Heron was more than circumstantial and extends beyond their shared political investments and activist orientation as writers.

Along with the Last Poets and Watts Prophets, Baraka's experimental collaborations with jazz musicians helped to innovate the kind of spoken-word recordings for which Scott-Heron would become famous.[7] Both artists, across several decades, used the LP format to synthesize popular art and vanguard politics. Their work was directed toward black audiences, and their poetic and aesthetic sensibilities were rooted in black vernacular forms even as they reached toward the vanguard. As an aspect of their blues-toned performances, both relied on humor to connect with audiences. They became known for their biting political satire, especially applied to popular entertainment, mass media, and consumer culture. Joyce A. Joyce asserts that Scott-Heron's work consistently denounces "the meretricious beauties that embody a capitalistic society." She identifies the "poetic-blues rap (or the satiric monologue)"

---

7. Baraka's early recordings with the New York Art Quartet, Sunny Murray, and the Jihad represent a further evolution of the form, especially the role and sound of the poet in collaborative musical settings.

as well as the "satirical lyric" as two of five major modes in his work (74).[8] Likewise, Baraka comments that satire "has always been present in my work," and that irony and humor are "characteristic of my view of things" (Melhem, "Revolution" 92). Tracing the ironic and satirical strains in their work reveals their sophisticated critiques of mainstream popular culture. Such ironic gestures throw into relief not only the bourgeois decadence, moral complacency, and aesthetic mediocrity of mainstream American culture, but also the fecklessness of American politicians and the sustained corruption of democratic ideals.

Set in comparison, Gil Scott-Heron's and Amiri Baraka's lyricism demonstrates the power of satire and vernacular humor traditions to affirm black consciousness and values. In the context of a hostile social and political environment, their satire aimed at provoking audiences to critically evaluate their world and, potentially, pursue changes to material conditions. Laughter provides catharsis, but a joke can also become a mnemonic for social critique. Gil Scott-Heron and Amiri Baraka engage with icons of consumer capitalism, mass media, and popular entertainment to break down America's fundamental contradictions. Their allusions to historical figures, entertainers, politicians, and fictional characters as well as to television and film titles, brand names, and slogans exemplify an element of the signifying tradition that Stephen Henderson calls "virtuoso naming and enumerating" (33). Through reversal and irony, signifying and the dozens, Baraka and Scott-Heron play with the masking trope of double consciousness and its literary manifestation: the ironic double voice.

According to Dickson-Carr, the African American trickster figure "consistently reifies the potential for the witty and idealistic to effect an alteration of material conditions," otherwise known as getting over (35). Baraka's and Scott-Heron's satirical vision of American culture and institutions uses vernacular humor, rooted in black values and folkways, to expose the hypocrisy of American society and its corrupt democracy. Tragicomic humor—an element of the blues aesthetic—serves as a bulwark against an oppressive, arbitrary world. Communal rituals of catharsis like dancing or laughing illustrate the true stakes of satire: to orient popular consciousness around principles of dignity, humanity (its beauty *and* ugliness), and agency, the right to control one's own destiny.

Baraka's "Look for You Yesterday, Here You Come Today" (*Transbluesency* 17–21) arguably exemplifies the concerns of his Beat-era poetry, but may also

---

8. The other categories are "the people's folktale, the musical poem," and "the mellow lyric" (74).

contain seeds of his later assault on Western values, symbols, and institutions.[9] It begins in a wry tone, full of layered allusions: eliotic verse peppered with beatnik humor. He name-drops high-art references including Lorca's *Poet in New York,* the playwright August Strindberg, and painters Leonardo, Bosch, Hogarth, and Kline. In the "terrible poems" (line 10) that arrive by mail, the speaker reads "Descriptions of celibate parties / torn trousers: Great Poets dying / with their strophes on" (10–12). These stimuli notwithstanding, existential dread and uncertainty prompt the speaker to a shocking realization: "There is probably no such place as BattleCreek, Michigan!" (62).[10] Television cowboys like Tom Mix and Dickie Dare are missing or dead and the speaker grows increasingly panicked:

> What is one to do in an alien planet
> where the people breath New Ports?
> Where is my space helmet, I sent for it
> 3 lives ago . . . when there were box tops.
>
> What has happened to box tops??
>
> O, God . . . I must have a belt that glows green
> in the dark. Where is my Captain Midnight decoder??
> I can't understand what Superman is saying!
>
> THERE *MUST* BE A LONE RANGER!!! (66–75)

Cowboys, spacemen, and superheroes are conjured by the speaker "as shields against culture's decline," and symbolize his "sentimental hope for the heroes of his radio days to lift up the culture's wilting frame" (Muyumba 30). The references evoke the false consciousness resulting from the alignment of mass media and industry through advertising and promotion schemes. The speaker's youthful anxiety over the arrival by mail of a space helmet or decoder ring illustrates the triumph of the capitalist fetish. The narratives and rituals of daily life have become completely structured by and oriented toward the market. The decoder is a decryption device that unlocks secret messages in

---

9. Watts identifies the poem's "endless introspections and explorations of the arbitrariness of personal histories, the inconsequentiality of life, and the meaninglessness of death" as indicators of Beat poetics (48).

10. Battle Creek, Michigan, nicknamed "Cereal City," is the home of Dr. John Harvey Kellogg, the medical doctor, health activist, and inventor of corn flakes. He was also a proponent of eugenics and scientific racism.

the media, but never points back at itself as a tool of instruction in the codes and values of the marketplace. The speaker grants that his musings may be "maudlin nostalgia" (78) or "sentimental" (81), but he blithely contends that this also "is part of my charm" (89).

While I concede that "Look for You Yesterday" is not the only, or even primary influence Baraka had on Scott-Heron's writing, I maintain that it offers an early glimpse of the kind of satirical allusions to mass entertainment that would become a hallmark of each writer's work. In "too soon too beat" (*Small Talk at 125th and Lenox* 49), Scott-Heron also portrays Western society as corrupt and exhausted, but still demanding sacrifices. The speaker asserts that exchanging integrity for social status is an act of self-denial: "soon, even your beating drums will have no / meaning. / soon, even your soul of souls will have no feeling" (lines 3–4). The necktie that marks professional identity and upward mobility is figured as a noose or slave shackles: "as sophistication soars and ties are tightened / collars will replace what music heightened" (5–6). The concluding couplet insists that any attempt to escape racial identity results in a *false* freedom dangled by oppressors hoping to ensnare the desperate and vulnerable: "in your search for freedom you left freedom behind. / chains once on your limbs are now binding your mind" (11–12). Transcending restraints on agency, mobility, and opportunity requires one to adopt the same bourgeois, white-supremacist value system that denies equality to others. Given Scott-Heron's ambivalent relationship to institutional education, the poem perhaps speaks to academic credentials as a dubious avenue to middle-class success. The qualifier "too beat" in the poem's title may also be an indirect swipe at Baraka's sojourn through the bohemian East Village—the retreat from blackness that he attempted to reconcile by moving uptown to Harlem and finally back to Newark.

In the years between Baraka's beat lyricism and his militant cultural nationalism, he regularly employed images and myths drawn from popular media, especially associated with the tradition of blackface minstrelsy. His book *The Dead Lecturer* (1964) contains "A Poem for Willie Best" (*Transbluesency* 62–69), who was a "Negro character actor whose Hollywood name was Sleep'n'eat."[11] Best's name appears later in the same book during the climactic moments of the iconic poem "Black Dada Nihilismus" (*Transbluesency* 97–100), where the speaker builds to the following dedication:

> For tambo, willie best, dubois, patrice, mantan, the
> bronze buckaroos.

---

11. This reference is the author's own footnote to the poem (*Transbluesency* 62).

For Jack Johnson, asbestos, tonto, buckwheat,
billie holiday.
    For tom russ, l'overture, vesey, beau jack. (lines 66–70)

Juxtaposing minstrel performers and stock characters with black revolutionary figures across history, the athletes and entertainers included occupy something of a middle ground. They inherited and sometimes fulfilled, but also
challenged and transformed restrictive stereotypes. Still, the poem suggests
that all these figures, including the poet's own grandfather, Tom Russ, were
battered by or succumbed to antiblack racism, some slowly, grindingly, and
others more violently.

Baraka's next collection, *Black Magic*, grows increasingly bombastic. Like
"Black Dada Nihilismus," poems like "The Bronze Buckaroo" (*Transbluesency*
135) and "Poem for HalfWhite College Students" (144) draw on pop culture
allusions framed by bitter irony, and each ends with violence, or the threat of
it. In the latter poem, the speaker accuses his addressees of imitating Hollywood actors rather than fashioning authentic selves—of "starchecking" rather
than "checking / yourself" (lines 8–9). One sister is "so full of Elizabeth Taylor, Richard Burton is / coming out of her ears" (14–15). The speaker implores:
"When you find yourself gesturing like Steve McQueen, check it out, ask / in
your black heart who it is you are, and is that image black or white, // you
might be surprised right out the window, whistling dixie on the way in" (21–
23). The pairing of humor and violence is perfectly in tune with the potential
for subversive irony in blackface minstrelsy, as in "A Poem for Willie Best,"
where the performer becomes "a renegade / behind the mask," and the performance "a renegade / disguise" (158–159, 160–161).

Scott-Heron's poetry is similarly invested in mediation and masking, but
the dominant metaphor of false consciousness in his work is the television
screen. Perhaps most vividly, his poem "omen" (*Small Talk* 22) opens with
an image drawn from a subway poster for the 1968 film *The Green Slime*: "a
giant eye zapped across the screen," its "tentacle type / feeler . . . / reaching
for someone, maybe me" (lines 1, 3–5). The trope of the screen carries heavier
symbolic weight in the poem "riot" (*Small Talk* 42–43), which bridges personal introspection and a radical critique of popular entertainment: "It probably won't happen tonight or / tomorrow or even next week. Things don't
happen / to your inside like they do in the mirror" (lines 1–3). The mirror
image in the initial lines sets up the further removal of the self from the visual
images through which we come to know, fashion, and evaluate ourselves. The
speaker projects the audience into a scene "right out of Richard Wright" (18),
where the television is ingeniously removed from the addressee by the store's

window, which functions as both a mirror and a second screen: "You'll be looking through the window of an / appliance store—a tv" (30–31), only to realize that "the hurt and hate will fill your mind. A window / will be broken" (34–35). A riot breaks out, "and you will never be able to go back to the / stick candy / land and talk shit about riots killing the movement" because "you will have been there" (40–42, 43). The poem's second person address ("you" and "your") and its use of the future tense ("will be") are striking precursors to the poem by which Scott-Heron would be most recognized in his lifetime, "The Revolution Will Not Be Televised." The concluding line of "riot" projects the completion of an as-yet-unrealized act of resistance by shifting into future perfect tense, "you *will have been* there" (43; emphasis mine).

In the final turn of "The Revolution Will Not Be Televised" (*Now and Then* 77–79), Scott-Heron's speaker gives the few positive, rather than negative, images of the revolution: It "*will* put you in the driver's seat" (line 76) and "the revolution will be LIVE" (82). Yet, until that point and despite the poem's insistence that the revolution will *not* be televised, the poem draws from the lexicon of advertising and entertainment to construct its perspective through the visual frame of the television screen. The opening lines revise Timothy Leary's famous ode to escapism: "Tune in, Turn on, Drop out." Scott-Heron says: "You will not be able to stay home, brother. / You will not be able to plug in, turn on and cop / out" (1–3).

Commercial sponsorship and interruption are unifying tropes: The revolution will not be "brought to you / by Xerox" (8–9) nor "The Schaeffer Award Theatre" (18). The speaker guarantees that the revolution will *not* "give your mouth sex / appeal" (19–20), "get rid of the nubs" (21), or "make you look five / pounds thinner" (22–23). The ironic function of negation is heightened as the imagery becomes more satirical and surreal. Though readers cannot help but imagine it anyhow, Scott-Heron insists that the revolution will *not* show us pictures of "Nixon blowing a bugle and leading a charge by / John Mitchell, General Abramson and Spiro / Agnew" 12–14). The same goes for Roy Wilkins's "red, black / and green liberation jumpsuit" (42–43).

The poem uses "instant replay" (37), "still lifes," and "slow motion" (41) to frame a television newscast: "NBC will not be able to predict the winner at / 8:32 on reports from twenty-nine districts," the speaker announces (32). The scene of "you and Willie Mae / pushing that shopping cart down the block on / the dead run" (27–29) or sliding a "color tv in a stolen / ambulance" (30–31) appears rapid-fire as if it were eyewitness footage on the "*Eleven / O'Clock News*" (55–56), though Scott-Heron notes that "there will be no highlights" (55). A kind of dark prophecy twists the conceit as the speaker doubles back on the lines "There will be no pictures of pigs shooting down / brothers / on the instant replay" (35–37). A bitter irony presents itself: Despite the proliferation of images and footage documenting police brutality, especially the killing of unarmed black citizens, even this vivid, brutal evidence has not stopped the state-sponsored violence. The revolution will not be televised.

Just as this critique of commercial media calls out across decades from its own time to our current moment, so do Scott-Heron's "presidential poems," which cover the time period between Watergate and Ronald Reagan's second presidential term. Taken together, these works tell a prophetic alternative history of the 1970s and '80s. Scott-Heron's first recording of "The Revolution Will Not Be Televised" was one of just a handful of lyrics to namecheck President Richard Nixon in his first year in office.[12] But with the administration unraveling in scandal, Scott-Heron returned the studio to follow up on the state of the union. His performance of the poem "H_2O Gate Blues" for his 1974 Strata East album *Winter in America* is both poetically ingenious and politically astute. The sequel, "Pardon Our Analysis (We Beg Your Pardon)," was released the next year, with another installment to follow in 1976, called "Bicentennial Blues." The latter poem coined nicknames for the new cast of characters: President Ford became "Oatmeal Man," then-governor Reagan was "Hollyweird," and President Carter "Skippy" (*Now and Then* 96–101, lines 96, 101, 108). Together they made "a blues trio" (111) and, with Henry Kissinger, "a blues quartet" (119). Scott-Heron continued serializing his satire into the 1980s with a poem for each of Reagan's elections: first "B Movie" and then "Re-Ron." Baraka called Scott-Heron's album *Reflections*, containing "B Movie," "a masterpiece" (*The Music* 239).

At the same time, Baraka was also populating his poems with public figures and political actors. Appearing together and separately across his book *Hard Facts* (1972) are Richard Nixon, Spiro Agnew, and Henry Kissinger. The Rockefellers and Kennedys also hold heavy symbolic value. Baraka's poems "History on Wheels," "Real Life," "When We'll Worship Jesus," "Horatio Alger Uses Scag," and "A New Reality Is Better Than a New Movie!" reference one or more of these figures. But not until 1979 did Baraka use a president's name in a poem to the extent that he did with Jimmy Carter's in the poem "Dope" (*Reader* 263–266). The central addiction metaphor refers literally to rising narcotic abuse in the post-Vietnam era, but also alludes to Marx's famous

---

12. Phil Och's song "Ten Cents a Coup" compares the president and vice president to Laurel and Hardy and emphasizes the role of television in shaping political consciousness. Charlie Daniels's "The Pope and the Dope" imagines sending Nixon as ambassador to Timbuktu, and excuses further racism with a haphazard denunciation of crony capitalism. Curtis Mayfield's bass-heavy jeremiad "(Don't Worry) If There's a Hell Below, We're All Going to Go" appeared on his self-titled album the same year, seeming to quote Nixon.

invective against religion as "the opiate of the masses." The phrase indicates that deferral of one's needs to the afterlife helps obscure class exploitation in this world. Baraka's vernacular refrain echoes across the poem: "It must be the devil" (line 20). It "cain be rockefeller" (31), and it "cain be / them rich folks" (38–39) because "theys good to us, i know, the / massa tolt me / so" (42–44), the speaker even "seed it on channel 7" (44) as well as "channel 9 i seed / it on channel 4 and 2 and 5" (45–46). Like television, the presidency is a national institution charged with affirming our collective faith in democracy and capitalism: "it ain't capitalism / naw it aint that, jimmy carter wdnt lie, / 'lifes unfair' but it aint capitalism" (67–69).[13] Echoes of "The Revolution Will Not Be Televised" are striking: Baraka's use of virtuoso naming (especially of politicians), his references to television, and his use of repetition and negation all echo Scott-Heron's masterwork. Baraka's recording of the poem demonstrates that he has a delivery and poetics of his own, but the poem engages in a tradition of signifying that begs us to put it in conversation with Scott-Heron's work.[14]

Both artists defied labels and transcended categories; their work must be understood as multifaceted and evolving. Despite often being reduced to their most famous or controversial lyrics, their work defies simplistic portrayal by relying on ironic reversals. From the long hot summers of the Black Arts movement into the twenty-first century, Amiri Baraka and Gil Scott-Heron created challenging, socially engaged art across forms and media that spoke to the struggles of everyday people. Their blues-toned modernism shared strong roots in black communities, and their black perspectives fortified them against the assaults of a hostile world. Against violence, false images, distractions, and oversimplifications, these artists pursued authentic self-knowledge whatever the cost. Daring to define themselves for themselves, they fought for their communities and widened the path toward self-determination.

---

13. The quotation perhaps refers to President Carter's response to a reporter during a 1977 press conference. When asked about abortion access for poor and working-class women, the president answered, "Well, as you know, there are many things in life that are not fair, that wealthy people can afford and poor people can't" (Carter 1237).

14. Baraka's recorded performance of that poem for the Folkways album *Contemporary Poets Read Their Poetry* has become one of his most well-known and reproduced readings.

13

"Pick Up Them Cliffords"

Amiri Baraka, Clifford Brown, and the Coinage of Currency

AIDAN LEVY

URIED IN BOX 22, folder 32 of the 219.5 linear feet of the Baraka archive at Columbia University's Rare Book and Manuscript Library was a 1,300-word typewritten document printed from a word processor on a dot-matrix printer with handwritten corrections, dated January 1994, with a nondescript title: "Essay/'Poem' on Money."[1] But the subtitle, "(from Why You Saying This: A Novel)" seemed more intriguing, and pointed to a mystery I intended to solve. It appeared to be a proof, similar to the proofs in an adjacent folder for *Funk Lore*, published in 1996, but for *Why You Saying This: Novel*, a text I had not read. Yet a quick internet search uncovered that there was no such novel. I asked anyone who might have heard of it, and no one had. The inclusion of an unpublished essay in Baraka's massive archive seemed plausible, but an errant fragment of an unpublished novel Baraka had never mentioned, with no ostensible provenance, was unlikely. The use of "novel" was somewhat clearly a catachresis—why would Baraka have separated it from the rest of the novel's manuscript? Why did it have the distinction "Essay/'Poem'" if it was excerpted from a longer work that was neither

1. This essay emerged from Brent Hayes Edwards's fall 2014 "Black Radicalism and the Archive" graduate seminar at Columbia University and a subsequent conference presentation at the Amiri Baraka Society's American Literature Association conference panel, "Digging: Amiri Baraka's Lesser Known Texts" (May 27, 2017). Grateful acknowledgment goes to Genji Amino, who was there when we first came upon the essay/poem, for his insights and archival savvy.

essay nor poem? The title seemed to recall the 1995 Afro-Modernist epic *Wise Why's Y's: The Griot's Song (Djeli Ya),*[2] the Beat Generation credo "How You Sound??," or the troubling of form and genre in *The System of Dante's Hell.* But was this misplaced "Essay/'Poem'" a trace of a lost novel, a postmodern genre joke, or an empty signifier, sans referent, placed to confound some credulous future archival researcher?

There may be no missing novel—not yet, anyway—but Baraka's "Essay/'Poem' on Money" has value nonetheless, illuminating how Baraka's theory of the relationship between jazz aesthetics, revolutionary politics, and US currency coalesces through his archival practice. The unpublished yet polished 1994 prose poem conflates the history of the penny and hard bop trumpeter Clifford Brown, positing a practical if ironic strategy for transforming pennies into dollars: simply pick them up. Baraka intends to return social and political capital to the people through self-determination efforts—at the literal grassroots level.

Embedded in Baraka's seemingly untenable provocation is a notion of the material penny as archive and a theory of the archive itself—what it signifies and could be. I argue that crucial to Baraka's liberation politics is what Arjun Appadurai calls the "diasporic archive," which resists the neoliberal, state-sanctioned model of "seeing the archive as the tomb of the accidental trace, rather than as the material site of the collective will to remember," as a kind of commemorative coinage that *co-memorates.* To obliquely reference Baraka's urban griot in the 1998 film *Bulworth,* the archive serves as the material repository not of a ghostly presence, but of a living spirit. For Appadurai, "the archive is a map," but for Baraka, it's also the buried treasure, in which "collective memory and the archive have mutually formative possibilities, thus allowing new traffic across the gap between the internalities and externalities of collective memory." To quote the promotional flier for Clifford Brown's June 1955 appearance at Music City in Philadelphia, part of Brown's living archive, "Brownie speaks to attentive listeners" (Glanden), and through his own archive, Baraka speaks. By tracing the penny imagery in Baraka's "Essay/'Poem' on Money" across his oeuvre, I will show how his archival practice constitutes not only the possibility of new traffic in Baraka studies, but an aspiration, a repository for his as-yet-unrealized Marxist idealism.

In the digital age, the term *archive* has evolved to mean, according to the *Oxford English Dictionary,* "to transfer to a store containing infrequently used files, or to a lower level in the hierarchy of memories" ("Archive"). To

---

2. See Kathy Lou Schultz, "Amiri Baraka's Wise Why's Y's: Lineages of the Afro-Modernist Epic," *Journal of Modern Literature,* vol. 35, no. 3, 2012, pp. 25–50.

archive something generally means to consign it to digital oblivion. I want to argue against this view of archiving as planned obsolescence, held in abeyance until eventual deletion. Rather, the brick-and-mortar archive can illuminate a hidden corner of an artist's history and development. Along these lines, "Essay/'Poem' on Money" becomes what Derrida refers to in *Archive Fever* as "consignation," not only "the act of assigning residence or of entrusting so as to put into reserve (to consign, to deposit), in a place and on a substrate, but here the act of *con*signing through gathering together signs" (3). Similarly, I want to read Baraka's essay as a consignation, not to what Schomburg calls the "dust of digging" (672), but to a nodal point in the history of Baraka's Marxist thought dating back to the early 1960s, an archival trace that unearths and unifies a circuit of imagery that recurs throughout his career. It is the *con*signing of an unlikely sign that accrues great value for Baraka: the US penny.

The essay opens with an anecdotal rumination, an idle moment of improvisation on the street transformed into an excursus on economic policy, using free associative rhetoric to construct what might be termed, as in jazz poetry, a jazz essay. Baraka recalls an everyday occurrence: picking up a penny on the street, traditionally an act of superstition, thrift, or resourcefulness, but which for Baraka naturally becomes figurative and polemical:

> I thought today about the last time I picked up a penny. It was near new & still determinedly shiny. People walked by whether they saw it or not. Brown so it blended with refuse & the bottoms of bushes, the dirt, left under leaves, "covered" by coming attractions of a skeleton's past.
>
> We cd be seen better through the cage of bones or better if the dead thing was blown away. We are mostly Brown! That is very beautiful, that mostly Brown—varying from various conditions. (During WW2 they took out the color & made us lead gray. The same color as bullets, the left arm of a demon. ("Essay/'Poem' on Money")

The penny is the essay's central metaphor, with Baraka by turns framing an alternative history of the penny, close reading the coin itself, and anthropomorphizing it as a synecdoche for black bodies, with this penny in particular representing jazz trumpeter Clifford Brown.

Baraka draws from several facts concerning the protean history of the coin he refers to as "the only colored money" ("Essay/'Poem' on Money"). One year after Emancipation, the Coinage Act of 1864 implemented several tangible changes to the currency: It legally altered the composition of the penny to increase the copper content of the alloy, interpreted by Baraka as "mostly Brown." This legislation introduced the phrase "In God We Trust" on US currency—according to Baraka, "so we don't blame nobody here"—as an addition to the Latinate motto "E Pluribus Unum" ("One from many"). It brought the two-cent coin into circulation, leading to a colloquial expression that, in Baraka's interpretation, devalues African American thought. "But think we was only 3 cents. That's why when we say something they say, 'Why you wanna put yr two cents in it?'" ("Essay/'Poem' on Money").

The penny shamelessly represented exploitation. It was not until 1909 that the government transitioned from the "Indian Head Cent," a perverse homage to settler colonialism, to the Lincoln penny. To Baraka, this meant "they want you to No. You are 1 cent. Used to have the native bro's head upon this low dog's brow. To say you are the same. And so we did mate, ourselves hurtling away from plantations—maroons (combines black and red. Dig?) and new brides and grooms" ("Essay/'Poem' on Money"). The notion of "maroons" evokes Glissant's concept of *marronage* but also a rusty penny. To Baraka, pennies, both who had access to them transactionally and literally on their faces, represented an imperialist system with the power to enslave, dispossess, or reify, but also the revolutionary potential to be picked up and repurposed for the creation of an autonomous maroon culture.

Baraka had warmer feelings toward the Lincoln penny, introduced in 1909 to commemorate the centennial of the birth of the man Baraka refers to as "our liberator. So I feel a we on that one cent" ("Essay/'Poem' on Money"). In 1943, the US Mint struck the steel cent in response to a copper shortage due to increased ammunition usage. As Baraka notes, "They needed the copper for war." Copper may be malleable and ductile, but it is a better conductor of heat than steel. The raw material for pennies was the same as the raw material for warfare.

In the "Essay/'Poem,'" Baraka intends to reclaim the penny's symbolic value. In an improvisatory rhetorical leap, he coins a new term for the penny—the Clifford—meaning Clifford Brown, the penny not as profit, but prophet. Alongside drummer Max Roach, Baraka's longtime biographical subject, Brown rose to prominence with Brown-Roach, Incorporated, forming a quintet that over the course of a mere two-and-a-half-year period redefined the jazz lexicon on the trumpet, bridging the innovations of Fats Navarro and Freddie Hubbard; shaped the hard bop idiom; and established a successful model of artistic self-determination. The Roach-Brown quintet, with George Morrow, Richie Powell, Harold Land, and then Sonny Rollins, represented "the cutting edge of post-bop elaboration of what the new music had taught," Baraka wrote (*Digging* 215). "Only the Miles Davis classic groups of the same period exist at the same intensity of artistic power and influence" (215). Affectionately known as Brownie, Brown died at twenty-five in a fatal car crash on

June 26, 1956, alongside Richie Powell and Powell's wife, Nancy.[3] Baraka's essay memorializes and politicizes this fallen prodigy as though emblazoning his image on the penny and imbuing it with his sound.

In the essay, as Baraka stoops to pick up the pennies, which he refers to as "Brownies" and then "Cliffords," he conjures Brown's memory: "I shd have heard 'Jordu' or 'Hymn to the Orient'—yet not even 'Parisian Thoroughfare.' Just the hot squeezed flashes of where I was" ("Essay/'Poem' on Money"). Baraka metaphorizes picking up pennies as a means of Marxist self-determination, just as the cultural capital signified by Brown could potentially be directed toward the same purpose. Brown is never mentioned explicitly by his full name; Baraka references his nickname and his repertoire, imagining the post-bop progenitor as a kind of immanent griot whose legacy could alter the way we listen if only enough people listened closely.

Through the conceit of discarded or lost pennies, "like a lost tribe run over a thousand times a day," Baraka insists that Brown's legacy be remembered, invoking "I Remember Clifford," the tribute composed by tenor saxophonist and composer Benny Golson:

> The only colored money. That's why people leave it walking past. I don't think I ever did. But now it's just I want to pick them up for definite. Like I tell people, like now forever, "Pick up them pennies." Hum, "I Remember Clifford." If it makes you. Pick up the colored money. ("Essay/'Poem' on Money")

The phrase "pick up them pennies," used pejoratively as a taunt, is here invested with a new meaning meant more to galvanize a political movement than to evoke jazz nostalgia—the penny as Clifford. This conceit recontextualizes the notion of jazz appropriation Baraka establishes in the "Swing: From Verb to Noun" chapter of *Blues People,* in which he claims that "*Swing,* the verb, meant a simple reaction to the music. . . . As it was formalized, and the term and the music taken further out of context, *swing* became a noun that meant a commercial popular music in cheap imitation of a kind of Afro-American music" (212–213). As Brown was commodified or "nounified," his music was reduced to mere pennies, exploited on the capitalist market, but in the context of Baraka's neologism—the penny as Clifford—he foregrounds his art as a material repository of political and artistic capital in which the

---

3. For a more in-depth study of Brown's life and aesthetics, see Nick Catalano, *Clifford Brown: The Life and Art of the Legendary Jazz Trumpeter.*

producers and listeners can absorb its artistically and politically generative surplus value.

The metaphor extended beyond jazz. "'Fat black bucks in a wine barrel room,' wrote Vachel Lindsay, the 'discoverer' of Langston. Like the poem covered us in Dis! So we are money. Bucks" ("Essay/'Poem' on Money"). Baraka's formulation of "Dis" is a recurrent trope, its meaning polyvalent: disrespect, dispossession, and the farce of dis-covery. Here, Baraka repudiates Vachel Lindsay as the "discoverer" of Langston Hughes; Hughes was Lindsay's busboy at the Wardman Park Hotel in Washington, DC. Baraka mines this linguistic slippage in Lindsay's "The Congo (A Study of the Negro Race)," in which the "black buck" constitutes the exploitation of African American culture on multiple levels, "to show we are part of the means of producing wealth. Not producers, but tools used by the producers!!" ("Essay/'Poem' on Money").

Picking up Cliffords meant returning the tools to their makers, a reversal of the exploitation Baraka describes in *Digging: The Afro-American Soul of American Classical Music* as "superexploitation." This term refers to artists cut off from their profits—"hit songs bought for a few pennies, while the corporations made millions" (*Digging* 79). Baraka's use of "digging" connotes the musician's slang ("you dig?") but also the process of reconstituting the past from lost fragments championed by Arthur Schomburg, the archivist and founder of the Schomburg Center for Research in Black Culture. In "The Negro Digs Up His Past," Schomburg writes that "a group tradition must supply compensation for persecution, and pride of race the antidote for prejudice" such that "the Negro historian today digs under the spot where his predecessor stood and argued" (670). This kind of archival digging is a kind of digging for pennies, and requires scrutinizing every last one; even the most innocuous-looking Cliffords may exceed their monetary value.

Yet in Baraka's utopian striving, his coinage as metaphor could also be literalized. In the "Essay/'Poem,'" he pushes for collective organizing and investment: "We shd pick them up. Save one a day. 35,00,000 a day. $350,000 a day. For Self Determination. For Self Determination for the oppressed Afro American Nation!" ("Essay/'Poem' on Money"). In this black nationalist polemic, Baraka refers to the approximately 35 million African Americans living in the US in 1994, sketching an admittedly utopian plan for populist revolution vis-à-vis a simple grassroots consolidation of capital through black consciousness and an insistence on collective organizing—everyone picks up a penny a day. "So pick up them Cliffords, & stash one a day, per person. In 10 years we got 3 million dollars for the plebiscite" ("Essay/'Poem' on Money"). Though a romantic vision in practical terms, Baraka illustrates a modus operandi analogous to the community-based ethos of the Black Lives Matter movement. To

Baraka, picking up pennies, figuratively and literally, meant fighting primitive accumulation, in which black lives were relegated to "the bottom of this order, the lowest, to be left in the street, ignored, thrown away as a game" ("Essay/'Poem' on Money"). One penny might be marginal, but all the pennies in the jar add up.

Perhaps more significant to Baraka scholarship, we can pick up pennies spread across the rest of his career.[4] In "Revolutionary Art," a lecture Baraka drafted several months after "Essay/'Poem' on Money" and delivered in May 1994 at the Poetry Project at St. Marks Church, then later that summer at the Jack Kerouac School of Disembodied Poetics at Naropa University, he suggests a riposte to superexploitation. "Where are the efforts that we ourselves control? You know what I'm saying?" he said during the Q&A at Naropa. "When we were growing up, like we say, there used to be a guy who would produce penny poems. You used to be able to walk around. 'Hey, you want to buy a poem?' A penny" (Baraka, "Lecture on Revolutionary Poetry."). Here, Baraka references the *Penny Poems* broadsheet series, published beginning in 1959, in which Baraka contributed three of the two hundred poems solicited nationally and distributed by students at Yale. Baraka's entries were "April 13 (for Tom)" (1959), an allusion to Thomas Jefferson's birthday, but possibly another poet in Baraka's circle, Tom Postell; "Spring & soforth" (1960); and "The Disguise" (1961). "Purchasers may plunk down a penny and take home a poem. They may not read before buying," read an article on the series. "There's no profit motive, say the Yale students" ("Yale Students"). This experimental reconceptualization of the literary market undermined a system of exchange that could quantify the monetary value of a poem; the penny represented each poem's unquantifiable symbolic value. Each entry in the series led with a graphical representation of *Penny Poems,* a drummer boy beating a bass drum labeled "PENNY"—perhaps, as Baraka might see it, banging on a Clifford.

In "Allah Mean Everything," a 1999 poem, Baraka echoes the "Essay/'Poem'":

Who invented money?
Why is money and slaves called a buck? Is a wooden nickel 3/5th of a
real one. Why is only a penny brown and got Lincoln on it? Is that why
they leave it on the ground. (*Allah Mean* 113–116)

He returns to the theme several times in 2003 in *Somebody Blew Up America,* first in "Beginnings: Malcolm," as well as the notion of "Dis":

---

4. See also Keorapetse "Willie" Kgositsile's "Whistle for Pennies" in *The Cricket* (1969), which Baraka edited; and *Money,* Baraka's 1982 jazz opera collaboration with composer George Gruntz. Amiri Baraka Papers, Box 27, Columbia University Rare Book and Manuscript Library.

> Even then, when he had left tht cage of sin,
> The Lamb sent a nightingale, wearing the red crescent
> of Marvin Gaye, mercy mercy me, O Lamb of Allah,
> of black sheep,
> of wooly feeling, oh nigger with only three pennies
> worth of Dis. (53–58)

In the title poem for the same collection, he uses money imagery yet again: "Who in disguise / Who had the slaves / Who got the bux out the Bucks" (22–24).

This double entendre recurs in "The Used Saver," a story in Baraka's 2007 *Tales of the Out and the Gone,* in which Eppsmith conflates himself with paper money:

> "I was born as the bank note was legal. I am the note." He laughed. "The Idea
>   is all it is, you know."
>   "It's paper," the white boy said. "You are invisible w/o it, but where are
>   you when you can't be seen?" (179)

Baraka's brief disquisition on the development of paper money as a symbolic store of value, a crucial step in the transition from any semblance of a C-M-C economy to an M-C-M economy in the spread of global capitalism, carries a secondary resonance with music in this passage. "I am the note" obliquely gestures toward the musical note as synecdoche for the musician, of a note worth more than its market value, currency with purchasing power endowed by the listener. This kind of note is non-fungible, a sui generis note, or a coin—the kind of prophetic note Baraka sounds in his rumination on the penny. To those who look and listen closely, a Clifford is not just a penny, and all the pennies are unique.

By 1994, when Baraka wrote the essay, the penny's value had long depreciated to the extent that it could be blithely discarded, not worth picking up on the street. In 2019, it cost nearly two pennies (or 1.99 cents) to make one penny,[5] but as of this writing, the penny nonetheless retains its worth, just as Baraka's archival Clifford has value. Part of the mission of Baraka's archival project, and archival recovery projects in general, is to allow for these coins to be brought back into circulation, or into circulation for the first time, and in polishing them, see what they illuminate. What ultimately, though, does

---

5. See Mike Unser, "Penny Costs 1.99 Cents to Make in 2019, Nickel Costs 7.62 Cents; US Mint Realizes $318.3M in Seigniorage," *Coin News,* 7 Feb. 2020, https://www.coinnews.net/2020/02/07/penny-costs-1-99-cents-to-make-in-2019/.

this conceptual mapping tell us? For one, it shows that the penny became a symbol with lasting currency for Baraka, and should therefore have lasting currency for Baraka scholars. Yet it has more significance than just another trip down the rabbit hole. This kind of archival project works toward collapsing the binary tension Diana Taylor describes between "the archive of supposedly enduring materials" and the "so-called ephemeral repertoire of embodied practice/knowledge" (19). To dig up those pennies, we must visit the archive, which is, after all, a kind of wishing well.

Baraka certainly felt that way. In 1997, three years after drafting the essay/poem, he instantiated these ideas through his involvement in the Newark Music Project, part of a national program called "Lost Jazz Shrines," which sought to "archive, record, perform, and create indigenous institutions and programs to reconstruct and present all the music produced in the city of Newark" (*Digging* 32). For Baraka, the living archive can breathe new life into a city—culturally, socially, and economically. "This archive will be organized to be studied, to entertain, but also as one avenue of economic and social development," he writes. "We will be raising a new city, a New Ark" (*Digging* 105). This archival (and Ark-ival) project brings Baraka's idealism into sharp relief, refusing to let a Clifford languish in the street, and deeply engaging in the project not just of remembering, but re-membering. There are more pennies, and penny poems, waiting to be picked up in the Baraka archive, and in the broader diaspora of black archives—always more digging deep in the pocket. But where does the money come from to recover these pennies, slipped into the breaks of the well-worn couch of history, to ensure that the legacy of someone like Clifford Brown, which cannot be quantified, will never die? This is where we see Baraka the realist, in for a penny, in for a pound. It takes change to make change. Perhaps the only surefire way, Baraka would say, is to pick up them Cliffords.

14

=

We Are the (Rhythm and) Blues

ANTHONY REED

AMIRI BARAKA, perhaps more than any other critic, helped shape our collective sense of black music as avant-garde, as cutting edge, cutting knowledge. In various writings, he refers to it as "the result of thought perfected at its most empirical," a "basis for thought," and a "cultural insistence, a feeling-matrix, a tonal memory" (*Blues People* 152, *Reader* 184, *The Music* 263). So powerful and influential are the arguments he and his Black Arts cohort made for the centrality of music to a self-originating, self-sustaining, self-referring black culture that they appear to us now fully naturalized. Such arguments for black art's "valid separation and anarchic disregard of" Western aesthetic standards and its function as a guard against "the sinister vapidity of mainline American culture" can make it difficult to appreciate the degree to which Baraka engaged "popular" or vernacular cultures (*Blues People* 225, 182). More pointedly, emphasis on separation as a noun can obscure his emphasis on the ethical and political imperative to separate. Crucially, too, while the music has its origins in slavery, Baraka emphasizes it as a post-emancipation modern phenomenon, claiming black vernacular musics as a hinge—a site of articulation, of joint and separation—between "Negro music" and "white America" rather than an indication of the essential relationship black people have to America. Through critical reflection, it becomes a site through which to reframe questions of subjectivity and consciousness. Framed as a "feeling matrix," a repository of intuitive subjective attitudes or stances through which to glimpse alternatives to racial capitalism emerging from the black proletariat, Baraka implicitly points to spaces for (re)invention within the culture industries, defined by the dominance of bourgeois norms and sensibilities. This essay situates Baraka's recording with the Spirit House Movers and his 2010 collaboration with bassist William Parker in a broader context of the simultaneous evolution of R&B and jazz in the 1960s and Baraka's own analysis of the relationship between bourgeois culture and the not fully dominated proletarian forms upon which it depends. He finds, within the obligatory recapitulation of alienated consciousness that for him and other Marx-inspired theorists of art characterizes the work of the culture industry forms of consciousness that, if not free, escape total determination. Baraka's relatively neglected R&B-inflected collaborations, for which recording is a key component, deconstruct the circularity of musical and rhetorical form and in that discrepancy reveal resources for the art to come.

In a 1980 interview with William J. Harris, Baraka makes a case for the importance of *recorded* sound:

> The page doesn't interest me that much—not as much as the actual spoken word. The contradiction with that is that I should be *recording* all the time, which I'm not for obvious reasons. I'm much more interested in the spoken word, and I think that the whole wave of the future is definitely not literary in a sense of books and is tending toward the spoken and the visual. (Harris, *Poetry* 147)

Harris had suggested that Baraka's Marxist poetry pursued an immediacy that made it more score-like, "less and less about the text," and more about the presumed immediacy of the voice. In context, Baraka seems to be pushing against a notion of sound as coincidence of object (music) and subject (musician), but also of writing as conditioned by the separation between subject and object. If we avoid the idealization of voice as fundamentally a sign of the self, and thus avoid the sense of poetry as a relay passing from world to subject to other subjects—if we read voice in terms of the radical implications of Baraka's claims for the Music—we might better grasp the stakes and contours of his arguments for black culture's vulnerable autonomy, but also his decision to engage the apparatuses of the culture industry. The *recorded* voice, like the written score, necessarily bears a sonority excessive to the intended message, a vibrational intensity whose separation from and potential displacement of the source is quite literal. Recording is a metonym for the culture industries (insofar as the "obvious reasons" seem to be bourgeois control of the means of technical reproduction), which have their own vexed histories as mechanisms of control and exploitation. What Ralph Ellison termed "democratic symbolic action" could well encourage reconciliation with or rationalization of US domination.[1] But it is also a history of incipient liberation, or at least recontextualization of the present by reshaping the sensorium, as Michael Denning's study of early sound recording alongside Baraka's own investment in recorded sound attest.

"Avant-garde," then, connotes refashioning aesthetic practice's ground in order to create practical and conceptual openings for new systems of value or thought in the intervals between the emergence of an alternative and its co-optation by the dominant power. The contradiction between black music as "populist high art" and the liberal democratic ideal typically championed by jazz critics does not derive from "black life being considered devoid of human quality," as Fumi Okiji has it, but from the glimpses of genuine human expression that gesture toward the authentic experience of freedom black life has always figured (*Jazz as Critique* 17). Okiji mobilizes to good effect Theodor Adorno's critique of jazz as an expression of the capitalist degradation and rationalization, and rightly critiques his exclusive emphasis on the bourgeoisie (with all other forms deemed derivative). I am not convinced either that "Black life can have no stake in the world and so is not party to the modes of deception that accompany" the ideology of individualism, or that "jazz emerged by way of a mode of subjectivity" (Okiji 26, 10). The former seems to me incorrect on its face, as the bitter history of Baraka's involvement in both pan-African and urban politics reveals. The latter posits jazz (and the blues) as autonomous forms appropriated by the culture industry rather than, as would be more accurate, forms whose apparent autonomy exists in dialectical relationship with the culture industries. The continual pursuit of what Baraka termed "uglier modes," aesthetics we call "out" because they seem to refer to social forms that have no immediate part within the thought–feeling matrix of consumer capitalism, speaks to the need for a social and political aesthetics defined not only by its opposition to society but by the positive vision of alternative social organization it makes available (*Reader* 174).

Baraka's first foray into recorded sound is an adaptation of "Black Dada Nihilismus," recorded with members of the New York Art Quartet (John Tchicai, woodwinds; Roswell Rudd, trombone; Lewis Worrell, bass; Milford Graves, percussion) in 1964 for their eponymous debut ESP-Disk recording. He continued to perform with them as an honorary fifth member. His most famous recording may be his adaptation of "Black Art," which first appears

1. Ellison refers to "democratic symbolic action" in an interview with John O'Brien collected in Graham and Singh, 222–234. For Baraka's rejoinder, see "Afro-American Literature and Class Struggle" in *Daggers and Javelins* 321–322.

(i.e., prior to its appearance in print) on a Sunny Murray record, *Sonny's Time Now,* on Baraka's own Jihad Productions, which would also release *A Black Mass,* featuring Baraka's adaptation of the Yakub myth accompanied by Sun Ra's Myth-Science Arkestra. The first recording Jihad released, however, was *Black and Beautiful . . . Soul and Madness,* which in the liner notes to the 2009 CD reissue Baraka characterizes as "word-music." That album opens with an uncharacteristic, within Baraka's recorded oeuvre, tribute to "Beautiful Black Woman." It is even more surprising to hear the Spirit House Movers (Freddy Johnson, Leonard Cathcart, Aireen Eternal, and Gilbert Monk) introduce the Miracles' 1965 hit "Ooo Baby Baby." Hearing the continuity between Smokey Robinson's group and doo-wop, and wanting to showcase Newark-based bassist Yusef Iman's group, the choice makes aesthetic sense if we consider it in the context of the many references to mass culture throughout his work of this period (e.g., Mantan Moreland, Herb Jeffries, et al.). But it also makes aesthetic sense. Where one might expect the interpolation of the rhythm and blues (R&B) cheater's begging lament ("I did you wrong" is the blunt explicit-but-euphemistic opening line) to be ironic, but Baraka retrospectively declares the Spirit House Movers' desire to "create word-music that reflected the Motown vibe" (Baraka, Liner notes, *Black & Beautiful*). The performance formally enacts the continuity Baraka and others in the moment claimed between the commercially ascendant R&B and the earlier forms it drew on, in this case doo-wop.

Part of Baraka's critique of rhythm and blues (and what he alternatively terms "bourgeois" or "middle class" art, the former apparently a synonym for "petty bourgeois") is its substitution of banal or stereotyped sentiments, whose spurious universality is an effect of their alienation from any real subjectivity. In this, he follows Adorno's concern for the isolation of the individual and the means by which all are encouraged to accept the simulacrum of individuality to mask the reality of capitalist production's exchangeable workers. Race is not external but designates a specific modality of a more general process for which voluntarist consciousness raising is as inadequate as the false consolations of nationalist or other thin universalisms. And yet, invoking Adorno's arguments with Max Horkheimer, even if the R&B ballad adapts only the simulacra of real feelings, we should hear songs like "Ooo Baby Baby" in their specific social and historical context, shaped in this instance by the Moynihan Report, in which black families appear hopelessly dysfunctional and black love non-normative. Appeals to love and forgiveness, the citation of black ongoingness, are a subversive ain't-studying-you riposte to the specific forms of discipline and social hygiene that target the black proletariat. Calculating within the terms of a patriarchal system to which she's attached even if it is relatively indifferent to her, the woman will likely choose to forgive this begging man, or at least take him back. This song, and others like it, confirm that it matters that she does.

As intertext, the song at once complements and complicates the poem (*Black Magic* 148–149). The Spirit House Movers perform only the introduction and the chorus, in effect suppressing the lead–background and verse–chorus dichotomy around which the Miracles—later Smokey Robinson and the Miracles—and other R&B groups structured their songs. More than that, they remake the *specific* narrative of romantic infidelity into a *general* account of black male–female relations. However, the poem maintains the play of abjection and objection, the play between "I did you wrong" and "You've made mistakes, too" that defines the source text's equivocal begging. "Beautiful Black Woman" is, as Ntozake Shange says in an interview with Marlon B. Ross, "like an Ave Maria" (Ross, "Interview" 487). It turns on a homophonic pun between "raining" and "reigning" in order to effect its final plea for intercession:

> Black
> queens, Ruby Dee weeps at the window, raining, being lost in her
> life, being what we all will be, sentimental bitter frustrated
> deprived of her fullest light. Beautiful black women, it is
> still raining in this terrible land. We need you. We flex our
> muscles, turn to stare at our tormentor, we need you. Raining.
> We need you, reigning, black queen. (lines 4–10)

Like the song it interpolates, one could read Baraka's tribute as merely instrumental, an attempt to acknowledge wrong and to convince black women to stay in the fold of hetero-patriarchal power relations as "daughter, wife/mother" (19).

R&B begging in the phonographic poem functions as the studium, a grammar-like structure that generates meanings irrespective of reference. In this instance, it's a grammatical structure of men speaking to or about women, inviting them into hetero-patriarchal visions of domesticity. The poem initially follows that pattern. The addressee of the poem's first part, the agent of failure, is presumably male—"Beautiful black women, fail, they act" (1), "we fail them" (3). Women weep long, grow "sentimental, bitter, frustrated," as "we all will be." The unexpected invocation of Ruby Dee, which marks the phonopoem's pivot to directly addressing women, disrupts both canny readings (this is a sincere tribute to black womanhood) and cynical readings (i.e., this is a perfunctory or generically necessary tribute). "Ruby Dee" is on one level a synecdoche for the black women and black womanhood the poem celebrates. Contemporary readers and listeners would probably first have thought of Dee's role on the prime-time melodrama *Peyton's Place*, which makes her name metonymic of those culture industry forces that deprive black women of their "fullest light." The proper name "Ruby Dee" is an audio-conceptual punctum, an excessive element whose irrepressible referentiality overflows and reroutes the studium's grammars. It brings together at once knowability and opacity. In this world, black women are surrounded by words traded among and between men (the presence of Claudette Rogers Robinson in the Miracles or Aireen Eternal in the Spirit House Movers notwithstanding); they occupy and sustain a world shaped by male desire in which they are invited to play a subordinate part. Weeping, without diagnosing or understanding the problem, at least indexes it, makes it clear that if she accepts the manipulations and false promises of *Peyton's Place*, "Ooo Baby Baby," and by implication "Beautiful Black Women," what she accepts is presumably not the offer to help or be helped with which the poem ends, but the implicit offer of a time, unimaginable within the grammars of address here, where she might speak on her own behalf.

If Smokey Robinson seems unlikely as an aesthetic partner, the encounter with Curtis Mayfield, another male falsetto singer who rose to greater prominence after leaving a doo-wop-based ensemble, dubbed by Aldon Nielsen "the very poet of the civil rights era," seems almost inevitable ("Belief" 172). Their delayed encounter takes place via collaboration with bassist William Parker, standard-bearer of the contemporary jazz avant-garde and self-proclaimed proponent of "the bigger tune called Peoples' Music." Part of Parker's project, like Baraka's, is to find the "inside song," deeper connections between forms of black art beyond what he elsewhere refers to as the "pasteurization of musicians through music education," which facilitates the co-optation of art and artist by the culture industry. Like Baraka, Mayfield drew on the insights vernacular utterance affords, making everyday usage the substance of thought, as when the persona of "Little Child Runnin' Wild" declares the pain is "getting worser day by day / and all my life has been this way." And yet, unlike Baraka, despite his chairing Cabrini Green's Committee on Alternative Social Thought, Mayfield's approach might be characterized, in Fred Moten's terms, by "an affective speaking that comes out of nowhere, as if said by nobody, as if about nothing" (*Consent* 69). In his approach, there's something we might characterize as less furtive than indirect, a "counterstrophic (non)violence," an off-to-the-side, there-but-I'm-gone ethereality that puts him on the margin of an era largely characterized by baritone belters and big talkers (69). Rather than simply cover Mayfield, Parker's group, including Baraka, vocalist Leena Conquest, pianist Dave Burrell, saxophonists Sabir Mateen and Darryl Foster, trumpeter Lewis Barnes, and either percussionist Hamid Drake or Guillermo E. Brown, among others (including choirs of as many as ninety children from the Parisian *banlieues*), re-create Mayfield songs in order to "present a full spectrum story that would be in tune with the original political and social message laid out by Curtis" (Parker). Part of that re-creation, recorded on stage between 2001 and 2008 in France, Italy, and the US, is the interpolation of poetry from Baraka alongside Parker's own poetry, performed by Conquest.

To conclude this essay, I will focus on one track from Parker's album, "I'm So Proud / Ya He Yey Ya," which takes Impressions-era Mayfield out into a modal, riff-based meditation on the song's themes and origins. The song is and is not about race pride, does and does not recapitulate an anxious, possessive patriarchy ("it would hurt to know if she ever were untrue"). Conquest's respectful rendering of the lyric smooths away the jagged edges of Mayfield's falsetto's "poor musical theater," while the ensemble, with Guillermo E. Brown substituting for Hamid Drake on percussion, performs a passable if restless version of 1960s R&B, members of the all-woman choir assembled for the occasion providing ethereal background vocals.

It's easy to miss the tension roiling beneath the ensemble's respectful cover until around the three-minute mark, when the initial vocals end and Parker begins a bass solo that moves one harmonic step away from what Mayfield wrote into a more open sound, propelled now by a polyrhythmic (12/8) ostinato that introduces Baraka. Once Burrell and Brown join, the ensemble release the tumultuous energy they'd been building, an uncoiling groove that stands as an auditory sign of the feeling matrix and tonal memory Baraka theorized. The shift of energy opens the way for the "inside song," that is, the out song, the song of the way out. Calmly, Baraka begins his otherwise unpublished poem: "We proud / I'm so proud / For you be what you see." With this intro, he reframes the Mayfield lyric into a different kind of tribute to black women.

Where one might expect her to be praised for resolving a contradiction between essence and appearance ("you be what you *seem*"), the line runs in a different direction. If certain phenomenological and poetic traditions start from the presumption of the subject's separation from the world, and thus stipulate its "intendedness" toward the world (and, implicitly, its mastery and subjugation of the world), to "be what you see" posits a mode of subjective experience outside this framework. Such philosophical moves will be familiar to students of Baraka's work, and the Music he championed, which so often proceeds from alternative or heterodox conceptions of the subject and its relation to the collective or common. But it immediately tips us off that this pride makes the satisfaction of illusory, socially necessary desires only apparently personal, secondary. Mayfield's "untrue," rather than referring to infidelity, now refers to a false relationship to the world. The rest of the poem carries out a meditation on the true and the beautiful, Baraka having recourse to the songfulness that lies on the "inside" of his verse, singing, "We are deeper than the surface / we are broader than the sky," holding out the "-er" with a surprisingly strong vibrato. He speaks in what appears to be Swahili, and when he repeats, a chorus of women's voices joins his, chant-singing "ya he yey ya" in loose unison as he reframes pride as "loving your wholeness." Baraka's poem continues to riff on these themes, worrying the lines but not substantially changing them. His voice gives way to Darryl Foster's soprano saxophone solo, which extends and intensifies what's come before it, but women's voices, atop Parker's bass, yield nothing, effecting a kind of demand or a conception of wholeness for which no models are forthcoming. It's not a model for alternative society, but sounds the struggle of continual self-abolition Baraka identifies in the music, its will to be other than itself.

At stake here and in the previous example is not politics per se, but something ante-political. Baraka's engagement with rhythm and blues sounds the call to relationships impossible within available understandings of the subject, the poem, or the (female-identified love) song. The space of writing and collaboration is here one of encounter that rather than "transcending" the self and leaving underlying assumptions in place, instead "kills" the self by including knowledge of the self that writes and performs as an internal limit of the project to be overcome in the finished text. We might, then, register rhythm and blues not as a stable repertoire of rhetorical and melodic phrases but as potential ways of relating poetically and performatively, alternative poetic and performative grammars. They operate not through modernist refusal and separation from bourgeois society, but by reminding that fulfillment of a desire always exceeds, differs, and defers the form of its demand: stay with me, get in the groove.

PART II

IN THE TRADITION

Reassessments, Recollections, Legacies

15

===

The Legacy and Place of
Amiri Baraka

LAURI SCHEYER

MIRI BARAKA built on the historical tactics of African American literature in his activist and politically instrumental view of poetry and poetics. This "conservative" motive allowed him to successfully insert African American poetry into the critical framework of American poetry and bring these previously divergent genres together. Though his methods were widely regarded as revolutionary, he strategically and consciously applied two defining characteristics of the African American poetry tradition to the contemporaneous moment: art as political action for the communal benefit and art as a performative multimodal space. By alluding in his aesthetic ethos of the 1960s to past practices and conditions, he became an inspiration for many African American poets who had been following diverse stylistic paths. He also irrevocably forced prominent figures in varied schools of the "new American poetry" to attend to the voices and presence of African American poets in the American poetry canon. Previously, African American poetry had no clear single guiding spirit in a comparable position. The trajectories of American and African American poetry had been regarded as unrelated or parallel paths, as amply demonstrated by the non-race-based anthologies that consistently contained either Baraka as the sole token representative of all African American poetry or no black poets at all. Following the 1960s, this pattern of exclusion slowly but demonstrably changed in its openness to including black poets in literary magazines and poetry anthologies in the US and UK due to Baraka's determined intervention.

In a long career marked by a succession of iterations and impacts, the era associated with the Black Arts Movement represented a watershed in the personal and professional life of Baraka. During this period, he emerged more prominently as an instigator of activist poetics among black poets and as a force to increase African American representation in American poetry. In *The Autobiography of Leroi Jones,* Baraka thoroughly documented his own origin story as an African American poet with certain "natural proclivities" in a white-oriented society. Early on, he recognized that "a political consciousness was lurking" beneath his interest in art and culture. Influenced by underrecognized and underappreciated (to this day) African American contemporaries like Allen Polite and A. B. Spellman, he was also "open" to "white poets of all faiths and flags," including the "schools" of the Beats, San Francisco Renaissance, Black Mountain, and New York (233). "Whitman and Williams and Pound and Apollinaire and the Surrealists were our prophets," he recalled (234), enumerating the breadth and depth of his influences at the time. In contrast with his own receptivity to everything that was interesting in aesthetic expression, Baraka was vocal about the absence of reciprocal enthusiasm among white poets and publishers toward a panoply of African American writings. He observed the prevailing climate of racism where he was often the sole black figure in publications, asking "what had happened to the blacks" and "How is it that there's only one colored guy?" (231). Regardless of Baraka's token inclusion, most collections of Anglo-American poetry maintained a pattern of racial segregation through the 1960s and 1970s. The slow but appreciable shift to new practices of racially diverse representation are in no small part the result of Baraka's adamant pursuit of aesthetic and stylistic justice.

•

Baraka was an energizing force for many African American poets whose aesthetics and politics previously had been maintained, or at least regarded, as separate entities. He had enormous impact on a surprisingly wide range of African American poets who are not typically associated with either the Black Arts Movement or with practicing a poetics of political witness and activism. Baraka as a monumental postmodern figure was a standard-bearer for the continuously confrontational, oppositional, and righteous history of African American poetry that addresses social issues, reveals the truthful realities of black life in America, adapts assertively to changing times and situations, contains blazingly direct honesty and outrage against lies and bad faith, devotedly preserves a consciousness of African origins, comments on African American communal needs and issues, and insists on being performed and heard inside—not on the outskirts—of the American political and literary landscape.

Through the connections and active outreach of Baraka, the relationship between the American "new poetries" and the varied trajectories of African American poetries began to shift in the 1960s. The inextricable relationship between art, action, performance, and politics that Baraka relentlessly modeled began to slowly infuse the various mid-century "schools" of American and African American poetry and poetics. African American voices were increasingly perceived as essential to the American and Anglophone poetry tradition. Simultaneously, Baraka served to ignite a spirit of political agency that resulted in the emergence of political themes in a diverse range of African American poets, including those who may have radically differed from his literary or personal style. The courses of both the African American and American literary traditions changed as a result of Baraka's own transformations in the 1960s and after. We become better able to see in a properly illuminated light how Baraka upheld and extended the revolutionary statements and styles of earlier poets like George Moses Horton, and ignited purposeful and focused rage and action among contemporaneous African American poets generally affiliated with radically different literary values and purposes. We are enabled to better appreciate how the paths of political engagement by white American poets were influenced by Baraka and how this impact was not isolated from his role as an instigator for African American poetry and poetics. Through the life and work of Amiri Baraka, especially in the 1960s, we gain an expanded and more accurate perspective of the correspondences among black and white politically engaged American schools of poetry in the late twentieth century, which too often have been artificially segregated based on racial assumptions about the authors.[1]

---

1. This topic is discussed at greater length in my essay, "Zero Hour and the Changing Same: Aesthetic Modernism and Black Nationalist Identity" in *Journal of Foreign Languages and Cultures*, vol. 4, no. 1, June 2020, Hunan Normal University Press, pp. 99–113.

16

Anthologizing the Poetry of Amiri Baraka, 1960–2018

Howard Rambsy II

THE EXTENSIVE CIRCULATION of Amiri Baraka's poems in anthologies over the last several decades is one of the great underreported stories in book history and American poetry. From nearly the beginning of his career to after his death, anthology editors chose to repeatedly reprint Baraka's poems. His poetry has appeared in so many collections for so long now that we might take his ubiquitous presence for granted. The possibility of a fiery black artist and political activist becoming one of our most canonical poets was still no easy feat. Yet, Baraka's poetry became a mainstay in American literature anthologies. To understand why and how, we might begin by following Larry Neal's directive about what to do when encountering an African sculpture in a New York art gallery—"Ask yourself: What is it doing there?" ("Shine" 648). Indeed, ask yourself: What is Baraka's poetry doing in all these anthologies?

In some cases, his poems contribute to a chorus of black poets. In other instances, he and his works perform the role of tokenism: diversifying a collection of nearly all white poets. In still other collections, his poems appear alongside various "Black Arts" compositions. In one anthology, he is the youngest contributor, and in another, he is one of the oldest. In one recent occurrence, Baraka's poem "SOS" serves as the title of an entire anthology. In dozens of collections, his poetry is there doing dozens of things.

Baraka is accurately described as a "widely anthologized" poet. Never-theless, scholars have not accounted for the nature of his frequent appear-ances in literature collections. Editors have collectively canonized Baraka and simultaneously constricted views of his dynamic creative output. A data analy-sis of his poems included in more than one hundred anthologies published over nearly six decades illuminates the ways editors made him one of our most frequently anthologized African American poets while at the same time conservatively representing the full range of his compositions. The history of Baraka's poetry in anthologies is the history of literary curation, that is, of editors selecting and regularly replicating selections made by previous editors.

A data set, not only a standard bibliography, creates new possibilities for understanding the transmission of Baraka's poetry. Digital software such as a basic Excel spreadsheet allows us to organize, tabulate, and quickly reconfig-ure hundreds of items associated with the publication of poetry. Since 1960, anthologists reprinted Baraka's poetic compositions more than four hundred times. A standard bibliography can provide a record of those publications. A data set, on the other hand, facilitates our abilities to quantify, rearrange, and visualize the multifaceted nature of Baraka's reprinted poems.

This essay reveals how digital tools and data analysis chart the transmis-sion of poems by a prolific African American literary artist, Amiri Baraka. The first section of the essay offers a brief numerical overview drawn from a Baraka poetry data set.[1] The section indicates the possibilities of quantifying aspects of bibliographic information. The second section explains why the appearances of Baraka's poems across a large number of anthologies consti-tute an extraordinary though limited representation of his work. Finally, the third section presents the implications of utilizing data management software to chart the publishing histories of black poetry. The propensity of dozens of editors to continually select Baraka's work for inclusion presents us with opportunities for exploring literary history in innovative ways.

A BARAKA POETRY DATA SET BY THE NUMBERS

Scholars describe Baraka as a consequential figure in black literary history. As Arnold Rampersad once observed, Baraka "stands with Wheatley, Douglass,

---

1. Many thanks to Kenton Rambsy for collaborating with me on several different data sets, including projects on Jay-Z, twentieth-century African American literature, and the con-tents of the *College Language Association Journal*. Those previous data sets shaped the design of my Baraka data set. For the initial phase of the project, I received invaluable contributions from my research assistant Rae'Jean Spears.

Dunbar, Hughes, Hurston, Wright, and Ellison as one of the eight figures who have significantly affected the course of African-American literary culture."[2] Baraka was a tremendously prolific writer, and just as important, editors persistently chose to reprint his works, ensuring that he would have an expansive reach. In retrospect, Baraka's productivity as a poet and his popularity as a contributor to anthologies determined that he would have a data-rich publishing history. In other words, a bibliography of his poems, not to mention his various other writings and criticism on his works, contains abundant information.

My Baraka poetry data set identifies 136 of his unique poems, which in total appear 481 times in 120 anthologies published from 1960 through 2018. The reprints of his poems vary. For instance, sixty-three of his poems appear in just one collection, while seventy-three of his poems appear in two or more anthologies. Moreover, twenty of his poems appear in six or more anthologies, and ten of those poems appear in ten or more anthologies. Baraka's "Preface to a Twenty Volume Suicide Note," "An Agony. As Now," "A Poem for Black Hearts," and "In Memory of Radio" are his most frequently selected poems, each appearing in more than twenty collections.

Although Baraka actively produced new poetry throughout his career, editors anthologized a majority (63 percent) of his poems that were first composed prior to the 1980s. His five most anthologized poems—"Preface to a Twenty Volume Suicide Note," "An Agony. As Now," "A Poem for Black Hearts," "In Memory of Radio," and "Black Art"—were all produced before 1970. During the twenty-first century, Baraka's "Somebody Blew Up America," concerning provocative claims about the September 11, 2001, terrorist attacks, sparked considerable debate. The poem subsequently became one of the poet's most widely discussed works over the last two decades. Nonetheless, that poem does not appear in any of the thirty-five anthologies published after 2000 that include poems by Baraka.

Like with numerous other poets, editors regularly selected just a few Baraka poems—nineteen anthologies include only one of his poems, twenty-six include two of his poems, and twenty-one include three of his poems. Still, in several cases, editors chose to publish even more, with fifty-four anthologies including four or more Baraka poems. Editors published eight or more of his poems in fifteen anthologies. Dudley Randall's *The Black Poets* (1971) includes eighteen Baraka poems, more than any other anthology. *The Poetry of Black America* (1973), edited by Arnold Adoff, includes fourteen Baraka poems, and *Call & Response: The Riverside Anthology of the African American*

---

2. Versions of the statement from Rampersad, which first appeared in *Amiri Baraka: The Kaleidoscopic Torch*, edited by James B. Gwynne, have circulated as book blurbs on Baraka books, such as *The LeRoi Jones/Amiri Baraka Reader*, and in articles.

Literary Tradition (1998), with Patricia Liggins Hill as general editor, includes thirteen Baraka poems.

Scholars and commentators generally refer to the 1960s as a defining moment in the production of African American literary history in part because of the Black Arts Movement. However, the 1970s, more so than the 1960s, were when editors reprinted a really large number of Baraka poems. During the 1960s, Baraka's poems appeared in fourteen anthologies, but his poems appeared in thirty-three anthologies during the 1970s. His poems appeared in nine anthologies during the 1980s, twenty-nine during the 1990s, twenty-three during the 2000s, and eleven during the 2010s. Anthologies published during the 1970s and 1990s account for approximately 52 percent of the books in the data set.

There are hundreds of anthologies with no black authors. A slight majority—sixty-two—of the anthologies in this Baraka data set, though, includes primarily African American writers.

An additional four anthologies—*Forgotten Pages of American Literature* (1970), *You Better Believe It: Black Verse in English from Africa, the West Indies and the United States* (1973), *Giant Talk: An Anthology of Third World Writing* (1975), and *Unsettling America: An Anthology of Contemporary Multicultural Poetry* (1994)—consist of a large number of ethnically diverse contributors. In these sixty-five anthologies, Baraka's works appear alongside those of dozens of other black poets. Conversely, Baraka is among a relatively small group of African American poets, which sometimes includes Langston Hughes, Gwendolyn Brooks, Robert Hayden, and Rita Dove, whose works appear in the fifty-five anthologies composed of primarily white writers.

Poetry anthologies account for the majority of collections in this data set. Overall, seventy of the total 120 anthologies focus on poetry, while fifty of the collections contain an assortment of poetry and prose. Among the sixty-two African American collections, thirty-five of the books focus on poetry, with the other twenty-seven including poetry and prose. None of the anthologies with primarily African American contributors were published during the 1980s. Among the anthologies that include Baraka's works, W. W. Norton and Company produced twenty-three of the collections, more than any other publisher in the data set.

BARAKA'S EXCEPTIONAL PRESENCE IN LITERATURE ANTHOLOGIES

Students who take survey courses on African American literature typically encounter a relatively small sample of works by poets. Limits of time and space make it difficult to offer expansive views of prolific poets. Accordingly, students who come across Baraka's work in a single anthology might not become aware of his exceptional presence in American and African American publishing histories. Even collections of Baraka's works such as *Transbluesency: The Selected Poetry of Amiri Baraka/LeRoi Jones 1961–1995* (1995) and *SOS: Poems 1961–2013* (2014), both edited by Paul Vangelisti, cannot adequately capture the extent to which Baraka's poems circulated across the decades in multiple anthologies. Recognition of the far-reaching transmission of his poems requires some consideration of his extensive publishing record in more than one hundred collections, spanning multiple decades.

A data set on the publication of Baraka's poems in anthologies confirms his associations with a wide variety of movements and literary periods. He appears in anthologies as a Beat poet, as a new American poet in 1960, as a new black poet in the 1970s, as a postmodernist poet, as a multicultural poet, and as an African American poet from the 1990s onward. Baraka is situated within the context of the Black Arts era in the three editions of the *Norton Anthologies of African American Literature* (1997, 2003, and 2014). As a nod toward his affinity for writing about music, Baraka appears as a contributor to *The Jazz Poetry Anthology* (1991), *Blues Poems* (2003), and *Jazz Poems* (2006). Baraka is the youngest contributor in *The New Oxford Book of American Verse* (1976), and he is the second oldest, after Sonia Sanchez, in *Of Poetry and Protest* (2016). Baraka's varied placements are suggestive of his unique adaptability over the course of six decades.

Like Wheatley, Dunbar, Hughes, and Brooks, Baraka is one of the most frequently included black poets in American and African American literature anthologies. Nonetheless, Baraka is notably distinct. Few, if any, other major African American poets were described as being a leading political or controversial figure the way Baraka was. For his biographical sketch in *Kaleidoscope* (1967), Hayden explains that Baraka "has become in a relatively short time the most controversial writer in America" (208). In the sketch on Baraka in *Black American Literature: Poetry* (1969), Darwin Turner notes that Baraka "has become a spokesman and a leader for many young black people who are rebelling against traditions of society and art" (119).

In *On Being Black* (1970), Charles T. Davis and Daniel Walden open their sketch on Baraka by noting that when he "writes poetry the words are weapons" (353). Stephen Henderson, in *Understanding the New Black Poetry* (1973), writes that Baraka is "the central figure of the new Black literary awakening" (380). The recurring presentations in 1960s and 1970s anthologies of Baraka as a leader and as controversial advanced a view of him as our most political major author.

The designation of Baraka as a leading poet also alerted the dozens of subsequent editors about why they should necessarily include the writer in their anthologies. Although dozens of poets published poems in Black Arts–era anthologies, only a small number of those writers had their works selected for regular inclusion in general, primarily white anthologies. Baraka was one of those poets. He in fact appeared in ostensibly white poetry anthologies prior to the formation of the Black Arts Movement. Nonetheless, his involvement with cultural and political movements of the mid- to late 1960s reinforced and extended his reputation as an essential poet for inclusion in subsequent black and white anthologies.

Baraka was not only viewed as a poet. Editors of general anthologies presented his plays, essays, and short stories, demonstrating that he distinguished himself in multiple genres. Some editors even signaled that his identity rested on issues beyond writing. In *Literature in America: The Modern Age* (1971), Charles Kaplan describes Baraka as "an activist and black militant" before identifying him as a literary artist. In the biographical sketch for *Black Fire* co-edited by Baraka and Larry Neal, Baraka is described as "poet, social critic, and dramatist" (Jones and Neal 664). The label "social critic" would persist and appear in biographical sketches on Baraka for decades.

Since the 1990s, biographical sketches in contemporary anthologies increasingly referred to Baraka as a primarily literary figure. In the 1960s and 1970s, though, the covert politicized nature of black artistic discourse was reflected in descriptions of Baraka. In *Dark Symphony* (1968), James A. Emanuel and Theodore L. Gross note that although Baraka "considers himself primarily a poet, his plays and essays have added hectic controversy to the arts." They go on to observe that his poetry "seems almost homicidal to some, certainly vitriolic to others, but also delicate and gentle to still others" (513–514). Abraham Chapman, in *Black Voices: An Anthology of Afro-American Literature* (1968), points out that Baraka "started out in literature as an avant-garde writer with a primarily aesthetic interest but has since became an active controversial black nationalist" (482). Four years later in *New Black Voices*, Chapman described Baraka as a "poet, playwright, novelist, essayist, social critic, music critic, anthologist, editor, and director of Spirit House, a Black community organization in Newark." The editor also identified Baraka as "a leading figure of the nationalist Black arts movement" (207–208). As Chapman's labels suggest, Baraka was presented by editors as occupying multiple subject positions.

Baraka's name changes make him additionally unique among almost all major black poets. Anthologies record the poet's name changes from "LeRoi Jones" to "Imamu Amiri Baraka" to "Amiri Baraka." Several anthologies labeled him "Amiri Baraka (LeRoi Jones)," and at least one, *The Heath Anthology of American Literature,* Vol. 2 (1990), referred to him as "Amiri Baraka (LeRoy Jones)" (Lauter et al. 2448). The cover of Donald Allen and George F. Butterick's anthology *The Postmoderns: The New American Poetry Revised* (1982) presents "LeRoi Jones (Amiri Baraka)" while presenting him as "LeRoi Jones/ Amiri Baraka" in the book. There was evidence of confusion, if not resistance, concerning how to refer to Baraka during the late 1960s and early 1970s as he was shifting his name. In *Afro-American Voices 1770s–1970s* (1970), Ralph Kendricks and Claudette Levitt identified the poet as "LeRoi Jones (1934–), or Imamu Baraka, as he now prefers to be called" (346). The editors were acknowledging the poet's new name but nonetheless choosing to still present his poems under "LeRoi Jones."

Since numerous editors arrange poets chronologically and by year of birth, Baraka's name changes did not lead to major shifts in where he and his works appeared in anthologies. Yet there were exceptions, as some books arranged authors alphabetically. Baraka appears as the first poet, for instance, in Keith Gilyard's *Spirit & Flame: An Anthology of Contemporary African American Poetry* (1997). For those anthologies that include biographical sketches at the end of the books, Baraka began appearing as one of the first writers, as opposed to appearing later among the contributors when he was arranged based on the last name "Jones." That change in positioning is small but does contribute to the larger discourse of shifts associated with the processes of anthologizing of Baraka across the decades.

Some editors linked Baraka's name changes to his literary and political viewpoints. In his biographical sketch on "Imamu Amiri Baraka," Stephen Henderson explained that "under the name LeRoi Jones he became famous as an avant-garde poet of the post-Beat school. Later, he declared independence from white cultural influences and deliberately set out to explore the revolutionary potential of Black Consciousness" (380). In *Anthology of Modern American Poetry* (2000), Cary Nelson points out that Baraka's "work and his system of beliefs have gone through several distinct phases." Noting the shift from LeRoi Jones to Amiri Baraka, Nelson goes on to write that "for several years he was a stunningly forceful advocate of black cultural nationalism, but by 1975 he was finding its racial exclusivity confining. He thus embraced the revolutionary forms of international socialism" (997). No doubt countless poets evolved and shifted positions during the course of their careers. Nevertheless, editors seemed especially committed to highlighting Baraka's transformations, more so than other writers.

The documentation of those changes is largely confined to the shifts that Baraka made during the early 1960s on to the late 1970s. As noted, relatively few of the poems that Baraka composed during the twenty-first century are repeatedly republished. Editors therefore rarely comment on changes that Baraka made post-1980. The erroneous suggestion by cumulative biographical sketches, then, is that the artist Baraka was in 1974 was who he was in 1984, 1994, 2004, and 2014. As a result, students encountering Baraka in anthologies might be led to downplay additional shifts in his artistry and politics.

Even scholars familiar with Baraka's work and career might not realize the particulars of his appearances in such a large number of anthologies. Baraka scholars regularly cite his poems "A Poem for Black Hearts" and "Black Art." However, his other poems, including "An Agony. As Now," "In Memory of Radio," "Ka'Ba," "I Substitute for Dead Lecturer," "A Poem Some People Will Have to Understand," and "The Invention of Comics," which appeared in multiple anthologies, receive relatively little attention. Those poems are apparently far more popular for anthology inclusion than scholarly analysis. The selection practices of editors who reprint Baraka's poems await thorough investigations. Hence, our collective knowledge about the circulation and selection history of his poetry is limited.

Scholars might also overlook the degrees to which the 1990s, not only the Black Arts era, were crucial to solidifying Baraka's status as a major poet. The publication of more than two dozen anthologies during the 1990s that contained Baraka's poems was vital to introducing his work to new readers, particularly students in American and African American literature courses. That time period is not usually referred to as a defining moment in Baraka's career or in the history of black literature. Yet, the release of all those anthologies between 1990 and 1999 featuring black poetry resembled the Black Arts era in terms of book production and poetry transmission. The works of large numbers of black writers were appearing together in common collections. In retrospect, the period was a kind of nameless literary movement.

During that time, Baraka's presence was pervasive. Kevin Powell and Ras Baraka's *In the Tradition: An Anthology of Young Black Writers* (1992), announcing a new generation of writers, took its title from an Amiri Baraka poem. Keith Gilyard, Michael Harper and Anthony Walton, Clarence Major, E. Ethelbert Miller, Jerry W. Ward Jr., and Al Young all edited anthologies that included Baraka's poems. The first edition of *The Norton Anthology of African American Literature* (1997), one of the most well-known collections of black literature, contributed to the collective effort of fortifying Baraka's presence in canonical history. The editors of the *Norton Anthology* include more poems by Baraka than any of the other writers in the "Black Arts Movement" section. In addition, Baraka is the only poet whose pre-Black-Arts-era poems are reprinted in the section. "Without doubt," Houston Baker Jr., wrote in the biographical note, "Baraka has been influential in the development of contemporary black letters, succeeding and building upon the work of such major figures as W. E. B. Du Bois and Richard Wright" (Baker, "Amiri Baraka" 1877). During the 1960s and 1970s, Baraka was described as a "new" black poet, and by the 1990s, he was positioned as a prominent and influential major literary and cultural figure.

With the benefit of hindsight, the surge of collections produced during the 1990s is even more important when we consider the paucity of African American anthologies from the previous decade. Comparatively speaking, the 1980s were a low point for the circulation of Baraka's poetry. The dearth of his republications corresponded with a lack of anthologies containing black poetry in general. Conversely, Baraka's appearances in anthologies in the 2000s continued the abundant reprinting of his poems from the 1990s. The twenty-year period between 1990 and 2010 constitutes a consistent presentation of Baraka's poetry. So far, the 2010s have just barely outpaced the 1980s in terms of Baraka reprints. Perhaps periods of dynamic production of anthologies is followed by periods of decreased activity.

Despite the extensive republication of Baraka's works and his status as a widely anthologized poet, aspects of his poetry somehow remain underpublished. *SOS: Poems 1961–2013* contains 192 poems, so the reprinting of 136 unique compositions in anthologies is in some ways quite impressive. On the other hand, *SOS* and other collected works by Baraka do not contain all of his poems. It is difficult to obtain and construct a full record of his voluminous publications and performances. Our bibliographies of his primary works have not kept pace with his prolific output.

Just as there are poems in Baraka's volumes that do not appear in anthologies, some of his poems in anthologies do not appear in his single-authored books. Baraka's "The Pause of Joe," which pays homage to "Philly Joe" Jones, a jazz drummer who died in 1985, and was first published in 1988, does not appear in his volumes. The poem was reprinted in Douglas Messerli's *From the Other Side of the Century: A New American Poetry, 1960–1990* (1994). Poems like that one do not circulate as widely as we would expect in general anthologies, despite the centrality of music and tributes to jazz musicians in Baraka's work. The limited publishing records concerning Baraka's poems composed during the 1980s give a work like "The Pause of Joe" added significance as we endeavor to document the transmission of his works.

Several seemingly noteworthy poems produced by Baraka during the late twentieth and early twenty-first centuries did not circulate widely. From the mid-1990s to the end of his life, Baraka regularly performed short, biting poems, which he referred to as "low coup," a pun on haiku. Despite the popularity of those poems in his public readings for close to two decades, hardly any low coup poems circulated in anthologies. Baraka's "In the Funk World" was published in Joanne Gabbin's edited collection *Furious Flower: African American Poetry from the Black Arts Movement to the Present* (2004), but for the most part, editors do not select his low coup for republication. Consequently, innumerable students and new readers who cover Baraka in anthologies remain unaware of his vibrant sense of humor as well as his willingness to lambast politicians.

While the lack of a larger number of his later-career poems published in anthologies is regrettable, an even tougher challenge involves scholars and editors devising ways to adequately indicate the full scope of Baraka's tremendous body of works in the future. The ongoing scholarly discourse and popular conversations about the latter stages of Baraka's career will ideally influence the ends to which editors will anthologize his poems. We will need to consider Baraka's transformations and developments well beyond the 1960s and 1970s. The tendency of editors to present materials chronologically and based on author birth year partially explains why Baraka and various other poets are so often represented by their earliest poems. Considerations about the limits of confining Baraka to a single historical era or even two could create important opportunities for rethinking how we anthologize his poems and the works of a wide range of additional literary artists.

DATA MANAGEMENT TOOLS AND THE PUBLICATION RECORDS OF AFRICAN AMERICAN POETS

Scholars and various commentators have long designated various poets as prolific. More now than ever before, we are in positions to adequately chart capacious publishing histories of these highly productive writers. The availability of user-friendly data-management tools can advance our abilities to pinpoint the nature of substantial creative output. The tools make it possible for us to move beyond standard, conventional bibliographies. We can create data sets to study and illuminate extensive publishing records.

A data set containing hundreds of items concerning the circulation of works by black writers can enrich our understanding of literary history. Rather than view a publishing record only in chronological terms, we could consider alternative configurations. We might study poets based on most to least reprinted poems. We could arrange works by book title, publisher, year or decade of publication, and number of appearances. Data-management tools facilitate our ability to create graphs and derive specific numbers and percentages concerning rates of republication.

All of these components of bibliographic management contributed to the construction and use of a data set on Baraka's poetry. In addition to his high productivity, Baraka was an author whose works were repeatedly included in collections across a long period of time. And as it turns out, the bibliographic elements of a prolific, frequently anthologized poet add up. The identification and use of an approach that would allow me to effectively manage and continually reconfigure a large body of information was crucial. Aside from providing me with a way of organizing and accounting for Baraka's poems published in 120 anthologies from 1960 through 2018, data-management tools motivated the very production of my Baraka data set. Awareness that the available tools could make a poet's massive publication record more easily manageable and possibly yield new and useful findings about the transmission of his poems gave me reasons to pursue so much bibliographic information, otherwise known as data.

Future studies might take into account the republication of Baraka's plays, essays, and short fiction. Doing so would capture even more of the works that editors selected to reprint. Additionally, we need comparative studies concerning the ways that a wide range of writers, including Phillis Wheatley, Paul Laurence Dunbar, Nikki Giovanni, Rita Dove, and Elizabeth Alexander, to name just a few, are anthologized. Considerations of how the circulation of compositions by Baraka coincides with and differs from others are critical to our abilities to make distinctions between various widely anthologized poets. Baraka's expansive and data-rich publishing record necessitates that we take up these innovative methods of pursuing literary history.

17

Black (Feminist) Art

Contemporary Black Female Poets
Speak Back to Baraka

LAURA VRANA

S UMMARIZING a widely held viewpoint, Aldon Lynn Nielsen recently
stated that Amiri Baraka remains significant for, yet serves "more as
inspiration than model" ("Roundtable") to, contemporary African
American poets. The terms of this distinction are imprecise, but Nielsen
asserts a difference between citing Baraka admiringly but from within works
that are not reflective of his views of black art—and fundamentally adopting
or adapting his aesthetic and ideological principles. Charles Rowell's recent
editorship of *Angles of Ascent: A Norton Anthology of Contemporary African American Poetry* (2013) buttresses such claims about black poetry today:
He denigrates Baraka therein and asserts that "the work of major post-Black
Aesthetic poets does not bear any of the traces of the poetry whose authors
devoted their art to the social and political ideology of the Black Arts Movement" (xl).[1] Thus this anthology implies that black poets now rarely grapple
meaningfully with the works and principles of Amiri Baraka.

While that anthology prompted considerable disagreement and many are
fruitfully reexamining Baraka's complex legacy, elements of these underlying

---

1. Rowell's preface and introduction make clear his disdain for poets affiliated with the
Black Arts Movement. He privileges contemporaries of that period that he categorizes as "outside the movement," suggesting that "the poets who argued for an art following the dicta of the
Movement demanded that black writers must create work 'of and for black people'" (xxv) and
dismissing "the prescriptive agenda of the Black Aesthetic" (xl).

beliefs about Baraka's essential irrelevancy substantially shape which contemporary black poets earn scholarly attention. Baraka's condemnation of *Angles of Ascent* renders visible one of the key assumptions that enables this limited view: "Rowell thinks the majority of Afro-American poets are MFA recipients or professors. Wrong again!" ("A Post-Racial Anthology?"). Many discussions of contemporary black poetry demonstrate this same unstated preference for "blackacademic" poets (Smith, *Robert Hayden,* 10), though fewer, fortunately, legitimize Rowell's connected notion that successful black poets have escaped the "fetters of narrow political and social demands that have nothing to do with the production of artistic texts" (xlvii). Such a notion proves antithetically opposed to Baraka's one relatively consistent value: his belief that meaningful art must help alleviate societal ills. The idea that this aspect of Baraka's legacy has lost relevance can only be supported by ignoring large swaths of recent black poetic practice. While such a focus may be efficacious when "blackademic" poets more readily find spots on syllabi and in canons, it denies Baraka's continuing impact on black poets, especially those who eschew that academic categorization and so are excluded by Rowell as (by implication) insufficiently "major."

This essay counters that exclusion by examining the legacy of Baraka for young black female poet-activists Jamila Woods and Aja Monet, both of whom have alluded substantially to his oeuvre. The form of their work could be positioned as antipathetic to Baraka allusions in the texts of better-known poets like Elizabeth Alexander, as they more comprehensively follow Baraka's lead in form and ideology. But looking closely at their careers helps explode the standard paradigm that pits "blackademic poets" against those aligned with performance, allowing us to explore Baraka as a model for much contemporary black feminist poetics. Woods's "Blk Girl Art" and Monet's indebtedness to Baraka in *My Mother Was a Freedom Fighter* (2017) elevate Baraka as a model for asserting an unapologetic black womanhood, one that counteracts the imposition on black female poets of both a politics of respectability and a politicized division of black poetry into academic and non.

FUCK POEMS

No history of twentieth-century African American literature is now complete without at least mentioning Baraka, nor are overviews of avant-garde American literature, which have long displayed him as their nonwhite representative in what Cathy Park Hong labels "tokenism at its most elegant." Yet relatively narrow views of his legacy can even dictate allusions to his work by brilliant black poets: Alexander's Pulitzer-nominated *American Sublime* (2005) includes a piece, "When," that rhapsodizes about "black men" in "the early 1980s" who "quoted Baraka's / 'Black Art'; 'Fuck poems / and they are useful'" (10). The past-tense nature of this brief poem frames this famed phrase as a historical artifact, representing a distant era that one may mourn but can never recapture or probe for contemporary relevance. Lauding Baraka as an ancestor primarily by referring to only those elements of his poetics and thought that can be easily decontextualized has become common among black poets and their critics and anthologists.

Of course, the recurring controversies surrounding Baraka render any deeper engagement with his legacy potentially dangerous. Yet Jelani Cobb highlights that although "the received wisdom about Baraka in his later years dismissed him as a relic of the sixties," he was "a singular figure whose work laid down the terms of engagement for many, if not most, of us who came to the craft after him" ("The Path Cleared"). One of the key lessons Baraka offers lies in this misreading: It is not true that he fails to provide a model for any black poets today, but it is surely true that those who take him as a model inherit his reception problems, dismissed as not "major" or read reductively at best. Poets who devote themselves to Baraka's key aesthetic and ideological principles thus are not yet benefiting from the (limited) posthumous surge in his currency.

Pinning down those principles certainly proved thorny, for he undeniably "discarded ideologies like a man tossing away wrenches that didn't fit the bolt he was desperately trying to loosen" (Cobb, "Path"). But the purposeful center of his art rarely shifted: As Cobb drew out in an interview, he wished to be remembered as "an artist who relentlessly sought better solutions" to ever-metamorphosing problems. A number of black poets today view that unwavering sense of the purpose of black art as an essential model, coupling it with ever-shifting approaches to institutional critique. However, their voices are rarely amplified or even heard by institutions that now treat a decontextualized, frozen image of Baraka reverentially.

This neglect is unsurprising, given exactly how these poets use Baraka's model. Woods and Monet enact formal experimentation reminiscent of tools Baraka honed to expose the systemic racism and violence of American institutions, highlighting similar facets of those institutions today: their targets too include white-supremacist violence enacted by our government, military, and schools. But they also use his methods to critique those problematic constructions of black masculinity that he at times perpetuated, such that their works may prove the ultimate evidence that his approaches remain effective. Aesthetically, these poets' choices—prioritizing performance as equally significant as textual publication, flouting conventional punctuation and capitalization, and privileging black musical inspiration—follow in a Black Arts Movement (BAM) legacy traceable to Baraka (and his female peers like Sonia Sanchez). Ideologically, their commitments to Baraka's model take two primary forms: aspiring to be dual poet-activists, and keeping black audiences at the forefront. Howard Rambsy has articulated that the "poet-as-artist model [of BAM] also prompted writers to actively seek collaborations with musicians, visual artists, dancers, and other writers working in a variety of genres in order to produce mixed-media black art. The conception of poets as activists equipped writers with a presumably higher, purpose-driven calling" (5), embodied by Woods and Monet. They also adhere to Baraka's principles by addressing themselves predominantly to black readers, though their understanding of that has adapted, reflecting increased willingness to recognize their class-inflected distance from the understanding of the black masses that was propagated by Black Arts Movement predecessors. Woods recently appeared at AfroPunk Fest in Brooklyn, and Monet's frequent performances at the Nuyorican Poetry Café affiliate her with audiences of people of color. Yet neither of them, nor like-minded peers, overtly reject white readership, and their increase in visibility as they begin to win awards and fellowships from historically white institutions does yield increased white audiences.

However, Woods and Monet certainly perpetuate the spirit of Black Arts Movement architects' efforts to make space for autonomous black art that refused white readers' aesthetic and social demands. While they may not be publishing with black-run presses, they persist in making sites where the diversity of blackness can be represented free of the "fetters" of white expectations: This poetry is defined by stories featuring black women and imagery and phrasing that resonate more immediately with those raised in black communities, even if Woods and Monet feel less compulsion to delimit their audiences. It is also key that they work to bridge divides between what most still perceive as divergent groups, poets associated with academia and those practicing in the everyday world. Urging all readers to see such a divide as exaggerated, by embracing affinity with both academic and performance-based lineages, is important to these poets' careers. Their refusal of external categories—even those Baraka himself espoused—in favor of reinventing black art from within serves as their truest fulfillment of Baraka's legacy of structural critique in contemporary contexts.

Younger black female poets' ability to draw on Baraka's aesthetics and ideas to investigate realms that he did not pursue demonstrates the power of his contributions, as well as their own capacity for looking beyond simplistic narratives about Baraka. Woods and Monet are subjected to similar respectability policing, especially as women, but their poetics merit sustained attention if we are to break down boundaries that "calcify our thinking about who we are and misname each others' work and intent" (Alexander, "New Ideas" 618). It misnames the "work and intent" of allusions to Baraka to ignore all the ways his legacy resonates, both for "blackademic" poets and those—like these women—who refuse that binary. They synthesize his influence with a range of other black poetic models, but denying his centrality to many contemporary black poets' oeuvres perpetuates reductive thinking about Baraka's legacies.

JAMILA WOODS

Jamila Woods might, based solely on a list of her awards and degrees, appear to be a poet Rowell would venerate: Though she has not (yet) published a full collection, she has attained acclaim from historically white institutions, including a 2015 Ruth Lilly and Dorothy Sargent Rosenberg Poetry Fellowship, a Pushcart Prize nomination, and publication in *Poetry*. Further, she graduated from predominantly white Brown University. But Woods's career does not differ as substantially from Baraka's model as it might seem, for she has also made a number of ideological and aesthetic choices that cleave to his legacy and render her less visible than her poetic peers more readily classifiable as "blackademic." For instance, she notes of her time at Brown that "all of [her] learning was very community-based" and that, contrasting with the experience of many black poets in creative writing programs, she chose Brown

> because [she] wanted to go to a place where there was a community of poetry. Not that the poetry program at Brown was really good, but that the city of Providence, where Brown is, has poetry. There's a poetry club and I think I never took a poetry class. . . . I think I'm still learning and I don't need to call a school, an institution to do that. I need communities and spaces like this, definitely, to do that. (Barney)

Similarly, her participation in the Dark Noise Collective[2] resonates well with Baraka's commitments to battling collaboratively the oppressive whiteness of publishing and American culture. And, perhaps most important, she operates at the interstices of genre in a mode overtly indebted to Black Arts Movement influences, as frontwoman of the Chicago-based soul duo M&O. Enacting the

---

2. The six writers of the Dark Noise Collective, Fatimah Asghar, Franny Choi, Nate Marshall, Aaron Samuels, Danez Smith, and Woods, have established multiracial, multigenre connections that update that BAM ethos for the twenty-first century.

dual role of poet-activist, she also helped found the Young Chicago Authors Teaching Artists Corps, a branch of the Young Chicago Authors organization, where as a child, "learning about Gwendolyn Brooks and other poets from Chicago really taught [her] that [her] story is valid" (Shifflett). In addition, the aesthetics and ideology of her thus far meager published output draw attention, in ways both indebted to and critical of Baraka, to the contradictions between ongoing respectability policing—which demands demure, apolitical conduct from black women—and external expectations imposed on visible black female artists, whereby they are virtually forced to address race-related topics.[3]

As an example, Woods's poem "Blk Girl Art" (261) cites Baraka in title and dedication, and the ideology underlying this poem is fundamentally the same as that which motivated Baraka: unwavering commitment to poetry as producing material consequences for the black community, if approached correctly by practitioners and readers. Yet Woods's update centers black womanhood—as is evidenced by inserting "Girl" into the title that thus evokes the recent social media hashtag "Black Girl Magic"—and highlights that adapting Baraka's ideas to the twenty-first century demands distinguishing between the individual and collective voices. As Smith insists, many Black Arts Movement poets like Baraka "placed themselves squarely in the folk milieu by liberally using collective pronouns of solidarity" (*Robert Hayden,* 70) that overstated their affinity with the everyday black masses; by contrast, contemporary poets drawing on Baraka's legacy recognize their distance from the so-called folk and seek ways to make poetry productive for larger audiences, across both racial and intraracial divisions.

The poem begins by echoing Baraka's "Black Art," opening: "Poems are bullshit unless they are" (*SOS* 149–150, line 1). Baraka then inserts a line break, before the sometimes violent metaphors:

> teeth or trees or lemons piled
> On a step. Or black ladies dying
> Of men leaving nickel hearts
> Beating them down. Fuck poems
> And they are useful. (2–6)

---

3. Hong refers to this double bind: "Mainstream poetry is rather pernicious in awarding quietist minority poets who assuage quasi-white liberal guilt rather than challenge it. They prefer their poets to praise rather than excoriate, to write sanitized, easily understood personal lyrics on family and ancestry rather than make sweeping institutional critiques. But the avant-gardists prefer their poets of color to be quietest as well, paying attention to poems where race—through subject and form—is incidental."

This pause after "unless they are" forces readers to consider the ontology of poems by lingering on "are," whereas Woods begins with a different break, suggestive of a distinct poetic ideology. Her first line barrels forward: "Poems are bullshit unless they are eyeglasses, honey / tea with lemon, hot water bottles on tummies" (lines 1-2). The immediate appearance of softer symbols like "eyeglasses" and "honey" refuse to allow the poem to veer near that ideological territory from within which Baraka marginalized the import of community love. Woods proceeds to four anaphoric sentences that open "I want" and describe poems affirmatively: "poems my grandma wants to tell the ladies at church about" (3), "orange potato words soaking in the pot / til their skins fall off, words you burn your tongue on, / words on sale" (4-6). These words too yield tangible consequences—"I want a poem in my fist in the alley just in case. / I want a poem for dude at the bus stop" (7-8)—and perform material help, as they can "grow mama's hair back" and "detangle the kitchen" (11).

Woods's ideal poems, then, serve as protection in instances of potential violence, palliatives for widespread ills like homelessness, modes of binding communities (particularly of black women), and everyday tools for necessary tasks. These functions closely mirror the ends to which Baraka hoped to deploy black poetry, merely reframed to prioritize black feminist values. Woods's poem in the fist "in the alley" is there "just in case," operating from a place of caring instead of preemptive violence; "detangl[ing] the kitchen" becomes not just the housework of black women but also the labor that must be poured into relationships between women if poetry, art, and politics have any chance of successfully attaining their aims.

Also of note is Woods's replacement of Baraka's "We want" with the singular "I want," a gesture that could be read reductively as representing the shift away from viewing (black) art as demonstrative of community needs and thus as indicating the irrelevance of Baraka's artistic ideology. Yet such a shift primarily demonstrates the adjustment between the period of Baraka's "Black Art" and our era, when the demand to represent the entire African American community has lost some of its exigency. Nevertheless, poets like Woods remain concerned with reforming those systems that still produce oppressive, violent conditions for black women—and so the change cannot be framed solely through differing contexts. All of Woods's poetry (and art) also portrays black women as singular individuals, not subsuming them under communal umbrellas.

This interpretation is borne out by the way the shift in Woods's final lines differs from that in Baraka's final lines: Her last sentence asserts that "I won't write poems unless they are" (12), listing positive definitions of poems that obtain if her voice is worth contributing. Baraka, by contrast, changes in his concluding stanza to a collective "we" that ends:

> Let the world be a Black Poem
> And Let All Black People Speak This Poem
> Silently
> Or LOUD. ("Black Art," *SOS*, 149–150, lines 53–56)

The confident tone required to assume the hortative mantle of commanding "All Black People" to perform a certain relationship to poetry is unlike Woods's unassuming declarations of individual relation to an art demonstrating similar values. These values are evidenced in her ending on a potential stereotype of black women as mules of housework, "I won't write poems unless they are an instruction manual, a bus / card, warm shea butter on elbows, water, a finger massage to the scalp" (12–13), which is followed by an undermining line break, "a broomstick sometimes used for cleaning and sometimes / to soar" (14–15). To reclaim sweeping as empowering, while also affiliating it with the often negative misogyn(oir)istic imagery of witches, enacts substantial ideological deconstruction. "Blk Girl Art" thus insists on the multifaceted elements of black female experience, rather than associating it just with invisible, respectable labor and politically acceptable quiet. The "soar[ing]" of a witch is, by contrast, a rising above those externally imposed constrictions.

This deconstruction of a masculinist approach to black art and politics is central to Woods's ode to Baraka. This twenty-first-century black female meditation on worthwhile poetry may focus on individual responsibility rather than collective blackness, but this does not mean it defines black art's social role wholly differently. Instead, Woods's piece mirrors Baraka's in its insistence on the social utility of black poetry if executed and consumed correctly. Asserting that this execution means prioritizing black women's needs is merely updating the philosophy for a new generation, one that Woods is helping define through multigenre output and her recent foray into editorship as co-editor of *The Breakbeat Poets Volume 2: Black Girl Magic*. Such editorial work, as Rambsy highlights, significantly defined the principles and goals of the Black Arts Movement, so in this way too, Woods follows Baraka's lead as a model for black poetics today.

AJA MONET

While Aja Monet's work less overtly evokes Baraka, she repeatedly insists in interviews and performances that Baraka should be more widely read and frames him as literary and spiritual ancestor. Monet's poetry in both print and performance thus demonstrates the essential nature of turning to ancestors like Baraka to develop effectual countermeasures against continually shifting versions of the societal ills he fought. The relevance of Baraka's principles to her artistic approaches is demonstrated by the arc of Monet's career as, much like Woods, first a performer and avowed poet-activist who only recently published her first collection, *My Mother Was A Freedom Fighter* (2017), that has now begun drawing critics' attention. She has long been known in certain circles as a performance poet who became in 2007 the youngest ever to win the Nuyorican Poets Café Grand Slam Championship. Indeed, many of the poems in *Freedom Fighter* derive from her performance repertoire; she writes in her "author's note" that "i have held onto some of them for far too long" (xi). Despite her undeniable success within performance poetry circles, Monet displays an anxiety here surrounding being judged differently (and by different individuals) for textual versions of the works than she has been judged for her much-acclaimed performances, illustrating the unspoken tenets that elevate "blackademic" print texts.

In parallel, her performance and print endeavors all center on unifying poetry and activism. Her visibility skyrocketed when she read the title poem of *Freedom Fighter* at the Women's March on Washington, DC, on January 21, 2017, showing Monet's commitment to art as an activist tool. Further, her desire to remain connected to working-class people for whom poetry might have material implications, rather than being pondered merely as abstract, evokes Baraka: Her website emphasizes that "she currently lives in Little Haiti, Miami, where she is co-founder of Smoke Signals Studio and dedicates her time to merging arts & culture with community organizing through her work with the Dream Defenders and the Community Justice Project" ("Bio"). These commitments shape her poetry, both performed and on the page—evidencing the desire to embody the dual poet-activist role Baraka sought, but in ways that ultimately challenge the binaries he often supported through prioritizing black women today.

Freedom Fighter is, as evidenced by its title, a collection of tales about maternal ancestors and their descendants, depicting the black female struggle as heroic even when quotidian or ugly. The humanizing portraits of black women grappling with complex concerns like whether to abort a child enable Monet to critique those institutional parameters that produce such impossible choices. Centralizing women's battles, joys, priorities, and experiences in deconstructing those institutions and ideologies adapts Baraka's tools to problems to which he was not always attuned. Monet's poems demonstrate the need to shift approaches to suit audiences for whom poetics might offer useful means of combating those institutions. For instance, her text eschews capitalization,[4] common among performative poets since her Black Arts Movement ancestors. Yet such a choice here reflects both that history and current conditions under which rejecting capitalization proves nearly ubiquitous in communication on the internet, social media, and phones.

It is not only these elements of Monet's poetics writ large that merit classifying it as Baraka-inspired. To turn to one specific example, "is that all you got" (*Mother* 110–114) transforms Baraka's tactics to the end of critiquing ideologies surrounding black masculinity—and how problematic behaviors prescribed thereby are blamed on black women. Monet cries out near the poem's end that treating black women well against societally condoned mistreatment requires that black men

> swallow that ego the white man done gave you
> ego never looked good on a black man
> he was never well suited for treating his woman this way
> musta been something he learned
> picked up in school
> his mama did not teach him that

> caution
> this is not a metaphor
> did you know she bleeds
> she bleeds monthly
> did you see the god in that
> her beauty is not an excuse for some
> flattery word poem
> do not romanticize. (lines 115–126)

The rejection of "metaphor" and "romanticiz[ing]" in favor of asserting that the black woman is "right now" bears traces of Baraka's philosophy about black art's material consequences. Further, Monet's unabashed calling out of "the white man" is a strategy that might feel out of place in Alexander's or many "blackademic" poets' work, but that is central to a Baraka-inspired, wholly unashamed and unafraid naming of toxic institutions.

"is that all you got" overall deconstructs societal demands both that black women subscribe to respectability that mandates they remain strong no matter what, and that black men perform a masculinity premised on maltreat-

---

4. Stylizing her title—ambiguously printed on the cover in all-capitalized letters—in the conventional mode may even betray her intent.

ment of "even the strongest woman." Portraying an archetypal black woman
who

> is tired
> she is tired
> she is tired
> she is tired of trying to be everything
> or everyone and nothing for herself. (60–64)

Monet ends this long poem demanding accountability:

> she is not a martyr for your cause
> you musta forgot you were a king
> musta forgot you were a king
> in her queendom
> her cause is ours
> not yours is ours
> > *is that all you got,*
> > *what the fuck is you broken for?* (134–141)

This refrain, italicized to indicate that she ventriloquizes demands commonly imposed on black women, assumes a different valence by these final
lines, where Monet frames the world as a "queendom" and seeks a communal embrace of responsibility across gender and race for black women. Con-
tradicting expectations that black female characters be depicted as behaving
in certain ways and black female poets eschew cursing or confronting institutional problems, Monet establishes the vibrancy of Baraka's influence for
a black poetic feminism that resists respectability policing and reveals the
unacceptable outcomes of narrow conceptions of gender roles among African
American communities.

In this and other poems, then, Aja Monet's work updates Baraka's strategies of performance, linguistic inventiveness, and framing black poetry as
politically useful to the pressing needs of black women whose material conditions have not substantially improved since the Black Arts Movement. Monet
thus demonstrates the ongoing utility of his legacy for black female poets,
especially those invested in tearing down ideologies that he unwittingly helped
perpetuate. Her shift in the last lines of "is that all you got" from a repeated,
accusatory second-person voice to the assertion that "her cause is ours" (113)
rings quite differently from how Baraka's collective voice in the final gesture of
"Black Art" reads today, for Monet's poetry is unapologetically for and about

black women—but rejects efforts to delimit black women's identities singularly or narrowly.

CONCLUSION

Of course, neither Woods nor Monet truly represents those Baraka had in mind in his critique of Rowell, for both are earning measurable success and some support from white-dominated institutions. However, their invisibility relative to the types of poets canonized in anthologies like Rowell's—which prove determinative of other texts, syllabi, and critical surveys—is worth remarking. Truly understanding Baraka's legacy requires widening our views of black poetics, and shedding light on lesser-known poets like these can only help grant validity to the non-degree-holding poets Baraka wished to venerate. Further, their circulation both in and beyond academic spaces demonstrates their adaptation of Baraka's views of the "masses" to the class circumstances of many black poets today, who seek not to efface the distance between their often privileged experiences and their readers' but to use that distance to positive ends. Nothing makes Baraka's ongoing vitality clearer than the engagement of black female poets with him, despite and through their condemnation of his masculinist perspectives. The fiery poetics of artists like Jamila Woods and Aja Monet—along with others like Harmony Holiday, who cites Baraka extensively in the soundtrack and notes that accompany her *Negro League Baseball* (2011)—illustrate the fallacy of implying that Baraka has become irrelevant.

Such poets' critiques break down conceptions of black masculinity and femininity still premised on respectability politics and misogyny—but scholarly conversations (or lack thereof) about their work also merit scrutiny, reflective as those discussions continue to be of the divisive tactics Baraka decried. Whom does it serve to view artists like Woods and Monet as meaningfully distinct from poetic peers like Alexander, if not the institutions that view Baraka's "Fuck poems / and they are useful" as merely a modified iteration of Marianne Moore's "I too dislike them," rather than a radical rejection of white supremacy and embrace of black love? Looking beyond the lacunae produced by labeling Baraka irrelevant to black poets today mandates recognizing affinities between "blackademic" poets and those less intimately affiliated with (white) academic institutions, or grappling with how some black poets like Woods move within those institutions but do not embrace the same understanding of black art that Rowell declares universal among recent black poets. His proclamation that "the work of major post-Black Aesthetic poets does not bear any of the traces" (xl) of poets like Baraka does not hold up if we expand our analytical purview beyond those already deemed major and likely would not hold up if we examined "major" poets more deeply. Ultimately, Amiri Baraka's devotion to dismantling the power of the white gaze is surely providing inspiration for the recent flourishing of black poetry, enabling such poets to be critical or embracing of his legacy with perhaps greater freedom than his own peers experienced.

18

Black Magic

Evolving Notions of Gender and Sexuality
in the Work of Amiri Baraka

AMY ABUGO ONGIRI

> For my part what is so horrible is that given the fact that I had
> a sister, only one sister of the blood, that the many plays I have
> written *should have* given her vehicles for her particular expres-
> sion of our total collective lives. Kimako did act and direct some
> of these plays. But I should have created works for her. For
> black women. To say and be, and all of us therefore, would be.
>
> —Amiri Baraka's eulogy for his sister Kimako
> Baraka, delivered April 20, 1984

WHEN AMIRI BARAKA delivered the eulogy for his murdered sister, he made the unusual decision to attack the coverage of her murder in the *New York Post,* which ignored her lifelong involvement in the New York Theater scene in identifying her as a distributor of Amway products and in questioning her right to live in a building primarily occupied by entertainment professionals. "[Amway:] This was a so-called real job. No, you can't be a director. That's why *The Post* had to question why my sister was even allowed in the Manhattan Plaza. The real job of Black women, according to these blood suckers, is prostitute" ("Kimako Baraka," *Eulogies* 52). He would further eulogize her saying: "And then to be black and female. Kimako wanted to be a director. She wanted to be on the stage. To dance to act. And when she cd no longer do these things, she wanted still to be close to them, to have a hand at bringing new meaning in the world, but you cannot be black you cannot be female and aspire to creativity" (52). Baraka did not hold himself blameless in Kimako's death, as he "began by citing our [collective] failure" (52). "What was it," he asked and responded: "That we have not created a context in which life can live, in which creativity can be spared and developed.

That we have not created a world in which something wonderful and blessed, Kimako Baraka, could exist" (52–53). For Amiri Baraka, his youngest sister's death represented a larger failure in which he was implicated of an inability to imagine a cultural reality in which black female creativity would matter and have an impact and it was also part of a larger cultural will for black women not to exist at all.

This essay will examine two specific moments of dramatic rupture in the life and career of Amiri Baraka: the murders, nearly twenty years apart, of Baraka's younger sister, Kimako Baraka, in 1984, and of his youngest daughter, Shani Baraka, who was murdered along with her partner Rayshon Holmes in 2003. It will do so in relationship to evolutions in Amiri Baraka's evolving notions of black women, the place of femininity in his construction of black culture and sexuality. These events were obviously moments of extreme trauma. Yet they also provided the catalyst for much introspection, reflection, and evolution in relationship to Baraka's ideas about black women and black female sexuality and the culture that he had personally done so much to create. Baraka eulogized both Kimako and Shani Baraka at their respective funerals and named after his sister "Kimako's Blues People," an art space he cofounded with Amina Baraka for Newark-based artists.

I will examine these events in relationship to Baraka's lifelong collaboration with Amina Baraka. Baraka was associated through collaboration and marriage with two women who were prominent in their own right as cultural workers. Hettie Cohen has documented her private and professional life with Baraka, then known as LeRoi Jones, in her critically acclaimed 1990 memoir *How I Became Hettie Jones*. Amina Baraka's life with Baraka and their creative and professional collaborations are much less well known. While married from 1966 until his death in 2014, Amina and Amiri Baraka collaborated on two chapbooks of poetry, an anthology of African American women writers, a book of essays on African American music, and countless other projects, including jazz performance pieces and the formation of the influential Spirit House in Newark. Amina Baraka was an important cultural worker in her own right as a proponent of African American women's writing and political organizing. She also served as a partner in the crafting of Baraka's public persona, speaking alongside of him or representing him alone at moments when their private trauma was public, such as during the trial of Shani Baraka's killer or the opening in Newark of a domestic violence center named in her honor.

Even Ishmael Reed, often an infamously harsh critic of Amiri Baraka, the Black Arts Movement, and Baraka's post–Black Arts Movement work, acknowledged the significance of his intellectual collaboration with Amina

Baraka, whom Reed labeled a "kook detector," claiming that "Baraka credited his spouse, Amina . . . for moderating his views about misogyny" (29). In "LeRoi Jones/Amiri Baraka and Me," a piece published at Baraka's death in 2014, Reed attributes the refinement of Baraka's most intellectually avant-garde positions to Amina Baraka:

> To call Baraka a complicated figure would be an understatement. He always wanted to be on the cutting edge, which sometimes put him in the company of dangerous crackpots. But he finally found his life partner Amina, whose level-headed maturity often kept him from going over the cliff altogether. (29)

Rather than view Amiri and Amina Baraka's collaboration as one in which she merely moderated his more extreme views, as Reed does, this essay will explore the centrality of that collaboration to the evolution of Baraka's own views on black women and sexuality.

There is literally no way to sum up broad topics such as gender and sexuality with an author and thinker as complex and prolific as Amiri Baraka. However, when literary critics have tried, they have most often reduced his immense legacy of complex thought to words like *misogyny* and *homophobia*, intentionally ignoring the complex ebbs and flows of thought and changes that were so much a part of his public and private persona. Evolution—personal and political and creative and intellectual—was a major hallmark of Baraka's career. More than any other intellectual of the twentieth century, Baraka invested in a very public working-through of positions, practices, and theory that he was enmeshed in, as is best symbolized by the evolution of his name from LeRoi Jones to Amiri Baraka and every iteration in between. Though Baraka's life and work were marked by constant growth, change, examination, and reexamination, it was also marked by many thematic and social constants. So for example, though he abandoned the black nationalist politics of the Nation of Islam that were generative in the creation of *A Black Mass,* one of his early experimental works for the theater, he returned to the themes over and over through various manifestations, from jazz performances conducted by the legendary Sun Ra and the Myth Science Arkestra to his continual revisions of themes of the tyranny and constructed nature of time that reoccur in work as late as his 2005 tribute to Thelonious Monk, *The Book of Monk.* In the 1966 play *Black Mass,* Baraka has a character say: "We have no need for time. In fact, brother, we have a hatred for it. It is raw and stays raw. It drives brothers across the earth. I think that it is evil" (*Four* 39). In 2005, *The Book of Monk* has Baraka running into Monk on a Newark street months after he has attended his funeral. When he questions him about his age in order to establish his identity, Monk warns him to stop telling people his own age or "people start to believe you believe in time" (24). Similar to the "changing same" of Baraka's interest in the construction of time, his investments in and understandings of women, black female sexuality, and its role in black politics and culture are far too complex to be adequately addressed by reducing it all to the concept of "misogyny."

Baraka's controversial assessment of Charles Rowell's *Angles of Ascent: A Norton Anthology of Contemporary African American Poetry* epitomizes his later position on African American women and their contributions to African American culture. Written for *Poetry* magazine and published the year before his death, the review uses the occasion of the release of the new poetry anthology to revisit the significance of the Black Arts Movement. Baraka writes: "This is a bizarre collection. It seems that it has been pulled together as a relentless 'anti' to one thing: the Black Arts Movement" ("A Post-Racial"). Baraka takes issue with Rowell's supposed rendering of the Black Arts Movement as "old school, backward, fundamentally artless" ("A Post-Racial").

Baraka's critique of Rowell's anthology is in keeping with his position on the importance of the Black Arts Movement as a community-based movement versus the "literary" poets that Rowell favors, who Baraka claims have the basis for their art in white academic settings. This position is unsurprising since it is one that Baraka has consistently articulated across a variety of formats since the movement ended. However, what is surprising is that in refuting Rowell's account of poetry, Baraka creates his own unique history of the Black Arts Movement that centers African American women, including many of those not typically associated with the movement. These include June Jordan, Sherley Anne Williams, Alice Walker, and Lucille Clifton, but also lesser-known writers such as Louise Merriweather and Aishah Rahman. Baraka's list of young poets who work out of the legacy of the Black Arts Movement includes Jessica Care Moore and Staceyann Chin, spoken-word poets who challenge the form's conventions around gender roles and sexuality. Baraka's acknowledgment of women's contribution and ongoing engagement with the Black Arts Movement legacy in this review is indicative of how far he had moved from his early positions on black women and cultural production.

Baraka's later work had as many thematic and aesthetic consistencies as it had evolutions. However, his later work evidences few examples of his early positions on women and black female sexuality. *Funk Lore,* a poetry collection; a series of chapbooks on Thelonious Monk and John Coltrane; *Un Poco Low Coupe,* a poetry collection with illustrations published by Ishmael Reed; and a spoken-word collaboration with jazz musician Billy Harper all evidence

Baraka's continued engagement with experimentalism and the avant-garde. His 2007 short story collection *Tales of the Out and the Gone* is typical for his later work in that while it showcases his latest evolutions, it begins with stories written in the 1970s and continues many of Baraka's lifelong thematic and aesthetic concerns. For example, even the phrase "the out" in the collection's title could be seen to invoke the extreme experimentation of 1960s free jazz that became known as "playing out," as in the title of Eric Dolphy's albums *Out There, Outward Bound,* and *Out to Lunch!* Similarly, Baraka's collaborations with Amina Baraka, which began with their work in Spirit House in the '60s and continued until his death, evidence a deep investment evolving notions of black women's role in culture.

BLACK MAGIC: BLACK WOMEN IN THE NEW BLACK POETICS

There has been a tendency to fix the ever-evolving Baraka within his black nationalist period as typified by his work in the influential poetry collection *Black Magic.* The reasons for this are complex and include the fact that this work, coming as it did during the waning years of the civil rights movement, proved the most challenging to a mainstream discourse on how the newly integratable black citizenry might be constructed. In the pages of *Black Magic,* in "A Poem Some People Will Have to Understand," Baraka (then Leroi Jones) declared: "I practice no industry. / I am no longer a credit / to my race" (6, lines 5–7). In "The People Burning" (10–11), he would warn, "They now gonna pretend they flowers. Snake stalked / large named vegetables, who have, if nothing else, / the title: World's Vilest Living Things" (lines 8–10).

Most impactfully, Baraka presented "Black Art" (116–117), a poem that would go on to define the Black Arts Movement with its invocation:

> Poems are bullshit unless they are
> Teeth or trees or lemons piled
> On a step. Or black ladies dying
> Of men leaving nickel hearts
> Beating them down. Fuck poems (lines 1–5)

"Black Art" would firmly assert that a new kind of poetics had arrived in keeping with the changing political climate. Larry Neal declared the Black Arts Movement "the aesthetic and spiritual sister of the Black Power concept" in a landmark essay on the new movement published in *The Drama Review* in 1968 (28). Neal echoed Baraka's call at the end of the poem: "We want a black poem. And a / Black world. / Let the world be a Black poem" (51–53), in his observation that "the Western aesthetic has run its course" (29).

The Black Power movement contended with gender construction in important ways, particularly in its desire to reconstruct black masculinity from its position of abjection as symbolized by the pre–civil rights tradition of referring to black men as "boy" or the fact that urban African Americans referred to white men as "The Man," as Black Panther Party co-founder Huey P. Newton noted. Newton claimed that this had significant consequences for gender relationships among black people, stating: "Black people who haven't been enlightened have defined the white man by calling him 'the MAN.' 'The Man' is making this decision. 'The Man' this and 'The Man' that. The black woman found it difficult to respect the black man because he didn't even define himself as a man!" (61). The Black Power movement lamented the abjection of black men and sought to restore black men to a power they were perpetually and systemically denied. When Ossie Davis eulogized Malcolm X, he famously mourned the loss because "Malcolm was our manhood, our living Black manhood!" He ordered the audience to use the moment to "stand up off our knees and address ourselves to the truth."[1]

In the first few lines of "Black Art," Baraka importantly invokes the image of "black ladies dying" to create the sense of visceral urgency and change that the new Black Arts Movement promised. In *Black Magic* and in *Four Revolutionary Black Plays,* which was also published in 1969, Baraka's main preoccupation is with the redemption of black men, to which black women are both very necessary and also ancillary. Black women's bodies are often figured in relationship to death or dying. For example, the title page of the book reads: "ALL PRAISES TO THE BLACK MAN" under the title and above the author's name, while the opening play *Experimental Death Unit #1*'s dedication reads: "for a used to be dead sister" (*Four* 1). The play revolves around a black woman who appears to be a prostitute in order to lure two white soldiers to their death. In the original 1965 production, the character was played by Barbara Ann Teer, who would go on to found the National Black Theater in Harlem that year. By this time, Teer had already had a brilliant and innovative career in the theater, including co-founding the Negro Ensemble Company in 1963. While her role in *Experimental Death Unit #1* is innovative in terms of scripting a woman as central to the project of black revolution, it is hard not to be struck by the irony that this innovation comes at the cost of continuing to perpetuate stereotypes of black women as sexually seductive and dangerous

---

1. *Democracy Now!* revisited the eulogy in a 2005 celebration of Malcolm X; see Goodman.

as a result, as best exemplified by the soldier's labeling of Teer's character as "a whore. A Black stinking mess of a bitch" (9).

Each of the rest of the plays in *Four Revolutionary Black Plays* continues the association of black female sexuality with seduction, danger, contamination, and death. In *Black Mass,* a play based around the teachings of the Nation of Islam, a black female character is the first one to be susceptible to the workings of an evil wizard when whiteness is unleashed on the world. The character and whiteness itself is likened to "anti-life" (*Four* 34). The only solution is that she "must be cut off from our people" (38). *Madheart* is a biting critique of the criminal justice system in which a black female character called "Devil Lady" proclaims, "I am dead and can never die" while in dialogue with a character labeled "Black Man," who responds: "You will die when I kill you" (70). He then attempts to kill her as a group of black women look on and try to make him stop.

Black nationalism in all its manifestations struggled to reconcile its wish for an empowered masculinity with wider cultural demands made by the women's movement for equity and the specific demands made African American women who were also empowered by the demand for self-determination made by the Black Power movement. Baraka had a more nuanced response to "the woman question" than some of the criticism surrounding his work might suggest.[2] Komozi Woodard notes that both Amina and Amiri Baraka contested policies that they found to be sexist within the Congress of African People (CAP) and the Committee for a Unified Newark (CFUN). Central to this debate were sexual practices and the role of women in the family. Woodard notes that "the battle against polygamy grew into a struggle against male chauvinism" (181). Woodard writes:

Both Amina and Amiri Baraka denounced the introduction of those practices in CFUN; at one point in 1971 in the internal *CFUN Newsletter* Imamu Baraka's editorial warned the men that the women were revolutionary comrades deserving nothing less than full respect and that in that organization it was impermissible to treat women otherwise. Before long, a few high-ranking former US members resigned, charging that Baraka was "revisionist" of the doctrine. (181)

---

2. Baraka authored and delivered a position paper on the newly formed Black Women's United Front in Detroit in 1975. (Black women's united front: Congress of Afrikan People on the woman question: position paper and speeches from meeting held in Detroit, Mich., January 25, 1975. Michigan State University Special Collections archive.)

Woodard mentions that this stance led to significant policy changes within both the CFUN and CAP and also challenged the US organization. Baraka had significant professional collaborations with both ex-wife Hettie Cohen and Amina Baraka that challenge the notion that he was simply a misogynist. The politics and poetics of the moment existed in a syncretic relationship in which Amiri Baraka's ever-evolving notions of women's roles were both carried and contained. While his 1969 work associated black women with death and disease, his collaborations with Amina Baraka in the early '70s—a period in which Amina Baraka organized a national women's conference at Rutgers University—already suggest a very different perspective.

5 BOPTREES: AMINA BARAKA AND THE EVOLUTION OF AMIRI BARAKA

When Amiri Baraka died, Hilton Als honored the moment by paying tribute in an essay titled "Amiri Baraka's First Family":

> We didn't know the late Imamu Amiri Baraka (LeRoi Jones), who died this week at the age of seventy-nine, as a famous poet who initiated the powerful Black Arts Movement in 1965, or as the man whose groundbreaking plays, ranging from 1964's "Dutchman," to 1969's "Four Black Revolutionary Plays," changed what was possible on the American stage; we just knew him as Kellie and Lisa's father, and Hettie's former husband.

Family life played a central role in Baraka's world view even as cultural, social, and political forces shaped and reshaped his notion of family. As with his personal and political struggle with polygamy, Baraka struggled to define revolutionary notions of family in the face of personal challenges that the real-life circumstances of his family presented.[3] This was especially true in relationship to Kimako's and Shani's homosexuality and the domestic violence that marked both of their deaths. Baraka famously used antigay rhetoric in his early work and also relentlessly pushed a hypermasculinity that actively derided the feminine as undesirable even when it celebrated women. So for example, in "DEATH IS NOT AS NATURAL AS YOU FAGS SEEM TO THINK" (18) from *Black Magic*, "fags" becomes synonymous with a kind of masculinity that is so weak it is actually dead. It is also equated to

---

3. Baraka discusses at length his personal struggles with the idea of polygamy as it became fashionable among black nationalists in the late '60s and '70s in *The Autobiography of LeRoi Jones*.

the black puritan
>   (Half-screamer
in dull tones
of another forest. (lines 2–5)

It is easy, perhaps, to dismiss these equivalencies as a product of their time and context. Als, himself a gay man, notes about Baraka: "The queasy remarks he's made about homosexuality over the years, for instance, bothered me less than they should have, but I knew he was speaking from a certain vantage point that was not unfamiliar to me: many black men of his generation didn't like who I was, certainly on that score, but that wouldn't stop me from being myself" ("Amiri").

However, the deaths of Kimako and Shani force us to face the actual specter of death surrounding the most marginalized in the black community. Or at least it seemed to for Baraka, who in his eulogy of Shani Baraka indicts in no uncertain terms both homophobia and male chauvinism as the causes for her death. In fact, Baraka used the word *homophobic* nine times and the word *chauvinist* seven times during the rather brief, grief-filled eulogy. In doing so, Baraka is indicting the actual murder of Shani as well as, in his words, "not only the actual ignorant negro homophobic male chauvinist black woman hating murderer, as a person, but as an idea, a philosophy, an ideology, roaming though so many minds" ("Who Killed"). Baraka importantly tied Shani's murder to the violence that killed Kimako twenty years earlier by reflecting on the patterns of violence that Shani herself recognized as tying them together. Baraka was shocked to learn upon Shani's murder that she revealed to a friend that she herself feared and predicted a similar end to the one Kimako faced:

> Like Shani, Kimako was an artist, a dancer and an actress, she was black, small and, like our little Shani, Gay.
>
> Shani! reminded both my wife and me of my sister. And Shani apparently had very deeply identified with Kimako, asking Amina many questions over the years about her. The way she was murdered. How I had felt about her being Gay. *But I never knew that she believed she would die the same way!* Murdered by a homophobic Negro maniac. She said she thought about that all the time and the last time Shani told the girl she thought such a thing would happen to her soon! ("Who Killed")

In tying Kimako Baraka's life and death to her own, Shani Baraka recognized a life defined by a pattern of male violence that limited her possibilities as it had limited Kimako's twenty years earlier. Knowledge of this realization caused Baraka to conclude:

> He murdered our little Shani and Ray Ray because they were Black, because they were women, because they were workers, because they did not live off stocks and bonds and other people's misery. But he also killed them, shot our little Shani and her companion Ray Ray, because he believed they were gay, he hated them because he thought they loved each other and this fake human with the mind of a nasty gob of spit on the floor felt that it was wrong for these two women to love each other, to want to be together rather than with him or with other men, black or white, like him. So this homophobic male chauvinist Negro hated them even more for that. For what he saw as a crime, being Gay, and rejecting his sorry Ignorant and very dangerous homophobic male chauvinist self. ("Who Killed")

Activist and writer Darnell L. Moore, who would subsequently arrange a first-time-ever meeting and conversation between Baraka and black lesbian poet Cheryl Clarke in Newark, called "the killing of black women, black women loving women, by black men . . . a clarion reminder that the want for power and the afforded privileges offered to straight/queer/trans men folk—black, brown, and white—has dangerous and violent consequences. Murder is but one" ("When"). Another significant consequence unnamed by Moore is erasure.

During this difficult time, Amina Baraka would often represent the Baraka family to the press. Her composure and her ability to articulate deep truths with the economy of words necessary for press interviews spoke to her years as a wordsmith, performer, and community organizer. In 2018, Amina Baraka would memorialize Shani Baraka and Rayshon Holmes in a long interview with the Queer Newark Oral History Project in which she attributed some of Baraka's previous attitudes to the limitations of the Black Power Movement, stating: "The Black Liberation Movement was—you talk about homophobic and sexist, you ain't seen nothin' yet" (Scorsone et al. 17–18). Amina Baraka says:

> He had a lot of stuff to regret in terms of—then he had to admit he wasn't good with women either. Then he began to reflect on that. He began to change, as much as he was gonna change, his relationship to women. Because he was definitely a chauvinist. He writes about him bein' a chauvinist. I can say that. (18)

In addition to giving intimate insights into many of Amiri Baraka's challenges and transformations, the interview presents one of the longest, most easily accessible examinations of Amina Baraka's own work as an organizer, artist, and activist that is currently available.[4]

In the interview, Amina Baraka talks in detail about the ways in which her own attitudes and experiences led her to different conclusions about black women and homosexuality. She also discusses the ways in which occasionally her challenges would have a transformative effect on Baraka, most notably in relationship to organizing black women involved in CAP and CFUN. In his *Autobiography of LeRoi Jones,* Baraka notes, "The thing that most changed my life at the time was marriage. It was Sylvia [now known as Amina] who showed me the craziness of my ways and struggled with me as hard as she could to get me to change" (268). It is clear from the text how deeply intertwined their creative and life choices are. In fact, the book's dedication reads: "For my wife, Amina, who is responsible for any truth in this, or in the chapters to come" (1). As early as 1981, Amiri Baraka noted a shift in perceptions of women's participation and importance in black liberation struggles, including in attitudes that he himself had formerly held. In an interview with D. H. Melhem, he stated that "there has been some kind of significant change and I would attribute that to my wife, principally" (Melhem, "Revolution" 95).

Despite these types of acknowledgments and the fact that Amina Baraka had a long history in the arts, including the founding of a school and numerous other cultural and political institutions in Newark, her work is relatively undocumented either in relationship to Amiri Baraka or as an artist and organizer in her own right. In his autobiography, Baraka notes the lack of attention to Amina Baraka, especially in relationship to his former marriage with Hettie Cohen. He writes: "Biographers never fail to mention it, though they sometimes leave out mention of my present wife of 13 years, Amina, who is Black and our five children" (20). Amina Baraka's books, including the stunning edited collection *Confirmation: An Anthology of African American Women,* are

---

4. It is hard to talk with any certainty and respect of allegations of Amiri Baraka's own experiences with homosexuality, which Baraka himself denied. However, in this interview Amina Baraka does seem to make some deeply coded references to friendships that were lost and deathbed regrets that might at least insinuate that there were complexities to several key relationships that have not yet been fully explored. The fullest exploration of the allegations of Baraka's homosexuality appear in Jerry Giafo Watts's 2001 book, *Amiri Baraka: The Politics and Art of a Black Intellectual.* In addition, Baraka faced his own allegations of domestic violence when he was sentenced to ninety days at the infamous Rikers Island prison for resisting arrest after a police officer claimed to have attempted to stop Baraka from hitting his wife on a New York street. Both Amina and Amiri Baraka claimed that they had only been arguing and that only the arresting officer had been violent.

almost all out of print and very difficult to access. *Confirmation,* which was co-edited with Amiri Baraka in 1983, remains one of the most comprehensive and visionary articulations of African American women's writing, from Toni Morrison, Gwendolyn Brooks, Alice Walker, and Audre Lorde to Gayl Jones and June Jordan. The anthology presents women who would go on to be very well known as well as women whose work still lies on the periphery of the literary canon. The anthology pushed the boundaries of genre by featuring artists such as Abbey Lincoln, Verta Mae Grosvenor, and Faith Ringgold, who were well known in nonliterary fields, and presenting their written work, some for the first time. It also featured original cover art by Elizabeth Catlett. Despite the tremendous achievement of this text, it went almost immediately out of print. Amina Baraka's other work, which was mostly published by small presses, is nearly impossible to find. In the 1992 chapbook *5 Boptrees,* Amina celebrates in "Slave Legacy" (1–2) the unseen labor of the generation who "wrapped their hurt in a cotton song" (line 3) and "took dirt, washed it clean" (13). Similarly, Amina Baraka's work is mostly knowable only in the traces it left beyond its original manifestations, in the transformations of Amiri Baraka and the community of Newark.

Through her interview with the Queer Newark Oral History project and in his eulogies for Shani and Kimako, both Amina and Amiri Baraka attempt to testify to the lives lost through the homophobic and misogynist violence that killed Kimako, Shani, Rayshon Holmes, and so many like them. Amiri Baraka seems most struck by what might have been and by those who "cannot be allowed to be" (*Eulogies* 51).

The more we pay attention to Amiri Baraka, the more the traces of these lost lives are evident to us. But we also benefit, as Baraka himself did, from the emotional, creative, and intellectual labor of the women who defined, challenged, spoke for, educated, and interpreted the world for and with him. These women haunt the many evolutions that Baraka made and are vital to acknowledge in advancing our knowledge of his work.

19

==

Amina Baraka

The Woman Who Guided the Ship

KIM McMILLON

ARRIVED ON Amina Baraka's doorstep in Newark, New Jersey, on June 6, 2017. I had never been to Newark and was strongly aware that I was in an African American city with lovely old homes and streets filled with black people, signs of neglect, urban renewal, and community. A police car sat in front of Amina's two-story home, and an African American female cop got out of the car and walked up the steps, announcing my arrival. Amina greeted me like a long-lost family member. This neighborhood became my home for the next two days. I opened the door to African and African American history sitting together, not quite in harmony, but understanding their roots and allowing each other their space. African artifacts were everywhere, along with books, art, and history. I am reminded of the words of Franz Fanon in *The Wretched of the Earth*: "When the colonized intellectual writing for his people uses the past he must do so with the intention of opening up the future, of spurring them into action and fostering hope" (167). Amina and Amiri Baraka were doing more than "fostering hope." Through their work in the community, they cultivated an ideological vision of a better world for African American people, opening the minds of many to the real possibility of black self-determination. Throughout the Barakas' home, the past and the present sit in compelling silence through art that speaks of revolution, of honoring the ancestors, and of using history to move a people toward freedom. The Barakas' African American art collection recalls the past, but demands that we reclaim our present through black pride and an acknowledging of our ancestral home, Africa. That is what Amina and Amiri did through the Black Arts Movement: They offered hope by providing words and art as ammunition for social change. Amina's roots are connected to the fight for equal rights for all, and the acknowledgment of the importance of the worker. Amina says of her advocacy, "My consciousness came from pain. Like an escaped slave. I said I am done" (Phone interview, June 22, 2019).

We sat down as sisters who had been away for too long, or perhaps had never met but knew we were connected. She, with her cigarettes, and I, with my camera, ready to document her story, her struggle for identity living with a man worshipped by so many. During the 1960s, Amina's late husband had become a symbol of black pride, black anger, and black revolution. Amina described it as worshipping at the "Cult of Personality." It is her belief that the deifying of Amiri Baraka was cult-like. In *Fighting for US*, Scot Brown cites Clyde Halisi as saying, "Sometime around 1968, Karenga gave Baraka the name/title 'Imamu,' for high priest" (139).

Amiri's art, marriages, and politics were often played out as living theater, performed by those closest to him. Amina has been profoundly affected by his art, to the point that she refuses to allow his most famous play, *Dutchman* (1964), to be performed in her lifetime. Amina hated the play and saw it as disrespectful to Amiri's first wife, Hettie Jones. Her view is that he used the character of Lula to humiliate Hettie. In Charles Reilly's "An Interview with Amiri Baraka," Amiri speaks of how the character of Lula was developed:

> Well, my model for Lula was an utterly whacked-out white woman whom I met during my early Village days. I called her Dolly in the Autobiography, and she was a deeply disturbed human being. . . . Personally, I can say Lula was modeled on a number of people. My ex-wife, who is white and who did marry me, would be a good bet to be one aspect of the character. (*Conversations* 254, 257)

I do not know if Amiri consciously used the character of Lula to hurt his ex-wife. Art, much like life, is complicated. In *Dutchman*, Amiri opens a painful door on racism. When the character Clay moves beyond the role of the "safe" black male, he is murdered by Lula. Amiri was speaking on the very real issue of black men being metaphorically, physically, and spiritually assassinated by a society unwilling to deal with its embedded racism. From reading Cohen's biography, *How I Became Hettie Jones*, I would argue that the emotions of Hettie and Amiri with regard to *Dutchman* are complex and based on issues of race that sadly still apply. She speaks of "glances of strangers" and feeling the question silently asked, "Who was that at the playwright's side—Lula the murderer, his white wife, or the former Hettie Cohen?" She says, "And then, as I'd dreaded, one day they all become one" (Jones, *How* 218). As a white woman, it could not have been easy living with a black man who racialized black–white, male–female relationships in his plays *The Slave* and *Dutchman*.

Amina explained that after Malcolm's death, Amiri felt guilty for living downtown with the Beat society, with whiteness. Amina saw his time with the Beats as an opportunity for them to become knowledgeable about what it means to be a black man in America. Amina felt that the Beats learned about black culture from people like Leroi Jones, and made the analogy that as African Americans, white culture was forced upon us. Amina believes the dominant culture has the luxury to discover and choose how much blackness they can accept. When Amiri left Greenwich Village, he had an awakening. A great many of his friends felt hurt because of his rejection of that life. Amina asserts:

> I did not know him when he wrote his early work. I did not have the same view. He thought the worst thing he could have done was marry a White woman, which I did not agree with. I did not know him. I had never heard of Leroi Jones. You can only know what you know at the time you know it. When he moved to Harlem, he thought he had done something wrong. He was embarrassed. I don't agree with that and I told him. I can understand how it would hurt her. The class element in this and the racial element. When he got to Newark, he was saying we were not Black enough. He was out of touch until he went to Harlem. He was trying. They were criticizing him wrongfully. He had to come back home. He wasn't welcomed in Harlem. (Phone interview, March 3, 2020)

Amina's view of Amiri is unlike that which is described in the memoirs of Hettie Jones and Diane DiPrima, which points to a pattern of male chauvinism that Amiri also displays in his autobiography, and that is evident in his treatment of the women closest to him. As an African American, Amina observed Amiri from the point of blackness. Perhaps this was not an area that he was able to share with Diane or Hettie, through no fault of their own. Time, place, and conditions play a large role in relationships, particularly in 1960s America with its racialized and patriarchal culture. Amina is right. There was no reason for Amiri to be embarrassed. Love is love and has no color. However, Amiri was creating a new identity, one based on living and breathing in blackness. To him, that identity did not entail a mixed-race marriage.

•

When you are married to a symbol, your voice can become lost, no matter how powerful, and Amina's voice is powerful. Amina was a part of Newark, New Jersey's Loft Culture. This was a movement of older working-class musicians who did what was called moonlighting. At the time, they were looking for a place to perform and Amina happened to come across an available loft at 22 Shipment Street, near Springfield Avenue. Before this, the musicians had been meeting in each other's homes. The loft was on the fourth floor. They paid $50 a month and had a café. People started coming from all across the country to listen to the artists. Amina explained, "There was a split in the politics of the artists, and so Art Williams, the founder and a bass player, created the cellar culture downstairs. The loft stopped existing and everything became the cellar" (Phone interview, March 3, 2020). What is essential about the culture that saw the emergence of spaces for black artists is that it represents the need and development of spaces for art and community that the Barakas eventually played a major role in developing throughout Newark.

Amina's love of community and Newark are on display as she describes her early life and joy in exploring the arts. Her mother was in the garment workers union, and her grandfather was in the construction workers union in Newark. Amina reminds me that she came from a working-class background and that support of unions was an important part of her early development. In fact, to understand Amina requires the knowledge of her roots, her connection to family that often includes her entire neighborhood. In my hours of conversation with Amina, I would identify Newark as a point of recognition, heart centeredness developed over a lifetime of working within her community for the betterment of African Americans, particularly African American women and children.

However, Amina's life work goes beyond community activism. Amina is a brilliant writer and major voice that was often silenced. This was the 1960s, and men did not marry women with the idea of promoting their art. In one of our conversations about Amiri, she shares:

> I had a collection of Billie's [Holiday] stuff before my first marriage. Amiri was surprised I knew so much about music. I explained to him that I came out of a musical family. When my mother sang, you couldn't tell whether it was Billie or my mother. I sacrificed my life, and I did it willingly. Every time I had a child, I wanted them to have. I schemed. I asked him to get me a publisher. (Phone interview, May 14, 2019)

Those are the words of an artist longing to be heard. Amina grew up in a household of musicians and vocalists. Every fiber of her being represents art in creation mode. She says she sacrificed her life willingly. When will women of all colors no longer have to sacrifice for love and family?

As an artist, Amina's contributions to the Black Liberation Movement and her community are immense. In his book *Amiri Baraka and the Congress of African People,* educator Michael Simanga says of Amina:

> To date no comprehensive study of her significant contribution to the Black Liberation Movement, especially as a leader in CAP [the Congress of American People], has been written. This lack of scholarship on her work and contribution and that of other women in CAP deprives us of a complete view of the important role they had in CAP and the movement. (79)

Simanga makes an excellent point about Amina's critical reception that this essay seeks to address: New scholarship on Amina Baraka is vital to understanding both the importance of women to the Black Arts Movement and her role in Amiri Baraka's formidable rise in the Newark community. The need for a definitive book on Amina Baraka's life and contributions to the Black Arts Movement cannot be understated. From spending only a few days in Newark and seeing the love Amina receives from her community, particularly from the young people, there is the realization that her life and work have made a difference to the Black Liberation Movement.

•

Amina's use of her life to tell our stories is evident in the anthology *Confirmation* and illustrates her deep connection to jazz. Amina discusses its creation:

> It was named after Charlie "Bird" Parker's tune, "Confirmation," and what was interesting about "Confirmation"—there are several different takes on the same tune. I saw in different people's writings; there were different takes on Black culture and Black life, and so on, and so I said, Well Bird could do it, he did a whole lot of different takes on "Confirmation." So, we named it Confirmation. (Personal interview, June 6, 2017)

Similar to the intricacy of Parker's "Confirmation," Amina weaves together a gathering of women speaking on blackness and gender inequality through poetry, plays, and prose. Franz Fanon uses the term "Combat Literature," describing it as literature that calls upon the oppressed to "join in the struggle for the existence of the nation" (173). *Confirmation* is combat literature. There is no waving of the white flag. This is literature that enlightens and seeks cultural justice for every black woman "in the margins." *Confirmation* is representative of African American woman stating their truths. The African American has been engaged in the struggle for self-determination since landing in the Americas. Anthologies like *Confirmation* speak to that struggle; it is a major undertaking with some of the most accomplished African American female writers.

However, what is problematic about the anthology is the introduction by Amiri. In "Old Friends, New Faces, and an Intruder," published in 1983, the same year as *Confirmation*, Evelynn Hammonds makes the point that "the introduction, by Amiri Baraka, is disturbingly at odds with the rest of the book. As feminists, we cannot ignore the presence of the introduction—especially if *Confirmation* becomes widely used as a text in Women's Studies programs (as well it should)" (6). Amina said that she did not have the opportunity to read the introduction before the publication of the anthology. While I understand Hammond's concerns, *Confirmation* was Amina's dream, and in 1983 America, Amina did not feel that this dream could take place without Amiri, as he contracted his publisher to print the work.

Even with its introduction, *Confirmation* stands alone as a significant contribution to American letters, and yet, you will not find it on bookshelves. Still, excerpts from the anthology are a regular part of college literature courses, most notably Toni Morrison's "Recitatif," her only short story. I asked Amina how the authors were chosen:

> You know what happened. . . . I was traveling around . . . and I met various women; poets, and writers, and dancers, and singers, and every time I would go somewhere, I would find somebody who just struck me, and this went on for years before I said, "Amiri, maybe we should do a book, and collect all these black women," and so I went through the gamut of the women that I had met, heard, and read. Some of them I had not met, but I heard them read, and then I had, by that time, understood that Abbey Lincoln was a writer as well, and she is in there, and Maya is in there, and Toni is in there, and Sonia is in there, and Jayne Cortez, I mean everybody—every time we went to a reading or something, I would find somebody else that I would like to collect, and put it in a book, so other women could have my experience. (Personal interview, June 5, 2017)

As she traveled, Amina collected the words of African American women, words that speak to the traditions, culture, and voices of black America. This is a form of ancestralness as each of the women represents her ancestors on a space-time continuum that allows for the interconnectedness, a refashioning of the black experience that at its core is nonlinear and infinite in its expressions. In fact, Amina's description of gathering the writers for *Confirmation* is reminiscent of the African priestess, assembling the women for a healing ritual, because black women reading the works of other black women is healing. It is an affirmation that the black woman's voice matters.

When Amina took up the mantle of *Confirmation*, she became a voice for the living and the dead, the dreams of the ancestors, black women who, in their lifetimes, were denied the right to speak their truth. Amina's voice is unique in its ability to speak truth to power. *Confirmation* more than affirms the black woman: It is a testament to the resilience of the black female creating art, literature, poems, and plays that reach into the heart of black womanhood. A syncretic examination of Amiri's view of black music as black history, which can be seen through Amina's naming the anthology after "Confirmation," challenges our perceptions of black history, and opens the door on the myriad of ways in which blackness is historicized. It is also indicative of how African American women have historically told their history through art. Just as Charlie Parker was able to extend the riffs in "Confirmation," the women are having a protracted conversation on black womanhood through the anthology *Confirmation*. Amina affirms black womanism by using text to tell the history of the black woman and threading the writings together in a way that correlates the musicality of Parker's composition. The women articulate black history through the written word; it is a history of black womanhood that affirms their worth, and that speaks to what it means to be a black woman in America.

Nevertheless, the absence of Amina's voice from the introduction is a reminder of the silencing of black women, intentionally or not. The voices of African American women in general are marginalized due to racism and gender inequality. Amiri points this out in his introduction by stating that "the Black woman is usually and notoriously absent (as are the other third-world women)" from American literature (*Confirmation* 15–16). Amiri makes the case that the black woman has been and continues to be ignored as one on the "bottom of the American social ladder . . . the slaves of slaves" (16). Amiri's quote "the slaves of slaves" points to what writers from Anna Julia Cooper to Angela Davis have described as the debasement of the African American female. Being a slave is horrendous, but being so low on the scale of importance that you do not even rise to the position of a slave is incomprehensible. Amina is a brilliant author who was married to one of the most exciting voices in American literature, and yet her voice and talent took a backseat to Amiri's art.

•

Amina's view of the United States and its power structure is dark, but this is a woman who has battled for the rights of women and men and for social justice from an early age. Her daughter, Shani Baraka, was murdered in August 2003. Her husband, Amiri Baraka, was beaten and arrested during the Newark Rebellion of 1967, and her son, Ahi, was shot in the head and lived. These are not the experiences of everyday Americans. The life experiences of Amina speak to the power of standing up no matter what, of walking forward when all you want to do is crawl. Amina is a survivor. She wears the mantle of history as a woman who has seen into the future and is reminded of the sins of our past. Her viewpoint from a global perspective is about the limitations placed on women, particularly those fighting to be heard.

The need to fight those who would oppress is at the heart of Amina's art and music. While lesser souls might give up and remove themselves from the fight for social justice, Amina fights and writes and speaks her truth on the marginalization of people, due to nothing more than skin color and features born of African ancestry. The women of the BAM worked alongside the men and saw themselves as comrades, even though many believed the men were misogynistic. Amina has never been one to shy away from her truth; she said, "You have to know enough about history and the politics of humans, and particularly the sexual politics of females and males. It is not difficult to understand that this is not only with the Black Liberation Movement, this is with all movements" (Personal interview, June 7, 2017). Why is there a need for dominance? Is this in the DNA of the male? Does the male believe it is his right to dominate the female due to spoken and unspoken belief systems of what it means to be a man? Amina clarifies her thinking concerning the men of the Black Arts Movement by saying she did not think they were conscious enough to know or understand what they were doing.

While I would agree that many of the men of the Black Arts Movement were not consciously working to marginalize African American women, the need to be seen, to stand out in a world where your very existence is questioned, is reminiscent of Amiri Baraka's quote, "the slaves of the slaves." The black man was carrying the burden of slavery and could not clearly see his light, and so sought to dim the radiance of the black female. Amina's understanding of this period in American history is from the standpoint of one who has been a major voice in the battle for black liberation. We see educators speaking in an erudite manner on this period. However, the power of the Black Liberation Movement was felt on a gut level. It was not cerebral. These men and women were committed to the Black Aesthetic. This commitment permeated their beings and essence as black Americans. They did not necessarily come from academia, but they understood the power of their message. They wore Afros and ethnic clothing, and saw their dark skin and features as magnificent.

I asked Amina if she saw herself as Amiri's muse, and if so, was her voice heard. It is her belief that it was not until she started fighting back that she gained voice and agency. As long as she stood in the background, on the side, and did not say anything or publicly speak out, or gather other people to defend her views, it was fine. Amina could say something to Amiri, but not reject his viewpoint in public. Her next words surprised me:

> There were many times I thought that the marriage was done. As I got older, and I learned more because it didn't have to do with my age; it had to do with the company that I was keeping meaning the more I moved to the left. The people I was beginning to get in contact with were in the Liberation Movement, and Marxist-Leninism, and also lots of women on the left. I began little by little to say, "I think they're correct," and I started on my own development, reading their works, and reading history, and so forth. So when I found myself in a place that was very uncomfortable because I found myself disagreeing strongly with some of the things that we were doing, he and I, and some of the things I had to watch other women bear that they shouldn't have had to bear, and in their inability to understand that this ain't the way it's supposed to be. (Personal interview, June 6, 2017)

As I listened, I thought of Amiri Baraka's autobiography, published in 1984. The reprint includes an introduction dated from 1996 that can be likened to an internal battle between Amiri's perceptions and beliefs about Amina as they pertained to their relationship. There is the question of ideological differences as well as grievances brought about by his actions that he acknowledges as chauvinistic, heightened by his involvement with the Congress of African People (CAP). He speaks of following the doctrine of Maulana Karenga that perceived women as "not equal, but complimentary to men" (*Autobiography* 149). Amina resigned from CAP, which Amiri saw as a betrayal (149). Amiri views Amina as an extension of himself, and therefore, has difficulty with her veering from his belief systems. Throughout the autobiography, he constantly acknowledges his "chauvinistic" behavior, although it does not appear to change. Much like an observer of his own life, Amiri comments and moves on.

•

Amina speaks of Harriet Tubman, Sojourner Truth, and Ida B. Wells in our dialogue on powerful black women. Harriet, Sojourner, and Ida stood their ground in ways that most men and women could not even imagine. Yet, all three were born slaves. The black woman at one time in US history was not thought of as a woman, or even as a person, but rather as property, marginalized in an effort to justify inhumane treatment. In *Women, Race & Class,* Angela Davis deftly defines the parameters of the black woman's existence, asserting, "The slave system defined black people as chattel. Since women, no less than men, were viewed as profitable labor-units, they might as well have been genderless as far as the slaveholders were concerned" (5). With the rape and abuse of the black woman's body, it might be asked how the female slave could be seen as genderless. As rape is not sex, but rather domination, the black body has become a site of torture and subjugation. So, when Sojourner Truth asks the question "Ain't I a woman," she is stating that the black female body, a site of torture, resists any acts of violence in her determination to self-define black female identity. These women speak to the truth of having a black body. They rejoice in their blackness, no matter the pain. When I say pain, I am speaking of a psychic pain and the realization that you are judged before entering a room. Our skin color creates an awareness that we must be vigilant with the full knowledge that the beauty of our blackness is not always seen or appreciated.

Amina speaks of wanting the voices of black women to be heard, no matter the cost:

I wanted them to hear the voices of the most oppressed. I wanted them to hear the voices of freedom writers, freedom fighters. I wanted them to hear our voices as women who bear children, who raise children, who marry, who don't marry; women who are struggling every day of their lives to become looked at, and appreciated as human beings which many times does not happen, particularly in the climate of the United States of America. (Phone interview, January 7, 2019)

There are people born to the revolution. Perhaps the tragedies that she has faced have led Amina to fight for freedom for all. This need to overcome obstacles is in her writing and in her approach to life. Amina's poetry is fierce in its determination to stare down adversity. Art is used as a weapon against the pain of living. Amina offers a means to heal through art and to show those who are healing that it is possible and probable that they will make it through the fire. In her poem "Sortin-Out," anthologized in *Confirmation* (74–75), Amina glides and stomps through pain, writing about "people [who] kept asking her "why don't you write a novel, / since you have had such an interesting & colourful childhood," (lines 20–21), and, more specifically, about "a girl pregnant at sixteen married at seven- / teen" (22–23) and "working in factories wanting to be a movie-star / or at least the mate to the Thin Man" (25–26). This woman ends up in "his big house, this famous man / & seven children" (28–29) only to wonder "why wasn't she somewhere working or in school / why did she lose her sense of direction / was it love that led her into this long adventure" (28–30), an experience "that not even she could understand" (30). Her conclusion reveals her heartbreak and confusion: "Was this the end / since she never made it to her dreams" (30–31) and " was it being raped at fourteen / or having to drop out of high school pregnant" (35–36). With "Sortin-Out" Amina has written an autobiographical poem that speaks to her dreams as well as her dreams deferred. She had the courage to write about rape long before the Me Too movement and women en masse began demanding justice for the sexual abuse by men in power and men in general.

I wanted Amina to speak on the major contributions of the women of the Black Arts Movement. Amina described Sonia Sanchez as vital to the movement, explaining:

> She was brave enough to say things in poetry, stuff that most women would not say, and she too has had an extraordinary life. In my personal point of view, Sonya was the mother of the Black Arts, and they said well what about so in so—so I say, "I'm not talking about that. I'm only talking about when I came in the room." You know how we tend to think history begins when we show up, and it was going on all along but that's when I showed up, and she was among mostly men. (Personal interview, June 6, 2017)

When I asked Amina what she would say about the Black Panther women, in her profound directness, she replied, "I'm glad they existed. Thank goodness they were born. Thank goodness they had the courage and thank goodness they lived. These women took chances—just like asking somebody what you think of Sojourner Truth or Harriet Tubman—what do you think of them because you're glad they were born so that you could be born" (Personal interview, June 6, 2017).

•

What Amina has accomplished in response to the Black Arts Movement is historical. However, I am not sure of Amina's dreams. In "Sortin-Out," Amina addresses being married to "the Poet, the Monkish One / the—famous one"

(59–60). Which, of course, is Amiri Baraka. She speaks of their "complicated sojourn" (61). Yes, it was complicated by people, music, children, art, lovers, and life, but Amina was living her life, the one with Amiri, of which she says in her 1968 letter to him: "You have given me all the things and taken me to all of the places I dreamed of sometimes I just can't believe I have you for real" (Letter). Amiri and Amina were artists painting the same landscape with different strokes and beliefs of what was important.

Amina uses her poetry as autobiography to speak of the past, her life, and black artists that have enthralled us. In her writings, she holds the keys that document the lives of black men and women artists, while Amiri's poetry is like white lightning, the backyard brew. There is darkness and light in his work. Amina, too, is not afraid to dwell in the darkness and the light. She uses words to deconstruct pain. Amina has boxes of poems that have never been seen, never been published. While her voice was not silenced, it was muted. I asked why the majority of her work is not published. She expresses that Amiri wanted to control her literary output and so she stored her writings in boxes and became one of the hidden voices. In his autobiography, Amiri acknowledges her pain, stating, "Amina feels that her own background as dancer, painter and sculptor . . . are hidden not only by the hostile system, but with even greater injury, by me as well" (*Autobiography* 328).

Amina states that things had been difficult near the end of Amiri's life—so much so that she questioned staying in the marriage. There was a pause. It was clear that as a seventy-five-year-old woman, Amina was finding her voice. This was not just any voice. Amina is a Marxist-Leninist who feels strongly about the rights of the worker, the everyday person. I could see her commitment to community as I met young people of all ages who called her "Mom" with a sense of pride and family. Amina had grown up in Newark, and it showed in the love the people had for this woman.

I write about Amina as being Amiri Baraka's anchor. An anchor sinks to the bottom of the sea, holding the history and treasures of the ship. An anchor is what allows the ship to not float away, insubstantial and unable to handle life's currents. I saw Amina as often steering the ship when Amiri might go off in a different direction, or insult a major literary figure, such as Nikki Giovanni.

I wanted to know how Amina viewed Amiri's legacy, and whether she saw herself as his anchor. Amina starts with the position that they were male and female. That in itself will often cause a difference in viewpoints. As mentioned, Amina worked alongside Amiri and yet felt that she was not allowed the freedom that he had. Amina could make an analysis of what was going on, watching from the outside and participating all at the same time. She came to different conclusions about the movement, started to fight back, and encouraged other women to do so.

I spoke of Amina as Amiri's anchor, and perhaps, at times, his conscience. She does not know if she was an anchor for Amiri, but she would disagree and try to persuade Amiri to understand that there had to be equality in order to have freedom. Amina was a safe harbor for women and men in the Committee for a Unified Newark (CFUN) and CAP who desired a means of working toward self-determination and political advocacy in their communities. I am continually reminded that this was the 1960s, and women of all races were fighting for equal rights.

•

Amina has experienced more in one lifetime than most people experience in two or three. She points out that, compared to those who lived through the Jewish Holocaust or, like Native Americans and other black Americans, survived genocide and slavery, she does not have too many troubles. My interviews with her revealed a woman who is open and accepting of all people with a philosophy of "If you don't hurt me, I won't hurt you." That might seem simple, but at a time of racial unrest and barriers to class and gender, it was not a simple rule. Amina Baraka has shown a real commitment to human rights issues. Amina says of her advocacy, "My consciousness came from pain. Like an escaped slave. I said I am done."

20

════

Amiri Baraka

Mentoring as Revolutionary Praxis

MICHAEL SIMANGA

FIRST MET Amiri Baraka on the page of a book. I was a boy in elementary school, and he was the poet LeRoi Jones. My mother cultivated a love of reading in her children and exposed us to the canon of black literature, and I often tried reading some of her books that were beyond my comprehension. Most I don't remember, but one has remained a significant marker in my consciousness, perhaps because it was the beginning of a lifelong relationship. I remember staring curiously at the copy of *Preface to a Twenty Volume Suicide Note* my mother had on her nightstand. I didn't understand the meaning of the title but felt compelled to open the book and read the first poem. What struck me as odd and fascinating was that the title poem was written for his daughter, Kellie Jones, born five years and forty-five days after me.

"For kellie jones, born 16 May 1959" was a statement in and outside of the poem preface. It sat in its own space with a title hovering above it and a poem lingering below it. A breath, in a song that suggested something about the poet, and resonated as I read the rest of the poem, especially the final lines:

> And then last night, I tiptoed up
> To my daughter's room and heard her
> Talking to someone, and when I opened

The door, there was no one there . . .
Only she on her knees, peeking into

Her own clasped hands. (*Preface*, 5, lines 12–17)

The poem, a spellbinding subtle survey of what must be faced beyond the protections of home, ends with a simple and profound act of love, a father tiptoeing up to check on his daughter, and the implication that for her sake, he must seek and find real answers. Although I read poetry regularly as part of the curriculum of black literature at home, I'm certain my reaction was just a feeling that reminded me of my father looking in on us after a long day of work. A reminder of the potential dangers outside of our door, and the security of our black community that held us close and imparted lessons to carry beyond its borders into the hostile world. A reminder that seeking God is a search for answers within and outside of oneself.

I've come back to the poem many times over the years, because it still speaks to me but also because it is where I first met Baraka. A reminder of how serendipitously, other than my family, he became the most significant intellectual, artistic, and revolutionary influence on my life. A teacher who taught me and others that mentoring is revolutionary praxis.

I was nurtured in black Detroit, the last stop on the Underground Railroad. The Detroit river was both beacon and boundary of slavery and freedom. During the Great Migration, it was a major settling place for southern blacks escaping the Jim Crow South and seeking jobs and a better life in the North. As a major producer of black culture, jazz and soul flew out of the crevices and dreams of the kitchens we cooked in and the basements we danced in, the porches where we sat and the assembly lines where we worked. Black teachers taught us with love in the de facto segregated schools. Black professionals supported civil rights and achievement.

Detroit was a black city because there was a highly developed black consciousness, like a heart beating collectively out of the miles of east-side and west-side communities with generations of stories of racist terror and our resistance and victories. It was a consciousness shaped by the civil rights and labor movements of the twentieth century, and the ethos of "do for self" that was cultivated in the black church, and the Detroit-born Nation of Islam and Shrine of the Black Madonna, Ed Vaughn's bookstore, and numerous community organizations devoted to the liberation of Africa's descendants.

In 1963, Detroit is where Dr. Martin Luther King previewed his "I Have a Dream" speech on June 23 before 125,000 people at the March for Freedom, two months before the March on Washington. On November 10, Malcolm X spoke at the Grassroots Leadership Conference organized by Grace Lee Boggs, Milton Henry, Reverend Albert Cleage, and other Detroit radical activists. It was the site of Malcolm X's searing critique of America and call for revolutionary change. That speech, "Message to the Grassroots," perhaps his most famous, was both a preview of his evolving politics and a precursor to his break with the Nation of Islam.

By the mid-1960s, Detroit was fertile ground for Black Power, with the Revolutionary Action Movement (RAM), Black Christian Nationalists (Shrine of the Black Madonna), the League of Revolutionary Black Workers, the Black Arts Movement, the Black Panther Party, and college and high school student movements all growing from the grass roots. It was also the time when the influence of Malcolm X could be seen in almost every Black Power organization program or demand. His focus and articulation of Black Nationalist–Pan-African–Socialist ideas pushed the black liberation movement past the demand for civil rights and toward a Black Power agenda in the wake of his assassination February 21, 1965.

In my hometown, the city of the largest urban rebellion of the '60s, I was baptized over and over in succeeding surging waves of the Black Liberation Movement. I grew up in the rising of the civil rights movement when its courageous working-class black people, students, teachers, ministers, and sharecroppers and their allies confronted the violent terroristic Jim Crow system in the South and in the North fought against racism and discrimination and for justice, fair housing, education, and jobs. By the mid-1960s, the modern Black Freedom Movement was into its second decade and had achieved significant civil rights victories, including the 1964 Civil Rights Act and the 1965 Voting Rights Act. I came of age as Black Power pushed the movement past the struggle to enforce the civil rights of black people through the writing, speeches, organizations, and actions around the surging demand for self-determination and liberation for African Americans and all African peoples. One such demand was for a new black nation in the south, a Republic of New Afrika.

I first met Amiri Baraka in person at the March 1968 founding conference of the Republic of New Afrika (RNA) in Detroit. I was a teenage activist soaking up the ideas and actions of Black Power. He was Imamu Baraka, a political and spiritual leader of the movement and the most well known of the architects of the Black Arts Movement. I followed him closely after that meeting. By 1971 I was preparing to attend the National Black Political Convention in Gary and to spend time in NewArk learning the ideology and methodology of the Congress of African People.

At that first meeting at the RNA convention, with the typical precociousness of Black Power youth, I approached Baraka and introduced myself as a poet and activist. A brother providing security for him looked at me and smiled quiet amusement and approval. Amiri shook my hand, and said something like, "You a poet, huh? To be a black poet means you are committed to black liberation." As he walked away to talk with someone else, he said, "What are you reading?" He didn't wait for an answer, but over the forty-five years of our relationship, he asked that question almost every time we talked. If he stayed at my house when he came to Detroit, and later Atlanta, or if he rode in my car, he always left something to read. If we were at internal organizational meetings, at conferences, on a plane, eating dinner, on the phone, that question was always asked, as he passed on a book, a pamphlet, article, flyer . . . sometimes with a note: "Pili read this!"

Those gifts included poetry, fiction, literary theory, political economy, history, Marxism, African philosophy, and whatever subject was on his mind at the time and whatever he thought I needed to begin studying. Often the material required me to do research and study to grasp what he was sharing. Beyond high school, many of us didn't have formal education, but Amiri was training us as independent scholars while also training those with formal education to think like revolutionaries. We were constantly assigned research projects that required statistical and archival research, sources, field studies, demographic trends, politics, economics, pedagogy. It wasn't until after his death in 2014 that I began to realize the deliberate and methodical way he mentored hundreds of activists, artists, and students, creating next-generation radical organizers, thinkers, scholars, and artists in the tradition he represented.

Baraka insisted we learn the critical relationship between work and study as a key element of our organizing methodology. He conducted classes and held individual conversations with those of us in organizations like the Congress of African People (CAP). He and Amina Baraka trained others to teach the organization's ideas, practices, and methods to develop independent capacity for leadership. And while there is often discussion about his shifts in ideology, at every stage of his political life, Amiri insisted that we not just agree with him, but that we learn independently, and if we disagreed, to defend it with scholarship. It was much later that most of us understood the graduate-level education and skills we received in the organization.

Baraka is usually studied as a literary figure, a Black Arts Movement principal, a political leader and influencer during the Black Power era, and a significant late twentieth-century black Marxist. There is often mention of the institutions he built with others to advance the ideas he was committed to, but there is minimum writing about the institutions and organizations as a part of his larger praxis of mentoring. The Black Arts Repertory Theatre and

School (BARTS), Spirit House, Committee for Unified NewArk (CFUN), the Congress of African People, the National Black Political Convention (Gary '72), and the National Black Assembly were all full of young people between fifteen and twenty-five, who were learning through work and study, including working with more experienced activists and studying their expertise, discipline, and commitment. The Gary Convention is an example of the effectiveness of the mentorship model that Baraka practiced and insisted on. There is almost universal agreement among participants and scholars that the Gary Convention would not have happened and would have imploded without the high level of organizational and administrative capacity of the Congress of African People and especially the women of the organization. CAP was an organization of committed young black revolutionaries who were smart, disciplined, and self-sacrificing. In Baraka's understanding of mentoring as necessary revolutionary praxis, he'd led the building of a model that collectively and individually gave us the skills to use our intellect and talents at a high level to contribute to black liberation and a just and humane world.

Although many of Baraka's books were published by major publishers, he was a persistent example of how to function as an independent artist. Throughout his artistic life, he self-published or published with independent presses like Third World Press and Black Classics Press, both founded by Black Power activists Haki Madhubuti and Paul Coates. He encouraged young writers to publish in whatever way possible and was a living example. Baraka was the famous writer still publishing chapbooks or photocopying an essay or new poem that he'd slap a cover on and sell for a dollar or two at his performances and speeches. He mentored and encouraged young writers to act like literary guerillas using available resources. He insisted that the work must reach the people directly, despite and often without the blessing and resources of major publishers.

Although widely read in the academy, he was also read by working-class black people, independent artists, scholars, activists, and others. Many days I was with Amiri when a baggage handler, a store clerk, a young person on the street would say, "You're that poet, right?" Sometimes they'd call others over to meet him. Older people would often say, "I first knew you as LeRoi Jones." Sometimes they told him about a poem or essay he'd written or a speech or reading they'd experienced. Musicians often referenced *Blues People* as critical to their development as artists. He traversed the formal world of academia and arts and letters, but he wrote from and for the people with calloused hands and swollen feet.

For Amiri Baraka, teaching and mentoring was as important as his creative production and political work. He was always engaged in developing next-generation revolutionary artists and activists. Teaching seemed almost reflexive, innate, something he was compelled to do, like writing a poem. Whenever I was with him, there would always be unexpected moments of confirmation of his praxis. Once, in a small jazz club, a young trumpet player with great technical ability was blowing a swirling blizzard of notes. The audience applauded wildly, approvingly. In the quiet after the clapping stopped, Amiri leaned over to me and said, "But can he play a ballad?" One of my favorite lessons. It ain't all heat; we need cool water too. Balance in thinking and acting: In life, there is beauty, not only pain; laughter, not only rage.

Amiri Baraka's mentoring is also much broader than those he touched directly. If we listen closely to his private and public discussions of ideas and the presence of fire and light in his art, we will remember he also mentored spiritually, whispering from what he left. That we, black people and the human family, must find beauty and seek love. It is why we struggle to make change, to defeat those who render our world ugly.

> Our world is full of sound
> Our world is more lovely than anyone's
> tho we suffer, and kill each other
> and sometimes fail to walk the air
>
> We are beautiful people
> with african imaginations
> full of masks and dances and swelling chants
> with african eyes, and noses, and arms,
> though we sprawl in grey chains in a place
> full of winters, when what we want is sun.
> ("Ka Ba," *Reader* 222, lines 5–14)

21

The Overlooked Spirit Reach of Amiri Baraka's Terribleness

KALAMU YA SALAAM

THE '70s were our out years. Way out. When we was deep in our feelings. Feeling ourselves. What we wanted to be. Quickly become. Different from the was that we had been for so long. Too long. Our rage against injustice and super-exploitation contained, constrained, covered up for long time so. But long sought change was not, in the immortal words of Sam Cooke, "going to come." Because, in fact, in the streets, change had already arrived. Like our dear brother Mayfield said, we now were moving on up. Trying to get over. Headed forward toward all the beauty we were aiming to create and be. The hoped-for black and proud, future us-es. All that we dared dream we could become. The '70s was that time.

In the '60s, we had been killed. And beat. Down. Lynched too (make no mistake, then was when routine police arrests, beatings, and cops shooting us replaced the rope). It's just that once we got past Malcolm (1965) and Martin (1968) being gunned down, the real nature of America was not difficult to see: The gun was aimed not just at black leaders but also at anyone seeking to create fundamental change. Thus, the rise of the Boston brothers, Jack and Bobby of the Kennedy clan, was aborted. As reality made clear, even though some thought the Kennedys could and would be righteous presidents, that was not to be. As history demonstrated, their opponents would rather shoot them (Jack in 1963 and Bobby in 1968) than let them serve. Thus, a major mark of the mid-twentieth century was the domestic murder of both black and white political leaders.

Moreover, in the '60s none of us believed in the always quoted description of the American legal system—that is, we were governed based on the rule of law. What laws? Certainly not the laws of freedom, justice, and equality? Those laws that were allegedly on our side, the side of those who are discriminated against, whether by race, class, or gender. After the '50s, in a self-serving turn of illegal, extralegal, and even some of the legal jurisprudence, reductively, what happened is simply that Jim Crow transformed into John Law. Self-righteously, the system came down in force not just on us, but also on colonial subjects worldwide, most conspicuously and ignobly in Vietnam. Thus, Lyndon Johnson's failure to keep a cap on anticolonial and anticapitalist commotions. Johnson led the country deeper into war while counterintuitively signing the 1964 civil rights legislation and the 1965 voting rights legislation, not to mention publicly singing (some say "croaking") the civil rights anthem "We Shall Overcome."

Check the timeline: In Birmingham (we called it "Bombingham"), Alabama, four little girls killed in a church bombing, September 15, 1963. Large and small conflagrations resulted. With limited resources and limited armaments, people nonetheless fought back during the ensuing "long, hot summers." Some point out that the 1964 and 1965 congressional actions were an insufficient response to deeply entrenched social problems of systemic poverty, overt and covert racism, and outright police repression. The '60s rebellions therefore were the years of our discontent openly expressed.

From August 11 to 16, 1965, what the establishment called the "Watts Riots" exploded. From the perspective of many of the participants, the battle was better described as the "Watts Rebellion." After the conflagrations in Los Angeles's inner city of Watts, as well as in cities large and small across the country, wherever significant populations of poor black people were located, the fires were burning full up. Neighborhoods, as well as businesses that served (and some add "exploited") the inner-city enclaves, burst into flames, culminating, but not ending, in what was unofficially dubbed the "long, hot summer" of 1967. Most infamously, Newark and Detroit erupted, which were just two of over 150 so-called race riots that raged in 1967, as documented by the Kenner Commission (officially, the National Advisory Commission on Civil Disorders), which released their full report in March 1968.

The Newark uprising was a precursor to Detroit by one week. Newark was the home of poet and activist Amiri Baraka. In 1967, three of Baraka's most incendiary poems appeared in *The Evergreen Review,* a radical, literary, and political journal of that era. These inspired rants were effective in terms of contributing to insurrection by inflaming feelings and attitudes of and for black sufferers, and openly against white oppressors. Far beyond the page, Baraka's urbane and often vulgar lyrics were used in court as evidence against the defendant, Everett LeRoy Jones (Baraka's birth name). The radical poet was initially convicted, but the rulings were ultimately overturned.

Read in the glare of ghetto fires and Molotov cocktails, Baraka's *Evergreen* literary compositions are more inspirational racial rants than were the usual literary calls for romanticized equality and fraternity. The poem "leroy" (*Black Magic* 217) concludes with a stirring counter-establishment observation:

> When I die, the consciousness I carry I will to
> black people. May they pick me apart and take
> the useful parts, the sweet meet of my feelings. And leave
> the bitter bullshit rotten white parts
> alone. (lines 11–15)[1]

Moreover, those sentiments are actually a mild autopsy compared to lines such as these from the poem "Black People!" (225):

> All the stores will open if you
> will say the magic words. The magic words are: Up against the wall mother
> fucker this is a stick up! Or: Smash the window at night (these are magic
> actions) smash the windows daytime, anytime, together, let's smash the
> window drag the shit from in there. No money down. No time to pay. Just
> take what you want. The magic dance in the street. Run up and down Broad
> Street niggers, take the shit you want. Take their lives if need be, but
> get what you want what you need. Dance up and down the streets, turn all
> the music up, run through the streets with music. (9–17)

Few of the poets in the English tradition of Shakespeare or Donne, or the more recent American texts of Dickinson and Whitman, sounded anything like this. But these were words of social struggle that identified capitalism and racism as twin evils.

A retaliatory venom dripped from these poems, making it difficult to assume Baraka had any good intentions toward whites in general, regardless of who may have been as immediately past associates and, yes, lovers. The

---

1. Editor's note: References to poems are taken from *Black Magic: Poetry 1961–1967,* unless otherwise noted.

third poem, "The Black Man Is Making New Gods" (205–206), ends with a chilling indictment and sentence:

> These robots drag a robot
> in the image of themselves, to be
> ourselves, serving their dirty
> image. Selling fried potatoes
> and people, the little arty bastards
> talking arithmetic they sucked from the arab's
> head.
> Suck you pricks. The best is yet to come. On how
> we beat you
> and killed you
> and tied you up.
> And marked this specimen
> "Dangerous Germ
> Culture." And put you back
> in a cold box. (35–49)

Immediately following Newark, the fires burned even higher, hotter. The Detroit uprising started as a conflict between police and residents on Detroit's west side following a Sunday, July 23, early morning police raid on what was commonly known as a "blind pig" (i.e., an after-hours bar, often unlicensed). Over the course of the day, the conflict with the police escalated into pitched battles. Ironically, the police raid was conducted on a party honoring, among others, two soldiers who had returned home from the Vietnam War. By Sunday night, five people had been killed and disturbances and fire-bombings were out of police control. Then-governor George Romney ordered the Michigan National Guard into the city in an attempt to "restore" order, but the situation continued to worsen, and President Lyndon Johnson had to send in the US Army's 82nd and 101st Airborne Divisions to quell the rebellion. During the course of the conflict, forty-three people were killed, over 7,000 people were arrested, and well over 1,300 buildings were burned. There was no longer any denying or covering up the fact that America had a serious problem with racial inequality and conflict.

During the tumultuous '70s, Baraka moved from an advocate of Black Nationalism to a staunch communist ideology grounded in Marxism, with an emphasis on the teachings of Mao Tse Tung replacing the Kawaida brand of black nationalism articulated by Maulana Karenga. Kawaida was summed up in the Nguzo Saba (the seven principles), which Baraka spelled out in a 1970 pamphlet titled "A Black Value System." Shortly thereafter, Baraka repudiated his black nationalist positions and formally turned to Marxism; 1973 seems to be the pivotal year of Baraka's political pirouettes.

In the '70s, we had been pontificating about Africa and motherships. What a dangerous combination: an ancient homeland and a not-too-distant, almost-here, futuristic existence. You could certainly hear these proclamations in the music of the Sugarhill Gang and their surprising hit, which is often identified as the inauguration of an entirely new and original direction for popular music: 1979's "Rapper's Delight." Moreover, by then P-Funk's legendary mothership had landed with an otherworldly stage show that absolutely astounded and delighted fans and critics alike. For those who did not get to see one of the mythical mothership landings, there was a joyous live album, "Live: P-Funk Earth Tour," and eventually a video.[2]

Sun Ra had made the suggestion: Suppose we came not just from Africa; suppose we also came to Africa. Which of course, raises the question, where were we coming from to get to the Africa in us? And, if you think about it, the real answer was not just Garvey's UNIA and the Black Star Liners. That was a good idea, but a bit premature, given the physical, psychological, economic, and political ravages of colonialism. We, the wretched ones, had some liberation struggles to win first, primarily in the motherland, Africa, as well as up and down the western hemisphere. Not surprisingly, the '70s were when we celebrated ALD (African Liberation Day—May 25, sponsored by the African Liberation Support Committee, which offered financial, material, and ideological support for movements that ranged from democracy-advocating political formations to armed guerilla struggle).

"A Luta Continua" (the struggle continues) became our watchword. A bunch of us in the US actively agitated for and organized around an updated notion of Africa for Africans, at home and abroad. In 1974, we were a large and strong delegation led by Jim Turner in attending the Sixth Pan African Congress in Dar es Salaam, Tanzania.

Although in the new millennium we do not often think about fiction providing a timeline of political struggles, the '70s was also when Toni Morrison, an eventual Nobel laureate, jumped off with a triplet of devastatingly insightful, psychological novels: *The Bluest Eye* (1970), *Sula* (1973), and *Song of Solomon* (1977). These books were an unmatched examination of the interior complexes (and conflicts) of a black identity within a white supremacist society.

---

2. Editor's note: A version of the mothership is now exposed in the National Museum of African American History, precisely on the fourth floor's exhibit on "Cultural Expression."

Oh, back then we had all kinds of ideas jumping out of our wooly heads. Rufus might even become the president, and Eartha be the first lady. Check the context: America was literally on fire. Black, brown, red, and even some white post–Cold War youth were in open rebellion against an older political and cultural establishment. Black civil rights and liberation activists were ascendant. That up-full movement inspired all other peoples and conditions, from bottom to top, in this society and, indeed, worldwide.

The spirit of resistance and self-determination was particularly important in fighting misogyny. Remember, if you can, and learn about the massive militancy of that era if you are too young to know about and, of course, were never taught in high school or college about major women's liberation moments. For example, Shirley ("Unbought and Unbossed") Chisholm ran for the Democratic nomination for president in 1972. Although she did not win the votes, she did significantly elevate the consciousness of women, as well as that of some men. Like I said, the '70s were the ish. Everybody was thinking and feeling that anything/everything was possible.

So that's the historical context of three major works from Amiri Baraka: (1) *In Our Terribleness* (1970), a hardback book of lyrics by Imamu Amiri Baraka (LeRoi Jones) with photographs by Fundi (Billy Abernathy); (2) *It's Nation Time* (1972), an on-fire LP of revolutionary music on the Motown Black Forum label; and (3) *Spirit Reach* (1972), a short collection of Baraka's poetry from Jihad Publications, out of New Ark, New Jersey. Unfortunately, this trio of literary and musical undertakings has been largely ignored, despite representing the zenith of Baraka's black nationalist creative work.

In the larger context of African American literary developments, *Terribleness* is creatively a follow-up to *The Sweet Flypaper of Life*, which featured words by Langston Hughes and photographs by Roy DeCarava. *Flypaper* is critically considered a literary and artistic classic. Significantly, the book's contents are presented as a monologue by Sister Mary Bradley, a grandmother observing and meditating on her people and their conditions in the '40s and early '50s in Harlem. Published in 1955, the poignant lyricism and sharp-eyed images reveal a deep love of the culture and lives of working-class black people. The vernacular social assessments articulated by the elderly woman are a masterpiece of both tenderly as well as firmly situating women at the center of black life.

Even though articulated by the words of a male writer and the vision of a male photographer, *Flypaper* champions the feminine voice and viewpoint. In contradistinction, *Terribleness*, perhaps unintentionally, silences black women, or at best presents women as the silent objects of the male gaze. On the other hand, in an important way, *Terribleness* parallels *Flypaper,* which concluded with a photo portrait of grandmother Bradley. The final two images in *Terribleness* are elderly women. Although both women are looked at and not heard from, it is nonetheless significant, even extremely so, that *Flypaper* portrays a woman as the witnessing narrator, while in contrast *Terribleness* privileges the male voice. The most salient aspect is *Flypaper*'s existence provides an important example not only that men can be feminists but also that, well before the '60s, there were black male artists who were thinking and articulating womanist attitudes.

Baraka is, of course, a poet, and is most comfortable literally speaking in the male first person. But beyond the eliding of the feminine, not to mention feminist voice in *Terribleness,* there is an important element that is often extreme in its articulation. *Terribleness* is written in a vernacular that mirrors how black people spoke on the street in the '60s and '70s.

By contrast, the first published African American poet, Phillis Wheatley (1753–1784), rather than in the vernacular, wrote in the literary style of her time period. Moreover, one of the most popular African American poets of any and all time is Paul Laurence Dunbar (1872–1906).

Many of Dunbar's poems are written in what became known as dialect, or Negro dialect, which eventually was looked down upon by readers in general and lovers of more formal poetry in particular. Also, while not denouncing dialect poetry, Dunbar expressed frustration that he was more celebrated as a dialect poet than for his standard English language creations. After all, he gave us two of the most famous African American literary images: "the caged bird" and "we wear the mask."

Leapfrogging ahead by two millennia, from Wheatley and Dunbar, we find that black poetry has bifurcated into spoken word and written word. Spoken word privileges the vernacular, in direct contrast to written word, which is generally presented in a much more formally structured, standard literary manner. *Terribleness* in the late '60s is a long, long way from poetry written in standard English, whether compared and contrasted to that of Phillis Wheatley, whose 1773 offerings marked the beginnings of African American poetry, or to the work of Tracy K. Smith, who became poet laureate of the United States in 2017. Both the clashing and the distancing between the spoken word and the written word are glaringly apparent in Baraka's work in "IMAGE," a selection in the unpaged book *In Our Terribleness:*

Our terribleness is our survival as beautiful beings, any where. Who can
   dig that? Any where, even flying through space like we all doing,

> even faced with the iceman, the abominable snowman, the beast
> for whom there is no answer, but change in fire light and heat for
> the world

To be bad is one level
But to be terrible, is to be
badder dan nat.

Baraka's 1972 *Nation Time* recording significantly ups the ante and widens the chasm between spoken word and written word. Perhaps because Baraka is reciting with wide-ranging musical accompaniment and not just solo reading the poems off the page, *Nation Time* is more dramatic and, often, more accessible, especially to an audience not steeped in formal poetry. The music includes a drum chorus, a female vocal chorus, an R&B band, and a modern jazz ensemble. Although long out of print, we are fortunate that the whole work is available online at YouTube.

One poem that is in *Terribleness* and also recited on *Nation Time* is "Answers In Progress," which we taught the pupils at our school, Ahidiana Work/Study Center (K through third grade), to recite from memory. "Answers" encouraged our young people to

Walk through life
beautiful more than anything
stand in the sunlight
walk through life
love all the things
that make you strong. be lovers. be anything
for all the people of
earth.

You have brothers
you love each other, change up
and look at the world
now, its
ours, take it slow
we've a long time, a long way
to go.

We have
each other, and the
world,

dont be sorry
walk on out through sunlight life, and know
we're on the go
for love
to open
our lives
to walk
tastin the sunshine
    of life.

Inevitably, sound carries much more emotion than does silently reading. Added to that truism is the fact that black culture has traditionally emphasized sound over sight, and emotional expressiveness over intellectual acuity. A major reason for the dominance of sounding over seeing is that from 1619 up through the Civil War, self-determined black vision and visual projections, such as paintings and sculpture, were outlawed in much of the southern US, where the overwhelming majority of our people lived. But black talk and music could not easily be circumscribed nor restricted by legislation or by establishment customs. Nevertheless, inevitably there was a major status quo response and attempt to demean black cultural expressions.

"ALL IN THE STREET" is text in the *Terribleness* book but also sound (narration with music) on the *Nation Time* recording. The poem appeals to us to use our imagination to go beyond the reality of time and space:

Can you imagine something other
than what you
see Something
Big Big & Black
Purple yellow
Red & green (but Big, Big & Black)
Something look like a city
like a Sun Island gold-noon
Flame emptied out of heaven
grown swollen in the center
of the earth
Can you imagine who would live
there
with gold streets
striped circled inlaid
with pageants of the rulers

victories . . . Imagine these streets
along which walk some people
some evolved humans
look like you
maybe walk, stroll

rap like you
but maybe a lil difference
maybe different clothes
hip mighta changed
a lil, but they shoes still glow
black and brown mirrors for things
in the street
to dig themselves
mounds of round sounds bubblin and bumpin
right out the ground
can dig it . . . uh?
can see it . . . uh?
can feel it . . . uh?
can be it . . . huh?
This is now-past what you touch today
can change black man behaving under
your touch the way you want it to.
Can you digit . . . uh?
See, feel, touch, be
it, uh?

The challenge is to move from the reality that exists in the early '70s toward a projected future state of black self-determination, which is far, far from the caricature of black life that the establishment proffered throughout the '60s and that was massively contradicted by the movement of black people in the streets and in self-developed institutions following the late '60s rebellions. Where the establishment championed '60s- and '70s-era minstrelsy, particularly as televised comedies and caricatures, in contradistinction, as Baraka exemplified in *Nation Time,* there was a distinctly different musical wave happening in the black community.

Significantly, minstrel shows were a popular form of American antebellum entertainment and after the Reconstruction period (1865 to 1877), minstrel shows were replaced by vaudeville (generally dated from the 1890s to the mid-1930s), which itself also included a lampooning of black people. Although minstrelsy in particular, as well as subsequent forms of popular entertainment, mimicked black performance styles, it is notable that these stage, and later on, screen productions were performed by whites. Indeed, the first "Hollywood talkie" was *The Jazz Singer* in 1927, featuring Al Jolson (who ironically was Eizer Asa Yoelson, a Yiddish-named, Russian-born Jew) performing in black-face. In the case of the minstrel show on stage and *The Jazz Singer* on the silver screen, this is specifically when "blackface" entered American consciousness in a popular form.

Most people were oblivious, or at least uncaring, about the obvious con-tradiction of the broad acceptance of whites in blackface happening at the same time as the legal, and extralegal, repression of black people was rampant in this society. Most of the audience was also oblivious to the fact that this approach contained a negative reaction to the political and economic gains of the aforementioned Reconstruction period.

However, it was not only whites in blackface who low-rated and dispar-aged black people. Baraka's early creative work is especially critical of the "tomfoolery" of black actors such as Stepin Fetchit and Mantan Moreland. From *Dutchman* (1964) to *Slave Ship* (1970), Baraka's drama is suffused with both racial and gender conflicts.

As a poet, Baraka the black nationalist peaks with *Spirit Reach* (1972), a twenty-eight-page booklet published by Baraka's own Newark-based Jihad Publications. Five of the twelve poems in *Spirit Reach* are recited on the *Nation Time* recording. Baraka was aware that much of his poetry had to be heard, and not just read on the page, in order to be fully appreciated. The sound/sight dichotomy embodied in Baraka's poetic voice contrasted against his written text.

Spirit Reach is not only lyrical; the book is the last time we see Baraka advocating religion and identifying himself as a religious leader. The third poem in the book, "STUDY PEACE" (*Selected* 204), opens with the declaration:

Out of the shadow, I am come in to you whole a black holy man
whole of heaven in my hand in head look out two yeas to ice
what does not belong in the universe of humanity and love. I am
the black magician you have heard of, you knew was on you in you now
my whole self, which is the star beneath the knower's arc, when the star it
self rose and its light illuminated the first prophet, the five pointed being
of love. (lines 1–7)

The last poem in the book is "SNAPSHOTS OF EVERYTHING" (*Black Magic* 227) and concludes (both the poem and the book) with the ecstatic proclama-tion "dont put us / down / as merely singers, we are the song" (16–18).

It is noteworthy that Baraka was also a nationally recognized organizer and political figure who achieved the acme of his political career as one of the organizers of the 1972 National Black Political Convention in Gary, Indiana. In black nationalist circles, Baraka was credited with saving the National Black Assembly (NBA) from self-destruction when he gave a stirring speech, informally known as his "Nation Time" talk, that was an emotional call for unity and an exhortation to action. Although it was not apparent at the time, that was the beginning of the end of Baraka as a national political force. In 1974, at the Sixth Pan African Congress held in Dar es Salaam, Tanzania, Baraka, on an international stage, broke from the popularity of his black nationalist phase and, as mentioned before, formally announced he had adopted Marxism as his political philosophy.

Also significant is that shortly thereafter, Baraka dropped "Imamu" ("spiritual leader"), and from then on would be known simply as Amiri Baraka. Here is where Baraka's contact with black nationalism is broken and irreparably severed. The Baraka of this period also rejects religion as a progressive, not to mention, revolutionary force. Philosophically, and ironically, wasn't it Stalin who pointed out that when anything reaches its zenith, that is precisely the moment it begins to diminish, specifically because its upward force is spent and gravity begins to pull it back down? This principle is not just relevant to physical conditions; "the zenith is the beginning of the end" is also a social principle.

While many, many followers and observers were expecting more and blacker statements and leadership from Amiri Baraka during the latter half of the '70s, what happened instead is Baraka confounded the nation he had encouraged and, to a lesser degree, of which he had been a principal assembler. By 1974, Amiri became a full-out Marxist and permanently renounced black nationalism.

Thus were the '70s when Baraka's fires of black nationalism were extinguished. His diminishment of nationalism was not just an analytical flameout. As was his wont over the twisting years of his long career, in his attire as well as in his attitude and associations, Baraka did not merely turn his back on his past; he felt it necessary to renounce old ways while he waved the flag of future directions. Surely, he had phoenix in his blood. Out of the ashes of self-immolation a new, or rather, "another" Baraka rose up in awe-filling flight. While such turns are apparent over the course of his long career, 1970 to 1973 was a pivotal period and, in many ways, marked the last major turning of LeRoi Jones to Amiri Baraka.

When we study *In Our Terribleness, Nation Time,* and *Spirit Reach,* we not only find a poet and creative writer at his height, but we also encounter a person about to make fundamental professional and personal changes. Understanding Baraka's social context and his personal response to political realities in the '6os and '7os is absolutely essential to grasping the fullness of one of America's most profound poets.

Here is the kicker: Some people are trying to erase, or ignore, the black Baraka. The evidence is written down. In 2014, Grove Press published *SOS POEMS 1961–2013*, selected by Paul Vangelisti. Note that the title is misleading because poems from *Terribleness, Nation Time,* and *Spirit Reach* are nowhere to be found in the 530-some-page book. You read right: Over five hundred pages of poetry culled from over five decades of work, and yet we get no "Answers in Progress," no "ALL IN THE STREET," no bunch of verse from Black Power–oriented Baraka. And worse yet, the preface of *SOS* does not even make mention or acknowledgment that selections from three important works are not included. They are not obscure, or even previously unpublished work. Instead they are poems Baraka published himself on Jihad Publications (*Spirit Reach*), and which he recorded on Motown (*Nation Time*), not to mention in a hardback with Bobbs-Merrill Company, a major publishing company of the time period (*In Our Terribleness*). What gives?

I will not even attempt to suggest why the exclusion, why the seemingly knowledgeable editor overlooked or did not include work that originates in an important period of Baraka's poetic career, especially given how dynamic Baraka was as a reader and reciter of his poetic creations. Here we have a whole album on one of the major recording labels of all time, Motown, and none of the poems from that recording are anthologized.

You know a couple of generations from now, those who study Baraka may entirely miss this Baraka who delighted thousands in his stirring presentations all across the country and even internationally. I understand the reality that when you don't have an audience of black people, especially when you perform overseas, there is a tendency to lean on poems that foreigners can easily understand or relate to. This proclivity is especially sharp when you are reaching out to people whom you want to embrace or respect, and among whom you want and hope those feelings are reciprocal.

I understand that Baraka often found himself among South Americans, among Europeans, and among other people for whom being black was foreign, but as human beings, they could understand and feel you when you talked in nonracial terms, which is what, we understand, a serious international stance requires. Especially when you moved beyond being a victim of American racism. You do not want nobody pitying you, feeling sorry for you. What we really want is respect and human acceptance.

I understand that there was a deep disappointment in the ways that black political movements turned out in the US. The appalling absence of a black nation. The seemingly enduring reality of the ghetto. And worse yet, the god-awful betrayals by black boogie politicians who cared less for black workers than did their so-called devil colleagues.

I understand how fiendishly difficult it is to negotiate survival and development when you get support from others and rejection from peers.

I understand that you can get a "goddamn academy award" (that's a quote from *Black & Beautiful—Soul & Madness*, a 1968 Baraka recording) or a Pulitzer Prize for what might be called militant integration, but hey, let's not pretend there was not a time when black Baraka advocated, wrote, and recited some really deep poems about him and his people being their own selves, in a space and a place of their own. Their own control. Their own community.

I understand, at a certain level, black independence is a pipe dream. We are part of the world. And more importantly, part of this nation. Been so since Crispus Attucks, a black man in 1770, was the first to die fighting in the American Revolution. It's a tough contradiction being here while not feeling completely *of* here. Wanting to be closer to yourself, while wanting to be away from all that surrounds and, yes, all that majorly contributes to you being the you who you are. Indeed, your whole identity is bound up, surrounded, and dominated by people and positions who are not you.

The dilemma of being African American is that to be fully one element of your historic being negates being fully the other. Yet, somehow, we must find a way to be both/and rather than either/or. Social syncretism is a bitch. We be something completely different from either of the two major parts of our bloody birth. And so, yes, I understand the liquidation of a Baraka whose circle is difficult to square with the social realities of what it means to be American, to be black in America, and ultimately, just to be here, and be black without having to be anything else.

I understand that not everyone saw each of Baraka's three phases as mutually exclusive. Rather than embrace the pretzel-like twists and turns with an element of salty separations that are descriptive of Baraka's career, those who remain a partisan of the artist Amiri Baraka focus on his intellectual acumen and aesthetic insights and innovations.

I understand. But there was a time, and we should never forget or negate that even though Baraka left his earlier positions, his love of black culture and black people remains at the heart of all his concerns.

Specifically, there was a time when in our race toward a mythical, unreachable, but not undreamed-about *Nation Time* we was *Spirit Reach*-ing *In Our Terribleness*. Our *Nation Time* was a *Spirit Reach* in all our *Terribleness*. Had to be in spirit because our oppressors and exploiters were never going to allow us in physical reality to be ourselves, not without serious opposition and consequences clouding, confusing, containing, condemning, and/or criminalizing our being, our *Blackness*. (And when we capitalize the "B" in *Blackness*, it means we are talking about not just complexion, we are also talking necessarily and more importantly about both culture and consciousness.) We was terrible in a terrible time. Our spirit was steady reaching, a brilliant, black, terrible *Spirit Reach* for us, ourselves, in a space and a place of our own-ness. Where we could be we, in all our terribleness!

Without denying the relevance of what came after, the terrible spirit reach of a nation time Baraka, that is the Amiri I celebrate: an eloquent, and yes, when necessary, militant, Amiri, who, at our best, we all are and aspire to always be.

Amiri Baraka as
Cultural Philosopher

TONY BOLDEN

A PECULIAR IRONY of literary criticism is that the pioneering black feminist scholar Barbara Christian arguably characterized Amiri Baraka's legacy as a prescient cultural philosopher when she stated in her essay "The Race for Theory" that "people of color have always theorized—but in forms quite different from the Western form of abstract logic. And I am inclined to say that our theorizing (and I intentionally use the verb rather than the noun) is often in narrative forms, in the stories we create, in riddles and proverbs, [and] in the play with language" (52). In his prolific writings as a poet, playwright, fiction writer, memoirist, and cultural critic, Baraka functioned as a Marxist cultural philosopher who formulated analyses in blues-tinted ontological archives. And while legions of writers have examined Baraka's radicalism and blues, relatively few have discussed these themes in relation to funk and dialectics in his later writings. His foregrounding of class politics and blues ontology in analyses of blackness enhanced his critical talents immeasurably. Many public figures, for instance, were shocked and baffled by the rise of ethno-nationalist white supremacy in America. However, Baraka presaged this development in such collections as *Transbluesency* (1995) and *Funk Lore* (1996). Indeed, fascism is a prominent theme in his writings.

Baraka's analyses of American political history suggest that the nationalization of neo-confederacy isn't an anomalous development in the US. Rather, it's a logical extension of capitalist political economy. Fascist imagery appears in Baraka's writing as early as 1959, when he published the poem, "In Memory of Radio." In an oft-cited passage, he writes: "I cannot even order you to gaschamber satori like Hitler or / Goody Knight" (*Transbluesency* 15–16, lines 12–13). The apparently oxymoronic allusions to Adolf Hitler and popular Republican politician Goodwin Knight are stunning. The young poet's pairing of Knight with Nazism evokes Caryl Chessman's death in the gas chamber at San Quentin Prison. Chessman, who published four books, including the novel *The Kid Was a Killer* (1960), while he was on death row, was convicted for kidnapping; and since he was accused of sexual assault, the crime was punishable by death at the time. Knight wasn't known as an extremist, but as governor of California, he refused to issue a stay for the execution, and his conservative rhetoric created an atmosphere that enabled "a machinery of injustice to grind" (Morgan 152).

But Baraka's passage is also notable because it foreshadows several of his abiding concerns that assume different shape in his later treatment of fascism. He demonstrated his interests in popular culture, morality, and contrast in blues aesthetics, racial injustice, and dialectics, respectively. He revisited the theme of fascism some twenty years later. By then, Baraka had become a full-fledged cultural philosopher who understood rhythms, melodies, and timbres of blues-oriented music as sonic illustrations that he transposed into black radical writing. For instance, in his poem "In World War 3 Even Your Muse Will Get Killed!" (*Stepping* 6), John Coltrane's music ("Trane & co.") facilitates critical ruminations on American politics. Ronald Reagan's presidency pushed the nation to a "crossroads," and his victory over progressive forces in 1980 enabled right-wing extremists: "I keep seeing / Nazis, no shit /Nazis!" Note Baraka's prescience. He riffed on the theme of fascism with added emphasis in the 1990s, titling one of his poems "Reichstag 2" in *Funk Lore*.

But what distinguishes Baraka's political analyses are his representations of slavery as a uniquely American form of fascism. The correlation between the antebellum South and Nazi Germany is especially evident in some of his later blues writings. As James Smethurst observed recently, Baraka transcribed Marxist philosophy within the parameters of blues aesthetics, which he distilled into literary form. And since the blues era is long gone, it may be helpful to remind readers that salient characteristics of blues aesthetics (e.g., the penchant for irony, balance, and empathy for mistreated identities) stand at variance with capitalist logic and values. In fact, the predilection for contrariety in blues is compatible with Marxist dialectics. For instance, in his 1991 essay "The 'Blues Aesthetic' and the 'Black Aesthetic': Aesthetics as the Continuing Political History of a Culture," Baraka analyzes the relationship between blues and funk, stating, "Any and Every—All are related to the *one,* part of a whole,

whole of a part. The hole and what goes in and out, the creatinginginging. . . . What is *funky* is history, what comes goes" (107).

We can observe how Baraka theorized black disfranchisement in blues ontology in the section titled "Wise, Whys, Y's" in *Transbluesency*. As suggested in his homophonic punning and titular allusion to Duke Ellington's 1946 composition "Transblucency," Baraka envisioned blues as a distinctive verse form that inscribed the composite history of the black working class (Bolden 33). And since the music is self-reflexive, the songs often delineated features of capitalist political economy that reproduced black underdevelopment. Baraka's poem "Y's 18" (*Transbluesency* 226–234) is a prime example. The poem, subtitled *"Explainin' The Blues* (Ma Rainey) 'Georgia Tom' Dorsey," is a metanarrative that not only describes black political history but also explains why African Americans have been so susceptible to the blues as such. Baraka treats Rainey's 1925 recording as an archival document. His central premise is that the horrors of slavery were historical "rehearsals" for the Jewish Holocaust (line 204). In this context, slave owners were primordial fascists: "The southern Himmlers, / & Goebbels" (136–137). Of course, this passage is tantamount to heresy for many white intellectuals. Since the word *fascism* rightly invokes moral outrage commensurate with crimes against humanity, the systemic, centuries-long murder and enslavement of African Americans are incongruent with the conventional denotation because the West doesn't recognize black people as fully human beings. As philosopher Charles Mills points out, quoting Norman G. Finkelstein, Hitler "explicitly located his *Lebenstraum* project within the long trajectory of European racial conquest" (93). In other words, writes Aimé Césaire, Hitler "applied to Europe colonialist procedures which until then had been reserved exclusively for the Arabs of Algeria, the coolies of India, and the blacks of Africa" (*Discourse* 14). Baraka therefore signifies with wry humor befitting Bessie Smith: "Fascism / wd come later / in Europe" (227–229).

Baraka's use of dialectics in blues led to remarkably lucid analyses. The antiphony in blues-oriented music is emblematic of the contrariety within blues logic, and Baraka improvised on this principle like a jazz musician. At times, his political commentaries emulate call-and-response. "It is No & / Yes, and not It for long," writes Baraka in "'There was Something I Wanted to Tell You' (33) Why" (*Transbluesency*, 248–251, lines 65–66), adding, "What betrays revolution is the need / for revolution" (75–76). He thus envisioned dialectics as a prerequisite for understanding the dynamics of American politics. Baraka notes that slaveholders' brutish violence and exploitation established the ground for their own opposition. Riffing on W. E. B. Du Bois's classic study *Black Reconstruction in America* (1935), the poet states that during the

Civil War, African Americans refused to perform delegated duties, and that black soldiers contributed significantly toward the Union's victory. Conversely, Baraka represents the Thirteenth, Fourteenth, and Fifteenth Amendments during Reconstruction as propositions for African Americans' full citizenship during Reconstruction—what he calls "social / valence" ("Y's 18," ll. 152–153). Then he points out that white supremacists responded by smashing Reconstruction ("Nigger/ Democracy," 81–82), and that black freedom was sacrificed on the altar of economic prosperity in the Gilded Age, which established the foundation for American imperialism in the twentieth century. And since Baraka's insight encourages extrapolation, we can infer that since the civil rights movement constituted a second reconstruction, COINTELPRO and other repressive measures that impeded black liberation were also predictable reactions. And, finally, although Barack Obama's eight-year presidency symbolized the fruition of the civil rights movement, his achievement triggered the metastasizing of hate groups and right-wing extremism throughout America.

Baraka's blues-inflected Marxist philosophy not only illuminated his political vision; it also informed his sensibility and ontological alterity. Just as blues musicians functioned as secular priests on Saturday nights, Baraka shouldered the responsibility of analyzing fundamental contradictions between global capitalism and working-class black folks. Consequently, he presciently thematized neo-confederacy in its embryonic stages while other critically acclaimed intellectuals either ignored or underestimated the far-right as a relatively meaningless irritant that American exceptionalism would presumably nullify. For instance, Cornel West stated in 2015: "Brother Bernie and Brother Trump are authentic human beings in stark contrast to their donor-driven opponents" (@CornelWest). The same year Jelani Cobb commented on the presidential race, offering wishful thinking in lieu of analysis. He said, "Trump stands almost no chance of gaining the Republican nomination, or ascending to the Presidency if he did" ("Donald Trump"). Of course, everyone miscalculates sometimes. My point isn't to besmirch West or Cobb but rather to contextualize Baraka's perspicacity by comparison. Shortly after his seventy-fifth birthday, he visited the University of Kansas. At one point in his remarks, Baraka asked, "Does anyone remember the regime in Germany before Hitler?" Then he said, "I do," and without referring to anyone specifically, he clearly suggested that the next president would be an autocratic figure ("Racism" 2009). Hence the prescience of Amiri Baraka as poet-philosopher.

WORKS CITED

Adoff, Arnold. *Harris Portable Journal.* 14 July 2018.

Alexander, Elizabeth. *American Sublime: Poems.* Graywolf Press, 2005.

———. "New Ideas About Black Experimental Poetry." *Michigan Quarterly Review,* vol. 50, no. 4, 2011, pp. 598–621.

Allen, Donald, and George F. Butterick, editors. *The Postmoderns: The New American Poetry Revised.* Grove Press, 1982.

Als, Hilton. "Amiri Baraka's First Family." *The New Yorker,* 11 Jan. 2014, https://www.newyorker.com/books/page-turner/amiri-barakas-first-family.

Appadurai, Arjun. "Archive and Aspiration." *Archive public,* https://archivepublic.wordpress.com/texts/arjun-appadurai/.

"Archive." *Oxford English Dictionary,* www.oed.com/view/Entry/10417.

Auerbach, Erich. *Scenes from the Drama of European Literature.* 1959, U of Minnesota P, 1984.

Baker, Houston A. Jr. "Amiri Baraka." *The Norton Anthology of African American Literature,* edited by Henry Louis Gates Jr. and Nellie Y. McKay, W. W. Norton & Company, 1997, pp. 1877–1879.

———. "Critical Memory and the Black Public Sphere." *The Black Public Sphere,* edited by The Black Public Sphere Collective, U of Chicago P, 1995, pp. 5–37.

Bakhtin, Mikhail M. *The Dialogic Imagination: Four Essays.* Edited by Michael Holquist, translated by Caryl Emerson and Michael Holquist, U of Texas P, 1981.

Baldwin, James. *The Evidence of Things Not Seen.* Rinehart and Winston, 1985.

Bambara, Toni Cade. "Working at It in Five Parts" (1980). *Realizing the Dream of a Black University & Other Writings: Part I,* edited by Makeba Lavan and Conor Tomás Reed, the CUNY Poetics Lost and Found Documents Initiative, Series 7, Number 2, Part 1, Fall 2017.

Baraka, Amina. Letter to Amiri Baraka, 19 Nov. 1968. Moorland-Spingam Research Center–Howard University Founder's Library.

———. "Slave Legacy." *5 Boptrees*, with Amiri Baraka, 1992, pp. 1–2.

Baraka, Amiri / Leroi Jones. *6 Persons. The Fiction of LeRoi Jones / Amiri Baraka,* Lawrence Hill Books, 2000, pp. 233–462.

———. *Allah Mean Everything!: Thus Spake Amiri Baraka,* edited by Chris Funkhouser, *Newark Review,* vol. 2, set 4, 1999. https://web.njit.edu/~newrev/v2s4/Allah.html.

———. "Amiri Baraka Lecture on Revolutionary Poetry." *Internet Archive,* https://archive.org/details/naropa_amiri_baraka_lecture_on.

———. "Amiri Baraka, the Revolutionary Theatre, *Liberator,* July 1965." National Humanities Center, 1965. http://nationalhumanitiescenter.org/pds/maai3/protest/text12/barakatheatre.pdf.

———. "Amiri Baraka, September, 2009." Liner notes. Amiri Baraka and The Spirit House Movers, Black & Beautiful, Soul & Madness, 1967; Sonboy Records, 2009.

———. *The Autobiography of Leroi Jones.* A Cappella Publishing, 1995.

———. *Black Magic: Poetry 1961–1967.* Bobbs-Merrill Company, 1969.

———. *Black Music.* Greenwood Press, 1980.

———. "The 'Blues Aesthetic' and the 'Black Aesthetic': Aesthetics as the Continuing Political History of a Culture." *Black Music Research Journal,* vol. 11, no. 2, 1991, pp. 101–109.

———. *Blues People: The Negro Experience in White America.* Morrow Quills, 1963.

———. *The Book of Monk.* John Lebow, 2005.

———. "Brief Reflections on Two Hot Shots." *Kulchur,* no. 12, pp. 2–5.

———. *Daggers and Javelins: Essays, 1974–1979.* William Morrow, 1984.

———. "The Dempsey-Liston Fight." In *Home: Social Essays.* The Dark Towers Series, edited by Gerald Early, Ecco Press, 1998, pp. 179–184.

———. *Digging: The Afro-American Soul of American Classical Music.* Berkeley: The U of California P, 2009.

———. "Essay/'Poem' on Money." Amiri Baraka Papers, Columbia University Rare Book and Manuscript Library, Box 22, Folder 32.

———. *Eulogies.* Marsilio Publishers, 1996.

———. "Exaugural Address." *Kulchur,* no. 12. 1963.

———. *The Fiction of LeRoi Jones/Amiri Baraka.* Lawrence Hill, 2000.

———. *Four Revolutionary Plays.* Bobbs-Merrill, 1969.

———. "Freddie's Dead." William Parker. *I Plan to Stay a Believer: The Inside Songs of Curtis Mayfield,* AUM Fidelity AUM062/63, 2010.

———. *Funk Lore: New Poems (1985–1995).* Littoral Books, 1995.

———. *Home: Social Essays.* The Dark Towers Series, edited by Gerald Early, Ecco Press, 1998.

———. *In Our Terribleness.* Photography by Fundi, The Bobbs-Merrill Company, 1970.

———. Introduction. *Confirmation, an Anthology of African American Women,* edited by Amiri Baraka and Amina Baraka, Morrow, 1983, pp. 15–26.

———. Introduction. *The Moderns,* edited by LeRoi Jones, Corinth Books, 1963, pp. ix–xvi.

———. *It's Nation Time: African Visionary Music.* Black Forum B457L, 1972

———. *Kulchur,* vol. 3, no. 12, 1963.

———. *The Leroi Jones/Amiri Baraka Reader.* Edited by William J. Harris, Thunder's Mouth Press, 1991.

———. Liner notes. Eddie "Lockjaw" Davis, *Bacalao*, Prestige PRLP 7178, 1960.

———. Liner notes. John Wright Trio, *South Side Soul*, Prestige PRLP 7190, 1960.

———. Liner notes. Sonny Terry, *Sonny Is King*, Prestige Bluesville BV 1059, 1963.

———. Liner notes. Thelonious Monk Quartet with John Coltrane. *Thelonious Monk Quartet with John Coltrane at Carnegie Hall*. New York, Blue Note 094633517325, 2005.

———. "A Post-Racial Anthology?" *Poetry Magazine*, 1 May 2013, https://www.poetryfoundation.org/poetrymagazine/articles/69990/a-post-racial-anthology.

———. *Preface to a Twenty Volume Suicide Note*. Totem Press, 1961.

———. "Racism, Imperialism, and the Obama Presidency." Public Lecture. Kansas University, November 3rd, 2009.

———. "Review of *Reality Sandwiches* by Allen Ginsberg." *Kulchur*, no. 12, pp. 86–88.

———. "The Revolutionary Theatre." http://nationalhumanitiescenter.org/pds/maai3/protest/text12/barakatheatre.pdf.

———. "September 2009." *Black and Beautiful . . . Soul and Madness*. The Spirit House Movers, 1968, SonBoy Records B002T4GX4M, 2009.

———. *The Selected Poetry of Amiri Baraka/Leroi Jones*. William Morrow, 1979.

———. *Somebody Blew Up America & Other Poems*. House of Nehesi Publishing, 2003.

———. *SOS: Poems 1961–2013*. Edited by Paul Vangelisti. Grove Press, 2014.

———. *Spirit Reach*. Jihad, 1972.

———, editor. *Stepping*. With Amina Baraka, Premier issue, summer 1982.

———. *The System of Dante's Hell*. Grove Press, 1965.

———. *Tales*. Grove Press, 1967.

———. *Tales of the Out & the Gone*. Akashic Books, 2007.

———. *Transbluesency: The Selected Poems of Amiri Baraka/LeRoi Jones (1961–1995)*. Edited by Paul Vangelisti, Marsilio Publishers, 1995.

———. *Un Poco Low Coup*. Ishmael Reed Publishing Company, 2004.

———. "Who Killed Our Little Shani?" *The Blacklisted Journalist*, 1 Sept. 2003, http://www.blacklistedjournalist.com/column96.html.

———. *Wise, Whys, Y's*. Third World Press, 1995.

Baraka, Amiri, and Amina Baraka, *The Music: Reflections on Jazz and Blues*. William Morrow, 1987.

———, editors. *Confirmation: An Anthology of African American Women*. William Morrow, 1983.

Baraka, Amiri, and The Advanced Workers. *Jazztage, 2. Konzert. Berlin, Germany, November 3, 1977. Jazz on Sunday: Amiri Baraka—Berlin 1977* [no label], *Roio from the BigO audio archive*. http://bigozine2.com/roio/?p=4043.

Baraka, Amiri, and Ed Dorn. *The Collected Letters*. Edited by Claudia Moreno Pisano, U of New Mexico P, 2013.

Baraka, Amiri, David Murray, and Steve McCall. *New Music–New Poetry*. India Navigation B00ZYB6QOY, 1982.

Baram, Marcus. *Gil Scott-Heron: Pieces of a Man*. St. Martin's Press, 2014.

Barney, Justin. "From Church Choirs to Performance Poetry: How Jamila Woods Found Her Voice." *NPR*, 17 Sept. 2017, https://www.npr.org/2017/09/20/551089270/from-church-choirs-to-performance-poetry-how-jamila-woods-found-her-voice.

Belson, Ken. "N. F. L. Settlement with Kaepernick and Reid Is Said to Be Much Less Than $10 Million." *New York Times,* 21 Mar. 2019, https://www.nytimes.com/2019/03/21/sports/colin-kaepernick-nfl-settlement.html.

Benston, Kimberly W. *Baraka: The Renegade and the Mask.* Yale UP, 1978.

Berlant, Lauren. *Cruel Optimism.* Duke UP, 2011.

Berliner, Paul F. *Thinking in Jazz: The Infinite Art of Improvisation.* U of Chicago P, 1994.

Berry, Faith. Introduction. *Good Morning, Revolution: Uncollected Writings of Langston Hughes,* edited by Faith Berry. Citadel Press Book, 1992, pp. xix–xxi.

Bieler, Des. "LeBron James Turns 'Shut Up and Dribble' Insult into Title of Showtime Series." *Washington Post,* 7 Aug. 2018, https://www.washingtonpost.com/news/early-lead/wp/2018/08/07/lebron-james-turns-shut-up-and-dribble-insult-into-title-of-showtime-series/?utm_term=.08c1639cee31.

Billy Harper Sextet. "Knowledge of Self." *Blueprints of Jazz Vol. 2 ("Amazing Grace"),* Talking House Records B001E4SF9E, 2011.

Black & Beautiful, Soul & Madness. Featuring Yusef Iman and the Jihad Singers, Jihad Productions JIHAD 1001, 1967.

Bolden, Tony. "Art and Struggle: An Interview with Amiri Baraka." *The Ark of the Spirit,* edited by Quo Vadis Gex Breaux, National Black Arts Festival, 1996, pp. 31–33.

Bracey, John H. "Coming from a Black Thing." *SOS—Calling All Black People: A Black Arts Movement Reader,* edited by John Bracey, Sonia Sanchez, and James Smethurst, U of Massachusetts P, 2014, pp. 650–655.

Bracey, John H., Sonia Sanchez, and James Smethurst, editors. *SOS—Calling All Black People: A Black Arts Movement Reader.* U of Massachusetts P, 2014.

Branch, John. "Why the N. B. A. and the N. F. L. Are So Far Apart on Social Justice Stances." *New York Times,* 22 Jun. 2018, https://www.nytimes.com/2018/06/22/sports/nfl-nba-social-justice-protests.html.

Brown, Fahamisha Patricia. *Performing the Word: African American Poetry as Vernacular Culture.* Rutgers UP, 1999.

Brown, Lloyd W. *Amiri Baraka.* Twayne Publishers. 1981.

Brown, Scot. *Fighting for US: Maulana Karenga, the US Organization, and Black Cultural Nationalism.* New York UP, 2003.

Browne, Mahogany L., Idrissa Simmonds, and Jamila Woods, editors. *The Breakbeat Poets Volume 2: Black Girl Magic.* Haymarket Books, 2018.

Bryant, Howard. *The Heritage: Black Athletes, a Divided America, and the Politics of Patriotism.* Beacon Press, 2018.

Carter, Jimmy. *The Public Papers of the Presidents of the United States. Jimmy Carter: 1977.* Vol. 2., Office of the Federal Register, National Archives and Records Service, http://name.umdl.umich.edu/4732130.1977.002.

Catalano, Nick. *Clifford Brown: The Life and Art of the Legendary Jazz Trumpeter,* Oxford UP, 2001.

Césaire, Aimé. *Discourse on Colonialism.* Translated by Jane Pinkham. Monthly Review Press, 2001.

Chapman, Abraham, editor. *Black Voices: An Anthology of Afro-American Literature.* Penguin, 1968.

———. *New Black Voices: An Anthology of Contemporary Afro-American Literature.* First Mentor Printing, 1972.

Chinitz, David E. *Which Sin to Bear? Authenticity and Compromise in Langston Hughes.* Oxford UP, 2013.

Christian, Barbara. "The Race for Theory." *Cultural Critique,* no. 6, 1987, pp. 51–63.

Clover, Joshua. *Riot. Strike. Riot: The New Era of Uprisings.* Verso, 2016.

Cobb, Jelani. "Donald Trump Is a Rapper." *The New Yorker,* 11 July 2015, https://www.newyorker.com/news/daily-comment/donald-trump-is-a-rapper.

———. "The Path Cleared by Amiri Baraka." *The New Yorker,* 15 Jan. 2014, https://www.newyorker.com/news/news-desk/the-path-cleared-by-amiri-baraka.

"Colin Kaepernick Foundation." *Kaepernick7.com,* https://kaepernick7.com/pages/mission.

"COMMENTS? FROM ABROAD." *Kulchur,* vol. 4, no. 15, 1964, pp. 104–105.

Conley, Craig. "Abracadabra." *Magic Words: A Dictionary,* Weiser Books, 2008.

@CornelWest (Cornel West). "Brother Bernie and Brother Trump are authentic human beings in stark contrast to their donor-driven opponents." *Twitter,* 24 Aug. 2015, 9:04 p.m. https://twitter.com/CornelWest/status/635996114060050432.

Count Basie and His Orchestra. *April in Paris.* 1955, Verve MG V-8012, 1957.

Crawford, Margo Natalie. *Black Post-Blackness: The Black Arts Movement and Twenty-First Century Aesthetics.* U of Illinois P, 2017.

Cullen, Countee. "Incident." *Color,* Harpers and Brothers, 1925, p. 15.

Dace, Tish, editor. *Langston Hughes: The Contemporary Reviews.* Cambridge UP, 1997.

Davis, Angela Y. *Women, Race & Class.* Vintage, 1983.

Davis, Charles T., and Daniel Walden, editors. *On Being Black: Writings by Afro-Americans from Frederick Douglass to the Present.* Fawcett, 1970.

Derrida, Jacques. *Archive Fever: A Freudian Impression.* Translated by Eric Prenowitz, U of Chicago P, 1998.

———. *Dissemination.* Translated by Barbara Johnson, U of Chicago P, 1981.

———. "Paul De Man." *The Work of Mourning,* U of Chicago P, 2001, pp. 69–76.

Dickson-Carr, Darryl. *African American Satire: The Sacredly Profane Novel.* U of Missouri P, 2001.

Dixon, Melvin. *Ride out the Wilderness: Geography and Identity in Afro-American Literature.* U of Illinois P, 1987.

Dorn, Ed. "A Cup of Coffee." *Kulchur,* no. 12, pp. 22–23.

Draper, Kevin, and Julie Creswell. "Colin Kaepernick 'Dream Crazy' Ad Wins an Emmy." *The New York Times,* 16 Sept. 2019, https://www.nytimes.com/2019/09/16/sports/football/colin-kaepernick-nike-emmy.html.

Du Bois, W. E. B. *Black Reconstruction in America: Toward a History of the Part Which Black Folk Played in the Attempt to Reconstruct Democracy in America, 1860–1880.* Routledge, 2017.

———. *The Souls of Black Folk.* Oxford UP, 2007.

Dunayevskaya, Raya. *Rosa Luxemburg, Women's Liberation, and Marx's Philosophy of Revolution.* U of Illinois P, 1991.

Durem, Ray. "A Decoration for the President." *The Heritage Series of Black Poetry, 1962–1975,* edited by Lauri Ramey, Ashgate, 2008, p. 246.

Eburne, Jonathan. *Outsider Theory: Intellectual Histories of Unorthodox Ideas.* U of Minnesota P, 2018.

Edwards, Brent. *Epistrophies: Jazz and the Literary Imagination.* Cambridge: Harvard UP, 2017.

Ellison, Mary. "Jazz in the Poetry of Amiri Baraka and Roy Fisher." *The Yearbook of English Studies*, vol. 24, 1994, pp. 117–145.

Emanuel, James A., and Theodore L. Gross. Eds. *Dark Symphony: Negro Literature in America*. Simon and Schuster, 1968.

Fanon, Frantz. *The Wretched of the Earth*. Translated by Richard Philcox, Grove Press, 2004.

Ferrara, Abel, director. *The Funeral*. October Films, 1996.

Flatley, Jonathan. *Affective Mapping: Melancholia and the Politics of Modernism*. Harvard UP, 2008.

Floyd, Samuel A. Jr. *The Power of Black Music: Interpreting Its History from Africa to the United States*. Oxford UP, 1995.

Fox, Maraglit. "Amiri Baraka, Polarizing Poet and Playwright, Dies at 79." *The New York Times*, 9 Jan. 2014. https://www.nytimes.com/2014/01/10/arts/amiri-baraka-polarizing-poet-and-playwright-dies-at-79.html.

Gabbin, Joanne V. *Furious Flower: African American Poetry from the Black Arts Movement to the Present*. U of Virginia P, 2004.

Gates, Henry Louis, editor. *Black Literature & Literary Theory*. Routledge, 1990.

———. *Figures in Black: Words, Signs and the "Racial" Self*. Oxford UP, 1989.

Gennari, John. "Baraka's Bohemian Blues." *African American Review*, vol. 37, nos. 2/3, 2003, pp. 253–260.

Gilroy, Paul. *The Black Atlantic: Modernity and Double Consciousness*. Harvard UP, 1993.

Gilyard, Keith, editor. *Spirit & Flame: An Anthology of Contemporary African American Poetry*. Syracuse UP, 1997.

Ginsberg, Allen. *Spontaneous Mind: Selected Interviews, 1958–1996*. Harper Collins Publishers, 2001.

Glanden, Don. *Brownie Speaks* (booklet). Directed by Don Glanden, Glanden Productions, 2014.

Glick, Jeremy Matthew. "'All I Do Is Think About You': Some Notes on Pragmatist Longing in Recent Literary Study of Amiri Baraka." *Boundary 2*, vol. 37, no. 2, 2010, pp. 107–132.

———. *The Black Radical Tragic: Performance, Aesthetics, and the Unfinished Haitian Revolution*. New York UP, 2016.

Goodman, Amy. "Ossie Davis Eulogizes Malcolm X." *Democracy Now*, 7 Feb. 2005, https://www.democracynow.org/2005/2/7/ossie_davis_eulogizes_malcolm_x_in.

Graham, Maryemma and Amritjit Singh, eds. *Conversations with Ralph Ellison*. University Press of Mississippi, 1995.

Grundy, David. *A Black Arts Poetry Machine: Amiri Baraka and the Umbra Poets*. Bloomsbury, 2018.

Hammonds, Evelynn. "Old Friends, New Faces, and an Intruder." *The Women's Review of Books*, vol. 1, 1983, pp. 5–6.

Harper, Philip Brian. *Abstractionist Aesthetics: Artistic Form and Social Critique in African American Culture*. New York UP, 2015.

———. "Nationalism and Social Division in Black Arts Poetry of the 1960s." *Critical Inquiry*, vol. 19, no. 2, 1993, pp. 234–255.

Harris, William J. "'How You Sound??': Amiri Baraka Writes Free Jazz." *Uptown Conversations: The New Jazz Studies*, edited by Robert G. O'Meally, Brent Hayes Edwards, and Farah Jasmine Griffin, Columbia UP, 2004, pp. 312–325.

———. *The Poetry and Poetics of Amiri Baraka: The Jazz Aesthetic*. U of Missouri P, 1985.

Harris, William J., and Aldon Lynn Nielsen. "Somebody Blew Off Baraka." *African American Review,* vol. 37, nos. 2/3, 2003, pp. 183–187.

Harris, Theodore. William J. Harris Facebook timeline, 4 Sept. 2019.Hayden, Robert, editor. *Kaleidoscope.* Harcourt, Brace & World, 1967.

Hegel, G. W. F. *The Encyclopaedia Logic.* Translated by T. F. Geraets, W. A. Suchting, and H. S. Harris, Hackett, 1991.

———. Preface to *The Phenomenology. Texts and Commentary,* translated and edited by Walter Kaufmann, U of Notre Dame P, 1977, pp. 1–5.

———. "Who Thinks Abstractly?" *Hegel: Texts and Commentary,* translated and edited by Walter Kaufmann, U of Notre Dame P, 1965, pp. 113–118.

Henderson, Stephen. *Understanding the New Black Poetry: Black Speech and Black Music as Poetic References.* William Morrow and Company, 1973.

Holier, Denis. "Hegel's Fool." *Semiotext(e): Nietzsche's Return,* vol. 3, no. 1, 1978, pp. 120–127.

Hong, Cathy Park. "Delusions of Whiteness in the Avant-Garde." *Lana Turner,* 7, 3 Nov. 2014, https://arcade.stanford.edu/content/delusions-whiteness-avant-garde.

Hughes, Langston. *Ask Your Mama: 12 Moods for Jazz.* 1961. *Collected Poems of Langston Hughes,* edited by Arnold Rampersad and David Roessel, Knopf, 1994, pp. 472–531.

———. *Collected Poems of Langston Hughes.* Edited by Arnold Rampersad and David Roessel, Knopf, 1994.

———. *Good Morning Revolution: Uncollected Social Protest Writings.* Edited by Faith Berry, Lawrence Hill, 1973.

———. Langston Hughes Papers: Series I. General Correspondence: Baraka, Imamu Amiri / 1958—65. Box 12, Folder 268. James Weldon Johnson Collection. Beinecke Rare Book and Manuscript Library, Yale University.

———. "The Negro Artist and the Racial Mountain." *The Portable Harlem Renaissance Reader,* edited by David Levering Lewis, Penguin Books, 1994, pp. 91–95.

———. *Selected Letters of Langston Hughes.* Edited by Arnold Rampersad and David Roessel, with Christa Fratantoro, Knopf, 2015.

———. *The Sweet Flypaper of Life.* Photographs by Roy DeCarava. Simon & Schuster, 1955.

Inwood, Michael. *A Hegel Dictionary.* Blackwell Publishers, 1992.

Jackson, Esther M. "LeRoi Jones (Imamu Amiri Baraka): Form and the Progression of Consciousness." *CLA Journal,* vol. 17, 1973, pp. 33–56.

Joans, Ted. "Le griot surréaliste." *Jazz Hot,* Juillet-Août 1969, pp. 22–25.

———. *Poet Painter / World Traveller, Part 1.* Edited by Wendy Tronrud and Ammiel Alcalay, Lost & Found, 2016.

Jones, Hettie. "High-Rise Eats Tenement." Interview by Kai Ma, *Intelligencer,* 24 Oct. 2007.

———. *How I Become Hettie Jones.* E. P. Dutton, 1990.

Jones, Kellie. *South of Pico: African American Artists in Los Angeles in the 1960s and 1970s.* Duke UP, 2017.

Jones, LeRoi, and Larry Neal, editors. *Black Fire: An Anthology of Afro-American Writing.* William Morrow & Company, 1968.

Jones, Meta Du Ewa. *The Muse Is Music: Jazz Poetry from the Harlem Renaissance to Spoken Word.* U of Illinois P, 2013.

———. "Politics, Process & (Jazz) Performance: Amiri Baraka's 'It's Nation Time.'" *African American Review,* vol. 37, nos. 2/3, 2003, pp. 245–252.

Joseph, Peniel E. *Stokely: A Life.* Basic Civitas, 2014.

Joyce, Joyce A. "Gil Scott-Heron: Larry Neal's Quintessential Artist" (introduction). *So Far, So Good,* by Gil Scott-Heron, Third World Press, 1990, pp. 73–83.

Kane, Daniel. *All Poets Welcome: The Lower East Side Poetry Scene in the 1960s.* The University Press of California, 2003.

Kaplan, Charles, editor. *Literature in America: The Modern Age.* The Free Press, 1971.

Karenga, Maulana. "Black Social Organization." *Introduction to Black Studies,* Kawaida Publications, 1982, p. 209.

Kelley, Robin D. C. *Thelonious Monk: The Life and Times of an American Original.* Simon & Schuster, 2009.

———. "What Amiri Baraka Taught Me About Thelonious Monk." *Let Loose on the World: Celebrating Amiri Baraka at 75,* The Amiri Baraka Commemoration Committee, 2009.

Kendricks, Ralph and Claudette Levitt, editors. *Afro-American Voices 1770s–1970s.* Oxford Book Co. Press, 1970.

Kim, Daniel Won-gu. "'In the Tradition': Amiri Baraka, Black Liberation, and Avant-Garde Praxis in the U.S." *African American Review,* vol. 37, nos. 2/3, 2003, pp. 345–363.

Kirkland, Frank. "Susan Buck-Morss, *Hegel, Haiti and Universal History.*" *Logos: A Journal of Modern Society & Culture,* vol. 11, nos. 2–3, 2012, http://logosjournal.com/2012/spring-summer_kirkland/.

Kofsky, Frank. *Black Nationalism and the Revolution in Music.* Pathfinder Press, 1970.

Kojève, Alexandre. "The Idea of Death in the Philosophy of Hegel." Translated by Joseph J. Carpino, *Interpretation: A Journal of Political Philosophy,* vol. 3, nos. 2–3, 1973, pp. 114–156.

LaCapra, Dominick. *History in Transit: Experience, Identity, Critical Theory.* Cornell UP, 2004.

Lacey, Henry C. "A Longish Poem About a Dude: An Introduction to 6 Persons." *The Fiction of LeRoi Jones/Amiri Baraka,* edited by Henry C. Lacey, Lawrence Hill Books, 2000, pp. 229–231.

Lauter, Paul, et al. *The Heath Anthology of American Literature.* Vol. 2, Heath and Company, 1990.

Lenin, V. I. *Collected Works.* Vol. 38, *The Philosophical Notebooks,* 1895–1916, https://www.marxists.org/archive/lenin/works/cw/volume38.htm.

Levertov, Denise. "Letter to LeRoi Jones." *Kulchur,* no. 12, pp. 29–31.

Levine, Lawrence. *Black Culture and Black Consciousness: Afro-American Folk Thought from Slavery to Freedom.* Oxford UP, 1978.

Liner, James. "The Different Persons of Amiri Baraka: Collectivity, Singularity, and Becoming—Minor." *symploke,* vol. 23, nos. 1–2, 2015, pp. 247–267.

Lowney, John. "Jazz, Black Transnationalism, and the Political Aesthetics of Langston Hughes's *Ask Your Mama.*" *American Literature,* vol. 84, no. 3, 2012, pp. 563–587.

Mackey, Nathaniel. *Discrepant Engagement: Dissonance, Cross-Culturality, and Experimental Writing.* Cambridge UP, 1993.

"Manifesto on Hungrealistic Poetry." *Kulchur,* no. 15, Autumn 1964, p. 104.

Marcoux, Jean-Philippe. *Jazz Griots: Music as History in the 1960s African American Poem.* Lexington, 2012.

Marcuse, Herbert. *Reason and Revolution: Hegel and the Rise of Social Theory.* Routledge & Keegan Paul, 1941.

McKeon, Michael. *The Secret History of Domesticity: Public, Private, and the Division of Knowledge.* John Hopkins UP, 2005.

McKirdy, Euan. "Racial Slur Painted on LeBron James' House: 'It's Tough Being Black in America.'" *CNN*, 1 Jun. 2017, http://www.cnn.com/2017/05/31/sport/lebron-james-racist-graffiti-incident/index.html.

McShane, Mike. "Three Questions About LeBron James' I Promise School." *Forbes*, 6 Aug. 2018, https://www.forbes.com/sites/mikemcshane/2018/08/06/three-questions-about-lebron-james-i-promise-school/#121f91bab97a.

Melhem, D. H. *Heroism in the New Black Poetry: Introductions & Interviews*. The U of Kentucky P, 1990.

———. "Revolution: The Constancy of Change." 1981. Reprinted in *Conversation with Amiri Baraka*, edited by Charles Reilly, U of Mississippi P, 1994, pp. 181–220.

———. "Revolution: The Constancy of Change: An Interview with Amiri Baraka." *Black American Literature Forum*, vol. 16, no. 3, 1982, pp. 87–103.

Messerli, Douglas. *From the Other Side of the Century: A New American Poetry, 1960–1990*. Green Integrer, 1994.

Mills, Charles. *The Racial Contract*. Cornell UP, 1997.

Monet, Aja. "Bio." Ajamonet.com.

———. *My Mother Was a Freedom Fighter*. Haymarket Books, 2017.

Moore, Darnell L. "When Black Lesbians Are Killed by Black Men," *Out Magazine*, 20 Mar. 2014, https://www.out.com/news-opinion/2014/03/20/when-black-lesbians-are-killed-black-men.

Morgan, Stephanie S. "In Memory of Radio." *Encyclopedia of Beat Literature*, edited by Kurt Hemmer, Facts on File, 2007, p. 152.

Moten, Fred. *Consent Not to Be a Single Being: The Universal Machine*. Duke UP, 2018.

———. *In the Break: The Aesthetics of the Black Radical Tradition*. Minnesota UP, 2003.

———. *Stolen Life*. Duke UP, 2018.

Mueller, Darren. "At the Margins of Music: The Early LPs of Prestige Record." *American History Now*, 23 Apr. 2014, http://americanhistorynow.org/2014/04/23/at-the-margins-of-music-the-early-lps-of-prestige-records/.

Mumford, Kevin. *Newark: A History of Race, Rights, and Riots in America*. NYU Press, 2007.

Murch, Donna. *Living for the City: Migration, Education, and the Rise of the Black Panther Party in Oakland, California*. The U of North Carolina P, 2010.

Muyumba, Walton. "Improvising over the Changes: Improvisation as Intellectual and Aesthetic Practice in the Transitional Poems of LeRoi Jones/Amiri Baraka." *College Literature*, vol. 34, no. 1, 2007, pp. 23–51.

Neal, Larry. "The Black Arts Movement." *Visions of a Liberated Future: Black Arts Movement Writings*, Thunder Mouth's Press, 1989, p. 64.

———. "The Black Arts Movement." *The Drama Review*, vol. 12, no. 4 (Black Theatre), 1968, pp. 28–39.

———. "A Reply to Bayard Rustin: The Internal Revolution." *Liberator*, vol. 5, no. 7, 1965, pp. 6–8.

———. "And Shine Swam On." *Black Fire: An Anthology of Afro-American Writing*, edited by LeRoi Jones and Larry Neal, William Morrow & Company, 1968, pp. 638–656.

Nelson, Cary, editor. *Anthology of Modern American Poetry*. New York: Oxford University Press, 2000.

Newman, Roberta J., and Joel Nathan Rosen. *Black Baseball, Black Business: Race Enterprise and the Fate of the Segregated Dollar*. U of Mississippi P, 2014.

Newton, Huey P. "Huey Newton Talks to the Movement About the Black Panther Party, Cultural Nationalism, SNCC, Liberals and White Revolutionaries." *Black Panthers Speak*, edited by Phillip Foner, Da Capo, 1970, p. 61.

New York Art Quartet. *New York Art Quartet*. ESP-Disk, 1964.

Nielsen, Aldon. "Belief in Lyric." *American Studies with American Studies International*, vol. 53, no. 4, 2013, pp. 171–179.

———. *Black Chant: Languages of African American Postmodernism*. Cambridge UP, 1997.

———. *Integral Music: Languages of African American Innovation*. U of Alabama P, 2004.

———. "A Roundtable on the Poetry of Resistance and Social Justice: Remarks." Unpublished conference paper, College Language Association Convention, Chicago, IL, 6 Apr. 2018.

———. *Six Plus One Persons: "A Longish Poem About a Dude."* 2018.

Nowatzki, Robert. "'Legitimate Black Heroes': The Negro Leagues, Jackie Robinson, and the National Pastime in African American Literature." *NINE: A Journal of Baseball History and Culture*, vol. 24, nos. 1–2, 2015, pp. 103–115.

Nwuneli, Lynn. "Variety of Styles and Complexity of Vision in Baraka's *Black Magic* Poetry." *Black Culture and Black Consciousness in Literature*, edited by Chidi Ikonne, Ebele Eko, and Julia Oku, Heinemann Educational Books (Nigeria) Limited, 1987, pp. 3–22.

O'Hara, Frank. *The Collected Poems of Frank O'Hara*. Edited by Donald Allen, U of California P, 1995.

Okiji, Fumi. *Jazz as Critique: Adorno and Black Expression Reconsidered*. Stanford UP, 2018.

Oppenheimer, Joel. "Some of My Best Peers." *Kulchur*, no. 12, pp. 23–27.

Ossman, David. "LeRoi Jones: An Interview on *Yugen*." 1960. Reprinted in *Conversation with Amiri Baraka*, edited by Charles Reilly, U of Mississippi P, 1994, pp. 3–7.

Ottenhoff, Patrick. "Where Does the South Begin?" *The Atlantic*, 28 Jan. 2011, https://www.theatlantic.com/national/archive/2011/01/where-does-the-south-begin/70052/

Parker, William. *I Plan to Stay a Believer: The Inside Songs of Curtis Mayfield*, AUM Fidelity AUM062/63, 2010.

Piazza, Tom. *Setting the Tempo: Fifty Years of Great Liner Notes*. Anchor, 1996.

Pisano, Claudia Moreno. *Amiri Baraka & Edward Dorn: The Collected Letters*. U of New Mexico P, 2013.

Rambsy, Howard II. *The Black Arts Enterprise and the Production of African American Poetry*. U of Michigan P, 2011.

Rampersad, Arnold. *The Life of Langston Hughes, Vol. II: I Dream a World*. Oxford UP, 1988.

Ratliff, Ben. Liner notes. Miles Davis, *Sorcerer*, Columbia Records, 1967, *Vinyl Me Please*, 2017, https://magazine.vinylmeplease.com/magazine/sorcerer-liner-notes/.

Reed, Anthony. "After the End of the World: Sun Ra and the Grammar of Utopia." *Black Camera*, vol. 5, no. 1, 2013, pp. 118–139.

Reed, Ishmael. "LeRoi Jones/Amiri Baraka and Me." *Transition*, vol. 114, 2014, pp. 13–29.

Reid, Calvin. "Amiri Baraka: Fierce Fictions, Radical Truths." *Publishers Weekly*, May 2000.

Reilly, Charles, editor. *Conversations with Amiri Baraka*. U of Mississippi P, 1994.

Remnick, David. "The Racial Demagoguery of Trump's Assaults on Colin Kaepernick and Steph Curry." *The New Yorker*, 23 Sept. 2017, https://www.newyorker.com/news/daily-comment/the-racial-demagoguery-of-trumps-assaults-on-colin-kaepernick-and-steph-curry.

Rhoden, William C. *Forty Million Dollar Slaves: The Rise, Fall, and Redemption of the Black Athlete*. Crown, 2006.

Robinson, Jackie. *I Never Had It Made*. 1972, Ecco, 1995.

"Roger Goodell's Statement on National Anthem Policy." *NFL.com*, 23 May 2018, http://www.nfl.com/news/story/0ap3000000933962/article/roger-goodells-statement-on-national-anthem-policy.

Ross, Marlon B. "Baraka's Truth." *Callaloo*, vol. 37, no. 3, 2014, pp. 471–476.

———. "Camping the Dirty Dozens: The Queer Resources of Black Nationalist Invective." *Callaloo*, vol. 23, no. 1, 2000, pp. 290–312.

———. "An Interview with Ntozake Shange." *Callaloo*, vol. 37, no. 3, 2014, pp. 486–490.

Rowell, Charles Henry, editor. *Angles of Ascent: A Norton Anthology of Contemporary African American Poetry*. W. W. Norton, 2013, https://wwnorton.com/books/Angles-of-Ascent/.

Sadoff, Ira. William J. Harris Facebook timeline, 16 Apr. 2018.

Saul, Scott. *Freedom Is, Freedom Ain't: Jazz and the Making of the Sixties*. Harvard UP, 2005.

Scheyer, Lauri. "Zero Hour and the Changing Same: Aesthetic Modernism and Black Nationalist Identity" in *Journal of Foreign Languages and Cultures*, vol. 4, no. 1, June 2020, Hunan Normal University Press, pp. 99–113.

Schilken, Chuck. "Colin Kaepernick Appears to Take a Shot at Jay-Z with Tweet." *LATimes.com*, 19 Aug. 2019, https://www.latimes.com/sports/story/2019-08-19/colin-kaepernick-jay-z-eric-reid-protests.

Schomburg, Arturo A. "The Negro Digs Up His Past." *Survey Graphic*, 1 Mar. 1925.

Schultz, Kathy Lou. *The Afro-Modernist Epic and Literary History: Tolson, Hughes, Baraka*. Palgrave MacMillan, 2013.

———. "Amiri Baraka's Wise Why's Y's: Lineages of the Afro-Modernist Epic," *Journal of Modern Literature*, vol. 35, no. 3, 2012, pp. 25–50.

Scorsone, Kristyn, Christina Strasburger, Whitney Strub, and Mi Hyun Yoon. "Queer Newark Oral History Project: An Interview with Amina Baraka." March 2, 2018. https://queer.newark.rutgers.edu/sites/default/files/transcript/2018-03-02%20Amina%20Baraka.pdf

Scott-Heron, Gil. *Now and Then: The Poems of Gil Scott-Heron*. Canongate, 2000.

———. *The Last Holiday: A Memoir*. Grove, 2012.

———. *Small Talk at 125th and Lenox: A Collection of Black Poems*. The World Publishing Company, 1970.

Sebree, Chet'la. "Natasha Trethewey: Finding Her Calling in a Wound That Never Heals." *Guernica*, 9 Jan. 2019, https://www.guernicamag.com/natasha-trethewey-finding-her-calling-in-a-wound-that-never-heals/.

Shange, Ntozake. "First Loves: Ntozake Shange." *Poetry Society of America*, https://www.poetrysociety.org/psa/poetry/crossroads/first_loves/first_loves_ntozake_shange/.

———. "An Interview with Ntozake Shange." Interview with Marlon B. Ross, *Callaloo*, vol. 37, no. 3, 2014, pp. 486–490.

Shifflett, Jonathan. "Jamila Woods Uses Poetry and Song to Reflect on Her Native Chicago." *The Frame*, 24 Apr. 2018, https://www.scpr.org/programs/the-frame/2018/04/24/62713/jamila-woods-uses-poetry-and-song-to-reflect-on-he/.

Shoemaker, Bill. "The Circle with a Hole in the Middle: Rare Vinyl Revisited." Review of *Bush Baby*, by Black Arthur Blythe, *Point of Departure*, http://www.pointofdeparture.org/archives/PoD-6/PoD6TheCircle.html.

Simanga, M. *Amiri Baraka and the Congress of African People: History and Memory*. Palgrave Macmillan, 2016.

Smethurst, James. *The Black Arts Movement: Literary Nationalism in the 1960s and 1970s.* U of North Carolina P, 2005.

——. *Brick Songs: Amiri Baraka, Black Music, Black Modernity, and Black Vanguard.* U of Massachusetts P, 2020.

——. "'Don't Say Goodbye to the Porkpie Hat': Langston Hughes, the Left, and the Black Arts Movement." *Callaloo,* vol. 25, no. 4, 2002, pp. 1226–1236.

Smith, David. "Amiri Baraka and the Black Arts of Black Art." *boundary 2,* vol. 15, nos. 1/2, 1986–1987, pp. 235–254.

Smith, Derik. *Robert Hayden in Verse: New Histories of African American Poetry and the Black Arts Era.* U of Michigan P, 2018.

Sollors, Werner. *Amiri Baraka / LeRoi Jones: The Quest for a "Populist Modernism."* Columbia UP, 1978.

Sorrentino, Gilbert. "A Note on the Muslims." *Kulchur,* no. 12, pp. 19–21.

Spahr, Clemens. *A Poetics of Global Solidarity: Modern American Poetry and Social Movements.* Palgrave MacMillan, 2015.

Spellman, A. B. "*Le Déjeuner sur L'Herbe.*" *Kulchur,* no. 12, pp. 5–15.

Stelter, Brian, and Nicole Chavez. "Michael Jordan Pushes Back After Trump Attacks LeBron James, Don Lemon." *CNN.com,* 4 Aug. 2018, https://www.cnn.com/2018/08/04/politics/trump-lebron-james-tweet/index.html.

Stuckey, Sterling. *Slave Culture: Nationalist Theory and the Foundations of Black America.* Oxford UP, 1987.

Sun Ra. *The Immeasurable Equation: The Collected Poetry and Prose.* Edited by James L. Wolf and Hartmut Geerken, Waitawhile, 2005.

——. "The Music Is Like a Mirror." *My Way Is the Spaceways,* Norton Records ED-391, 2013.

Szwed, John F. *Space Is the Place: The Lives and Times of Sun Ra.* Pantheon Books, 1997.

Tate, Greg. "Foreword: Vicious Modernism." *The Fiction of LeRoi Jones/Amiri Baraka,* edited by Henry C. Lacey, Lawrence Hill Books, 2000, pp. vii–xviii.

Taylor, Diana. *The Archive and the Repertoire: Performing Cultural Memory in the Americas.* Duke UP, 2003.

Teague, Jessica E. "Black Sonic Space and the Stereophonic Poetics of Amiri Baraka's *It's Nation Time.*" *Sound Studies,* vol. 1, no. 1, 2016, pp. 22–39.

Thomas, Lorenzo. *The Collected Poems.* Edited by Aldon Nielsen and Laura Vrana, Wesleyan UP, 2019.

——. *Extraordinary Measures: Afrocentric Modernism and Twentieth-Century American Poetry.* U of Alabama P, 2000.

Thompson, Deborah. "Keeping Up with the Joneses: The Naming of Racial Identities in the Autobiographical Writings of LeRoi Jones/Amiri Baraka, Hettie Jones, and Lisa Jones." *College Literature,* vol. 29, no. 1, 2002, pp. 83–101.

Toews, John E. "Review: History in Transit: Experience, Identity, Critical Theory by Dominick LaCapra." *The Journal of Modern History,* vol. 78, no. 3, 2006, pp. 684–686.

Trethewey, Natasha. "Incident." *Native Guard,* Houghton Mifflin Company, 2007, p. 41.

Turner, Darwin T., editor. *Black American Literature: Poetry.* Columbus, OH: Charles E. Merrill, 1969.

Tuttle, Brad R. *How Newark Became Newark: The Rise, Fall, and Rebirth of an American City.* Rivergate, 2009.

Van Deburg, William. *New Day in Babylon: The Black Power Movement and American Culture 1965–1975.* U of Chicago P, 1993.

Waldman, Anne, "'Surprise Each Other': Anne Waldman on Collaboration." Interview by Lisa Birman, *What Is Poetry? (Just Kidding, I Know You Know): Interviews from the Poetry Project Newsletter (1983–2009),* edited by Anselm Berrigan, 2017.

Watts, Jerry Gafio. *Amiri Baraka: The Politics and Art of a Black Intellectual.* New York UP, 2001.

Weiss, James. *Always in Trouble: An Oral History of ESP-Disk: The Most Outrageous Record Label in America.* Wesleyan UP, 2012.

Weusi. Liner Notes. *Black and Beautiful . . . Soul and Madness.* Featuring Yusef Iman and the Jihad Singers, Jihad Productions, 1967.

White, Simone. *Dear Angel of Death.* Ugly Duckling Press, 2018.

Williams, Robert. "Reflections of an Exiled Freedom Fighter." *Kulchur,* no. 12, pp. 15–19.

Wills, Katherine V. "Heteroglossia." *Still Paying Attention Ten Years Later: A Bakhtinian Reading of the National Information Infrastructure Initiative Agenda for Action,* 2006, http://www2.bgsu.edu/departments/english/cconline/wills/hereroglossia.html.

Windham, Donald. "New Songs Will Be Misunderstood." *Kulchur* no. 12, pp. 27–29.

Wolfe, Cameron. "Stills Criticizes Jay-Z: He's Never Been on a Knee." *ESPN,* 19 Aug. 2019, https://www.espn.com/nfl/story/_/id/27421748/stills-criticizes-jay-z-never-knee.

Woodard, Komozi. *A Nation Within a Nation: Amiri Baraka (LeRoi Jones) and Black Power.* U of North Carolina P, 1999.

Woods, Jamila. "Blk Girl Art." *The Breakbeat Poets: New American Poetry in the Age of Hip—Hop,* edited by Kevin Coval, Quraysh Ali Lansana, and Nate Marshall, Haymarket Books, 2015, p. 261.

"Yale Students Hold Sale of Penny Poems." *The Evening Independent,* 4 Apr. 1959, *Google News.*

Yugen, no. 7. Masthead. Edited by LeRoi Jones and Hettie Cohen, Totem Press, 1961.

Zirin, Dave. *A People's History of Sports in the United States: 250 Years of Politics, Protest, People, and Play.* The New Press, 2008.

CONTRIBUTORS

TONY BOLDEN is Associate Professor of African and African-American Studies at the University of Kansas. He is the author of *Afro-Blue: Improvisations in African American Poetry and Culture*, as well as the editor of *The Funk Era and Beyond: New Perspectives on Black Popular Culture*. He is also the editor of *The Langston Hughes Review*. His upcoming book is entitled *Groove Theory: The Blues Foundation of Funk*.

JEREMY MATTHEW GLICK is Associate Professor of African Diaspora literature and Modern Drama at Hunter College. He is the author of *The Black Radical Tragic: Performance, Aesthetics, and the Unfinished Haitian Revolution*. His second book project is entitled *Coriolanus Against Liberalism / Lumumba & Pan-Africanist Loss*. He is a longtime friend of the Baraka family.

WILLIAM J. HARRIS is Associate Professor Emeritus at the University of Kansas. He is the author of *The Poetry and Poetics of Amiri Baraka: The Jazz Aesthetic*. He is the editor of *The LeRoi Jones/Amiri Baraka Reader* and *Call and Response: The Riverside Anthology of African American Literary Tradition*. He is also a poet.

BENJAMIN LEE is Associate Professor of English at the University of Tennessee, Knoxville and the author of *Poetics of Emergence: Affect and History in Postwar Experimental Poetry* (University of Iowa Press, 2020).

AIDAN LEVY is a doctoral candidate at Columbia University in the Department of English and Comparative Literature with a subfield in jazz studies. He is the author of books on Lou Reed, Patti Smith, and a forthcoming biography of Sonny Rollins.

His writing has appeared in the *New York Times*, the *Village Voice*, *JazzTimes*, and *The Nation*.

JOHN LOWNEY is Professor at St. John's University. He is the author of two books on twentieth-century American poetry: *The American Avant-Garde Tradition: William Carlos Williams, Postmodern Poetry, and the Politics of Cultural Memory* and *History, Memory, and the Literary Left: Modern American Poetry, 1935–1968*. His recent monograph is *Jazz Internationalism: Literary Afro-Modernism and the Cultural Politics of Black Music*.

JEAN-PHILIPPE MARCOUX is Professor of American Literature at Université Laval in Québec, Canada. He is the author of the monograph *Jazz Griots: Music and Historiography in the 1960s African American Poem*. He is currently working on a study of the Umbra poets and workshops titled *Interplay: The Poetics and Politics of the Society of Umbra*. He is a founding member of the Amiri Baraka Society.

KIM McMILLON is a scholar who produced the Dillard University–Harvard Hutchins Center Black Arts Movement Conference in September 2016 in New Orleans. She is the editor of the upcoming *Black Fire–This Time* anthology.

FRED MOTEN works in the Department of Performance Studies at New York University. His latest book, co-authored with Stefno Harney, is *All Incomplete*.

MICHAEL J. NEW is Assistant Professor of English at Saint Anselm College, where he teaches courses in American and African American literature and culture. His current book project, *Instrumental Voices: Poetic Experiments in Jazz*, focuses on writers like Amiri Baraka, Gil Scott-Heron, Jayne Cortez, and Sarah Webster Fabio.

ALDON LYNN NIELSEN is the George and Barbara Kelly Professor of American Literature at Penn State. He is the author of numerous books, including *Reading Race, Writing Between the Lines, Black Chant, Integral Music*, and *C. R. L. James: A Critical Introduction*. He is also the co-editor with Lauri Ramey of the anthologies *Every Goodbye Ain't Gone* and *What I Say: Innovative Poetry by Black Writers in America*. He is the co-editor of *The Collected Poems of Lorenzo Thomas*. Finally, he is an accomplished poet, with nine volumes published so far. Nielsen was a student of Baraka at Howard University. He is a founding member of the Amiri Baraka Society.

AMY ABUGO ONGIRI is Assistant Professor in the English Department and Film and Media Studies Program at the University of Florida. She is the author of *Spectacular Blackness: The Cultural Politics of the Black Power Movement and the Search for a Black Aesthetic*. Her numerous essays and articles have appeared in *The Journal of African American History*, the *Los Angeles Review of Books*, and *Postmodern Culture*, among others.

GRÉGORY PIERROT is Associate Professor at the University of Connecticut at Stamford. He co-edited *An Historical Account of the Black Empire of Hayti*, by Marcus Rainsford, with Paul Youngquist. He also published a translation of, and wrote the introduction to, *Free Jazz / Black Power* (originally by Philippe Carles and Jean-Louis

Comolli). His most recent book is *The Black Avenger in Atlantic Culture*. He is a founding member of the Amiri Baraka Society.

HOWARD RAMBSY II is a Professor of Literature at Southern Illinois University Edwardsville. He operates the website Cultural Front, and he is the author of *Bad Men: Creative Touchstones of Black Writers* (2020).

ANTHONY REED is Associate Professor of English at Vanderbilt. His first book is *Freedom Time: The Poetics and Politics of Black Experimental Writing*. His new study of the recorded collaborations between poets and musicians during the Black Arts era, entitled *Soundworks: Race, Poetry, and Sound in Production*, is forthcoming from Duke University Press.

EMILY RUTH RUTTER is Associate Professor of English at Ball State University. She is the author of *Invisible Ball of Dreams: Literary Representations of Baseball behind the Color Line* and *The Blues Muse: Race, Gender, and Musical Celebrity in American Poetry*. Along with Tiffany Austin, Sequoia Maner, and darlene anita scott, she co-edited *Revisiting the Elegy in the Black Lives Matter Era*.

LAURI SCHEYER is Xiaoxiang Distinguished Professor at Hunan Normal University. Her books include *Slave Songs and the Birth of African American Poetry* (Palgrave Macmillan), *The Heritage Series of Black Poetry* (Routledge), and *A History of African American Poetry* (Cambridge). Her new books are *Theatres of War* (Bloomsbury) and *Selected Poems of Calvin Hernton*, co-edited with David Grundy (Wesleyan). She co-edited *Every Goodbye Ain't Gone* and *What I Say* with Aldon Lynn Nielsen (Alabama).

KATHY LOU SCHULTZ is the Catherine and Charles Freeburg University Professor at the University of Memphis, where she directs the Women's and Gender Studies Program. She is the author of *The Afro-Modernist Epic and Literary History: Tolson, Hughes, Baraka* and four poetry collections. Her upcoming monograph focuses on Claudia Rankine.

MICHAEL SIMANGA is an activist writer and cultural worker who teaches in the Department of African American Studies at Georgia State University. He is the author of numerous books, including *Amiri Baraka and the Congress of African People: History and Memory*. He is also a co-editor of *Brilliant Flame! Amiri Baraka: Poems, Plays, Politics for the People*. His most recent work is *David Franklin: The Art Politics and Business of Black Empowerment* (2019). He is a friend of the Baraka family.

JAMES SMETHURST is a Professor in the W. E. B. Du Bois Department of Afro-American Studies, University of Massachusetts Amherst. He co-edited *SOS—Calling All Black People: A Black Arts Movement Reader* with John H. Bracey Jr. and Sonia Sanchez. He has written several books, including *The African American Roots of Modernism: Reconstruction to the Harlem Renaissance*, *The Black Arts Movement: Literary Nationalism in the 1960s and 1970s*, and *Brick City Vanguard: Amiri Baraka, Black Music, Black Modernity*. His history of the Black Arts Movement in the South will appear in Spring 2021.

LAURA VRANA is an Assistant Professor of English at the University of South Alabama. She has written numerous articles and book reviews that have appeared in *Obsidian: Literature and Arts in the African Diasporic, Journal of Ethnic American Literature,* and *College Language Association Journal,* among others. She is the co-editor of *The Collected Poems of Lorenzo Thomas* with Aldon Lynn Nielsen.

TYRONE WILLIAMS is a Professor in the English Department at Xavier University. He is the author of several chapbooks and six books of poetry, including *c.c., On Spec, The Hero Project of the Century, Adventures of Pi,* and *Howell.* His most recent book of poetry is *As iZ.* He has also published many critical essays on American and African American poetry.

New Orleans native KALAMU YA SALAAM is a writer, activist, and filmmaker. His most recent books are *The Magic of Juju: An appreciation of the Black Arts Movement; New Orleans Griot: The Tom Dent Reader* (2020 one book/one New Orleans selection); and *Be About Beauty* (winner of the 2019 PEN Oakland Award).

INDEX

Surrealists, 178
Szwed, 138, 140

Targ, William, 36–37
Tate, Greg, 39, 45
Taylor, Breonna, 145n15
Taylor, Cecil, 83–84, 87
Taylor, Diana, 165
Teague, Jessica E., 117
Teer, Barbara Ann, 209–210
Termini, Iggy, 83, 85
Termini, Joe, 83
Terry, Sonny, 125–126
Tertullian, 78–79
Third-World Marxism, 47–48n2, 53, 101; and
    Baraka, 61, 89, 96. *See also* Marxism
Third World Press, 8, 233
Thomas, Dylan, 39
Thomas, Lorenzo, 31, 85–86, 89, 101; "An Edu-
    cation," 85–86
Thompson, Bob, 31
Thompson, Deborah, 38, 50–51n13
Threadgill, Henry, 98, 102
Tillich, Paul, 70
Toews, John E., 34
Tolliver, Charles, 131
Tolson, Melvin, 89, 101
Totem Press, 17, 19, 67n1
Touré, Askia, 130, 146n1
Trethewey, Nathasha, 10; "Incident," 48–50,
    52–54
Truman, Harry, 86
Trump, Donald, 63–64, 254
Truth, Sojourner, 225–226
Tubman, Harriet, 225–226
Turner, Darwin, 184
Turner Ward, Douglas, 24
Turner, James (Jim), 239
Tuttle, Brad, 147n2

Umbra (Society of), 5, 30–31
Underground Railroad, 230

Union of God's Musicians and Artists Ascen-
    sion (UGMAA), 102
Universal Negro Improvement Association
    (UNIA), 239
Unser, Mike, 164n5
US Organization, 50n12, 211

Van Deburg, William, 5
Vangelisti, Paul, 8, 184, 247; *SOS: Poems 1961–
    2013*, 8, 184, 188, 247
Vaughn, Ed (Edward), 230
Village Vanguard, 92, 99
Voting Rights Act (1965), 231, 236
Vrana, Laura, 11

Walden, Daniel, 184
Waldman, Anne, 17
Walken, Christopher, 67
Walker, Alice, 207, 215
Waller, Fats, 102
Walrond, Eric, 49n7
Walton, Anthony, 187
Ward Jr. Jerry W., 187
Ware, Wilbur, 84
Warhol, Andy, 25
Warren, Butch, 84
Watts (uprisings), 136, 145, 236
Watts, Jerry Giafo, 113–115, 119–120, 151n9,
    214n4
Watts Prophets, 149
Welburn, Ron, 148
Wells, Ida B., 225
West, Cornel, 254
Weston, Randy, 84, 98
Weusi, 113
Whalen, Philip, 19
Wheatley, Phillis, 181, 184, 190, 241
White, Simone, 142n12
Whitman, Walt, 178, 237
Wilkins, Roy, 23, 154
William Morrow (Publishing), 36, 94
Williams, Art, 219
Williams, Martin, 123

CPSIA information can be obtained
at www.ICGtesting.com
Printed in the USA
LVHW010042210721
693208LV00003B/39